The Geologic Model of Religion

THE GEOLOGIC MODEL OF RELIGION

Andrew Clifford

◆

GMReligion.com ◆ Saffron Walden

Dedicated to
Trisha & Christopher

*Thanks for your support and putting up with all the days
and nights of hearing the sound of me tap, tap, tapping away…*

Cover Illustrations:

<u>*Front: Geologic Model*</u>
Graphic with symbols of major religions within worldviews and afterlife paradigms:

Inner Core Religion: *Animal Renewal Traditions, Plant Renewal Traditions, Stone Breathing Traditions, Red Ochre Tradition*

Outer Core Religion: *Enhanced Rebirth Afterlife, Rebirth Feedback Belief*
Lower Mantle Religion: *Baha'i, Japanese, Chinese, Egyptian, Mesopotamian, and Megalithic*

Upper Mantle Religion: *Islam, Christianity, Judaism, Zoroastrianism, Sikhism, Buddhism, Jainism, and Hinduism*

<u>*Back: Egyptian thirtieth Dynasty architectural relief ca. 370 BCE [British Museum]*</u>
The pharaoh Nectanebo receives the renewal powers of an egg to achieve long life. It is showing religious belief drawn from the Natural Spiritual Traditions.

CONTENTS

INTRODUCTION

The Journey Begins

If the traveller cannot find master or friend to go with him, let him travel alone rather than with a fool for company.

– Buddha, from the *Dhammapada*

In films the cobwebbed black curtain gets ripped from a mystery that has endured through uncounted years. It results in instant news. Everyone pays attention. We all know that life and the real world is far more complex than simple celluloid dreams. So when I tell you that I have unravelled the great mystery of religion, surely the greatest cultural mystery, in our real world. I hope you read this book – having bought it at least! And if you think the concepts are sound, I hope you tell others about it too.

I have spent many years both scornful and scared of religion. I was scornful of its irrationality, scared of its hold on people I knew, its hold on society and indeed our whole civilization. For a long while I would not enter a church for the dismissive reason of "the roof will fall in" at the proud building encountering such an unbeliever. Am I describing you too? Perhaps, but I have moved on since. I now maintain my sceptical credentials but I also appreciate what religion has done for humanity. And now, when I enter a church it is with the eye of a detective, scanning for the evidence of the religions which pre-date Christianity. Fragments of them are still with us, even today.

Writing a book should be motivated by reading another, and happily this is true here. *The Geologic Model of Religion* (abbreviated to GMR), was motivated by *The God Delusion.* When Richard Dawkins published his work in 2006 I eagerly devoured an early copy expecting, like Dawkins may have done, that it would be a seminal milestone in the declining influence of religion. But, for me, something more important happened. It got me thinking and reading about the subject, every day. Then in January 2007 I had a moment of epiphany:

2 – Geologic Model of Religion

Religion and society are mutually reinforcing like steel and concrete in a skyscraper.

Yet, Dawkins calls religion a parasitic virus of the mind. Everything in human culture is arguably a mind virus, but this trivializes very important matters. There is much more to religion than meets the eye. Religion as a mystery warrants full and in-depth research. I had long considered the invisible "Id monster" scarily depicted in the 1956 film *Forbidden Planet* as a metaphor for the world's religions. Religion is very large, of uncertain shape and origin, resisting critical analysis. Scientists and authors attacking God and religion fire logical arguments like laser beams but they bounce off and the beast presses on. Rather than attack, I want to understand, to present a study of religion, independent of the atheist attackers and defending believers who line both sides of this battle. It transpires that Dawkins is mostly, but not entirely, right. At a minimum, if religion is a virus of the mind, it is different in the crucial respect of being very beneficial.

By early summer, June 2007, I realized that religion had several distinct layers:

First, it comprises beliefs either arising directly from the human condition, for example afterlife, or the social condition, for example judgment. These are also the important parts of eschatology.

Secondly, religion had developed through codifying the prevailing worldview, such as in scripture and creation myths.

Thirdly, that there is a layer in religion that is motivated to answer science, for example intelligent design and beliefs with roots which develop even in science fiction: Scientology and UFO cults.

Everything in religion could be placed in these very general categories. I needed a pictorial representation – preferably capable of further granularity which, as it turned out, was needed. The earth itself came to mind. It has a core, mantle and crust. The earth is permanently active due to the radioactive decay of uranium and thorium. This produces heat energy, radiating from the core, powering earthquakes, volcanism, tectonic movement and the magnetic field. Without radioactive decay our planet would be a dead world, impossible for complex life.

By analogy, awareness of personal mortality and self-importance maintains the heat energy of world religion powering the whole edifice of it. Even in the face of rationalism, secularism and scientific method religion is strongly persistent for the simple reasons that humans are still mortal and very much value their identity.

During five years of reading all I could absorb of archaeology, anthropology and history which had import to religion, and also reading the prior analysis of comparative studies, eventually I determined that the core, mantle and crust of the GMR is best considered as different worldview paradigms or models of reality. The earth's core has two distinct parts: an inner core of iron, solid from extreme pressure, and the outer core of liquid iron. By analogy the core, or life-force worldview, in the GMR also has two parts which group religious traditions with two different classes of rebirth afterlife belief.

Further, the earth's mantle is divided into liquid and plastic rock. It occupies the largest volume of the planet. Similarly, the spiritual worldview in the GMR is analogous to it. Mantle Religion is divided into two layers, again to represent different belief either in a spiritual or physical afterlife. It is within Mantle Religion that the visible form of religion is seen: churches, temples and mosques full of believers surrounded by iconography and tradition. It is a vast, historical canvas. This is the majority of cultural religious thought.

The earth's crust is solid rock consisting of large but thin tectonic plates which float like rafts on the mantle. Religion invented in the scientific era is thin, compared to pre-scientific Mantle Religion. Tectonic Religion is religious belief and doctrine which arises purely to answer science.

In researching the GMR I have always followed where the evidence drew me and discarded hypotheses which didn't add up. It sure made for a lot of rubbing out and rewriting, but it was worth it! What is the point of defending a theory when the evidence mounts overwhelmingly against it? Very quickly I realized that archaeology has, for years, danced around an obvious truth. Red ochre (also spelt ocher) has been found in prehistoric graves in all parts of the world. Yes, it has been recognized as early symbolism, but recognition of it as an ancient religious belief system is missing from the literature. The prototype of all religion, the Red Ochre Tradition, is crucial to the understanding of the origins of religion itself. This understanding leads to the paradigm shift that is spirituality and how the higher Abrahamic and Dharmic religions finally developed. Once on the trail many other fundamentals became apparent. There are several other distinct belief systems all over one hundred thousand years old, constantly appearing in archaeology – but never properly identified.

If you have no familiarity with the GMR, it is worth reviewing the illustration on the cover. A picture really does convey a thousand words as what I will achieve in writing serves just to flesh out detail in the model. Fortunately, the essence of the whole model can be grasped in just a minute of examination. Here, the monolith of religion is separated into layers for analysis. The inner layers are older and primitive where beliefs originate and feed up to each successive layer which is newer and accounts for the complexity in it.

The GMR weeds out pseudo-religious philosophies, enables clear analysis of the famous Abrahamic God of Western civilization and finally creates a context for the advancements made by reincarnation and resurrection beliefs. It shows that science and religion are harmonious and work in partnership for the betterment of mankind. It explains the origin of the moral imperative within religion and why religion appears to cause wars, but really doesn't.

If the analysis represented by the GMR is to be generally accepted then millions of words will flow in comment and argument. This should take years. In order to spark the debate more is required than argument by nervous suggestion. It requires the force of conviction. Every time I review the GMR I find that it feels more right than wrong. Hence I have the strength of conviction to present it to you. Consider this:

Religion has been instrumental in setting up conditions fostering a 1000-fold multiplication of the human population over its natural level.

The whole of world civilization exists only because of the buttressing effect of religion upon society. Without stable society the world population would fall to the hunter-gatherer distribution with some small settled groups. It would number millions, not billions and humans would be little better than intelligent animals, science would not exist. In fact, we would be living today worse off than we were ten thousand years ago. Religion is functioning like a beneficial environmental force in evolution. Yet in modern literature it is under continuous attack for sound, undeniable, logical and scientific reasons. Can this be the greatest disconnect of all time? The powerful glue of human civilization is not only illusory but irrational. This simply demands explanation!

What is the point of an understanding if we do not use it improve our grasp of the future? After presenting the GMR I go on to describe a redefinition of death itself in the context of advanced science. Death is not what most people think! The partnership between religion and science will eventually solve the quest for immortality. Finally, we can see how religion will simply fade away and even predict when it will happen.

Conventions

Because of my Western European ancestral heritage and similarly that of the bulk of the readership of the GMR I have adopted the following convention. Throughout this work the capitalised "God" refers the monotheistic supreme God, primarily the Abrahamic God of Judaism, Christianity and Islam, but also of Sikhism, Baha'i and Ahura Mazda of Zoroastrianism. All other religious gods are the lower-case noun. Hebrew Biblical quotes are from the Masoretic Text, and Christian Biblical quotes are from the King James Version. The quotes from the Holy Quran of Islam are from the 1934 Yusuf Ali translation.

Other conventions are designed to reduce confusion in terminology.

Atheism is disbelief in God specifically. Because God is central to monotheistic religions with one supreme deity the term atheism in the West is popularly interpreted as a rejection of religion in general. I touched on the general sense earlier in the introduction, but hereafter I will use it in the specific sense. For example: the early Indian religious school of Samkhya was atheist, i.e. a religion without any gods. Therefore, it is more accurate to define a disbeliever in religion completely as a physicalist. More is said on physicalism in the epilogue as this is outside the history of religion.

Eschatology is the branch of theology concerned with afterlife and judgment which is the principal theme of the GMR. Often this is a study of religious end-times, i.e. an end of material kingdoms and beginning of divine rule on earth. This is apocalyptic eschatology. I limit its use to discussing the religions which hold to a final resurrection.

The Neolithic not only saw the development of permanent settled societies, the domestication of animals, invention of agriculture, and pottery, but it also saw a transformation, multiplication and flowering of complexity in religious belief. There are serious difficulties however, in using the term when discussing global changes. Some researchers think of the "Neolithic Revolution" as a sudden change like the Industrial

Revolution, which it was in Northern Europe, but others stress its much more gradual development and prefer "Neolithic revolution" instead, with a lower case "r" to emphasise slow progression.

This is the convention I think is appropriate in most contexts in Southern Europe, Anatolia, Mesopotamia and the Levant where the Neolithic was roughly 10,000 BCE to 3500 BCE followed by the Bronze Age. Elsewhere in Asia, Africa and the Americas, the Neolithic is not fully recognized and it is better to consider the term "neolithic" simply for grouping settled, agrarian, and pottery using cultures that did not have metal-working skills. Australian Aboriginals who live in the traditional manner are the last major Palaeolithic culture to survive.

Throughout the GMR "spirit" is used as an umbrella term for a disembodied identity in religion. The majority of religions conceive of a duality – the physical body and an immaterial spirit which survives the death of the body. Therefore, *spirituality* defines the overarching worldview for the belief that disembodied identities can exist.

Spirit is analogous to "breath" or "wind", an immaterial essence that brings life in the first place. Often the *soul* is considered equivalent to spirit, but not always. The Old Testament scriptures of Judaism and Christianity use different Hebrew terms for spirit and soul, while the Christian New Testament scriptures use different Greek terms for both. The translations into English follow this distinction. The soul of a person might be considered *psyche* or *mind,* distinct from spirit, but also sometimes means simply that the person is "alive" as in the cry of shipwreck victims, "Save our souls!"

Although Hinduism is a spiritual religion, the key break between the great Dharmic religions is the Buddhist rejection of deity and therefore rejection of the concept of spirit. This is a doctrine known as *anatman.* Instead Buddhism assumes the presence of either a disembodied, *physical-mental state, or a mind or consciousness,* but there is no clear agreement even amongst scholarly adherents to Buddhism as to how identity is preserved.

From the perspective of comparative religion there is no useful distinction between disembodied spirits or minds. Consciousness obviously does exist within our skulls, and its electro-chemical nature is also explored when discussing scientific physicalism.

Rebirth in the GMR is always used in the simplest sense of dying and being reborn with no proper concept of continuation of previous identity. When discussing the Dharmic religions and others with a similar belief in *reincarnation,* this latter term is always used because *continuation of personhood* as a disembodied identity is always assumed.

I will be presenting substantial evidence of religious belief from the late Middle Palaeolithic era. It was a time when we co-existed with the Neanderthal. There is a seismic shift occurring in palaeoanthropology which is the recognition that the species *Homo neanderthalensis* is misnamed. Recent DNA evidence of successful, though limited, interbreeding means that they were a sub-species, not an entirely separate species of human.[1] So I use the term "modern humans" for *Homo sapiens sapiens* and "Neanderthal" for *Homo sapiens neanderthalensis.* Note that the Neanderthal was *robust.* Fully modern humans are *gracile* and individuals with intermediate characteristics *semi-robust* or *early modern.*

Anthropologists normally refer to preparation of a deceased's corpse and subsequent burial, cremation etc. as *mortuary* ritual but throughout the GMR I refer to *funerary* ritual – there is an important but subtle distinction. Mortuary practices are detached from the emotional aspect; it is a technical procedure. Funerary ritual better captures the holistic sense of the grief, loss and sorrow which accompanies physical treatment of the deceased. It includes the expression of religious belief in assisting with the process of coping with death.

Perhaps it is fitting for a book about religion to start with a curse. And for the GMR it is the "curse of the *three letter acronyms"* (TLAs). I apologize in advance for this necessity to save space and make easy reference to key ideas. The Geologic Model is composed like the earth, in layers, and these layers are referenced often, similarly the distinct Palaeolithic religious traditions are also clearly identified by name and acronym. So where an acronym is introduced and is specific to the GMR it appears also in the table of contents and chapter and section headings, and the *glossary.* Acronyms seen elsewhere will be one of common usage in anthropology and other disciplines, for example, "kya", for *thousands (kilos) of years ago.*

Because the history of religion encompasses distant pre-history through historic periods I will use the convention in anthropology of kya for dates earlier than the invention of agriculture: the Neolithic Revolution at 12 kya or 10,000 BCE, and the Common Era convention thereafter. Many dates in source literature are provided in Before Present (BP) form which is before 1950 CE. These are converted to BCE as accurately as possible and rounded to reflect the margin of error in dating the site under discussion. Chronological tables are presented with the earliest period at the top reading down to the latest period at the bottom.

Determining the number of adherents to both living and dead religions is a notoriously imprecise activity, more art than science. For the sake of consistency I will cite numbers only for living religions and use *adherents.com* as the source.

I am well aware of the many differences between British and American English spellings and have deliberately chosen a careful fusion of the two in order to make this work least jarring to most people in an international audience. Perhaps I have succeeded, perhaps not.

References are more focused upon the analysis of archaeological literature related to prehistory. In the historic period these are restrained. Additionally, ideas are pulled together from many sources, and perhaps some of my ideas (at least the framing of religion into three progressive worldviews and two quasi-worldviews, formally collating six different Palaeolithic traditions in one place, and the Neolithic origin of spirituality) are original. I believe that the holistic synthesis of them is certainly completely novel – and that is most important. So a balance is struck between readability and the visual weeds of embedded references.

Note

All quotes in this work are to be taken as self-contained. They are reproduced simply to provide emphasis or illustrate another perspective relevant to the paragraph where they appear. Sometimes they require critical analysis in the light of conclusions from this work. None of those quoted are to be read as endorsing the principles of the GMR which is a completely new model presented for the first time.

1 ♦ THE GEOLOGIC MODEL OF RELIGION (GMR)

The Central Concept in Religion

Religion is so vast that it seems impossible to know where to begin in the analysis of it. Anyone who has put pen to paper on the subject would have leant back, taken a deep breath and considered hard. Where to begin? What is the first step? Well, the first step must be to determine what it does. What is religion for?

Scenario Ranking

We want to identify the central concept of religion. It should not be difficult, yet people debate even this point. Consider analogies. Aircraft are varied and complex, a Boeing 747 might have a million pieces, but the central concept of aircraft is simple: rapid, long-distance transportation. The roots of language are lost in the mists of time, and some 6900 of them exist, but we don't need to know more than one to determine the central concept behind language. It is to enable the exchange of information. Yet, if you wanted an explanation of the history and design of aircraft or the history and development of language you could fill whole libraries with books on these subjects.

The same applies to religion. Central concepts can always be written in a few words. So, again, what is the central concept or the one primary purpose which religion is actually for? Many people will immediately say "to overcome death", but others will respond "to find God". Perhaps the compromise is to argue for both at once: "Finding God before and after death", although many religions have no gods of importance. Whatever anyone says about the central concept or primary purpose of religion: belief, life, death, gods and afterlife cannot be ignored. So we test them and proceed from the result. Right now we will begin with the thought experiment illustrated next:

GMR: PURPOSE OF RELIGION BY SCENARIO RANKING

PEOPLE AND THEIR BELIEFS MEET DEATH
EXPECTING BELIEVED OUTCOMES

(a) Your Life + God + Afterlife → (Your Death) → God + Afterlife

(b) Your Life + Physicalism → (Your Death) → Oblivion

(c) Your Life + Atheism + Afterlife → (Your Death) → Afterlife

(d) Your Life + God → (Your Death) → Oblivion

Rank all four scenarios in order of desirability of the whole scenario. Whatever your beliefs, religion, or non-religious stance, try to be objective and assess what religion should achieve. In preferential order what do most people really want from it?

Note that an atheist is a disbeliever in God only, whereas a physicalist is a disbeliever in all of religious belief which is not supported by evidence from the corpus of mainstream science. Take a moment here to pause and consider your answer.

There are other, somewhat weaker, purposes for religion such as "ensuring providence" or "providing meaning to life" or "explaining the universe"; more on these shortly. Consider our analogies. The purpose of a Boeing 747 is not the same as the purpose for all aircraft. We can't just say a 747 is an aircraft and find purposes for those alone. We must consider the subject, not an example object. Religion with God present is an example of a type of religion. Additionally we can't get side-tracked with by-products and epiphenomena. We can't define the purpose of language if we are focused upon how it facilitates social cohesion, is useful for finding a mate or exercises the brain.

So this is an important matter. We are determining the road to take, not just a single step on the road. It is easy to see how we cannot make any progress unless we answer a basic question: What is religion for? The thought experiment helps break this log-jam.

In the test above we focus on the words at the right which symbolise our expectations. My guess is that most people prefer *(a)* or *(c)* as afterlife always trumps oblivion. So the central concept in religion is immediately apparent. *It is the promise of afterlife. Religion exists to overcome death.* It exists to solve the ancient and disturbing discovery of *personal mortality.* Surely this is not a complete surprise to anyone.

What this result clearly shows is that afterlife is more important than God. Part of the fog of mystery over the origin and persistence of religion is that cause and effect is usually mixed up. God is commonly thought of as a cause and cited as the "prime mover". We will see that God is more of a religious effect, not a cause of religion. Analysis of religion requires a clear distinction between causes and effects.

Now you might, and others will say that personal mortality is an old chestnut and has been explored ad nauseum by authors analysing religion. So there is always a temptation to search for something else, some other mystical spark. That is getting the road right and then crashing off, going wrong straight-away. How can we be so sure? Through this book we will see compounding evidence at every turn that religion is an empty shell if it does not address personal mortality. Every religion in the world has a functional afterlife belief or it is not a religion – just a philosophy or a pseudoscientific hypothesis.

The formulation of the test itself will seem unsatisfactory to many believers, atheists and physicalists alike. Although some objections will be valid points they are highly unlikely to produce a completely different conclusion. In the meantime we have our answer, although more questions arise out of the thought experiment.

One you might already pose is, "How can there be afterlife without God?" This is voicing the assertion that only option *(a)* in the test is valid.

Afterlife is a theoretical *process* whereas God is a theoretical *person.* Afterlife as a process is the preservation of complexity – which might even stand up to scientific scrutiny. In the *Many Worlds Interpretation* of quantum mechanics, a front-running theory of how the universe works, many versions of each individual survives the death of others of the same individual. [2] This is an unconventional form of afterlife, even if it is true, which is far from certain at the present time, but it is wholly independent of God belief. So afterlife in the broadest sense of preservation of life after death is a scientific matter even if religion never existed to culturally codify it. Additionally, science requires a robust definition of death and religion does not.

So option *(a), God with afterlife,* is the default position of resurrection religions: Zoroastrianism and Abrahamic Judaism, Christianity and

Islam. This is because God is believed to be essential to the afterlife process. The reason for that is the difference between *spiritual afterlife* and *resurrection afterlife*.

In the ancient spiritual religions – ancestor worship or those with spiritual realms such as Mesopotamia, Pharaonic Egypt and Greco-Roman Antiquity – there was a natural progression to a spirit realm after death. Afterlife was normally seen as inevitable however, the process could be assisted with grave goods and rituals. It is only after this process is underway that gods become involved to judge or direct the fate of the dead – if they could be bothered, as often they weren't.

In the official reference book of Roman Catholicism, the *Catechism of the Catholic Church,* Article 5 asserts:

> *The frequent New Testament affirmations that Jesus was "raised from the dead" presuppose that the crucified one sojourned in the realm of the dead prior to his resurrection. This was the first meaning given in the apostolic preaching to Christ's descent into hell: that Jesus, like all men, experienced death and in his soul joined the others in the realm of the dead.* [3]

Spiritual progression is still seen as a natural process by the higher religions today. The advance in thinking described by resurrection builds upon spiritual afterlife. It is the further proposition that after a period of spiritual afterlife, in a sky or underworld realm, deceased spirits can be raised up and reunited with a new physical body. It is the final step that requires the hand of God in the afterlife process.

Option *(b), oblivion,* is the humanist and physicalist position. Richard Dawkins in his work *Unweaving the Rainbow* makes the case for oblivion by pointing out that this is the default state for all the trillions of people who have never existed in the first place. For each of us there was only a slim probability that aeons of chemical and genetic events could finally lead to our own existence. [4] Although rational this is a minority view because it excessively reduces the problem of personal mortality. Having come into existence, as intelligent beings, most of us are unhappy giving up the experience of life.

Intelligence demands the preservation of intelligence even if irrational ideas need to be embraced.

The epilogue is devoted to analysing the problem of oblivion and shows that there is indeed a scientific solution to personal mortality.

On a personal note, this is why I believe that religion and science are both amazing products of intelligence, as together they have saved the sanity of humanity!

Option *(c), afterlife without God,* includes the earliest form of all religion: prehistoric rebirth. It is also the position of the Dharmic reincarnation religions of Buddhism and Jainism. Even in Hinduism and Sikhism with a supreme God, the cycle of death and reincarnation (*samsara*) is considered a natural process. Karma is believed to be decisive upon an individual's future path through samsara. Usually the god Yama is involved in interpreting the results of karma and executing the appropriate afterlife reward or punishment. Escaping the cycle of reincarnation to a state of brahma or nirvana can be interpreted by some as union with a god head – but all of this is additional to the process of afterlife.

The native Australian Aboriginals have a rich and vibrant traditional religion which could not be denied by the nineteenth century Europeans who then searched the Dreamtime mythologies for the presence of God, but failed and eventually gave up. It is only after 200 years of Christian missionary preaching in Australia that some interpreters of Aboriginal religion now detect a "God-like" presence in their beliefs.

It is through the prism of the resurrection religions that God is required for post-spiritual afterlife. Hundreds of millions of people have lived and died believing in afterlife but not believing in God.

Option *(d), God without afterlife,* is rare but not unknown. The Sadducees were a Jewish aristocratic sect, flourishing from 200 BCE to 70 CE, who subscribed only to the five books of Moses which set out laws for society and asserted the primacy of God. They took inspiration from the scepticism of Classical Greece a few hundred years earlier, therefore rejecting any idea of spirituality, afterlife, supernatural beings (angels, demons) or resurrection. Their debates with Christ are mentioned in Biblical scripture but their almost atheist views did not survive long into the Christian era.

More recently *Deism* is the belief where reason and the complexity of nature leads to the conclusion that God created the universe but has since let it run with no intervention. In the strictest form of this belief religion is rejected completely. Although Deism has been intellectually fashionable for a couple of hundred years, it is a minority belief. In reality this description of Deism is close to the Strong Anthropic principle of fringe science. The GMR is clear on the point that if God is described outside of religion then this is no longer God being discussed but a theory drawn from pseudoscience. This is explored further in Chapter Eight, Concepts from Science.

Some Deists still subscribe to afterlife belief, and when they do it means their form of Deism is no more than a standard religion with spiritual afterlife.

One rare culture without any afterlife belief is the primitive and nomadic tribe known as Hadzabe who live in Tanzania. They are one of the world's last hunter-gatherer societies and roam around the shores of Lake Eyasi of the central and eastern Great Rift Valley, just south of the equator. Numbering about 300 fully nomadic and 700 semi-nomadic people they hunt for game with poisoned arrows and forage for fruit, honey and edible roots. Theirs is a timeless existence, yet under threat from intrusions of the modern world. When a family member dies the body is unceremoniously left for hyenas or, only recently, buried. They have a few historical myths about giants but even these are not gods to them.

If god belief was central to religion, and afterlife optional, then there would be many examples throughout world cultures and history. This isn't the case.

Other objections arising from the thought experiment may be grouped as defences for the importance of creation, explanations, meaning, morality, and so on. I am going to address those now, and objections to the whole thought experiment itself, by way of a diversion to an important writer and thinker about sociocultural anthropology and psychology. Pascal Boyer in *Religion Explained* presents a comprehensive list of possible reasons, within four categories, of why religion exists. In brief the categories: first that religion provides explanations for natural phenomena, dreams, origins and good and evil etc. Secondly, that religion provides comfort about personal mortality and anxiety. Thirdly, that religion provides social order holding society together, hierarchies and morality. Fourthly, that religion is an illusion because people are simply superstitious, want to have faith, or that religion is simply irrefutable. [5]

Of the four categories the first three are all correct, but not equal, and the last can be junked. Boyer calls it "unsatisfactory" so we agree there. Category two, religion as a comfort for personal mortality is primordial and most important. Boyer recognizes it is a special case:

*All religions, or so it seems, have **something** to say about death.*
People die but their shadows stay around. Or they die and wait
for the Last Judgment. Or they come back in another form. [5]

So surely, by definition, if religion always has something to say about death then this is the fundamental element of it? In the GMR, religion as a psychological comfort, an antidote for death and therefore religious practices concerning death, is essential to the whole model. Boyer assumes that supernatural agents are also universal in religion, but we will see this is only in the spiritual worldview.

Boyer's third category, social order, has grown hugely in importance since the Neolithic revolution, and is a key element of Mantle Religion. Boyer's first category, religion as an explanation, is actually part of the spiritual worldview. This is also a fundamental in the GMR. Each of these is fully addressed later. The reality is that religion first evolved to solve one problem and expanded over thousands of years to solve many others.

More important than agreeing a list of secondary reasons why religion exists is observing Boyer's cognitive-template and inferred-concept model for religious belief. This is a valuable insight. However, and this is expressed in the GMR, Boyer has gone farthest in explaining the technical mechanics of how religion works but much more needs to be said about how religion is structured within worldviews and afterlife paradigms and even more must be said about how it enabled large societies and civilizations to develop.

The purpose of religion is now clear: the promise of afterlife. I am thinking back to Dawkins' frustration. He is firing at the wrong target and should be writing instead about *The Afterlife Delusion*. If everyone suddenly decided that afterlife is untenable then god belief would quickly wither too.

A lot still needs to be said about God, explanations, meaning and morality, but that is for later. For the moment all we need to know is that contrary to popular opinion, by millions of religious believers, atheists and physicalists alike, *God is not central to any religion.*

Theocentric and Afterlife-centric Religion

A large number of books about religion, written by physicalists, such as Dawkins' *The God Delusion* and Stenger's *God: the Failed Hypothesis*, focus their analysis upon God, the deity. It is the same for believers such as McGrath's *The Science of God*; Polkinghorne's *Science and Providence* and Winston's *The Story of God*. Similarly, analytical works like Humphrey's *The character of God in the book of Genesis* focus upon God.

They assume that he is central to religion and attack, promote or analyse him relentlessly. The louder the discussion becomes the less progress is made. Christopher Hitchens in *God is not Great* puts God at the centre in the title but correctly identifies religion as a much wider subject. So he opens up his guns on all fronts.

The debate over the primacy of God is reminiscent about the events in determining the correct nature of the Solar System. It is worth exploring a little as this also became a defining moment in the relationship between science and religion.

The five planets out to Saturn were known of for many thousands of years but it was Ptolemy of Alexandria, who lived ca. 87-150 CE, who applied robust mathematics in demonstrating how the sun and the five planets orbited the earth. Then it started getting complicated, requiring epicycles to explain puzzling retrograde motion of the planets. The Sun and planets had to perform a total of 80 strange dancing loops in their orbits around the earth. Yet the Ptolemaic geocentric system worked in making predictions so it remained the peak of knowledge about astronomy for 1,400 years. Despite that success, the matter would not rest.

Nicolai Copernicus was a canon at the Cathedral of Olsztyn in Poland. He studied Ptolemy's observations and mathematics and in 1513 made an important discovery. If the Sun was at the centre the planetary orbits would be circular. This explains why Mars appears to reverse direction. It is because the earth's orbit around the sun is shorter, so, orbitally speaking, our planet catches Mars up and passes it once each earth year. It explains how Mars can be invisible when it is behind the Sun. It was far simpler. The heliocentric model turned out to be true, only requiring the smaller final modification of circular to elliptical orbits.

The same problem of displaced primary importance still exists with religion. Most people think that it revolves around God, but it doesn't. It revolves around afterlife. Religion where God is at the centre is the equivalent of the Ptolemaic Earth-centred system. It might look fine to begin with, but the more that is discovered the more unworkable it becomes. God-centred religion is theocentric, yet many religions do not have an important god. When God assumes the role of facilitating afterlife and judgment, God seems integral to afterlife and seems central to religion. Arguing that this proves religion is theocentric is like adding epicycles to save a failing theory.

Religion where afterlife is at the centre is a clear and refreshing determination, like the heliocentric Solar System. There does not appear to be an appropriate adjective invented for "afterlife centred" so *afterlife-centric* is used in the GMR to refer to religion with afterlife at its centre and God further to the periphery. If this is difficult to accept for some then there it gets harder because the GMR shows that *judgment in afterlife* is also more universal in religion and also more important than God.

Norman McClelland, Zen dharma master, in choosing the name of his *Encyclopedia of Reincarnation and Karma*, by default identifies the two most important elements of religion. He might as well have named his work *Encyclopedia of Afterlife and Judgment*.

Lao-Tse, the founder of Taoism around 500 BCE, wisely said, "Even the longest journey must begin where you stand". A simple metaphor as this is true of all endeavours, whether it is in relationships, science, commerce, education and so on. Even more than that, the first step is crucial as it gets you going in the right direction. If the first step is wrong then your journey may never end and your endeavour fails.

The decision-making behind the first step is most important and for each subsequent step slightly less so. The reason is that in taking a correct step the probability tree of wrong paths is invisibly pruned. By the time you are 99 per cent through your journey the end is so obvious that neon signs are flashing and the last step is a formality.

I assert that most of the thousands of books written about religion have gone wrong at the first or second step. Most authors, from East or West, whether from scientific (anthropological, sociological) or religious (theological) perspectives have launched themselves on their journey at a tangent by not recognizing the fundamental importance of afterlife and judgment. There are a number of deserved exceptions, and their valuable insights are introduced in the right context and referenced later. Generally though, their overall picture is incomplete.

Many of the remaining authors have wound up lost in the mountains and ravines of the religious landscape, like desperate Himalayan climbers, gasping for the oxygen of coherence and freezing without the warmth of reality. I do not want to waste your time - so upon this journey to uncover the origins, persistence and future of religion we must follow the evidence and evaluate it dispassionately to stay on track.

The GMR asserts afterlife-centric religion, restoring the most important element of it to the centre so that everything else revolves around. Now we are in a position to understand the whole.

Afterlife at the Centre

If you were to destroy in mankind the belief in immortality, not only love, but every living force maintaining the life of the world would at once be dried up. Moreover, nothing then would be immoral; everything would be lawful, even cannibalism.

– Fyodor Dostoevsky, *The Brothers Karamazov*

Afterlife can only be important because it answers the problem of personal mortality. Do we risk being caught in a circular trap where afterlife is important because personal mortality is important because afterlife is important – ad nauseum? Not if we listen to Fyodor Dostoevsky, the great 19th century Russian writer and thinker who often expressed his own views through his characters. He makes it clear that immortality (afterlife) is the prop under our morals and civilization. If we are truly mortal then we are reduced to living as animals. Mortality comes first in importance, afterlife next and everything else follows.

So the first critical test of afterlife as the engine of power of religion is to establish whether all religions have an afterlife belief.

This is obvious in Christianity and Islam. Their engine of power is afterlife by resurrection. Let's not tarry with easy cases. Let's go immediately to the difficult, apparent disproofs. Consider Shinto, the traditional belief system in Japan; although it must be noted that it is actively practised by only a few millions of Japanese, most have a weak adherence to Shinto or are atheist. In Japan, while marriage and life ceremonies are performed with Shinto rites, their funerals are always

Buddhist. Shinto is devoid of its own afterlife tradition, but it is still a religion as it has borrowed one! At least 80 per cent of Shinto adherents will believe in the Buddhist afterlife traditions, the remainder hold to ancestor veneration where the dead exist spiritually at a shrine. The Buddhist afterlife belief is so embedded that many Japanese do not even realize that Buddhism is a completely separate religion in its own right. Afterlife is the engine of power of Shinto as well.

Two difficult cases are both from China. Taoism in its varying forms and often apparently absent afterlife belief, and Confucianism without a recognizable afterlife belief at all and subject to a 100 year debate about its religious status.

First though, the principal religion in China, for the majority, is ancestor worship. Not just everyone's ancestors - for each person it is the ancestors of their own extended family, plus many historical and mythical figures worthy of veneration, which could even include Lao-Tse or Confucius. There are millions of ancestral shrines throughout China.

This is traditional or folk religion and is woven throughout Chinese culture dating back at least 5000 years. An important distinction between Chinese ancestor worship and the Abrahamic and Dharmic religions is that in folk religion judgment is delivered upon the living by the dead – instead of being delivered upon the dead during afterlife based upon their deeds while alive. It is only since communism, industrialization and wholesale migration to the cities in recent decades that major disruption has occurred to the network of families and their ancestral roots supporting this important religion in China.

Taoism, also called Daoism, emerged from the traditional folk religions and adopted a vast complex of life-directing themes, selfless philosophy, goal of physical immortality through herbal and natural means, as well as ideas of reincarnation from Buddhism and concepts of afterlife punishment and paradise. It became the state religion of the imperial dynasties. So Taoism does have afterlife, and some judgment beliefs, but they vary significantly depending upon the school of thought. Famously, the Taoist Dongyue temple in Beijing, dating from the thirteenth century, has life-sized wooden statues illustrating grisly afterlife punishments.

Confucianism is first a moral, ethical and attainment-oriented philosophy codified by Confucius who said he wanted to benefit society above all. He also said nothing of afterlife except that ancestors should be venerated. The pressure to determine whether Confucianism is a religion comes purely from the Western mind which observes that this belief is of lifelong importance to millions of Chinese – so must be considered a distinct religion. The reality is that Confucianism is a life-directing philosophy.

A philosophy is a different intellectual discipline which covers wisdom and ways to live one's life in harmony with family, society and enlightened thinking. This life-affirming philosophy is commonly practiced by those who also believe in spiritual afterlife as part of ancestor worship, but also many Taoists, Buddhists and adherents to Shinto follow Confucian philosophy in day-to-day life.

Of the remainder in China, who do not hold to the folk religion, they are atheist, or adherents to the major religions: Taoism, Buddhism, Islam or Christianity.

Why is astrology not considered to be a religion? In the West, it is because it does not have anything to say about afterlife or judgment. Likewise, if a religion is found to consist of a belief in nature spirits which emerge from the forest to cause misfortune, and that is all there is to it, then this is a magical superstition not a religion.

So the GMR stands clear on this distinction. A religion must have afterlife belief, its own or borrowed, because if it doesn't then it is a philosophy, superstition or pseudoscience which people are confusing as a religion. None of this is ground breaking, as many people have considered afterlife as primary to religion, perhaps none more so than subscribers to a theory of religion which we need to consider next.

Terror Management Theory

> *Here, in the decisive moments of existence when man first becomes man and realizes his immense loneliness in the universal, the world-fear reveals itself for the first time as the essentially human fear in the presence of death . . . here too the higher thought originates as meditation upon death. Every religion, every scientific investigation, every philosophy proceeds from it. Every great symbolism attaches its form language to the cult of the dead, the forms of disposal of the dead, the adornment of the graves of the dead.* [6]

– Oswald Spengler

The *Terror Management Theory*, also known as TMT, has all of culture including religion and science as a worldview to defend intellectually against the terror of personal mortality. Proponents of the TMT take to heart the views of the historian and philosopher Oswald Spengler.

At first thought, death as a "terror" seems an exaggeration. That personal mortality lies, for most people, between being a concern and a fear. After all, we do not think of it every day. Further, at the extreme, there are many people who have given their lives in defence of their family, group or state. And what higher price can be paid? Surely though, all those who give their lives in battle are reassured by the thought of afterlife.

The commonly repeated aphorism is that there were no atheists in World War I trenches. It is extremely rare for someone to go into battle expecting to be rewarded with oblivion. The acceptance of oblivion requires years of careful personal introspection. Islam has some adherents who easily give their lives for an earthly cause, rightly or wrongly. They are comforted in paying the ultimate price because of their afterlife belief.

Consider the scenario where religion never developed. What kind of society would people create? Perhaps the answer is "disastrously bad". In a situation where everyone knows, and everyone firmly believes, that there is no afterlife then death is final. Whatever one does, however upright one is – it is all for nothing. Even having children is bittersweet; they are brought into the world just to have their hopes and dreams dashed on the black cliffs of inevitable oblivion. This describes a world without hope, a place of despair, dread, anger and anarchy. It is not an exaggeration to suggest that societies would fail to advance even to the stage of the agrarian revolution, even to form villages and towns without the benefit of any religious cohesion.

So Spengler is right that there is a world-fear, but it is not apparent because it is always masked behind a buffer.

In contrast to the TMT, the GMR holds that religion is the buffer against the terror and the rest of culture, including science, lies beyond the buffer and can develop independently of the terror.

Religion and Suicide

Afterlife as a solution to personal mortality is a good solution, but not perfect. It allows for the idea that suicide is a sensible answer to survival hardship in order to start life over again. There are two types of desired outcome from suicide – although both resulting in the same actions:

1) Where the individual has a problem with life itself and simply wants oblivion.

2) Where the individual is having problems in their present life and wants a quick exit to a better life in the afterlife.

Clearly widespread acceptance of this second mindset would be damaging to the stability of families, tribes and society. However, in a non-religious society only the first case would be seen, so it appears that religion makes suicide more likely as it permits a wider rationalization of it. Despite this, the opposite seems true.

Studies of the degree of religiosity within suicidal persons are rare, although some have been carried out, including by the psychologist Joseph Hovey who concluded, "High religiosity may play a protective role against suicide." [7]

Another study is by the psychiatrist Kanita Dervic who also concluded:

> *Religious affiliation is associated with less suicidal behavior in depressed inpatients. After other factors were controlled, it was found that greater moral objections to suicide and lower aggression level in religiously affiliated subjects may function as protective factors against suicide attempts.* [8]

These studies contrast with that done by Benjamin Beit-Hallahmi which had the neutral result of no significant difference in suicide rates between religious and non-religious persons. [9]

Turning to religion itself we find no equivocation. Suicide is regarded as a major sin in Christianity and is forbidden in Islam. The loophole which comes to mind is martyrdom. Extremists in any religion will always be able to rationalise this option, but few take this fateful step. On balance it is safe to conclude that religion is life-affirming and beneficial in maintaining lower suicide rates than would otherwise prevail.

Earlier, in the scenario ranking exercise, one purpose popularly considered for religion was briefly mentioned: providing meaning to life. Usually God is considered the meaning, but in afterlife-centric religion this must be tangential. Seventy billion people have lived and died already. Most of them desired continued life, whether afterlife or immortality. Hence the meaning of life is more accurately considered to be the pursuit of more life!

This is on the surface simply: life for the sake of life. The deeper consideration is that life is fungible. With life all other things are possible: self-awareness, memories, relationships, reproduction, exploration, experiences, pleasure and pursuit of knowledge. Desiring life for all life experiences is a hallmark of self-aware intelligence.

Dawn of Religious Belief

> *At all times and everywhere man's intense desire and determination to destroy death and "put on immortality" has found expression not only in his ritual behaviour but also his mythology.* [10]
>
> – E.O. James

Many authors struggle to identify the beginnings of religious belief, but it can be seen here that James is absolutely correct with his definition. The "putting on" of immortality fuels religion even today. The desire for immortality characterized by the belief in afterlife and ritual practices to achieve it defines all the layers of the Geologic Model.

Other opinions on the dawn of religion vary widely. The anthropologist James George Frazer wrote:

> *Religion defined: it is a propitiation or conciliation of superhuman powers which are believed to control nature and man.* [11]

Frazer is only narrowly right assuming he was thinking of ancestor worship. Propitiation to ancestors is an important early religion which is explored in detail in the GMR, but it is not the earliest. If Frazer was thinking of nature gods this is well removed from the origin of religion.

The philosopher Daniel Dennett has a viewpoint which is at once dismissive and more general:

> *...to attribute agency – beliefs and desires and other mental states – to anything complicated that moves.* [12]

He is closer, as this is a description of naturalistic animism where the whole environment was considered to be alive. Both Frazer's and Dennett's explanations also touch on the broader concept of worldview and the further requirement to have an explanation of the natural world in the absence of science.

In the GMR several very different worldviews are defined and these provide the conceptual framework within which all of religion exists, including how afterlife belief is expressed.

The writer Daniel Haycock in his work on the human intellect, *Being and Perceiving*, observes:

> *We cannot turn to archaeology when seeking information about the roots of religion. Instead, we have to examine those beliefs and practices which are most conserved in societies across the world, and tribal societies in particular, and then conjecture about prehistoric religion on the basis of the most universal of those conserved characteristics.* [13]

In contrast, the GMR shows that afterlife belief has left a truly monumental archaeological record that reads like a book. We shall see that every culture left the fingerprints of its religion in the cold earth. Further, no culture in the world today practices religion as it was found everywhere 20,000 years ago. Finally, analysis which begins with the assumption that God is central to religion is fundamentally flawed.

Many writers start with God, as a prime mover, which is unfortunately starting late in the development of religion. God is a spiritual concept, and holds prime importance only in the higher religions, so does not advance the understanding of what were the original beliefs.

The Edwardian physician Albert Churchward also identifies propitiation to superhuman powers, clearly deferring to Frazer, but he quickly introduces his own theory involving personal mortality:

> *Religion proper commences with and must include the idea or desire for another life. The belief in another life is founded on the Resurrection of the Spirit. The belief in the resurrection of the Spirit was founded upon the faculties of abnormal seership, which led to Ancestor Worship in all lands at one time.* [14]

This is another opinion which is on the right track, but the flaw in this description is once more that belief in spirits was primordial. We will see evidence in the GMR that spirits and spirituality are known only from the Neolithic and this has a profound impact upon how the history of religion can be deciphered and presented.

Geologic Model of Religion – Paradigms

Religion has frustrated many attempts at analysis as there has been no obvious structure within which to properly capture its elements. The GMR has this visually simple structure. It has onion-like layers, more usefully named analogous to that of the earth's internal structure. So the innermost section is the core followed by the mantle and then the surface, or tectonic layer of crust.

The GMR is holistic, concerned with all facets of religion. This is more than just the structure of belief systems and why they exist and what they do. It is also concerned with the environment of religion which is the scientific basis for how religion itself persists, develops and spreads. Why a model at all? The whole point of one is a framework with which to encapsulate prior understanding as efficiently as possible and to improve future understanding, explain long-standing anomalies, and even predict future changes.

Three Worldviews and Two Paradigm Shifts

Afterlife is the essence of religion but it is not the place to start from. Before any religion can be properly decomposed and fitted into a model the prevailing worldview paradigm must first be determined. A worldview in this sense is the overarching understanding, or model of reality which was universally accepted at the time.

Afterlife and aspects arising from the worldview, such as creation myths, will all conform to the prevailing worldview paradigm. Knowing the paradigm which applies in a given culture is most critical to understanding all the aspects of its religion.

Table 1.1 (next page) illustrates the distinct paradigms – the sequentially prevailing major models of reality – which have existed.

GMR: 1.1   **WORLDVIEWS AND PARADIGM SHIFTS**

WORLDVIEW	ORIGIN	LIFE AND AFTERLIFE	LAYER
Life-Force	Palaeolithic	The whole environment is alive and consists of living things	Core Religion
First Great Paradigm Shift	Mesolithic / Neolithic Boundary	Quasi-worldview: The environment has a landscape which is alive and is inhabited by living things with intangible doubles (spirits) which become ancestral or nature spirits	Core-Mantle Boundary
Spiritual	Neolithic	The environment is dead but inhabited by living things with intangible doubles (spirits) which become ancestral spirits, nature spirits or even gods. Spiritual worlds may also exist	Mantle Religion
Second Great Paradigm Shift	Modern Era	Quasi-worldview: The spiritual worldview includes elements of pseudoscience. Religion has principles of science applied outside of the accepted corpus of science	Tectonic Religion
Science	Modern Era	The step by step description of nature	External to the Geologic Model

We humans have always been fully self-aware and aware of the environment, so we have required a model of reality, of the world in which we find ourselves. Within human history there has developed three distinct and therefore two merged but temporary paradigms of worldview. All the current and dead religions of world are framed by one of the worldviews which occur sequentially in time.

Of the three worldviews only the first is extinct. The first, where the environment is considered alive, is *naturalistic animism,* defined in the GMR as "life-force" as there is no general definition of animism without including the possibility of spirituality. Animatism is sometimes used in this regard.

Of the latter worldviews, spirituality and science operate concurrently today. In human history there have only been two major worldview paradigm shifts which are transitional phases where elements of the old and new paradigms are concurrent.

The two worldview paradigm shifts are life-force to spirituality, and spirituality to science. Analogous to a phase shift, such as the transformation of crystalline ice into water, all the ideas within the old paradigm are quickly *transformed or destroyed* in the new one. It is because the first paradigm shift occurred before recorded history that prehistoric religion has been an opaque mystery, until now that is. The second paradigm shift is still underway; we are living in the time window of approximately 500 years which it will take to complete.

Because paradigm shifts take hundreds or even thousands of years then the many generations of people who live in them usually accept the transitional phase as a true worldview in its own right which means a few religions exist wholly within a temporary worldview. In the GMR the paradigm shifts are also called quasi-worldviews.

Because of the isolation of the Australian Aboriginal peoples their worldview developed without the effects from diffusion which occurred everywhere else on the planet. They have a worldview called *Dreamtime* which encompasses their traditional religious beliefs. It is presently transitional between the life-force and spiritual worldviews. This is the last significant surviving example of the First Great Paradigm Shift. In the GMR the Dreamtime is specifically Aboriginal; a dreamtime-like, merged or quasi-worldview may have briefly existed in Eurasia, Africa and the Americas, at various times, during the paradigm shift from the life-force to the spiritual worldview.

Today, within the Second Great Paradigm Shift, science is accepted unanimously by religious believers and physicalists alike, although believers will also consider that spirituality exists. If someone accepts only the science worldview then this is physical monism. If someone accepts the science worldview but also accepts another, earlier, worldview then it is this overlap of worldviews which makes necessary concepts such as Cartesian Dualism where body, mind and spirit are separate yet still interacts.

Within the Geologic Model the worldview paradigms are analogous to the rock and iron substrate of the earth upon which the model is based.

It is the different worldviews which create the separate Core, Mantle and Tectonic layers which are used to decompose religion into its main parts. The life-force and spiritual worldviews are environment-oriented as they attempt to explain what can be detected with the human senses (including any supposed "sixth" sense). In the chapters dealing with the main layers of the GMR aspects of worldviews are separately described. These comprise belief systems usually grouped as religious which is *not* specific to afterlife and judgment.

The life-force and spirituality worldviews predate all of science so these are an explanation for reality without it and they framed religion itself. Within these worldviews magic is the substitute for science and technology. Both are needed to harness an essential of the human condition which is the impulse to control the natural world.

In practice, the vast majority of beliefs in religion are within the spiritual worldview and this is the bedrock of Mantle Religion. The GMR shows how spirituality developed from pressures of the social condition. The spiritual worldview frames the religious explanation of the natural world through gods of creation, providence, sky, earth, wind, rain, fire, love, war and many others. It includes religious doctrine which directs the legal code, day-to-day rules of life, food restrictions, rites of passage, marriage protocols and other general traditions which support the control of society over individuals. Pressure from the social condition makes religion become a substitute for history and the rule of law, history and genealogy: origins and myths of ruling families and society itself. The more rules and regulations over how people are to live their lives then the more successful is a religion at buttressing the society it is part of. This is when individual morality and behaviour is controlled, allowing important group-level benefits of society to arise.

Science is nothing more or less than a description of nature. It is a step-by-step explanation of the fabric of the universe in which we happen to find ourselves. It does not start with any prejudices and does not end with doctrine. It is simply an accumulation of knowledge. Knowledge that can usually be obtained only by practical application of previously learned science. Science is also different because it uses *instrumentation* to go far beyond the human senses. So the study of nature includes things such as quasars, radio waves and nuclear particles, all completely outside the human sensory environment. Science itself is outside the scope of the GMR, and assuming this model, as a hypothesis for explaining the structure and history of religion, becomes widely accepted as valid, it will come to include the GMR too.

Prior to the scientific era, concepts of magic prevailed within worldviews, especially variations of sympathetic like-for-like magic. What we consider as symbolism was truly functional representation, ubiquitous through the layers of Core Religion and Mantle Religion. Tectonic Religion describes a quasi-worldview, where religion absorbs concepts from science, magic becomes transformed into pseudoscience.

Four Afterlife Paradigms

Afterlife is of course elaborated by doctrines which get to the heart of religion – its solution to personal mortality. Associated is judgment of the dead, quality of afterlife and funerary rituals and gods which facilitate afterlife-related concepts such as a god of judgment. Any analysis of religion which does not say much about these subjects misses the point of religion entirely and might as well be describing a philosophy, superstition or pseudoscience.

Belief in afterlife is the radiant heat energy which permeates the layers of worldview and keeps alive the persistence and power of religion itself.

Having established the major layers of the model by different types of worldview the next step is to fit the various types of afterlife into the model. During the process of examining each religion to separate out the afterlife and judgment beliefs it becomes apparent that belief in the method of progression from physical death to afterlife is consistently from four categories or afterlife paradigms.

These are summarized in Table 1.2 (next page).

To be clear, the term "rebirth" throughout the whole of the GMR is meant only in the simplest possible sense: death, then a short while later being reborn with only the vaguest connection between the new and previous existence. Despite persisting for several hundred millennia, rebirth is fundamentally flawed as it wipes the slate clean of an individual's previous existence.

Once someone has reached adulthood and invested decades into their memories and personality they will lose everything if afterlife is simply a restart from infancy. There can be no progression.

GMR: 1.2   **AFTERLIFE PARADIGMS IN RELIGION**

PARADIGM	PRINCIPAL RELIGIONS	AFTERLIFE & IDENTITY	LAYER
Rebirth	Natural Rebirth Traditions & Enhanced Rebirth Afterlife & Rebirth Feedback Belief	Life-Force Worldview Life, death, rebirth in a simple cyclic manner. Oblivion of prior adulthood and identity (personality, memories) Physical afterlife from infancy. Palaeolithic origin	Core Religion
Spirituality	Ancestor Worship (Tribal / Native, Chinese and Japanese traditional), Mesopotamian, Egyptian, Greco-Roman & Mesoamerican.	Spiritual Worldview A single physical life then transfer to a totemic site, allowing partial reincarnation, but poor preservation of identity. Or, transfer to a realm of the dead, with ethereal afterlife, but identity is preserved. Neolithic origin	Lower Mantle Religion
Reincarnation	Dharmic (Hinduism, Buddhism, Sikhism & Jainism)	Spiritual Worldviews Life, death, rebirth cycle with preservation of adulthood identity as spirit / mind. Spiritual afterlife during karmic judgment. Physical afterlife from infancy. Iron Age origin, ca. 800 BCE	Upper Mantle and Tectonic Religion
Resurrection	Abrahamic (Judaism & Christianity & Islam) Zoroastrianism	Spiritual Worldviews Single physical life then reconstitution to life anew. Spiritual afterlife with preservation of adulthood identity. Physical afterlife as an adult with identity preserved before final judgment. Iron Age origin, ca. 600 BCE	Upper Mantle And Tectonic Religion

As humanity developed in cultural sophistication so did its afterlife beliefs. Identity is the essence of each individual: the personality and memories that are so important to us all. The importance of identity relates to the degree of preservation of personal identity – survival of oneself in the afterlife. There has been a significant improvement in the perceived preservation of individual identity through the afterlife paradigms.

Rebirth afterlife, which was universal in the Palaeolithic era is unknown in today's religions for the reason that the modern mind will only accept afterlife belief which offers some degree of preservation of personal identity.

Preservation of identity in afterlife is not to be confused with *quality of afterlife* which is represented by existence in Heaven or Hell, or reincarnation into greater or lesser animals or, acceptance and rejection by ancestral spirits, or consignment to oblivion - all occurring after religious judgment.

The path forward for afterlife belief is preservation via spirituality, as a disembodied identity; this originated and spread globally with the Neolithic revolution, except in a few areas such as Aboriginal Australia where it was independently developed.

Yet, spiritual afterlife is not as satisfying as renewed physical life so during the Iron Age two new afterlife paradigms were overlaid upon spiritual immortality. First: reincarnation. By the eighth century BCE Hinduism, arising in India, adopted the concept of repeated physical lives, but of preserving personal identity through these lives in a spiritual form. In the Dharmic religions the term *rebirth* is commonly used to mean the same as reincarnation, and this confusion is avoided in the GMR. Reincarnation belief always assumes that *some* preservation of previous identity occurs, usually by spirit or mind. Even the rejection of spirit by Buddhism is more of an intellectual minority view not held by the vast majority of believers who are "Folk" Buddhists.

Secondly, the final afterlife paradigm is the concept of a single new and immortal physical life with identify preserved: resurrection. This is first seen in Zoroastrianism in Persia and Mesopotamia, and seen in Judaism in the Levant from the sixth century BCE.

It is through the hard evidence of funerary ritual, grave goods, that most of our knowledge is acquired about the prehistoric religious approach to handling personal mortality. The older a religion is, the more basic is the believed degree of survival of individual identity after death. Over thousands of years the concept of self-importance has continually gained within human cultures. This has driven the advancement of religious belief in different afterlife paradigms over a similarly long time. Each level of progression achieves a superior preservation of identity.

Geologic Model of Religion – Structure

Because the prevailing worldview paradigm completely frames the structure of religious belief itself the Core and the Mantle layers are characterized by fundamentally different worldview paradigms. The final, Tectonic, layer exists within a quasi-worldview which is religion developed as a response to science.

In the cover illustration of the GMR the life-force worldview is the bright, yellow core, with symbols of the major Palaeolithic religious traditions. The spiritual worldview is the darker, red mantle. Symbols of Neolithic, Bronze Age, Iron Age, and higher major religions of today are in black. Science is external but influences the outermost layer of the spiritual worldview.

In the GMR it is essential to separate the worldview framework around religious belief from the beliefs themselves. So, Core Religion is a description of the life-force worldview which rises from the human condition with drivers to religious belief. Whereas Inner Core Religion and Outer Core Religion are the actual belief systems separated by two discrete processes of afterlife progression.

Similarly, this principle is true of Mantle Religion. Mantle Religion is a description of the spiritual worldview which rises from the social condition with drivers to religious belief. Whereas Lower Mantle Religion and Upper Mantle Religion are the actual belief systems separated by two discrete processes of afterlife progression.

The exception is the quasi-worldview of Tectonic Religion where the science worldview is itself a driver, reinterpreted into pseudoscientific religious belief.

The assumptions the GMR has are few – just that cultural behaviour, which is religion, arises from the human condition in individuals and, when in large groups, the social condition. All existing, living and dead religions fit within the model – so it encompasses all known observations. Finally it has predictive and retrodictive capacity. It supports predictions and explains previously puzzling phenomena.

Core Religion (CR)

Core Religion (CR) describes the *life-force worldview* and how it rose from the *human condition* providing the framework for the religions of *rebirth.*

The simplest concept in religion is generated from the human condition at the level of the individual: awareness of personal mortality driving afterlife and the simple afterlife mechanism of rebirth. There is no preservation of adulthood or identity, and afterlife is by way of a new physical life. The physical attributes of blood and breathing which are seen to be life-giving are critically important in rebirth religions.

The key element of worldview in CR is that the environment was thought to be alive: animals, plants, streams, clouds, sun, moon; even rocks were all imbued with a life-force. This is naturalistic animism. The life-force worldview in the Geologic Model is analogous to the iron in the core of the earth.

CR is the inevitable consequence of self-aware intelligences living in the natural environment. It overlaps two layers which are different systems of religious belief.

Inner Core Religion (ICR)

Inner Core Religion (ICR) describes *rebirth afterlife* and the belief systems to attain it.

The religions of rebirth do not have a formal orthodoxy so it is best to describe them as religious traditions. There are four main ones, all inspired by the observed renewal power of nature. As a group they are the Natural Rebirth Traditions. These are essential for understanding hunter-gatherer religious belief systems as they held sway everywhere with the major phase of decline during the Neolithic revolution. The archaeological evidence for these prehistoric traditions is overwhelming. Their symbolism is still seen in modified forms in religions today.

Outer Core Religion (OCR)

Outer Core Religion (OCR) describes *enhanced rebirth afterlife* and the belief systems to attain it. If also includes the hypothesis of belief in *rebirth feedback* which may have had a profound effect upon the recent physical evolution of modern humans.

Rebirth afterlife was not a static belief. Prehistoric peoples developed it further, commonly expressing the idea of enhancing the next life. Mortuary treatment was often specific to improving the strength and skills of the deceased, when growing-up after rebirth. The archaeological evidence for this is also overwhelming.

Mantle Religion (MR)

Mantle Religion (MR) describes the *spiritual worldview* and how it rises from the *social condition* providing the framework for the *spiritual* religions.

The existence of the invisible atmosphere and necessity to breathe air originally provided the logical basis for the belief in spirituality and the possibility that a spirit realm exists.

MR also includes the set of religious concepts arising from the effects of multilevel natural selection. This acts specifically upon competing groups, societies and settlements, becoming the principal influence upon the human social condition. This is evident in religious belief which apparently benefits groups at the expense of individuals: the enhanced moral imperative and judgment in afterlife and various mechanisms of judgment. Belief in judgment necessitates the template concept of quality of afterlife where the inferred concepts of spiritual sky and underworld realms arise. Judgment also drives the meme of martyrdom, self-sacrifice for group-level considerations.

Importantly, an overall benefit from effective societies exists for individuals through improved living standards and reproduction. This outweighs the cost of individual submission to group-level considerations.

Nevertheless individual submission to group-level considerations has a reactive effect upon individual self-importance. Self-importance is the driver to enhanced personal survival through adulthood in afterlife and therefore spiritual afterlife is logically required to provide a context where individuals may continue to persist. Spiritual afterlife allows the preservation of adulthood, which rebirth can't, but the price of this is that there is no new physical life until the afterlife paradigm develops further.

The key element of worldview in MR is that the environment of animals, plants, oceans, mountains, sky and so on, was no longer alive but instead thought to be inhabited by the intangible spirits of ancestors. Even stars were imbued with a spiritual essence. This spiritual worldview in the Geologic Model is analogous to the rock in the mantle of the earth.

Judgment in afterlife became a critical concept enabling development of large societies, indeed civilization itself. Mantle religions are heavily focused upon it and provide rituals and doctrine for navigating judgment successfully. MR has two layers which are different systems of religious belief:

Lower Mantle Religion (LMR)

Lower Mantle Religion (LMR) describes *spiritual* afterlife and the associated belief systems or religions to attain and navigate it.

Ancestor worship is the original spiritual belief, essential to the megalithic cultures of the European Atlantic coast, Chinese traditional religion, American Indian, Australian Aboriginal, Polynesian and many African tribal religions. Partial reincarnation was a transitional concept between ideas of rebirth and full reincarnation where ancestors may be reborn but their prior identity is only temporarily and imperfectly preserved. This was also a common belief in ancestor worship. A spirit realm for the deceased is essential to many major but now extinct religions such as those of ancient Egypt, Greco-Roman Classical Antiquity, Scandinavia and Mesoamerica.

Upper Mantle Religion (UMR)

Upper Mantle Religion (UMR) describes *physical afterlife with adulthood preserved* and the associated belief systems or religions to attain it. UMR belief mainly comprises the higher Abrahamic and Dharmic religions which dominate the world today. These are very successful worldwide and it is because they offer believers an afterlife doctrine which preserves personal identity and also offers a new physical existence. Their spiritual preservation of adulthood is inherited from the older LMR religions.

So UMR is a combination of spiritual and physical afterlife in a single paradigm. There are three discrete forms of the spiritual/physical paradigm which allow belief in physical afterlife with identity preserved: reincarnation, resurrection and translation. In practice, the first two are almost ubiquitous and the third extremely rare.

Reincarnation assumes the spiritual preservation of identity and adulthood but allows for cycles of new physical life from infancy. Judgment is performed spiritually and determines temporary spiritual reward or punishment then the form taken in the next physical life (if any). An important development within UMR is that of physical-mental states as an alternative to spirit. This is seen primarily in Buddhism.

Resurrection also assumes spiritual preservation but allows for only one new physical life which begins at adulthood, and is often thought to be rejuvenated adulthood with aging reversed. Unlike reincarnation, final judgment is performed after physical resurrection, although spiritual judgment usually occurs before resurrection.

Translation afterlife is a rare type of resurrection where a living person may be translated directly into a resurrected and immortal afterlife state. This is physical resurrection without death and an intermediate spiritual state. This belief is not standard in any major religion. Mormons believe that some people have undergone translation but the normal path to resurrection is via spiritual progression.

Tectonic Religion (TR)

Tectonic Religion (abbreviated TR, and *not* to be confused with pagan German Teutonic religion) comprises formalized religious belief which develops as a response to the corpus of accepted scientific knowledge. This layer of belief exists because, for at least 400 years, both the spiritual worldview and scientific worldviews have been operating concurrently, and will for some years yet. Because TR has existed for many lifetimes it has become a quasi-worldview in its own right and includes pseudoscientific concepts which are incorporated into religion.

The modern ideas of "creation science" for the origin of the world and humanity, and Intelligent Design as a rebuttal to evolution, are examples of TR. A number of modern religions are inspired by science fiction and these are also part of the TR quasi-worldview.

Because the bulk of formal science is very young this makes TR very thin, and datable. This is the outer layer of the GMR. Further, TR beliefs must be part of a religion with afterlife belief otherwise it is just stand-alone pseudoscience or philosophy.

Templates and Memes

Before proceeding to detail the layers of the GMR it is necessary to see how religious ideas form and spread in the first place. At the heart of religious belief are abstract templates, the framework for ideas or concepts, which arise from the human and social conditions. The persistence and spread of ideas follow patterns of natural selection, and the emerging science of memetics describes how.

Abstract Templates

Afterlife, spirituality and judgment are templates, although only afterlife is seen in all religions, whereas spirituality and judgment is seen in most religions. Templates cannot usefully be broken down into simpler constructs, so they are atomic and are common across human cultures, even if they are culturally defined in formal religion so that they appear very different.

The essence of a template is that it is an abstract framework present in the human mind which can be quickly used to package new information. Templates contain the common elements found in real-world objects and intangible subjects, and are also subsets of worldview paradigms. So, in the example of the spiritual worldview the framework for the idea of spirits, invisible doubles of humans and animals etc., is an incomplete mental image, a template structure.

Pascal Boyer illustrates this by using the example of the "animal" template which everyone has in their mental library. He shows how a template is used by asking you to consider a statement about a rare type of animal which you have never heard of before. Immediately however, without knowing anything about this novelty, because of your mental animal template you can infer that it reproduces, has legs to move around, and requires food and water. So the animal template has "filled in" a lot of personal knowledge gaps about the new animal just discovered.

Even when this animal proves mythical the template still holds and there is an attribute which distinguishes real from mythical ones.

Afterlife is also a template because it is filled in before it can be used. Rebirth, reincarnation and resurrection are different inferred concepts or paradigms fleshing out the afterlife template into a form that can exist in religious belief. No religion holds to afterlife in the abstract fashion of the afterlife template, they will instead present a consistent understanding or orthodox paradigm about how the afterlife process works, although adherents will still debate the details.

The number of templates people have in their minds in order to make sense of the world is relatively small compared to the number of inferred concepts which arise. One reason is that templates exist due to causal drivers from the human and environmental conditions.

Drivers from the Human Condition

The GMR incorporates the principle that religion is a *response* to fundamental aspects of the human condition as individuals, and also a response to the social condition of human groups. These responses are the impetus for abstract templates which are associated with religious belief, if they are part of the solution to personal mortality. The templates are filled in later with inferred concepts, the common paradigms of belief itself which underpins the world's belief systems.

The relationship between important mental and physical factors or causal drivers give rise to the template of afterlife, utilizing either life-force (naturalistic animism) or spirituality which are shown in Table 1.3 (next page). This is cause and effect, spark and fire, the engine of religious belief – we could say. The aspects of the human condition which have a direct response in belief systems, specifically afterlife and the essential afterlife mechanisms, are seen in all religions.

Causal drivers are some familiar and essential attributes of being human: breathing air, self-awareness, self-importance and, above all, personal mortality. The afterlife templates in response to these drivers are abstract, but once they are mentally accepted they are filled in with inferred concepts and these are part of formal religious belief systems and practice.

GMR: 1.3 DRIVERS AND TEMPLATES IN BELIEF SYSTEMS

HUMAN CONDITION	RELIGIOUS TEMPLATE	LAYER
Personal Mortality	Afterlife	All
Self-Awareness and movement in the Life-Force Worldview	All natural objects are alive (Naturalistic Animism)	Core Religion
Breathing and air in the Spiritual Worldview	Spirituality Spirits, deities present in the environment (Animism and Totemism)	Mantle Religion
Self-Importance	Adulthood in Afterlife Preservation of personal identity	Mantle and Tectonic Religion

So, afterlife conceptualized as rebirth is a religious belief and the systems associated with it are grouped within Inner and Outer Core Religion of the GMR. Rebirth is the earliest form of afterlife and prevailed as its major paradigm for several hundred thousand years, only being replaced by spiritual afterlife as a gradual process across the world eleven to four thousand years ago.

Adulthood in afterlife is a template which is enthusiastically embraced because it asserts *preservation of the individual*. Therefore, the template of spiritual afterlife is continuously reinforced because adulthood can only be preserved spiritually after physical death. This is an essential part of both reincarnation and resurrection beliefs of Upper Mantle Religion.

Once religious templates arise through these conditions a multitude of inferred concepts develop and build up formal religions. Not all concepts are used at once in any religion, and different cultures infer different concepts. So we need to gain an understanding of how these concepts can become embedded and widespread in human cultures. The persistence of religious concepts cannot just be parasitic in nature as they have persisted since prehistory, there must be some benefit, a positive feedback response to people who accept them. The GMR holds that the flux of concepts and ideas in religion are memes, although we do at first consider the alternative of the religious instinct.

Instinct

An instinct is any inbuilt complex pattern of behaviour, like mating, hunting, fleeing and vocalization. Instinctive activities, commonly seen in animals, can be quite specific: the spawning of salmon, food burial by squirrels and dogs, nest-building by birds. A newborn kangaroo knows innately to make the climb to the safety of its mother's pouch.

Over a hundred years ago, when science first attempted to explain the tendency for religious belief in humanity, researchers turned to patterns of instinct. In 1897, Henry Marshall, lecturer in aesthetics in New York, wrote *The Religious Instinct,* [15] and in 1905, Herbert Barraclough, a medical practitioner, developed the theme, emphasising that it can be normal or pathological. Barraclough, obviously influenced by his medical background, was theorizing that the religious instinct could become psychosis and illustrated this by way of a sect in the United States who had predicted an imminent "end-time" and were preparing for it. [16]

However, the first hurdle was to prove that human instinct existed, before religious instinct could even be properly identified. After a promising start the balloon of human instinct as a branch of psychology was soon wobbling badly. In 1910, Sigmund Freud wrote his first paper defining instinct as a psychic (mental) response to organic (biological) stimulus, but for years afterward he muddled through with several varying definitions. [17] Eventually he recognized two instinctual drives: "eros" and "thanatos", the life and death instincts, although other researchers recognized more and more of them until thousands were identified. Thus, the stage was set until the 1960s when the hissing noise of escaping air could no longer be ignored. The set of instincts were being progressively eroded through analysis until the consensus today is that humans have no instincts after about three months of age.

A key attribute of instinct is that it cannot be consciously overridden. Confusion arises because the word "instinct" is abused in popular culture to refer to subconscious behaviour. Pulling on a steering wheel to avoid a car crash might be subconscious, but never instinctive. In the strictest sense humans do not have instincts because we can modify all behaviour through learning and make arbitrary conscious decisions. We have done what animals cannot and that is use intelligence to unlearn the baggage of primordial instincts.

If one is casting about to salvage the theory of human instinct then a powerful one commonly suggested is the survival instinct, but even that proves to be a mirage. The main reason any animal wants to survive is pleasurable feedback about being alive in its environment. Humans have instead intellectually decided that survival is an essential human quality. What can be decided can be undecided, otherwise how is the following explained?

In late September 2005, at an apartment tower in southern Paris, two 14-year-old girls, Marion and Virginie, called their friends into a room. As the door opened, immediately the pair jumped, hand in hand, from the seventeenth floor balcony. One of the girls left a note which read, "Life isn't worth it." The whole of France was shocked by this double suicide and days later the many bouquets of flowers almost covered the sawdust on the blood-stained ground.

Yet there is more to this story. Both girls were at the margin of their community and peer group at school, having few friends they immersed themselves in Goth culture, heavy metal music and black clothes. The music lyrics they listened to were all about hate, death and suicide. They may have heard about the deaths which happened in January 2005 (or any of the 500 teenage female suicides in France each year) where two girls, aged 14 and 15, Clémence and Noémie, jumped together off the cliff at Cap Blanc Nez in Normandy. These two had similar interests and had written passages and poems about death on their blogs.

What happened to the human survival instinct in these sad cases? If human instinct is a mirage, then religious instinct can't exist either, so we back to square one unless there is a better theory. Fortunately there is.

Memes

> *The most interesting thing about memes is not whether they're true or false: it's that they are the building blocks of your mind.* [18]

> – Richard Brodie

To explain the persistence of concepts at the heart of all religious belief we need to begin with a clean slate. Returning to the chain of teenage suicide events in France we see a common thread. It is that of a set of ideas spreading from mind to mind via imitation or copying:

memes. So the human "survival instinct" is itself a set of memes, part of our intellectual culture, and can be suppressed by a set of suicide memes.

A meme is an idea or behaviour in one individual which is seen or heard by another – and copied.

Even this is a working definition as it is not complete. It is possible to think of a meme which is something else and detected differently, but this is still pretty comprehensive for the purpose of analysing religious belief. We want to look at a set of cultural memes, not explore the extremes of *memetics* which is the branch of science concerned with all memes and how they spread. Nevertheless, we need a reasonable overview of this subject before we can make use of it to describe how the corpus of religion persists and spreads.

Richard Dawkins coined the word "meme" in his 1976 work *The Selfish Gene,* emphasising their viral nature. A successful meme is one that spreads easily through a population. In our globalized culture memes can even spread very quickly throughout the world. *Virus* is mentioned a lot in memetics, not because memes are biological or damaging, but simply because of how they spread. Anything which uses something external to replicate is a *replicator* and hence a virus is a replicator and a meme is a mind-virus. A common misconception is that a virus is always damaging to the host. Dawkins seems to let this misconception ride when writing about religion because he cannot see the benefit of it. Interestingly, his detractors, like Alister McGrath, the theologian and writer, then fall down the manhole of rejecting a memetic explanation for the transmission of religion because of the viral and parasitic connotations which are implied. We will see later in Chapter Five, on the Spiritual Worldview, how the inferred concepts arising from the *judgment in afterlife* template spread as memes and are hugely beneficial. It is a cornerstone in the development of towns and civilization, just as important as the invention of agriculture. So we need to reconcile the parasitic nature of mind-viruses with the apparent benefits of some of them.

Richard Brodie, IT specialist, wrote *Virus of the Mind* in 1993, the first book devoted entirely to the understanding of memes and how they operate in human minds and become cultural. His definition of a meme aids our understanding of what at first glance appears to be a very slippery subject. He writes:

> *A meme is a replicator which uses the medium of our minds to replicate. Meme evolution happens because our minds are good at*

copying and innovating – ideas, behaviours, tunes, shapes, structures and so on.

Unfortunately, if memes are analysed to discover which ones are beneficial to human minds and which ones are detrimental, it is not as simple as separating the true and false ones. Certainly, even if religion is comprised mostly of false memes, which is what the science worldview is currently implying, then this does not take away the colossal benefit which religion has afforded humanity and world civilization.

What is a good example of a meme? There are tens of thousands but one I like is the Mexican Wave because it encapsulates the life-cycle of a meme in a visual manner. At a crowded football match a few people jumping up and signalling are trying to start a wave by expressing the Mexican Wave meme. There are two states for everyone else, the meme is dormant in their mind or absent entirely. Where it is dormant there is a predisposition to copy the action and amplify the wave. Many will. Once the wave reaches a critical mass even those who are unaware of the meme are taking notice and some imitate it. The wave has momentum and then spreads through time and distance to a different set of people who have no idea who started the wave or when. Eventually, when everyone is losing interest the wave loses momentum. After the wave ends the Mexican Wave meme has spread because it is now dormant in more people than before. More people are predisposed to participate in a wave next time a suitable situation arises. Memes have some power as once they spread many people undergo a modification of their thoughts or behaviour. *After memes spread people are changed!*

All aspects of human culture are variations on this theme. Memes can be any attribute of culture which spreads by imitation, such as the habit of smoking, wearing jewellery, driving on one side of the road or me-too consumerism (buying things you don't need with money you don't have to impress people who don't care). However, imitation alone will not advance cultures over the long-term. There must be a process of invention and learning which adds incremental improvement to cultural knowledge before further imitation adds to the "fitness level" of the whole culture.

Even templates behave like memes when they are invented. They are abstract mental frameworks which also undergo natural selection and memetic behaviour, even if they are populated with ideas which are themselves memes, before they can be used.

Intergenerational transmission of memes is not limited to religion. Prior to the Neolithic period all humans lived by hunting and foraging. For physical reasons, usually but not always, the men hunted and women foraged. Society today reflects this ancient demarcation between the sexes. Men, usually but not always, like sports or competition, because they are predisposed to perform hunting tasks. Women usually, but not always, like shopping because they are predisposed to perform foraging tasks. Clearly the hunting and foraging memes are very ancient and typically spread from adults to children of the *same* sex (which is memetic predisposition) generation after generation.

Memes are often trivial and appeal because they represent counter-culture. Actor Mike Myers' enduring contribution to the English language came from applying the suffix "Not" to sentences to reverse their meaning. He created a meme which entered popular culture and has travelled quickly from one human mind to another. It doesn't enhance language and appears entirely parasitic.

Because parasitic memes exist, does not mean beneficial ones don't. Biologists have for a while recognized that viruses are sometimes beneficial to their hosts. This area is a hot topic because while the pathological role of viruses in diseases like hepatitis, rabies and herpes is well understood the beneficial and perhaps critical roles of other viruses in biological processes can be very subtle and remain undetected.

Marilyn Roossinck, plant pathologist, has identified nine virus groups each with a specific example of their beneficial role to plants, fungi, bacteria, insects and mammals. [19] It is interesting to note that early in the evolution of mammals an ancient retrovirus infection became so symbiotic that it spliced with mammalian DNA and now codes for growth and protection of the placenta. Sheep with this genetic sequence knocked out cannot reproduce due to miscarriages. [20]

Memetics and Memeplexes

Memetics is a new and still somewhat controversial branch of the psychological sciences as it deals with how memes originate, compete, spread and evolve. The working assumption is that memes operate under natural selection when they propagate from person to person analogously, to how genes are naturally selected for in competition between living organisms.

Memes are, of course, not alive, but their spread follows high-level processes which are seen in biology – in particular viruses. Memes are mental viruses which use the human brain as an external medium to replicate.

Genes, computer viruses and ideas (memes) use external resources to spread. They are not alive (we normally associate life with the ability to replicate) but the universe does have non-thinking structures which replicate. There are two overarching processes in our universe, *entropy* which is the tendency of order to disorder, and *evolution* which is a tendency of disorder to order. Entropy is thermodynamic and is the "main current" whereas evolution is like an eddy, a smaller reversing current. Memes evolve as they spread and the successful ones move typically towards a more ordered state.

I like Brodie's pithy summary: "*Evolution is a battle for resources by replicators.*"

So, the inferred concepts or paradigms which fill religious templates are most accurately called memes as they are readily copied from person to person and undergo natural selection within cultures.

Typically a meme is small, concise and cannot easily be broken down without making it meaningless. They are atomic. It is when they operate as a group with interconnectedness that they become a set of memes: a *memeplex* also known as a *meme-complex*.

The utility of money is a memeplex. This comprises numerous atomic memes which everyone has mentally accepted to fill in the template of equitable exchange. There is a meme where money is thought of as a medium of exchange. So, if someone does an hour of labour and receives a twenty dollar banknote then a meme must be prevailing in society that this note is exchangeable for labour, food and other products. There is another meme that the note is a *unit of accounting* so it can be exchanged for smaller denominations or deposited and turned into electronic money at the bank. There is another meme that the note or electronic deposit is a *store of value* so that it does not need to be spent immediately. All these together are a memeplex which makes intangible money acceptable for tangible transactions. Ultimately, the success of this memeplex depends upon trust. Trust that everyone else shares this structure of concepts. Its success is not guaranteed and the money-memeplex may fail. When this happens people will rely on the gold-meme, which has an intrinsic store of value and can't be printed, or untainted foreign currency, or the cumbersome barter-meme that products are better exchanged directly for other products.

The corporate image and branding of General Motors Corporation is a memeplex and the ideology and ethos of the Chinese Communist Party is another memeplex.

Natural selection in biology is a model for how memes spread and change. Since beneficial symbiosis is seen in biology it is very hard to imagine how memes could behave differently and always be parasitic. Further, it is even harder to imagine how any memeplex could be wholly parasitic, although many individual memes within it may be trivial or parasitic. As part of a memeplex they are part of a cultural structure which has benefits outweighing its detriments.

Religion as a Memeplex

Natural selection of competing ideas is an important component of memetics and this is reflected in the GMR. Within Core Religion the most important drivers are reflexes from the human condition. At the level of individuals this selects individual preferences in religion. Within Mantle Religion it is individuals selecting ideas only because of drivers, reflexes from the social condition, which arise from group level benefits. Mantle Religion therefore describes religions which have developed a combination of individual and socially beneficial memeplexes. These result in both the promise of afterlife modified to ensure the priority of social cohesion. Tectonic Religion is primarily a new set of memeplexes because religion is responding to the vast memeplex we know as science.

There are objections to memes as the building blocks of religion and these basically fall into two arguments.

First, that memes are trivial, implying that religion is too important to be reduced in this way. Because memes are often trivial it is hard to see them underpinning belief systems, but who is to say what is trivial? And religion is thousands of memes working together – some of which are extremely important: concepts about afterlife, spirituality and judgment. Furthermore, even powerful templates, such as the emerging spiritual worldview, which was fundamental to the success of the Neolithic revolution, still behaved mimetically as it spread from the Fertile Crescent.

Secondly, that memes are parasitical, recognizing that religion is too complex and pervasive to be categorized this way. Religion has been hugely beneficial to humanity by subduing the universal concern about mortality, also by enabling the development of civilizations and stable conditions within which science can flourish. So, far from being a parasite, religion is a hugely beneficial developmental force in its own right. This was addressed earlier when beneficial viruses were discussed. Memeplexes can only be enduring when they serve in a positive feedback loop, hence they grow or wither by Darwinian natural selection.

For example, Christianity is a memeplex. It is a superset of accepted memes which describe a religious orthodoxy. It has many memes comprising the whole. As well as the memes of inferred concepts which populate the afterlife and judgment templates there are stand-alone memes such as the virgin birth, another for the Bible as word of God, another for male-only priests (rejected in Protestantism), a meme for consecrated ground and for Sunday as a holy day. Many more exist. So a religion is something much more complicated than a single meme.

Every other world religion is a memeplex but it will not add to our understanding to discuss them individually in this fashion for the simple reason that all of human culture is a memeplex of one sort or another. Even God is a memeplex and the thinking behind his origin will be detailed later in this work.

The GMR rests upon religious templates arising from the human and social conditions. These templates are filled-in with culturally specific inferred concepts. These concepts are religious memes which undergo natural selection, singly and in combination, to produce the most successful memeplexes.

Magic and the Pre-Scientific Worldviews

The life-force and spiritual worldview paradigms developed before science so belief systems utilized common "functional representations" to understand and harness the natural environment. Effectively, this was a belief in what is known to have an unscientific basis, or, what in the modern era is known as magic.

Magic as Proto-science

Any sufficiently advanced technology is indistinguishable from magic.

– Arthur C. Clarke

Clarke's point is actually quite narrow. As a very successful science fiction writer he was thinking of advanced cultures meeting primitive ones, or even modern humans encountering alien intelligences. Until recent centuries there has been an overarching principle relevant to all cultures. It is that *magic is the substitute for science in a pre-scientific world.* This was not long ago. All early peoples developed magical practices in the absence of the corpus of science to draw upon.

The magic we refer to is not the stage magic of Houdini and modern day television performers. Pre-scientific era magic comprises functional representations, ritual, sacrifice, divining the future, appeasing gods, casting spells against enemies – all intended to understand or control the human environment in day-to-day life.

Today science is so vigorous and ubiquitous in our lives that we struggle to imagine life without its technological benefits. What was it like thousands of years ago? People could never live in a knowledge vacuum. As soon as they objectively assessed their natural world then it became a requirement to have a reasonable level of cultural knowledge about where they lived, their origins and how nature worked.

Whether as hunter-gatherers or small settled communities or whole civilizations, basic questions about nature have always been present. What forces drive the existence of day and night, the sun and moon, spring and autumn? How did it come to pass that there are animals and plants to eat? What causes the rain and wind? Important are questions about the environment which intelligent people simply can't just accept as happenstance without a deeper understanding. Further, once the environment is understood within a life-force or spiritual worldview, the desire follows to control it via the acquired knowledge. Before the science worldview emerged people relied upon magic to understand and exert control over the natural world. What the modern researcher might consider being an example of ancient symbolism, the carvings on a bone perhaps, is more accurately considered as an ancient tool. Its makers imagined a functional representation, within a belief system, which held it as being effective in the physical world. Magic is believed to be functional.

In 1890 James George Frazer published the first major book on comparative religion, *The Golden Bough*, which received a lot of attention in its day, especially as Christianity was often included in his comparisons. The shock and criticism about this is understandable as the Victorians very much viewed Christianity as a religion of divine origin whereas all others were thought to be invented by man. Frazer's knowledge of religious and superstitious trivia was profound because he could reel off numerous examples from all parts of the world to illustrate the smallest point.

Today Frazer is a footnote on the road to the scientific basis for religion. Although, he was the first to appreciate the importance of magic. Frazer recognized that magic was often integrated into religion; also that it was older, and substituted for science. He recognized that magic springs from the attempt to find logic in the structure of nature and make use of this knowledge. Unfortunately for magic it was doomed from the start because whenever it was wrong it remained magic but whenever it was right it became science! Frazer identified classifications within magic for decomposing parts of religious belief: magic as theoretical (pseudoscience) and magic as practical (pseudo-art). Within the latter is positive magic (sorcery) and negative magic (taboo). Then Frazer went well off-track. He assumed that magic was gradually replaced by religion. The reality is more complex. Some magic has stayed within religion, for example: transubstantiation of wine into blood and wafer into flesh –revelation and miracles.

It might be thought that it was hard for any magic to become science, and this was true, but examples exist, such as medicinal plants. For example mandrake (*Mandragora officinarum*) was surrounded with magical beliefs. Although poisonous, small amounts of the juice in a boiled preparation is a good anaesthetic and was used in ancient times before starting a surgical procedure. Some magic has long been outside religion, such as astrology. Some magic became alchemy and some alchemy became science. Famously, Isaac Newton was part scientist and part alchemist; he developed and calculated the Law of Universal Gravitation while spending a lot of time working on the Philosopher's Stone, clandestinely, because it was illegal as the government did not want gold to be easily made.

GMR:1.4   CATEGORIES OF MAGIC IN RELIGION

MAGIC	PARADIGM OF ACTION
Sympathetic Homeopathic	Like-for-like Like-makes-like
Sympathetic Contagious	Association by Touching Association after Separation
Divination	Interpretation of Current Events Prediction of Future Events
Propitiation	Sacrifice and Offerings Worship and Prayer
Miraculous	Divine Interventions
Revelation	Divinely Revealed Knowledge Holy Scripture

While we might look back and want to detect black and white distinctions, this is purist thinking. Change was gradual over lifetimes and there was early co-development of magic with religion, just as there has been a later co-development of science with religion.

The earliest magic was sympathetic-homeopathic or like-for-like and this type was virtually ubiquitous in prehistory and is the main one fundamental to afterlife belief. In funerary rituals it is used to facilitate rebirth in the life-force worldview, or used to facilitate spiritual progression in the spiritual worldview.

The Red Ochre Tradition, which is described in Chapter Three, is certainly the first use of magic by humans. It works by sympathetic-homeopathic magic and involved a sequence of concepts:

Interpretation: the pre-scientific discovery of blood as the "life-force" dividing the animate from inanimate in humans and animals.

Association: like-for-like, of red ochre functionally representing blood because of its colour and liquid consistency when mixed with water. Red ochre deposits in the ground could be magically interpreted as blood of the earth as this is consistent with the life-force worldview.

Application: The funerary ritual of applying red ochre to corpses, exercising human control over afterlife and rebirth.

Magic wasn't only associated with funerary rituals to overcome personal mortality. Most magical applications were to explain and control nature. Magic became proto-science, a substitute for science, and is therefore worked alongside religion in the prevailing worldview. In the example of the oracle bones in Shang China, divination was used to determine the intentions of ancestral spirits which amounted to a form of spiritual judgment.

Revealed knowledge is an important quality of all religions which can take a lifetime to learn. For example, the Four Noble Truths and Eightfold Path of Buddhism are central to dharma (law and knowledge). Revealed knowledge is magical in its origin as it was not obtained by scientific inquiry.

An example of magic as part of the Dreamtime quasi-worldview is traditional Aboriginal rock art in Arnhem Land, north Australia. The television reporter Colin Simpson describes its functional, like-for-like purpose:

> *Why did they paint? Were they like children, setting down whatever left a shape and excitement within the mind's eye? No. […] most of the art in the rock galleries of Inyaluk seems to have been motivated by purposes entirely beyond the realm of childish thinking. Much of it appears to express beliefs based in need and desire. To say that the aboriginal never practiced cultivating and growing things is wrong. He grew and cultivated all his foods, animal and plant – or believed he did – by magic. What we call art to him was often a means to that magic. A kangaroo painted was a kangaroo brought nearer to his spear.* [21]

The conceptual parallel with Palaeolithic European cave art has long been made. No effort was spent on landscapes, trees, mountains, rocks and rivers. All of it is about the animals, running, leaping, and sometimes harried by stick figure hunters. In Australia like-for-like hunting magic was intended to bring the animals forth from the earth and *nearer to the spear*. In Europe the magic was not quite the same, and this is explored at the end of Chapter Two.

Magic became bound into religion because it was religion that needed to answer the greatest question, "What of personal mortality?" Yet, how could it answer the greatest question and then be silent on lesser, day-to-day matters, still important to survival?

There are many issues concerning daily life, providence, warfare, ancestry and so on. Regaining control over fate is especially important when something goes wrong and people are starving and dying: the disappearance of herds or excessive dry weather or infertility. How can the elders of any community save face when their people are suffering and dying and looking to them to do something? Inevitably magical practices were absorbed into the prevailing religion of ancient societies. Priests and shamans were one and the same.

When religion came to include magic it was then seen as a substitute for science. Religious knowledge largely filled the role of a corpus of understanding wherever science was lacking. This is the root of much unfair criticism levelled at religion – particularly by physicalists today.

Our twenty-first century perspective is much more mature and balanced than a hundred years ago. Early writers were very dismissive of the ignorance and savagery of belief in naive magic, whereas today we study prehistoric artefacts for evidence of developmental symbolism, language and art – including magic. These artefacts would have been magical to their creators and owners. Although they are dusty and dead pieces of bone and wood to us, they still reveal evidence of sophisticated cultural belief systems within the worldview in which so many long forgotten people once lived.

2 ◆ CORE RELIGION: LIFE-FORCE WORLDVIEW

Emergence of the Life-Force Worldview Paradigm

The awareness of death and our attempts to transcend it have haunted humanity for at least the last ten thousand years and probably the last million years.[22]

– Mike Parker Pearson

Core Religion is contained in the life-force worldview which developed during the early period of human conceptual thinking, perhaps as long as one million years ago. This was where the nature of the environment first came to be considered and during this period the implications of personal mortality also became clear. Religion itself later emerged and then spread as naturally selected memes, as a behavioural response arising from awareness of mortality. Abstract thinking within belief systems had also begun to influence human evolution.

Life-Force or Naturalistic Animism

A horse in the dusk shies at the threatening form of a tree-stump beside the road, although in daylight he would not notice it at all. In his imagination it becomes a strange living being with power perhaps to injure him; the instinct of self-preservation, therefore, prompts him to be on his guard against the unknown.[23]

– Rafael Karsten

Belief in life-forces present in the elements of the environment is *naturalistic* or *psychological animism*. In this worldview all discrete environmental objects such as animals, trees, clouds, streams and mountains are thought to possess their own non-human self-awareness and are alive. This is the earliest worldview paradigm for all archaic humans, very likely predating our own species. As the intelligence of prehistoric humans improved it was an inevitable process to objectively consider nature and try obvious approaches to understanding it. Neither spirituality nor science is immediately obvious; the life-force worldview of naturalistic animism is much more obvious as a mirror to self-awareness. For hundreds of millenia hominins must have held the simplest "everything is alive" explanation of nature.

Analogies exist. The most advanced software components of artificial intelligence, when first run, will transition through an infantile phase while evaluating its environment for the first time. A toddler will chew a crayon before realising that it can be used to draw with.

Richard Clark makes this observation in his work *The Multiple Natural Origins of Religion,* but he prefers the term "animatism" instead of naturalistic animism:

> *Animatism is the attribution of mere personality to objects, processes or locations, so that one acts as if beings are there which are potentially aware of one's presence and as if one could relate to those beings rather as one person to another. The personality is not initially regarded as a soul or soul-like spirit.* [24]

All of the Palaeolithic and Mesolithic religious beliefs build upon the fundamental apprehension of naturalistic animism which creates and perpetuates the life-force worldview. Everything is alive.

Chris Fowler, archaeologist, explores how the identification of one-self, personally, often leads inexorably to animism in various cultures and concludes:

> *Animism in particular involves highly relational personhood, including open negotiations with non-human persons. Finally, interactions between entities are carried out within particular attitudes. In fully relational personhood, where animals, plants and rocks might be people, we would expect very similar attitudes to extend to interactions with all these people.* [25]

There is general confusion over whether the animism which followed from self-identification was at first naturalistic, spiritual, or both. However, in the GMR it is held that naturalistic animism first followed from self-identification and this later *transformed* into spiritual animism and totemism during the Neolithic spiritual worldview paradigm shift. So, in the GMR it is Core Religion which is defined by naturalistic concepts. It is Mantle Religion which is defined by the spiritual worldview including spiritual animism, totemism and ancestor worship.

The difference between animals and humans with regard to personal mortality and animism is simple: *conceptual thinking*. The development of this has been a multi-million year journey started before the *Homo* genus became distinct approximately 2.4 mya (million years ago). There are faint glimpses in the archaeological record to the degree of conceptual thinking performed by archaic hominins. Faint glimpses also hint that *Homo erectus* may have conceived of mortality, animism and the life-force worldview. If he did not then the earliest *Homo sapiens* certainly did.

Conceptual Thinking in *Australopithecus*

Long before modern humans existed, before the *Homo* genus itself, a hairy arm reached into sparkling clear river water and removed a red jasper pebble for close inspection. Behind quizzical eyes intelligence stirred. Recognition, association and meaning: the linkages of conceptual thought meshed in a new way. *Australopithecus africanus*, or his near-cousin, saw an abstract face, in the rounded pebble, and more perhaps – symbolic significance in the red colour that is also seen as blood dripping from the cut bodies of the living and dying. At a stretch it may have reminded him of a newborn infant, but more likely just an awareness that the pebble had an "australopithecine-like" quality, a quality in the stone that we would say as "human-like". If there is a birth certificate for conceptual thought then this is it – the moment this pebble was being examined the whole earth passed into the hands of a non-human intelligence.

This was an evolutionary milestone. Four billion years of mindless natural selection had reached the point where intelligence had become *self-referential*. Evolution made a paradigm shift and would never be the same again. In fact it has become supercharged because on that distant and sunny African day imagination became a new force in natural selection. *A. africanus* stood up clutching his find and carried it to his rockshelter about ten kilometres away, where it was kept and covered by the debris of habitation.

Nearly three million years later, in 1925, 250 km north-east of modern-day Johannesburg, South Africa, the area was excavated and the pebble found. It became called the *Makapansgat Cobble.* Coincidentally, Raymond Dart's archaeological team had found and named the first *Australopithecus* species only a year earlier. It was 50 long years later when Dart wrote about the cobble, and its significance properly seen as proof of emerging hominin intelligence. [26] It is the earliest known manuport, the earliest unworked but carried object. So how does *A. africanus* compare intellectually with humans and other large-brained animals?

The Encephalization Quotient (EQ) is the ratio of actual brain mass to a theoretical brain mass based upon body mass scaled across a zoological class where a rating of 1.0 is "normal". The domestic cat has an EQ of 1.0. Outliers like the hummingbird exist, EQ rated 9.0, but their brain of just one gram will never exhibit high intelligence. When only considering mammals the EQ is a reasonable approximation for the level of intelligence. By this measure modern humans rate 7.5, the highest of all mammals. At 5.0 *Homo erectus*, the first hominin to disperse from Africa, exceeded that of dolphins, which are between 4.0 and 4.7. Chimpanzees are a lowly 2.3. [27] So *A. africanus'* rating of 3.2 [28] was greater than that of all modern apes. (There is no standard calculation of EQ, so *A. africanus* is adjusted here for consistency with the animal values).

The complex behaviour of chimpanzees is well known, and their ability to learn symbolic association, from human teachers, supports the argument that *A. africanus* was capable of conceptual thought and had the potential to go beyond the capacity of chimps and apes. Extinct hominin species are troublesome because their remains are so fragmentary that their body mass is inexactly known. Tragically, the rich deposit of Australopithecus bones at Makapansgat were used for lime production in the 1920s!

So, the Makapansgat Cobble is good evidence indicating that the *Australopithecines* had crossed the threshold in achieving conceptual thinking. Yet the evidence for *Australopithecus* itself is so fragmentary that having already found a significant manuport so soon would tend to suggest that conceptualization was widespread in their population. There is no evidence that they had tools or art, let alone religion. Important questions remain unanswered. Was *Australopithecus* aware of his own personal mortality? Did he ever contemplate his own death? We may never know with any probability. Phrased another way we can see how a prototype of advanced intelligence could make the transition from animal to human. Did *Australopithecus* always live in the present? Because animals live in the present, it is a human quality to spend a lot of time contemplating the past and the future. This is also the power of abstraction. As soon as anything in the real world becomes abstracted, a hominoid face seen in a rock for example, then the mind is compelled to probe into the past or future in order to gain further meaning from the abstraction.

How much further progress in symbolic and abstract thought was made by *Australopithecus* is unknown but they went extinct about half a million years after the cobble was first found by them. Their intelligence was apparently insufficient to allow them to compete with the newly emerged and spreading *Homo* genus. This genus, known collectively as humans, likely arose from the Australopithecines. [28] It has been suggested that the sub-species *Australopithecus garhi*, found in Ethiopia, is a possible link. [29] The recent find of *Australopithecus sediba* in South Africa is another possibility. The hominin fossil record is a two-hundred-year work in progress – still ongoing, so debate over the detail rumbles on.

The *Homo* genus is characterized by a rapid succession of advancing sub-species of two successful primary species: *Homo erectus* and *Homo sapiens*. They both dispersed far across the globe. Yet the cognitive groundwork for their cultural development, the effect of imagination on natural selection, had been laid by evolution before humans appeared.

Conceptual Thinking in *Homo erectus*

> *There are indications at two earliest Acheulian sites in east Africa that Homo erectus of ca. 1.5 Ma B.P. was interested in red mineral pigment. At Terra Amata, near Nice, 75 shaped pieces of red ochre were found with the earliest European Acheulian industry (ca. 0.3 Ma B.P.). This occurrence indicates that to an Acheulian society red mineral pigment had great symbolic value.* [30]

> – K. P. Oakley

For the *Homo* genus, was proto-religious thinking an early solution to the greatest of abstract problems?

Homo erectus first appeared about 1.9 mya and died out as late as 50 kya (50,000 years ago) where evidence from Ngandong in Java is the last that strongly indicates they were still living. *Erectus* was the first human to have spread throughout Africa, Europe and Asia, later followed by *Homo sapiens*. They first tamed fire for cooking, scaring predators and warmth. They also knapped stone tools and may have been the first of any humans to wear animal skins and pair-bond monogamously for life. In Asia, their skeletal remains are the famous evidence of *Peking Man* and *Java Man* but for decades these were thought to be a separate species from the humans in Africa. However the 1997 discovery of a partially animal-chewed *erectus* skull in Awash, Ethiopia, dated to 1 mya confirms that they were one widespread species, as these remains are similar to Asian examples.

Homo erectus had a range of brain-size with the largest of them overlapping that seen in adult modern humans today. Nevertheless, the later members of this species suffered a gradual replacement by *Homo sapiens*, first in Africa, then Europe and finally Asia. *Erectus* did not bury their dead or leave any relics which might be associated with formal religion, but proto-religious roots were being laid down by them.

They had compassion for the sick, and this is firmly evidenced by the skeleton KNM-ER 1808 from Kenya, dated to 1.7 mya, and described by the paleoanthropologist Alan Walker as a "nightmare". This adult female had such an advanced condition of vitamin A overdose, from consuming carnivore livers, that all her bones were terribly diseased and deformed. She spent her last month in agony as blot clots ossified into bone. She was unable to obtain food by herself and required frequent care, with food and water brought to her and predators being kept away, day after day, week after week. [31]

Apart from the level of empathy shown, a further question arises, which is, how did these unusual remains fossilize? If this was an exceptional medical condition, isn't it a coincidence that she was one of the handful of largely intact skeletons from this era overlooked by scavengers? The possibility exists that she was finally euthanized as a mercy killing, or deliberately cached, in the muddy shallows of a watering hole. From the point of death her remains were not available to scavengers.

Two areas stand out as evidential of *Homo erectus'* conceptual thinking:

1) Red colour symbolism in Africa: Oldowan Bed II ca. 1.7 mya and Wonderwerk Cave ca. 900 to 800 kya
2) Deep-water rafting in Asia: Indonesian islands ca. 1 mya to 850 kya

It seems these humans recognized the colour red as special, and this is highly significant as it is the first step on the road to religious belief.

In the early 1950s the archaeologists Louis and Mary Leakey found two intriguing pieces of reddish volcanic rock (which they misidentified as ochre) at raised ground, possibly a place of habitation. It was near a rich archaeological hunting site of bones and stone tools known as Bed II which they also called the "Slaughter House". Clearly it used to be a swamp where *erectus* drove a great many animals, trapping, despatching them, and cutting them up for food. The Leakey's first considered that the "ochre" could have been used for body painting – as they saw on tribespeople when in Kenya. [32] Because of the antiquity of the find they dismissed body-painting, but the fact that the pieces were not ochre makes the point moot. Instead, and we shall see in context later, a more likely explanation is that reddish stones were thought to be functional representations of blood.

Further significance, perhaps also of blood symbolism, this time from red ochre, is implied elsewhere in the continent at the Wonderwerk Cave of South Africa which has ochre pieces in habitation layers dating back to between 900 and 800 kya, well before *Homo sapiens* appeared. This cave has by far the longest period of human occupancy of any site in the world and has yielded worked stone artefacts dating back several hundred thousand years. Humans collected reddish stones at their habitation site for a reason and that may well be that their blood-like quality held significance. For example, they could be interpreted as ensuring the area would continue to be a rich hunting ground, with plentiful animals for consumption. This might be the first evidence of magic. The concept of "like-makes-like", which was introduced in the previous chapter, may have been first put into practice by *erectus*.

This is not the only suggestion of symbolic thinking in this long-extinct species. Robert Bednarik of the *International Federation of Rock Art Organizations* and prodigious author on palaeoanthropology details radical but convincing arguments. He is attempting to prove that *erectus* was capable of more advanced symbolic thought, organization and communication than that generally credited to him by the anthropological community. One area of focus is the mystery of how *erectus* came to inhabit islands too remote for normal coastal migrations.

It is a mystery of real significance. David Cameron, anatomist, and Colin Groves, archaeologist, make this observation:

> *So there is reason to think that humans, more than three-quarters of a million years ago wandered unusually far east, crossing the sea as they did so. Does this mean that they had boats? We don't know. But the only humans in Southeast Asia at this time, as far as we knew, were Homo erectus. So our beetle-browed cousin was not such a slouch after all.* [33]

Most bird, mammal and reptile species were halted at the eastern shore of Bali. This boundary is part of the invisible Wallace Line, named after a nineteenth century biologist Alfred Wallace, who rivalled Charles Darwin, and identified the sharp distinction between the variety of animals in western and eastern Indonesia because they had evolved independently. However, at least five of the Lesser Sunda Islands: Lombok, Sumbawa, Sumba, Flores and Timor were populated by *erectus*. They had crossed the Wallace Line to an area which had never been joined to mainland Asia. The gap across the Lombok Strait in Indonesia cannot have been less than 20 kilometres even when ocean levels were lowest. How was it done?

A subsequent sudden tectonic movement sinking a former land bridge can be ruled out as there are five islands in question over a wide area, particularly also as Timor is part of the Australian plate and has been slowly rising for millions of years. However, Jan Lucassen, historian, still objects that *erectus* had not achieved anything special because ancestral stegodonts (primitive elephants) have also colonized the same islands but similarly not further east towards New Guinea. [34] Bednarik counters this by pointing out that elephants are excellent long-distance swimmers. They have been observed for up to two days crossing large African lakes and have colonized many islands elsewhere. *Erectus* did achieve something special, as humans cannot cross the sea without some form of technology. Bednarik proposes that it was by rafting. He has even experimented with ocean-going rafts, reminiscent of Thor Heyerdahl's *Kon-Tiki* adventure, to demonstrate viable deepwater bamboo rafting across the Lombok Strait. [35]

All the colonized islands are detectable from the previous one because of sightlines to peaks. So it might be thought that *erectus* didn't even need a lashed raft when a large tree trunk floating in the sea may have sufficed. A group could cling to it as they paddled to an island at the horizon. In reality sea conditions are rarely that favourable. There is a treacherous lateral current in the Lombok Strait which carries the greatest volume of tidal water in the world. Anyone helplessly drifting can be easily swept out to open sea. The survival time of individuals immersed in water depends upon temperature. The normal range in these islands is 19 to 26°c giving a period of 18 to 60 hours until death by hypothermia. [36] A stable raft at least gives the occupants time to paddle and rest without being immersed for a day in saltwater, but some attempts must have ended in failure and drowning. Also, it is remarkable in that many families must have successfully completed these trips to establish viable groups for resuming a hunter-gatherer existence.

Circumstantial evidence of ocean-going rafting implies that *erectus* exhibited conceptual thinking, planning, social organization and communication at a time before *Homo sapiens* had even evolved. If this much thinking was going on then surely *erectus* was also aware of his own mortality and might even have been bothered by it! Did they have afterlife beliefs? There is no evidence for this except the beginnings of the proto-religious red colour symbolism.

Interestingly, as a side note, it is known that large animals sometimes revert to a pygmy form after many generations confined on an island, and this may have happened to *erectus* on Flores, shrinking in size, becoming the recently discovered and named *Homo floresiensis*. This recently surviving species of genus *Homo*, who lived almost up to the historical era, was extinct at 12 kya, long after the Neanderthal had vanished in Europe. It would be fascinating if any archaic red-hued manuports were found on Flores.

The Origin of *Homo sapiens*

Homo erectus made the first dispersal from Africa about 1.9 million years ago. To be clear, the early Out of Africa theory of *Homo* origins and subsequent migration is unassailable. This was originally suggested by Charles Darwin over 150 years ago and has never been in real dispute. The first dispersal was not really a migration as it was driven by natural selection because *erectus* had become largely carnivorous, whereas the earlier Australopithecines were largely plant-eating. In order to maintain body size and population numbers *erectus* needed to be more spread out and this happened by 1.4 mya when much of Eurasia had been reached.

Archaic *Homo sapiens* diverged in Africa, either from *Homo erectus*, or a parallel species *Homo rhodesiensis* or *Homo heidelbergensis* at about 700 to 600 kya. DNA evidence supports this based upon mutation rates of genes. [37] Physical evidence of finds at Lake Ndutu in Tanzania also indicates a transitional phase between *erectus* and *sapiens* during 600 to 400 kya. Around then, a migration to southern Africa occurred and also a second migration into Europe and Asia, this time by archaic *sapiens.* Eventually a third migration occurred, also of *sapiens*, apparently of early modern type.

Perhaps this last major wave was represented by those living at Qafzeh Cave in Israel about 100 kya. There are many remarkable discoveries at this site, but one that is less commonly mentioned is that there were two types of human living at the cave at about the same time with the same burial practices. Half were semi-robust with Neanderthal-like features. Their teeth had archaic characteristics and their skulls had fairly prominent bony eyebrow ridges, yet they also had a modern pelvis shape compared to Neanderthal, and the thumb was more modern. Others were early modern humans, much closer to how we look today.

When it is considered that fully archaic Neanderthal lived at the nearby Kebara cave, thirty thousand years *later*, it is evident that human evolution was in a state of flux for a long time. There are two main competing theories of human evolution:

The older Multi-Regional Continuity Model assumes that modern humans developed locally in Europe, North Asia and South East Asia from descendent populations from either the first, *Homo erectus* migration, or the second, archaic *sapiens* migration.

The newer theory, Out of Africa Replacement Model, is that the third migration, of modern *sapiens*, wiped out the earlier populations completely. This proposes that modern humans originated in Africa by 100 kya and slowly spread to Europe and Asia, replacing all existing archaic humans and the older robust remnants of *sapiens*. This was when the Neanderthal was pushed into the Iberian Peninsula and seemingly breathed their last in a cave with their backs to the Atlantic Ocean. In the 1980s this theory gained immensely from DNA evidence – statistical analysis of human DNA variations in living populations – which suggested that all modern humans are descended from ancestors who were living in Northeast Africa around 200 to 150 kya. This analysis pointed to separate female and male "chokepoints" in the form of Mitochondrial Eve and Y-Chromosome Adam, both in Africa well before the final migrations. It became the consensus view of palaeoanthropology.

The theory of replacement always had problems such as explaining how early modern humans were in Australia at about 50 kya, but failed to complete their migration in Europe until 25 kya; the opposite would be expected based upon the distance from Africa. Also, the last Neanderthal remains in Europe show hybrid features with modern humans. A possible hybrid of Neanderthal and modern was found at Abrigo do Lagar Velho, Portugal, dated to 24.5 kya. Recent DNA evidence shows limited interbreeding, where Neanderthal DNA is present in people today, fatally weakening the total replacement theory. If there were two quite different species then interbreeding would only have occurred early on, not at such a recent period. The latest interpretation is that a partial replacement model is warranted. [38]

The full replacement theory prevailed until recently. Now there is irony as the theory benefited from DNA analysis; yet now DNA analysis has effectively demolished it. In 2002, geneticist Alan Templeton proved that modern humans have some DNA from archaic humans. Later research shows specific Neanderthal genetic variations present in Europeans and Asians but missing from modern Africans. So cross-breeding between Eurasian archaic humans and early modern humans from Africa took place outside Africa.

The Assimilation Model, which can be considered a variation of the Out of Africa Replacement model, still requires a recent migration of early moderns from Africa – but allows for limited interbreeding. It grows in support. Katerina Harvati, paleoanthropologist and Terry Harrison, anthropologist, after exhaustive analysis, conclude that humans from Africa and the Eurasian Neanderthal were capable of breeding to produce viable, fertile offspring. Also, Neanderthal genes are diluted because the population in Africa was always larger than in Eurasia because, for a long time, large parts of the great northern continent was under glaciers or consisted of frozen tundra. [39]

So, the real debate concerns how much assimilation took place. Africa was always the reservoir population, with its tropical climate which speeds up evolution, so it appears that African genes largely swamped the archaic genes in a 95 per cent to 5 per cent ratio. This is well over the numerical bias needed to favour migrating Africans over local populations to create the illusion of a replacement event after tens of thousands of years.

The GMR supports the Assimilation Theory of human evolution for the completely different and yet hitherto unconsidered reason that the evolution of religion is almost seamless through the demise of archaic humans, especially the Neanderthal, and the appearance of modern humans. This strongly suggests a peaceful and gradual process rather than a sudden extermination.

Implications of Personal Mortality

As Rank argued, consciousness is both a social and historical process, with increasing self-awareness over time, culminating in what Freud, Geza Roheim, Susanne Langer, Ernest Becker, and others claimed is the most significant event in the evolutionary history of humankind: the explicit awareness of death as a natural and inevitable event. [40]

– Sheldon Solomon, Jeff Greenburg, Jeff Schimel & Jamie Arndt

Awareness of death as an end-point for life is not the same as awareness of personal mortality. Awareness of death is apparent in higher animals such as elephants, cetaceans and primates. Lesser animals know it simply as the moment when their prey stops moving. When a cat is prodding a dead mouse it shows that true recognition is lacking in these animals.

Primatologists know that awareness of death as an end-point exists amongst bonobos, chimpanzees and other monkey and ape species. Instances are witnessed where they have shown strong recognition and unusual behaviour when one of their number succumbs to a lifeless state. Howling and circling and pawing actions sometimes accompanies the event of a death. Yet, even in primates the picture is mixed. Indifference to it is very common, and also a sudden transition from care to indifference when death claims the terminally wounded. What is not done is caching or burial of the corpse as a mark of respect by any animal. Elephants, however, have been known to cover their deceased with branches.

So much is lost to pre-history, including the moment when the first human sat and contemplated his or her own mortality, one long forgotten day as the sun beat down and tall gold grasses shimmered to the horizon. Perhaps it was in the Great Rift Valley or nearby savannahs which are part of modern-day Kenya and Ethiopia. This person may have been resting after a hunt, sad that a family member had died the same morning. Every animal has an instinct to preserve its own life when threatened, however, for the first time in the history of the earth an individual considered the inevitability of their own death while unthreatened. And the thought was not pleasant.

It may have been a hundred years later before a second person considered their future mortality in the same way. Certainly this was before the development of symbolic language. So, for tens of thousands of years everyone was locked in a prison in their own minds, taking what comfort seemed right about mortality, unable to properly share their feelings. Eventually such thinking became more common and eventually symbolic communication was sufficient to convey this abstract concern. Once people can communicate to each other about symbols and abstract ideas of mortality then proto-religious beliefs can develop as a defence.

The GMR is in full agreement with TMT theorists that the discovery of personal mortality is the single most important intellectual development in human history. It transcends events like the invention of the wheel or recognition of the counting numbers. The influence of mortality on the mental environment of humans is not neutral. Individuals can easily become depressed, anarchic, embittered and resigned due to this discovery. Emergence of intelligence, which then uncovers mortality, meets a negative factor upon the survival of the species. Natural selection would then favour an evolutionary adaptation which overcame the negative effects of mortality. It might seem insoluble. As animals become more intelligent they become fully aware of mortality and this works against their desire for life and reproduction and co-operation in groups. Evolution would seem to have hit a brick wall. Is there any path available for natural selection to advance intelligent, yet mortal, species?

Just as the problematic awareness of personal mortality arose from the abstract thinking of intelligent minds, so did the solution: afterlife. Belief in afterlife is an antidote to mortality. Acceptance and fleshing out of the afterlife template is the evolutionary adaptation driving the formation of religion. The invention of afterlife is the second most important intellectual development in human history.

It may even have dramatically skewed the evolutionary development of our human sub-species from its natural path of robustness to a gracile form, and this hypothesis is detailed in Chapter Four in the section on Rebirth Feedback Belief. Today we think of the human impact on the planet in terms of climate change and species domestication and extinction. The invention of afterlife has probably had a similarly profound effect upon humanity itself.

Two attributes of being alive must have become obvious in the remote past: blood and breathing. This goes well beyond awareness of death as an end-point and is recognition that there are physical qualities essential to being alive. The ancient symbolisms for both of these are explored in the following sections. We have now opened the book on the deep and ancient history of humanity reflecting upon mortality.

The GMR identifies fully flowering religious belief in *Homo sapiens* at one hundred thousand years ago, which is much earlier than most accepted dates. To support this early date we would expect to see evidence of a long history of general conceptual thinking and proto-religious thinking in extinct human species: *Homo sapiens neanderthalensis, Homo heidelbergensis* and perhaps *Homo erectus* before them. And we do, the evidence is fragmentary, but it exists!

Blood Symbolism

Red Blood and Red Ochre

Neanderthals are also known to have collected quantities of non-utilitarian aesthetic items such as the shells of non-edible species, and heavy pieces of iron pyrites, as well as ochre lumps and 'crayons'; all such behaviour can be seen as artistic expressions, probably related to ritual contexts. And the usage of ochre, already underway for many hundreds of millennia, increased markedly in the Middle Palaeolithic. During the period from 200,000 to 30,000 BC, such pigments became increasingly

*frequent and abundant, not only in occupation deposits but also
in burials which occurred for the first time.* [41]

– Paul G. Bahn and Jean Vertut

The primary reason for hundreds of thousands of years of red colour symbolism is certainly due to *red materials as a functional representation of blood*, and recognition that blood is vital to life, ensuring movement and animation. The knowledge that blood is one of the two essentials to life in humans and animals is advanced thinking well beyond the capability of animals.

The great antiquity of red colour symbolism begins before the emergence of *Homo sapiens,* as indicated in the previous section, but largely parallels the development of our species. Its importance is that it is the precursor to the Red Ochre Tradition, the world's oldest belief system. Additionally, the presence of red colour symbolism in many cultures is compelling evidence that humans drew significance from the colour of blood, surely because it was seen as fundamental to life. If they were thinking about a fundamental of life then they were concerned with mortality and therefore had awareness of personal mortality. In the GMR we want to explore what happened when mortality surfaced in archaic humans, because as soon as something was done about it, by way of afterlife belief evidenced by funerary ritual, religion was first invented.

Red ochre is a natural mineral, a mixture of iron oxide (haematite, FE_3O_2), clay and silica. In a hydrated form it is yellow, but in the anhydrous, dried or burnt, form it is red. If the dried form is crushed and mixed with a little water it has the colour and consistency of blood.

The colour red being regarded as special by several different species of Palaeolithic humans is abundant in the archaeological record and summarized in Table 2.1 (next page).

This table is a chronology of important sites where red colour has had cultural significance. There are a number of observations to be made. First, that the spatial range is huge: southern Africa to Europe to India. Further, the time range is truly vast, extending through the whole of the evolutionary period of the *Homo* genus. The only comparable activities in respect of time and space are the taming of fire and knapping of stone tools.

GMR:2.1 RED COLOUR SYMBOLISM BY ARCHAIC HOMININS

LOCATION	RED COLOUR SYMBOLISM EVIDENCE	PERIOD
Makapansgat, South Africa	Red jasperite face-like cobble manuport. [42] Possible symbolism by *Australopithecus africanus*.	3 – 2.5 mya
Olduvai Gorge, Tanzania	Two fragments of reddish volcanic tuff found in Oldowan Bed II habitation layer. [32] Possible symbolism by *Homo erectus*.	1.7 mya
Wonderwerk Cave, South Africa	Red ochre fragments found at every level in context with artefacts of human habitation through nearly a million years [43]	900 – 800 kya
Sima de los Huesos, Spain	Pink quartzite hand-axe as solitary artefact in cache of 32 *Homo heidelbergensis* skeletons [44]	500 – 350 kya
Terra Amata, Nice, France	60 red, yellow and brown ochre pieces found at occupation levels. Many with artificial wear markings. Possible firing in hearths [45]	300 kya
Kabwe, Zambia	Red ochre fragments and an ochre stained spherical stone possibly associated to *Homo heidelbergensis* [46]	300 kya
Tugen Hills, Kenya	70 red ochre fragments in habitation layer at sedimentary / volcanic Kapthurin Formation [47]	284 kya ± 12
Twin Rivers, Zambia	Red ochre fragments found in habitation layer of *Homo heidelbergensis* [48]	270 – 170 kya
Becov, Czech Republic	Striated red ochre fragment, smoothed rubbing stone and ochre stains at site [49]	250 – 200 kya
Hunsgi, Karnataka, India	Red ochre fragments (transported 25 km from source) in an Acheulian-era site including one, crayon-like, with wear marks [50]	250 – 200 kya
Maastricht-Belvédère, Netherlands	15 powdered stains of red ochre, at least 40 km from source, in association with lithics [51] *Homo sapiens neanderthalensis*	250 – 200 kya
Sai Island, North Sudan	Many red ochre fragments, ochre adhering to stone tools, found in habitation layers [52]	220 – 180 kya
Pinnacle Point, South Africa	57 red ochre pieces, some with rubbing wear [53]	164 kya
Lion Cavern, Swaziland	Red ochre (and specularite) mining with hundreds of tonnes removed over millennia [54]	110 – 70 kya to Holocene
Blombos Cave, South Africa	2000 red ochre fragments including two incised with cross-hatching. Large shell "paint-pots" [55]	100 – 70 kya

The distinction here is that red colour symbolism, or functional representation, is cultural and not of utility value important for day-to-day survival.

Secondly, of the earliest sites, only at Sima de los Huesos is the symbolism directly associated with human remains. Most sites are silent on identifying the humans who imagined symbolic associations of red colour enough to spend time working such stones. We can sometimes infer which sub-species of human were involved by contemporary remains from nearby. There can be no doubt that apart from the two most recent sites, Lion Cavern and Blombos Cave, likely early modern sites, the rest are all from archaic humans.

Thirdly, even with this limited data-set a progression is evident from the start. The Makapansgat Cobble, just an unworked natural pebble, was collected because it was unusual to the point of conveying meaning. The next oldest evidence is a million years later and this time comes from *Homo erectus*, a very successful species of early human, closer to modern humans than Australopithecus. Yet, it is not a find of red ochre, just reddish rock. Were these fragments representative of blood or blood renewal? Quite possibly *Homo erectus* had a concept of the special power of blood long before modern humans evolved.

Fourthly, it should be remembered that archaic humans were culturally-challenged when first developing abstract and symbolic thinking. There must have been a positive feedback cycle to reward such thinking and sustain a developmental process. Communication, sharing of symbolic concepts and deriving activities, must all have been possible at a minimum level and have had a net positive return to the group, especially for ensuring that symbolism took root. Early symbolism must have developed into proto-culture, become shared and persistent. It seems that red colour symbolism was considered positive, for a very long time, across several sub-species. The only universal driver capable of such a long-term and widespread persistence is personal mortality.

Some authorities put the age of recognizably modern human behaviour at 250 kya, while others assert that the process was not really complete until "mental wiring" enabled full abstract thinking perhaps by 60 kya. This, of course, must be far too recent. The physical evidence we have points to a million-year history where early humans drew symbolic meaning from the colour red. It implies a longstanding capacity for general abstraction as well.

Fifthly, sharing symbolic thinking implies proto-language, some ability to communicate what is being symbolized and why. The discovery of a Neanderthal skeleton at Kebara Cave, Israel in 1983, with an intact hyoid bone, was a milestone as it strongly indicates, but is not proof, that the Neanderthal was physically able to speak. This was about 60 kya, but could they have had the power of speech hundreds of thousands of years earlier? Michael Morris, journalist and writer, investigates the fossil evidence and concludes:

> *In typical mammals the voice box is high in the neck and the base of the skull is flat, resulting in a short pharynx that can only produce a rather limited range of sounds. Research suggests that a fully modern vocal tract first arose in Africa about one million years ago. The Homo heidelbergensis skull from Kabwe in Zambia, for instance, has an arched cranial base, suggesting that this ancestor was capable of fully modern speech.* [56]

Vocal tract tissues are never fossilized so inferring language capability from skeletal remains is never going to be conclusive. Indirect evidence, such as hundreds of thousands of years of red colour symbolism, is itself an indication of language capability, even if one of limited vocabulary. Symbolic language must have existed at a level sufficient to describe abstract concepts such as *life, blood as life-giving, mortality and rebirth.* Expression of concepts in early belief systems certainly provided impetus to the development of language and advancement to conveying abstractions and symbolism. Perhaps the drive to communicate important symbolisms arising from knowledge of mortality turbocharged the evolution of language itself!

More needs to be said about red ochre before we continue. Many cultures mined and collected red ochre or collected yellow ochre and used fire to dry and redden it. Fortunately for anthropology it is persistent in the ground and in stains so that pieces which are worked or found out of natural context are reliable scientific evidence of human activity. Although ochre is inedible it does have a number of uses in primitive society. It is antibacterial and can preserve hides in tanning processes, red being much more effective than yellow. When mixed with plant resins it can help with adhesion for hafting: attaching points to shafts. Cave and rock art show it was used extensively as a pigment and in painting. Usage for body painting, apart from being decorative, does have the technical benefit of deterring insect bites.

Sixthly, red ochre, although common, is not always near habitation sites and it sometimes had to be carried long distances. Very early examples of this include the Hunsgi site, where the source of ochre was 25 km away (tragically, this site has been destroyed in the last decade by modern farming and many known, but undocumented, sites of similar antiquity in India are being destroyed too). Another example of ochre transportation is at Belvédère, Maastricht in the Netherlands where the source could have been up to 100 km away. At Qafzeh, in Israel, the ochre was transported tens of kilometres at 100 kya. Clearly a lot of effort was expended recovering this material and implies that it was for important, ritual uses, not mundane day-to-day use.

The most remarkable evidence of the sheer determination to acquire ochre is seen at sites of *Homo sapiens sapiens*. John Wymer, archaeologist, wrote about the ochre mine at Lake Balaton in Hungary:

> *There were also bone picks and shovels, and hollow long bones in which the precious crushed ochre had apparently been stored. Such intensive effort to obtain this material can only show that it was of great significance to nearly all the known types of communities of this period. It might be described as Upper Paleolithic "gold", but it is doubtful that any concepts of trade or personal wealth had been acquired.* [57]

Isn't a solution to mortality a form of wealth? The ancient red ochre mine in Swaziland which was first worked when semi-robust humans were still present in Africa yielded many tonnes. It has a parallel in Western Australia at Wilgie Mia where ochre was mined at least from an estimated 27 kya. This mine is still regarded as the source of the finest ochre in Australia and once supported a long-distance network of ochre trade in pre-European times. There is a creation myth for the mine site about a red kangaroo which was wounded and later died spilling a lot of blood which became the ochre deposit. It is necessary to be careful about projecting the beliefs of a contemporary Palaeolithic culture into the remote past but the Aboriginal association of ochre and blood is highly consistent with the global red colour symbolism as a precursor to the Red Ochre Tradition.

Authors from diverse disciplines have noticed the cultural importance of prehistoric red colour symbolism and make inferences. Andrea Vianello, archaeologist, writes about the origins of symbolic thought and how it is evidenced in archaic humans by the usage of red ochre some time before 230 kya, and that we, the anatomically modern *Homo sapiens* (AMHS), progressed with symbolism which existed before we became evolutionarily distinct:

> *To sum up, the archaeological evidence proves that hominins have had symbolic behaviours, but these varied for long before some fixed patterns could be recognized. Thus, there are two different periods in human history in relation to symbols. In the first period, which predates AMHS, self-consciousness, the capacity of abstraction and symbolic systems as well as a few of the traits used to describe modern behaviour appeared. In the second period, patterns in symbolic behaviours can be identified and the traits increase exponentially. On one hand, there is no evidence that this change has been directly fuelled by biological changes because the path bringing humans to use symbolic systems began at the time of Homo heidelbergensis or perhaps already the late Homo erectus and progressed in different species such as Neanderthals and Homo sapiens. On the other hand, it is evident that AMHS progressed further than any other hominin, resulting in their definitive evolutionary success.* [58]

Sacha Kagan, art historian, echoes Vianello's viewpoint. He writes about the origin of art and rejects the "Big Bang" hypothesis that artistic skills suddenly flourished in modern humans at about 40 kya. Instead, by examining numerous Palaeolithic artefacts he concludes that functional artistry existed at 1.7 mya. He notes its close correlation with red colour symbolism with a first acceleration between 400 to 300 kya and a second acceleration at 100 to 40 kya. [59]

Susan Lanyon, a professor of human evolution, writes about the origins of language citing clear evidence from the archaeological record that most of what we recognize as fully modern intentional and symbolic behaviour arose in southern Africa 100 to 90 kya. As well as tools and perforated shells, many sites have an abundance of red ochre for colouring or are incised with geometric lines as well as association with ceremonial burial. Early humans were engaging in symbolic behaviour and language was possible. [60]

To conclude and tie together the relationship between mortality and red colour symbolism we return to Sheldon Solomon and his collaborators. In their paper *Human Awareness of Mortality and the Evolution of Culture* they speculate that some of the 15 species of archaic humans became aware of personal mortality but lacked the language to express it, and also couldn't develop death-denying or afterlife beliefs. They suggest that this was mentally crippling and affected their ability to compete and raises the possibility that several entire archaic human species died of fear. They conclude:

> *This suggests that with the dawn of awareness of mortality, hominid groups with particularly compelling spiritual beliefs and individuals particularly capable of sustaining faith in such beliefs would have had adaptive advantages; therefore such groups and individuals have thrived ever since.* [40]

Was there ever an adaptive advantage for humans with afterlife beliefs against those without? Probably so because the evidence of red colour symbolism present in several archaic human sub-species shows that this had adaptive advantages. It indicates that the significance of blood as life-giving was long known, implying knowledge of mortality and early language to express these concepts. Yet, it was not limited to the one successful sub-species, modern humans. This concept was shared by several species and therefore must be a pro-forma discovery when brain size and intellectual capacity passes a certain threshold.

In the GMR red colour symbolism, although highly significant, is not itself religious until it finds practical application in afterlife rituals or worldview rituals in parallel with an afterlife belief. Most specifically for red or blood colour evidence, religion begins by application of ochre in funerary ritual, practices to ensure renewal in afterlife, overcoming personal mortality. The inference of religion from red colour symbolism in funerary ritual is detailed in the *Red Ochre Tradition* in Chapter Three.

Breathing Symbolism

Landscape Cupules

> *Cupule: small cup-shaped marks deliberately pecked out of a rock surface. Their purpose and symbolism is not known, although there are some suggestions that in Scandinavia at least they are*

> *female signs. Also known as pits, dots, and cup-marks in rock art*
> *studies.* [61]

– Oxford Dictionary of Archaeology

The earliest cup-shaped depressions, known as cupules, were "pits" made in stone anvils which were used by *Homo erectus* to hold the stone of new hand-axes while they were knapped and these are commonly seen in Oldowan sites in Africa. Even then, many pits are deeper than necessary, and a few are unexplained, in particular, a pebble with four pits joined by an artificial groove dating to about 1.7 mya.

Cupules, also known as cup-marks, as rock art eventually developed and these are usually 2 to 6 cm wide, made by hammering and grinding the point of a usually harder stone into the surface of a softer one. They are the most common type of rock art in the world, and are found in a great many Palaeolithic, Mesolithic and Neolithic sites. Some are pounded into granite and took many hours of work, up to 30,000 blows! Most cupules are clearly of symbolic significance, as they have no utilitarian usage. Some were produced from within religious belief systems as they also exist in a burial and funerary temple context.

James Ritchie, antiquarian, studied the megalithic stone monuments in North East Scotland and was particularly interested in the phenomenon of large landscape rocks and exposed bedrock with cup-marks which had never been part of a megalithic monument:

> *But the marks are also found on rock surfaces, unconnected with*
> *stone circles, where, as far as we can judge, no burials have taken*
> *place, but in whose neighbourhood there undoubtedly must have*
> *existed a considerable population, probably a village.* [62]

Their purpose as landscape decoration, or upon megalithic stones, has never been satisfactorily explained, yet there must be an overarching, primary reason for this ancient class of artistic expression. How could a cup-shaped depression be so significant?

The GMR introduces the "Breathing Holes Hypothesis" (BHH) interpretation that Palaeolithic and Megalithic cupules are breathing holes made for bringing bedrock and isolated rocks alive, making the landscape itself alive, sympathetic and confirming of the life-force worldview. Making rock become alive was completing the environment as everything else moved and was considered as "living". This may have had several perceived benefits such as ensuring tribal fertility and providence for hunting. Perhaps it was also a defence against personal mortality as it was better to dwell in a fully living landscape. These are termed in the GMR as landscape cupules. Dust from hammering which is temporarily suspended in the air could be interpreted as the rock already "breathing" while the cupule was being made.

On the Narmada riverbank, India, a partial cranium was found similar to *Homo heidelbergensis*, and dating to about 200 kya. This is the only archaic human remains found in the whole of South Central Asia. Just 40 km away is the Bhimbetka site with hundreds of rockshelters, which has tools and flakes from archaic human activity. Bhimbetka was used from as early as 700 kya and also has some of the earliest known rock art, with eleven cupules present in rocks at Auditorium Cave, which are a minimum of 100 kya but could easily be several times as old. One excavated rock from below an undisturbed Acheulean layer has well-preserved markings, a single cupule and a meandering groove issuing away from it. [63, 64]

Assuming the cupule is a symbolic breathing hole then the meandering groove is a flow of air, as if imitating a meandering coil of smoke – visible "air". Lines are the most common glyph associated with cupules worldwide and could, in many cases, be indicative of air or smoke.

A site even more suggestive of symbolizing life forces is at Sai Island, Sudan, where eight 1 cm diameter cupules were found on a sandstone slab in layers dating to 200 kya, with red and yellow ochre fragments close by. The ochre, as symbolic of blood and cupules as symbolic breathing holes seen together, are more likely to be ritually associated with these two essential attributes of human and animal life.

A 3 cm-wide piece of red ochre found at Klasies River Mouth shelter, Howieson's Poort, in South Africa, and dates from layers about 75 kya, has several cupules present and also links both types of symbolism.

Landscape cupules are a common and early form of rock art in North America and must have been a tradition carried by the original migrants from Eurasia. Edward Lenik, archaeologist, assesses those seen at Bald Friar, Maryland:

> *The numerous cupules at Bald Friar, including the pit and groove form, may be the oldest glyphs at the site. Such glyphs in the Great Basin of the United States, for example, are believed to be between 5,000 and 7,000 years old (Heizer and Baumhoff 1962). I suggest*

> *that the cupules at Bald Friar may represent fish eggs and their carving was a metaphor for fertility.* [65]

However, it is unlikely that most ancient people were aware of the biological significance of fish eggs, especially as shells were thought to have this function, as we will see later.

One Australian Aboriginal myth explains cupules as the result of percussive hammering on a special rock to enhance spiritual fertility. Generally cupules are too regular and deliberately formed to be incidental side effects of hammering. Their formation was consciously intended and where subsequent groove or line patterns occur these are clearly outside what is certainly a more modern explanation of spiritual increase. A few cupules are seen in Scandinavia: rock art representing the female vulva as they are in context with human stick figures. Again this is a local, more modern interpretation.

Cupules in rock art worldwide often appear in pairs. If a cupule was a breathing hole representation then pairs were likely to represent nostrils. Cupules also appear in several pairs or large sets. Many were always considered more powerful than a singleton.

We shall see later in the chapter on Natural Rebirth Traditions that the idea of numerical strength was prevalent in funerary ritual, and also that there is at least one clear example of the Neanderthal employing a stone with cupules in a burial, as well as examples in prehistoric cultures of modern humans. The BHH defines this type as funerary cupules.

Charcoal in Art

Charcoal had significance, similarly to cupules. Air is normally invisible but, to the prehistoric mind, smoke and possibly flames, makes air visible and would therefore be associated with breathing symbolism. Charcoal was considered a source of air. Black is symbolic of charcoal which is seen, of course, in the remains of fires. The Neanderthal used manganese dioxide as a black pigment alongside the red of ochre, mostly between 60 and 40 kya. The exuberant paintings at Lascaux Cave in France, from about 15 kya, by modern humans, include an ochre-coloured standing horse with a trail of black dots issuing from its nose and flowing on past its body. This horse is depicted as breathing. Other animals have sprays of black dots either inside or outside the face, or on the body, which represent breathing and air flow.

Charcoal is sometimes associated with burials in many cultures worldwide. It is possible that the black hue of both bitumen and obsidian also helped give these materials a symbolic importance beyond their utility value. Obsidian, like ochre, was often sourced at distances of tens of kilometres from where it was finally used.

The inference of religion from breathing symbolism seen in funerary ritual is detailed in the Stone Breathing Traditions in Chapter Three.

Funerary Ritual

The strong evidence of red colour as blood symbolism and the more speculative evidence of cupules and charcoal as breathing symbolism together give us a picture of a million year history. It is a history of humans recognizing the physical essentials required to remain alive and therefore having awareness of mortality and using embryonic logic to make sense of this discovery. At some point, perhaps even from the beginning, such functional representations within belief systems, supported rebirth afterlife – where religion itself came into existence.

Religion began at the moment when afterlife was conceived, death-denying beliefs became a solution to personal mortality. Rebirth may have remained an intangible belief for hundreds of thousands of years. It is only when special treatment of the dead occurred, to help the deceased achieve afterlife, that physical evidence for religion can be found in the archaeological record. The earliest methods for disposal of the dead were developed during the life-force worldview when it was considered that everything in the environment was alive.

Excarnation

Logically, the earliest funerary practice was excarnation. In prehistoric times the process of disposal would have been simple, carrying the dead to an elevated or exposed site and allowing carrion eaters, vultures and hyenas to dismember and remove the corpse. The excarnation method of disposal of the dead is still seen today, infamously in the "Towers of Silence" of the Zoroastrian Parsis in India. It is their belief that the dead are unclean and shouldn't be buried or burned. So corpses are laid out on high platforms within circular stone towers for the sun and scavenging birds to consume. Excarnation is still done by the Hadzabe and Masai of Africa. Some Australian Aboriginal cultures have long practised leaving their dead in trees, and after the bones are disarticulated will cache them in rockshelters.

It is inconceivable that archaic *Homo sapiens* or even *Homo erectus* would have lived day-to-day with the rotting corpse of a family member on the other side of the cooking fire. They would have disposed of their dead. The problem for archaeology is that deliberate exposure of a corpse to nature eliminates it from the fossil record. We can only speculate as to whether funerary rituals were observed, such as sprinkling blood or red ochre onto the corpse before it was left to the elements. If enough ochre was used its association with the life-giving power of blood may have been boosted. It has antibacterial properties and slows down decay.

Excarnation includes the practice of defleshing which involves cutting away the soft tissue, leaving just the bones for funeral treatment. At Herto, in the Awash region of Ethiopia, several individuals of *Homo sapiens idaltu* have been found. This sub-species is probably closest to modern humans. As well as hand-axes and cutting tools three skulls dating to 160 kya, were found with cut marks from sharp stone edges, which are evidence of defleshing. Cut marks on Neanderthal bones at La Quina, Charente, South West France, show the practice was being continued at 60 kya, yet this time by a different human sub-species.

The possibility that defleshing was a prelude to cannibalism cannot be ignored either as there is evidence of a Neanderthal "cannibal feast". In 110 kya, at a cave near Moula-Guercy, in the Rhone Valley in France, six Neanderthal individuals (two adults, two teenagers and two children) were systematically butchered with sharp stones. Cut marks on their bones are similar to those on many animal bones present, suggesting the recovery of meat. [66] Elsewhere, the theory of Neanderthal cannibalism at Krapina, Croatia, has been analysed many times and the latest interpretation is a case of defleshing for possible burial of bones only. [67] However, because of the context of the Palaeolithic belief in rebirth afterlife, this makes any attempt of interpretation of it as a secondary burial very unlikely.

The modern mind finds the thought of cannibalism horrific and repugnant. We may have religion to thank for the reality that cannibalism is extinct in all cultures. The prospect of afterlife for the dead automatically warrants a respectful funeral for them too. This is the default position, a universal cultural meme, and even in extremis, enemies killed in war are buried, cremated or discarded – not eaten.

Caching

Prior to burying the dead, which required a certain amount of organized labour to dig and refill a hole, the practice of *caching* where the bodies of the deceased were carried away then deposited in a rocky crevice, was normal.

There is a particularly compelling example of caching from northern Spain. At Atapuerca, Burgos, a pit was discovered in the 1980s. It was swiftly named Sima de los Huesos, "The Pit of Bones", when the remains of 32 individuals were found in a side-chamber at the bottom of a 14 metre shaft. These remains were of an archaic human, *Homo heidelbergensis*, first discovered in Germany. The most complete reconstructed skull from the site, known as Atapuerca 5, shows some Neanderthal brow and facial features, but the shape of the cheekbone is similar to modern humans. So, it may be better identified as a *Homo sapiens heidelbergensis*, an archaic *Homo sapiens* sub-species. Their presence at the site is dated to about 350 kya. Despite this very early date the argument for deliberate caching is strong on two points.

First, the possibility that the remains were washed into the pit by flooding waters, concentrated at a low point, can be ruled out as there would be a mixture of human and animal bones present. Carnivore bones were found (perhaps attracted by the smell) but no herbivore bones.

Secondly, there is clearly red-colour symbolism present. It is because the only artefact found in the pit was an unusual bright pink quartzite hand-axe. Sometime during the long usage of this site, one of the bodies thrown in was immediately followed by a hand-axe. Was it a memento or something with a much deeper meaning?

The Atapuerca Cave site is discussed further in the following chapters.

Burial

> *These results indicate that the Tabun Neandertal woman is indeed the earliest burial known at present and, therefore, invalidate claims for the precedence of modern humans in regard to this kind of funerary practices.* [68]

– João Zilhão

After caching came inhumations – burials. The earliest evidence for religion is to be found in the graves of the dead. This is where the tangible context of afterlife belief is found and must be the starting point for determining the history of formalized belief systems.

Primary burial is where the whole body is interred or entombed soon after death. Palaeolithic burials, during the life-force worldview, were always primary. Secondary burial is where bones are collected after a long period of excarnation or temporary burial and then entombed. Secondary burials were always limited to the Neolithic and emergent spiritual worldview.

João Zilhão, archaeologist, identifies about 30 deliberate Neanderthal burials and concludes that the oldest is Tabun 1 dating to about 130 kya. Indeed, this makes untenable the common suggestion that the Neanderthal in Europe learned burial practices while observing modern humans.

Accepting Zilhão's assessment of Tabun means that the next earliest known burials, which are generally accepted to be deliberate, are at Qafzeh Cave approximately 100 kya. The Skhul Cave at Mount Carmel, also in Israel, is contemporary although various dating techniques give somewhat different results and the Skhul 9 burials are likely from about 90 kya. The Skhul are semi-robust *Homo sapiens*. Archaeology in Israel is a popular occupation and may partly explain why several archaic sites are known in a relatively small area compared to the rest of the Middle East. Of course the Levant is the primary migration bridge from Africa to Eurasia but it does suggest that many sites exist elsewhere in the region, still unknown to science, and may yield earlier burials.

Deliberate burial is not evidence of religion. It can often be interpreted as simply the tidy disposal of an unpleasant, fly-ravaged corpse. This is certainly correct in some cases. Anthropologists are quick to make this point and further, that grave goods is the best evidence of deliberate burial implying the likelihood of religious belief. [69]

Erik Trinkaus records the progressive increase in grave goods:

The changes in mortuary practices during the southwest Asian Upper Pleistocene do not as yet indicate a major cultural shift from Middle to Upper Palaeolithic. The use of red ochre, if the qualitative observations can be translated into quantitative aspects, indicates an increase during Upper Palaeolithic times. The same is true for marine shells, which are found in almost every site and assemblage from around 25,000 B.P. [70]

The physical position of the deceased and grave goods left behind help build a picture of what people were thinking, thousands of years ago, when they saw a loved one, a family member, for the last time. This begs the question, just what are the types of grave goods which signify religious beliefs?

Beads and arrowheads are unequivocal, but just as important are red ochre, shells, teeth, charcoal and animal bone. Also important is the "virtual" grave good of corpse positioning such as foetal flexing. Once these are fully recognized their religious significance can be assessed.

Concerning the earliest burials however, there appears to be researchers who are too selective in the definition of "grave good". A typical view is expressed by Paul Mellars:

But to suggest that the burial act must be seen as necessarily symbolic seems difficult to sustain. In the absence of either clear ritual or unambiguous grave offerings associated with the documented range of Neanderthal burials in Europe, it must be concluded that the case for a symbolic component in burial practices remains at best unproven. [71]

Except, however, the symbolism exists! Red ochre is unassailably symbolic. Flint, animal bones, antler, cupules or shell with a corpse are all symbolic, as is foetal positioning. All these exist across the spectrum of Neanderthal burials and deserve full recognition.

Thomas Levy observes that there are only a few Upper Palaeolithic burial sites in the Levant. The rarity of burials for this period is likely because they were placed in very shallow pits and suffered from erosion, a common cause for the loss of archaic remains globally. Those found were principally flexed burials, a practice commonly expressed in the later Neolithic Natufian culture as a likely continuation of the ancient foetal representation within the rebirth belief systems.

> *A flexed, fetal or sleeping position of the dead suggests that they were not supposed to be active in the afterlife.* [72]

The GMR identifies a foetal positioning for the dead, in the life-force worldview of naturalistic animism, as preparation for rebirth afterlife. Rebirth from the womb, soon after death, can simply be thought of as a natural progression after internment in the ground. With rebirth as the first afterlife paradigm means that all the hunter-gatherer burials were performed before any concept of spirituality came to exist.

The Null Hypothesis of MP Burial: Rejected

Some researchers argue that no Middle Palaeolithic (MP) burial, which means before 35 kya, was deliberate, purposeful or reasoned. It is a minority view. Paleoanthropologist Robert Gargett heads this cause and despatches several important sites as the result of natural processes, i.e. accidental burial. [73] He addresses Qafzeh (100-90 kya), Saint-Cesaire (36 kya), Kebara (61-59 kya), Amud (47-45 kya) and Dederiyeh (70-50 kya). This is in effect the null hypothesis for early human burial, and would imply that religious practices were minimal or non-existent at the time. This hypothesis is also a straw-man because evidence of deliberate burial at the oldest site he considers, Qafzeh, would allow the possibility of deliberate burial at all the other sites – even if not evidenced. However, upon investigation we find very good evidence for deliberate burial practices at all these sites except for the youngest, Saint-Cesaire.

At Qafzeh Cave in Israel the remains of several individuals were found with a high concentration of deliberately collected red ochre and seashells. One individual, Qafzeh 11, had deer antlers interred too.

Red ochre and shells were the ultimate grave goods for thousands of years and the case for this is detailed in Chapter Three on the Natural Rebirth Traditions. The presence of these items in close proximity with human remains, far from their natural sources, rolls back the argument for accidental burial completely. Some of the shellfish were inedible, so were not brought into the cave for food. [74]

At Dederiyeh Cave in Syria the skeleton of a two-year-old Neanderthal child was found, reportedly at the bottom of a 1.5 m pit. An approximately rectangular limestone slab present behind the child's head, triangular flint located at the heart, the arms straightened but legs flexed all suggest a deliberate internment. Further, the limestone piece has several "pit-marks" reminiscent of cupules with contrasting dots in the area closest to the child's skull. Unfortunately, analysis of this feature is absent in the best study, but evidenced in photographs. [75]

At Kebara Cave in Israel the largely complete skeletal torso of an adult male Neanderthal was recovered from a pit cut through two hearths. There was limited movement of the bones as the flesh decayed and no marks from hyenas that had gnawed many other bones scattered nearby. All points taken together strongly suggest deliberate burial. [76]

At Amud Cave, a burial quite clearly has a red deer maxilla (upper jaw) over the pelvis, seat of human reproduction, which makes certain of deliberate burial, and is very early evidence of afterlife belief.

The Neanderthal skeleton at Saint-Cesaire may have been accidentally buried but another site in France, La Chapelle-aux-Saints is dated 25,000 years earlier. It has convincingly deliberate burial and red ochre in context. So Saint-Cesaire proves nothing about whether early burial practices were deliberate or not.

The anthropologists, Matt Cartmill and Fred Smith, in *The Human Lineage* describe the debate in archaeology about the presence of funerary ritual in early modern humans and the supposed absence of it in the Neanderthal:

> *Shea sees the Tabun C Mousterian as showing signs of modern human behavior not found in the Neandertal sites (Tabun B). He notes, however, that these signs (use of grave goods, red ochre and long-distance transport of marine shells) disappear from the Levant during the succeeding cold-snap period of Neandertal resurgence and do not return until the establishment of "fully modern" behaviour at ~50 kya.* [77]

However, Ofer Bar-Yosef, the archaeologist who excavated and led campaigns at Qafzeh disagrees and sees no differences.

Sarunas Milisauskas, anthropologist, also observes that deliberate burial by the Neanderthal is evidenced by whole skeletons, flattened bottoms of burial pits and common positioning on their sides. He concludes:

> *So while there may be little definite evidence of elaborate cults or ritual among the Neanderthals, it does seem reasonably clear that they did, in fact, bury some of their dead. These included men, women, children and infants.* [78]

Recognizing this too, the GMR completely rejects the hypothesis that deliberate human burial was unknown before 35 kya.

Aspects of the Life-Force Worldview

Afterlife belief was the important part of belief systems in the life-force worldview, but during the Upper Palaeolithic and Mesolithic it was not the only part. Because spirits had not been conceived of, then gods weren't either, but there were nature forces greater than humans and naturalistic animism was fundamental in day-to-day life.

Powerful Life-Forces

> *Highly polished axes made of jade from a particular mountain top in Northern Italy have been found all across Europe. These precious, elegant objects are charged with metaphor, power and status; one example was placed as an offering underneath a wooden trackway in Somerset, Britain which has been dated to around 4000 BC (MacGregor 2010a).* [79]

> – Eva Ritter

High mountains appear to have been considered powerful earthly beings during the life-force worldview and hand-axes came to be sourced from the largest of them. As Ritter indicates, they were prized for holding power and must have been traded long-distance.

Miranda Green, archaeologist, observes similar beliefs at hand-axe sources in Britain:

> *At Great Langdale there was evidence that, particularly in the later part of the Neolithic, axe rock was being deliberately quarried from some of the most dangerous parts of the mountain, which may have increased the magical qualities of the axes.* [80]

This practice is an example of contagious magic: association after separation. Hand-axes are of course a very stable artefact and the evidence for beliefs in other powers of the environment and nature will be harder or impossible to detect archaeologically.

Trepanation is evidenced in some Palaeolithic human remains. This was the earliest, and also a most mysterious, "surgical" procedure where living people had holes bored in their skulls. Some even survived afterwards. A hypothesis to explain this practice comes from the life-force worldview by way of analogy with cupules. Perhaps some people had mental or physical disability, and trepanning was an attempt to improve their health by boring extra breathing holes into their heads.

Fertility Beliefs

Green also writes about the tradition of making small human figurines, seen at the Grimaldi Caves, Italy and elsewhere, about 25 kya. These images had artistic features of nudity, female and hermaphroditic forms, pregnancy, exaggerated sexuality and newborns:

> *This group of images is of considerable significance on many counts, not least because they form part of a Gravettian (Upper Palaeolithic) tradition spanning a huge region from Russia to France, a distribution that argues convincingly for a shared artistic and - perhaps - a shared cosmological perception.*

In the GMR the shared cosmological perception described here is naturalistic animism, the life-force worldview, where rebirth is the afterlife paradigm. The figurines are certainly representations of fertility magic, not just to ensure rebirths, but to ensure any birth occurs to maintain tribal numbers.

Sham menstruation is a fertility strategy, not a fertility belief, but it is theorized to be conserved in the context of rock art, myth, ritual and the first "gods". More importantly, it is also theorized to have originated between 500 and 150 kya, involved the usage of red ochre, from 200 kya, and may have been a causative factor in the speciation of modern humans and the development of language. Rudolf Botha and Chris Knight describe the two stages of the sham menstruation strategy:

> *Female coalitions would have used the strategy opportunistically*
> *to attract and retain male support, deterring any male*

> *philanderers' attempts to monopolize menstruating females. [...]*
> *As soon as male mates respond to ritualized signaling by going*
> *hunting to get access to female coalition members – effectively*
> *performing brideservice – they are actively investing in that*
> *female coalition (and their own offspring).* [81]

Where the hypothesis of sham menstruation is accepted, this ritual is sometimes considered to be the original usage of red ochre, particularly in Africa. This is very unlikely as the evidence of red colour symbolism, stretching back to the era and domains of *Homo erectus*, indicates that the primary purpose for ochre was a functional representation of blood as a defence against personal mortality, so sham menstruation was a later, secondary usage.

Providential Beliefs

The best surviving Palaeolithic rock art is in caves, because outside rock art gradually disappears through erosion from weathering, plants and unfortunately still – vandalism. Therefore, much outside rock art is Neolithic in origin and executed during the spiritual worldview. For that reason we consider just the European cave art here.

It is structuralist to consider the choice of caves for art where it would never be easily seen and perhaps only initiates were allowed to view it, most of the tribe would never enter the caves very far. This art was not for general viewing, it had another purpose.

Hunting magic was for a long time the main theory about the reasoning behind Palaeolithic cave art, although it has been marginalised by structural analysis and shamanistic theories since. The shamanistic theories assume that primitive priests in drug-induced trances illustrated on cave walls the distorted visions they saw. This theory is firmly dismissed by Paul Bahn, archaeologist specializing in rock art:

> *They firmly rejected theories of hunting magic or fertility magic,*
> *but in fact the number of therianthropes, or 'sorcerer` figures, or*
> *even of animals apparently emerging from or entering walls is*
> *tiny – a smaller minority even than those which seem to have*
> *arrows or missiles on them, or than figures of a sexual nature. In*

*the context of the tens of thousands of images in Ice Age art, they
are utterly insignificant.* [82]

Hunting magic was not originally put forward, such that it operated on its own. It was proposed as part of a wider set of beliefs which included fertility magic and destructive magic. The latter was needed to explain the prevalence of carnivores and other animals not hunted in art.

However, it is suggested here that even hunting magic is an inaccuracy and that fertility magic is closest to the best explanation of providential magic. Prehistoric hunter-gatherers would have always been concerned about providence – that there was enough food to be found or hunted. Hunting, per se, was never a direct concern; if the animals existed then they could always be hunted.

In the life-force worldview, if caves are wombs of the earth then rock art could be for the purpose of ensuring that the landscape remained populated with all animals, including people – which are assured by the presence of so many handprints. Human handprints are common and they were made by the artists blowing red ochre (as blood symbolism) or black manganese dioxide solution (as breathing symbolism) around their hands to create a negative image. In doing so they invoked contagious magic to ensure that providence in the environment always included people as well.

There is an additional reason that carnivores and other uncommon prey animals would be painted, and this was a matter of control. By painting predator animals, humans demonstrated superiority over them and therefore exercised some level of management of them. Magic in art ensured that bears, large cats and other competitive animals were limited in their ability to disrupt the day-to-day life of people.

3 ◆ INNER CORE RELIGION: REBIRTH AFTERLIFE

Natural Rebirth Traditions (NRT)

We are now in a position to unravel the earliest archaeological evidence of religion in Palaeolithic and Mesolithic burials. Time and again it is apparent that intervention, *funerary ritual within religious traditions*, is always consistent with the paradigm of rebirth afterlife within the life-force worldview. The GMR has the religions of rebirth collectively known as *Natural Rebirth Traditions*, and these comprise all of Inner Core Religion (ICR).

Rebirth Afterlife of the Life-Force Worldview

The conclusion is that there is a direct connection between intentional burials and living places, the reason for which is contained in the now unfathomable thoughts of these people. [57]

– John Wymer

Once the abstract template of afterlife as an antidote to personal mortality had taken root in human minds it was inevitable that people used nature to infer a working paradigm for afterlife. The first, or at least, the most successful paradigm was rebirth and this concept spread through human populations as a meme. As each person died it was imagined that they were to be reborn as an infant, presumably within the same family or tribe.

John Wymer wrote about Upper Palaeolithic peoples in Eastern Europe and the unfathomable reason that they buried their dead below their living spaces. In the rebirth afterlife paradigm the reason was to ensure that their loved ones would remain close to where they would be reborn.

Technically, as soon as rebirth became a belief religion itself came into existence. The date when this first happened can only be estimated by interpreting indirect evidence. We have already explored early red colour symbolism, cupule rock art, compassion for the sick and the complex activity of deepwater rafting. Human intelligence seems to have become capable of conceptualizing rebirth afterlife belief sometime between 1.7 and 0.8 mya, the era of *Homo erectus*.

For a long time, many hundreds of thousands of years, this must have remained a passive belief perpetuated by the shared blood and breathing symbolism of reddish stones and cupules. Then eventually the idea of intervention came about; people thought that they could advance or improve the process of rebirth for the deceased. Most likely this was a step-change developed only after the speciation of *Homo heidelbergensis* and *Homo sapiens* branches from *Homo erectus* as the earliest evidence suggestive of intervention in the process of afterlife is the presence of a pink quartzite hand-axe at Sima de los Huesos, Spain, deposited in a cache of deceased remains, by *heidelbergensis* about 350 kya. Intervention later became fully developed by way of funerary ritual, including grave goods.

Stephen Mithen, archaeologist, considers the early caching example from Spain and correctly dismisses supernatural religion:

> *..that religious ideas, or at least those which are shared, are born out of art, for without material symbols they cannot be sufficiently anchored into human minds. It is on this basis, therefore, that I feel we can be confident that ideas about supernatural beings did not exist within people's minds before material symbols were made. Whatever Neanderthals were doing when they placed individuals in pits, or whatever H. Heidelbergensis was doing at Atapuerca that led to the accumulation of bodies at Sima de los Huesos, it could not have involved shared beliefs in supernatural beings.* [83]

However, the GMR holds that art *did* exist by way of ochre usage and cupules, but also that rebirth was never a spiritual religion so there cannot be any supernatural beings in Palaeolithic religious belief. Supernatural beings are conceivable only in the spiritual worldview paradigm. Another important insight into the prehistoric mind is the positioning of the deceased, this time seen of the Neanderthal, noted by Nicholas Barton, palaeoarchaeologist:

> *While we may never know the direct significance of the body settings it is tempting to interpret the foetal positions and the*

gestures of sleeping / reawakening as metaphors for entering and leaving the world. [84]

This posture clearly demonstrates that Palaeolithic afterlife belief was that of rebirth. Foetal burial mimics the posture of an unborn baby and the newly dead are therefore most readied for return to the world as a new-born even without any grave goods. The positioning was not a mere metaphor for birth and death; it was a functional representation (like-for-like magic) for overcoming death by physical rebirth.

E.O. James comments that the Neanderthal was not familiar with internal anatomy, but surely they can be given more credit on that score. Foetal curling could well have become cultural knowledge. These were people who spent their lives butchering animals and would have often seen their unborn foetally curled.

The archaeologist d'Errico and colleagues examine the Neanderthal burial of a foetus at La Ferrassie and interpret wider significance from the treatment of premature stillborns:

> *The fact that they took care of such a young individual seems indicative of human emotion, and certainly a high degree of social discourse, which is difficult to conceive without the existence of a complex language. It is notable that, in modern human societies, with our complex and diversified systems of communication, we do not always bury foetuses.* [85]

It might seem strange that a foetus receives a formal burial, but it is likely that the foetus was interpreted by the Neanderthal as a recently deceased adult who had almost succeeded in achieving rebirth – but failed and required another chance!

Natural Rebirth Traditions (NRT)

> *Both the Neanderthal and the Stone Age Homo sapiens had the potential capacity for symbolic behaviour. This is confirmed in the Levantine Middle and Upper Palaeolithic by the Mousterian burials and the ochre. The use of powdered ochre and marine shells in the Upper Palaeolithic supports this suggestion.* [72]

> – Thomas Levy

Table 3.1 identifies the four classes of NRT, with their different origins and subsequent expression in funerary ritual.

GMR:3.1   **NATURAL REBIRTH TRADITIONS (NRT)**

BELIEF SYSTEM	ORIGIN	FUNERARY ARTEFACTS
Red Ochre Tradition (ROT)	Blood in humans and animals maintains life. Symbolism: 900 kya Funerary Use: 100 kya	Red ochre Haematite
Stone Breathing Traditions (SBT)	Breathing in humans and animals maintains life. Symbolism: >200 kya Funerary Use: 70 kya	Cupules in stone at burials Charcoal pieces and layers Modern humans: Cupules in stone at temples Holed stones and mortars Fossil Ammonites
Animal Renewal Traditions (ART)	Antlers renew annually. Funerary Use: 100 kya Bird and reptile eggs create life. Funerary Use: 100 kya	Antler parts in burials Modern humans: Eggs, seashells, teeth, ivory, turtle and snail shells Egg abstractions: oval stones, moulded clay, egg-imagery Bird, snake and turtle imagery
Plant Renewal Traditions (PRT)	Plants renew annually and seeds create life. Funerary Use: 8000 BCE	Modern humans: Green stones. Jadeite, malachite beads Flowers

After determining that intervention was possible, humans have employed funerary ritual to overcome oblivion and improve the chance of immortality, by at least another life, for the newly deceased. The Natural Rebirth Traditions (NRT) – formalization of religious belief encapsulating rebirth afterlife – were universal until the Neolithic when the paradigm shift to a spiritual worldview began. These beliefs permitted human control over the rebirth process, accelerating the time-scale or making sure it actually happened.

Observation of nature was to progressively reveal the four natural methodologies by which renewal of human life could be assisted or even guaranteed in a funerary ritual. During the Palaeolithic it was observed that blood is the carrier of life in humans and animals and that breathing was also essential for life. They also noted that birds and reptiles spring forth from the life-creating power of eggs and deer antlers grow anew each year. Finally, evidence is fragmentary, but, because of its association with agriculture, plant renewal as a life-giving tradition, developed later, at the Mesolithic and Neolithic boundary. This was only a few thousand years before all the NRT were radically transformed in the wave-front of the emerging spiritual worldview.

The belief systems identified as Natural Rebirth Traditions were shared by both *Homo sapiens neanderthalensis* and *Homo sapiens sapiens* and this is implied, unless noted otherwise in the table.

Apart from plant renewal, the NRT are old enough to be globally diffused. Therefore the conclusion from the GMR is that these belief systems were carried around the world on the long, slow human dispersals.

The NRT are fundamental to unravelling prehistoric belief systems and their global reach. There is convincing evidence, expressed by funerary ritual, of the Red Ochre Tradition (blood renewal) and Animal Renewal Traditions (shells, teeth and antlers) in the Levant region encompassing Qafzeh and Skhul, dating 100 to 90 kya. Seeing two distinct belief systems with four different elements used at this date implies a probability that at least one of these funerary practices predates those sites by tens of thousands of years. Multiple belief systems expressed in funerary ritual at one site strongly imply much earlier phases of at least one of the traditions.

In the GMR, substantial evidence will be presented for the significance of funerary usage of red ochre, shells and animal parts within afterlife belief. Many researchers downplay these artefacts, and fall back upon less important but more obvious conclusions. Robert Bellah, sociologist, has an opinion which is typical of many:

> *What is of particular interest from our point of view is that McBrearty cites evidence for red ochre and shell beads from well over 100,000 years ago. Of course we can't know for sure what these were used for, but ethnographic evidence suggests that they were almost certainly used for personal adornment as body painting and bead ornaments.* [86]

In that case just what funerary evidence would be deemed worthy of recognition as religious symbolism? Especially when we see, for example, at Sungir, skeletons still smothered in red ochre, with thousands of beads – far too many for mere ornamentation. This was closer to 30 kya than 100 kya, however, cultural development is unlikely to have trivial ornamentation slowly becoming ritually serious symbolism. It is more likely to develop the other way around, that ochre and beads have early importance and only slowly become ornamental.

Another viewpoint which casts a smokescreen over the understanding of prehistoric religion is that of projecting disharmony between early humans and their environment. Ian Hodder, archaeologist, has proposed an antagonistic interpretation between humans (domestic, life) and nature (wild, death). He divides the habitation space of prehistoric peoples into distinct conceptual regions and imagines antagonism between the regions. This is an interpretation which is embraced and expanded upon significantly by David Lewis-Williams and colleague David Pearce, cognitive archaeologists, in their work *Inside the Neolithic Mind.* They assume strong shamanistic traditions in Neolithic peoples. They may well be correct within the spiritual worldview, but not any earlier.

I disagree with these theories being applied to the Mesolithic or Palaeolithic and see it as a modern perspective projected onto the remote past. In the life-force worldview prehistoric people were at one with their environment and did not see a conflict between nature and humans. This is a viewpoint nicely summarized by Richard Bradley, archaeologist of prehistory, who also rejects the early antagonistic interpretation:

> *The distinctive character of Mesolithic burials in north and north-west Europe suggests that instead of this antagonism between culture and nature we might think in terms of a reciprocal relationship, more akin to the animistic beliefs so often reported among hunter gatherers. The dead were accompanied by the symbols of fertility and regeneration and Mesolithic communities may not have recognized the distinction between the human and animal kingdoms.* [87]

When considering the grave goods in Mesolithic and earlier Palaeolithic burials as regenerative for future life, a lot of what is perplexing quickly makes sense. Only then are we well on the way to understanding the prehistoric mind.

Some archaeologists investigate burials for ethnographic evidence of social differences and strata within a society, high-status and low-status and so on. This approach often draws a blank when focusing upon grave goods associated with the NRT for the reason that funerary rites to assist with afterlife progression cut across social boundaries. Similarly, the withholding of funerary privileges, part of ritual judgment, will also cut across social boundaries. Geoff Bailey, an archaeologist of prehistory, describes the inconclusive results of such projects at the Iron Gates burial grounds on the Danube riverbank:

> *However, apart from the presence of red ochre in many graves, burial goods are few and provide no clear evidence of social distinctions within the communities. Distinctions according to sex or age are difficult to discern. Ochre was associated with the burials of men, women, and children, and the practice of excarnation seems to have been applied to adults and children alike. A few of the burials at Schela Cladovei and Vlasec were accompanied by cyprinid pharyngeal teeth and/or marine shell beads, but again there are no clear associations according to sex and age.* [88]

We would expect inconclusive results when trying to discern social distinctions from grave goods which are fundamental to the perception of the afterlife process. High status people will have more of these grave goods but they cannot be of a completely different nature.

All archaeological evidence has a taphological time-lag, the complete loss of evidence through decay and decomposition, from the period of first use to the first surviving example. Organic evidence such as leather and fabric decays quickly, others like stone tools can last over a million years. We are fortunate that some of the best evidence of NRT is red ochre, teeth and shells which have a low rate of taphological decay and therefore a shorter time-lag of evidence after first use.

Because a mixture of NRT beliefs are seen at many sites, in order to present its discrete elements, it is necessary to refer to the same burial site in different places. This is a partitioning of the archaeological data by class of artefact, instead of the more usual technique where a site is considered in its entirety, in layers. For example the Paviland burial has red ochre, shells, ivory rods and a mammoth skull present, all of which have separate symbolic origins and meaning within blood renewal, animal renewal and rebirth enhancement. Inevitably it means this site is discussed in several places where each part of it is in a relevant context.

So, in sequence we will explore the archaeological evidence for each of the NRT belief systems which builds a comprehensive picture of prehistoric rebirth afterlife belief which was always seen as a physical event. It is a central assertion of the GMR that naturalistic animism, the life-force worldview, prevailed in the Palaeolithic and Mesolithic. Spiritual afterlife was unknown until the Neolithic.

Red Ochre Tradition (ROT)

In the GMR the Red Ochre Tradition is used to describe the belief system where red colour symbolism or representation employed in funerary ritual was intended to facilitate rebirth. By far the principal substances used for this was red ochre and haematite. Red organics discoloured and reddish stones were rarely preferred. Regardless of substance, it was the colour of blood that was significant in order to harness, by functional representation (like-for-like sympathetic magic), the life-giving power of real blood to facilitate rebirth afterlife.

Blood Renewal

> *We have seen that the use of color, especially red, in mortuary ceremonies is practically universal in time and space over the earth among prehistoric and primitive peoples.* [89]

> – Charles Peabody

It was obvious to prehistoric men and women that babies are born, loudly crying their way into the world, splashed with blood. Also they knew that blood can only flow from living bodies. Animals they hunted gushed forth blood in their death throes when sliced with stone tools. Menstruation in women was further proof of the importance of blood.

Their conclusion was that blood is the carrier or power of the vital force of life itself. Further proof to early humans is the rapidly stiffening corpse of a family member who has died. When cut, it shows that vital blood has abandoned a body which it reliably animated for many years.

There lay the link to birth, life, death and personal mortality. Observing the importance of blood is the application of logic and embryonic science. It is certainly the significance behind approximately a million years of red colour symbolism, discussed in the previous chapter.

There are three principal groups of substances used within the ROT in funerary ritual:

1) Organics

Human and animal blood, and red plant pastes and resins were likely ritual substances. However, any organics used in the Palaeolithic are very hard to detect archaeologically as they decay so quickly and are difficult to distinguish from associated non-ritual organic contaminants. Although it is a reasonable assumption that real blood was the first substance used in burial rituals to attempt to ensure rebirth occurred.

2) Red ochre and haematite

Haematite is iron ore, which may be reddish with grey and black shadings. Ochre is simply a natural mixture of clay with powdered haematite. In practice, pure haematite is rare in burials. Because ochre is found relatively easily and strongly colourfast, it is such a good blood substitute that not many alternatives have been used worldwide. Ochre has a very long history of use in death rites, rites of passage, fertility and rock art. Perhaps unsurprisingly, of all historical pigments it has by far the greatest and most widespread significance. Most of the red colour symbolism evidence is ochre.

3) Porcelanite and various reddish stone types

These are also seen and are "ochre-like", however, different processes of colour-change over thousands of years may hide their significance during excavation.

Cinnabar (mercury sulphide ore) and jasper are absent from Palaeolithic and Mesolithic burials, but are often used as red symbolism in the Neolithic, within spiritual beliefs and are not part of the ROT.

Red Ochre as Blood Symbolism

Researchers emphasise the deeply symbolic and diverse meanings of the colour red, mainly expressed in the burial context. The colour red is reminiscent of natural substances sharing the same colour, such as blood. The presence of the colour red in burials is regarded as being connected with the concept of death and with

> *the preservation of the energy of life, providing magical force for the route to the world beyond.* [90]
>
> – Ilga Zagorska

The period of ochre use in funerary ritual is truly vast, extending through the whole time that early modern and fully modern humans have existed. Its symbolism pre-dates the emergence of *Homo sapiens* and very early on ochre became the premier blood substitute for ritual usage. Table 3.2 (next page) gives a chronological overview of red colour symbolism specifically in a funerary context.

Just the span in years between the "Red Lady" (Paviland) and the "Fox Lady" (Dolni Vestonice) is longer than that from the first Mesopotamian town to today. When we consider that only a small fraction of burials avoid complete disintegration, and the number of sites found, we can conclude that ochre in funerary ritual was extremely common and widely practised.

The use of ochre to symbolise blood began long before the last dispersal out of Africa, so there is a strong case for global diffusion. A find at Ushki Lake, Kamchatka dating to 14 kya, and another in Alaska at 11 kya are particularly interesting as they are at the time of the Bering Strait crossing, known as Beringia, which was open during the last Ice Age. The ancestors of the Native Americans arrived from Asia through this route and were enthusiastic users of ochre up until European colonization. They developed many cultural variations such as sprinkling it on corpses before internment in trees.

The literature on theology and the great modern dictionaries of religion fail (at the time of writing) to recognize red ochre traditions as a distinct religion or even informal belief system. I searched the sixteen-volume *Encyclopaedia of Religion* in vain for even a useful mention of the significance of red ochre. The authors happily describe lesser-gods of the most obscure extinct sects but completely miss the oldest and globally widespread belief system up until European colonization took Christianity throughout the world. Truly, humanity has collectively forgotten its deepest religious beginnings.

The literature in cultural anthropology occasionally investigates the usage of red ochre but rarely are the global ramifications of it adequately discussed, and the hypothesis that this is an important Palaeolithic belief system is rarely presented.

GMR:3.2   RED OCHRE TRADITION IN FUNERARY RITUAL

LOCATION	BURIAL OR FUNERARY CONTEXT	PERIOD
Qafzeh Cave, Israel	Lowest layers have red ochre associated with early modern human burials [74, 91]	100 – 90 kya
Border Cave, South Africa	Early modern 4 to 6 month infant burial stained in red ochre [92]	90 – 66 kya
La Chapelle aux Saints, France	Neanderthal cave burial. Ochre pieces found within undisturbed burial layer [93]	60 kya
Lake Mungo, Australia	Mungo 3 - red ochre sprinkled over early modern adult human remains [94]	40 kya ± 2
Gower Peninsula, Wales	"Red Lady." Paviland Cave burial of modern male with large quantities of red ochre [95]	34 kya
Krems, Austria	Twin infant and single red ochre burials [96]	27 kya
Pavlov Hills, Brno, Czech Republic	"Fox Lady." Dolni Vestonice triple burial: red ochre on pelvis and male heads. [97]	26.6 kya
Abrigo do Lagar, Velho, Portugal	"Lapedo Child." Neanderthal/modern hybrid burial. Red ochre present [98]	24.5 kya
Zhoukoudian caves, China	Burial pit containing skeletal remains of several individuals with quantities of red ochre [99]	19 kya
Irlich, Germany	Adult and two children, burials with red ochre [100]	12.5 – 11.2 kya
Taforalt, Morocco	Cave with 40 burials, many containing red ochre [101]	12 – 11 kya
Bulgaria and Balkan area	Red ochre deposits in many burial sites [102]	6300 – 4850 BCE
Lake Onega, Russia	Mesolithic island cemetery with 500 burials, many with red ochre [103]	6300 – 5600 BCE
Labrador, Canada Maine, USA	Native American cultures, e.g. Beothuk, Moorehead. Red ochre extensive in burials [104]	5500 BCE – 1500 BCE
Bøgebakken, Denmark	Vedbaek cemetery. Burials with red ochre sprinkled throughout. Ochre stained objects [105]	4500 BCE – 4000 BCE

Charles Peabody, archaeologist and great-nephew of George Peabody who founded the Peabody Museum at Harvard, was first to identify red symbolism in mortuary ritual as a global tradition. His 1927 paper *Red Paint* explored dozens of examples of red symbolism, typically using ochre, in North and South America, Europe, Africa, Asia, Australia and Oceania. His conclusion was cautious but he noted that it is probable that the colour red represents blood, and blood recalls death, and finally:

> *This purpose, I say, remains unknown, but it is highly probable that it was in one of two senses apotropaic: (a) to ward off evil influences from the dead and the grave; (b) to ward off evil influences from the survivors; (c) to keep the dead man's ghost from returning to plague the living.* [89]

What Peabody completely overlooked was that people of all cultures were primarily concerned with obtaining afterlife in the first place and, in the case of rebirth, was not worried about what they might find there because they viewed it as another earthly life. So Peabody failed to pen what might have been: *(d) to assist and ensure the natural process of afterlife by rebirth within a naturalistic animism worldview; (e) to assist and ensure the progression to spiritual afterlife or achieve partial reincarnation within a spiritual worldview.*

Peabody was not aware of another distinction. During the spiritual worldview, secondary burials occurred where bones were recovered and painted with red ochre before re-entombment, as part of ancestor worship. This is not part of the Red Ochre Tradition but part of the Natural Spiritual Traditions. These are detailed in Chapter Six on spiritual afterlife.

In 1980 Ernst Wreschner wrote his provocative paper *Red Ochre and Human Evolution: A case for discussion* on the significance of red ochre highlighting its symbolic significance in burials. However, his scatter-gun approach assumes a continuation in all red symbolism. [106]

Rebecca Morris, historian and anthropologist, in her book *A Shroud of Ochre*, has produced a most comprehensive account on this phenomenon. It is specifically upon the subject of ochre symbolism for both an academic and lay audience with a global preview but detailing North America only.

Jones and MacGregor comment in *Colouring the Past* that the argument for blood symbolism with red ochre is forceful but partial.

Adding that it does not explain why red ochre is applied to the head, for example. [107] There are several answers to this reservation.

Specifically, red ochre is used on the head to facilitate rebirth afterlife as usually the head appears first during birth. Ochre use was often concentrated on the skull, but not always; perhaps if there was not enough available to cover a whole body it made sense to focus on the important areas. The head must have been recognized from early times as the seat of personal consciousness. Particularly as this is where vision operates and 80 per cent of our information about the outside world comes from this one sense.

Generally, red ochre can be applied anywhere that a culture sees fit. It is the like-for-like association between blood and renewal which is important, so just to have ochre in context with the burial can be thought of as sufficient. In many cases the ochre is a pebble or lump positioned next to the corpse. Often the pelvis was chosen, and this is, of course, the seat of human reproductive capability, so ochre was effective on the pelvis for making rebirth happen. Ochre powder is best as a blood substitute when mixed with water, and splashed over the corpse. There might be a trace amount, or conversely, as at Paviland, several kilograms of ochre used to cover the corpse completely. It is the presence of red colour as a functional representation of blood in a burial which is important for this belief system, not the local, culturally specific interpretation of how it should be applied.

Red ochre is more persistent than bone so we would expect to see it preserved in burials and art throughout a long period, and indeed this is the case. After water is long gone, the ochre remains as a fine red stain. In Finland and southern Mexico some burials show ochre in the acidic soil but with the bones having dissolved completely. It is also possible that bodies were covered in it and then wrapped in animal skins for burial too.

The ROT implies early social organization, individuals who were in charge of red ochre. It required coordination for ochre foraging, mining, recovery to base, proper storage and respect for this group property. Those who dispensed ochre in funeral rites maintained the tradition itself and passed it down the generations. It required religious education, no less, with enough symbolic sophistication of spoken language to convey this cultural knowledge.

During the life-force worldview which prevailed until the Neolithic revolution, staining of the bodies of deceased family members was done for one reason: to improve the process of rebirth – to hasten and ensure their physical return back to the world in a new human body as soon as possible – and defeat death. During a funerary ritual the dead body could be sprinkled or covered with red ochre or buried with ochre pieces. It was applied immediately in primary burials.

The following overview of significant red ochre sites in the world is intended to illustrate the commonality of this religious tradition, and its huge spatial and temporal ranges. There is a bias towards Europe, likely because archaeological research has been much more thorough over a longer period than in other areas.

The story does not even begin with modern humans, but our cousins and part ancestors of Europeans and Asians, the Neanderthal.

Neanderthal and the ROT

> *The death of others recalls our own fate to us and forces us to prepare for it in some fashion. For these – and a thousand other reasons – we cannot allow the death of those close to us to pass unmarked. Therefore, these middle Palaeolithic period burials are prima facie evidence that, at least on this very fundamental topic, the Neanderthals thought as we think and acted as we act.* [108]

– D. Bruce Dickson

The Neanderthal evolved from archaic *Homo sapiens* in Europe by 300 kya, exhibiting "classic" traits by 160 to 120 kya and surviving until about 30 kya. They certainly had an early interest in ochre as evidenced at the Maastricht-Belvédère site which was in use from about 250 to 200 kya, and was where bright stains exist from ochre mixed with water which fell as droplets. The ochre was non-local and may have been sourced from 40 to even 100 km away. So, at this site they went to a lot of trouble to make red liquid – for an unknown purpose.

Remains of over 400 Neanderthal individuals have been found from Portugal to as far east as Iraq and Uzbekistan. The evidence for intentional burial for most of them is absent although about 30 have very strong indications which, taken together, are convincing that the Neanderthal had a tradition of burial in some places during the Middle Palaeolithic or Mousterian period.

There is much anecdotal comment that red ochre is strongly evidenced at various Neanderthal burials but, upon examining the scientific literature detailing each find, it becomes apparent that what ochre usage existed in their funerary ritual is fragmentary at best.

The earliest evidence is at La Chapelle aux Saints, France, from 60 kya, where a few ochre pieces were found in context with a deliberate burial. At Grote de Spy in Belgium, animal bones which have ochre stains were recovered close to where a pair of skeletons lay, dating to 36 kya. Unfortunately, the early discovery of this site, before 1900, means that a lot of the context is lost. The report of ochre at Le Moustier does not seem supported by early descriptions of this site.

Their last burial, which also has ochre, is the Neanderthal and modern human hybrid at Lagar Velho, Portugal at 24.5 kya. Indications are that this body was also wrapped in a cloak or hide before being sprinkled with ochre solution. [98]

So, although the Neanderthal was arguably aware of ochre symbolism it is weakly evidenced in their burials. This may be due to a combination of their burials being shallow and poorly covered, and that they preferred animal parts as grave goods. There is a further possibility – that the Neanderthal always accepted rebirth as a given and were thinking beyond it to the concept of enhanced rebirth afterlife. This is explored in Chapter Four, Outer Core Religion: Enhanced Rebirth.

However, the ROT was in an accelerated phase at the time of the demise of the Neanderthal, from 34 to 24 kya, as evidenced in burials of fully modern humans, the gracile *Homo sapiens sapiens*.

Europe

The widespread custom of coating the corpse with red ochre clearly had a ritual significance. Red is the colour of living health. Therefore, as Professor Macalister has pointed out, if the dead man was to live again in his own body, of which the bones were the framework, to paint them with the ruddy colouring of life was "the nearest thing to mummification that the Palaeolithic people knew; it was an attempt to make the body again serviceable for its owner's use. [109]

– E. O. James

The Red Ochre Tradition can only be described as pervasive in Europe, from the Gravettian to the Neolithic. Evidence has been found in sites from Iberia to Greece, Wales to Lithuania and uncounted points in between. The time range, spanning nearly thirty millennia, is truly remarkable. The list that follows is chronological and gives a flavour of the diversity present in this powerful belief system.

The find by Buckland in 1823 at Goats Hole Cave, Paviland, Wales, is the earliest archaeological find of a red ochre burial and the earliest discovery of a modern European human skeleton as it dates to 34 kya. It was spectacular when intact, comprising a male burial with huge quantities of ochre, some 50 periwinkle shells and fragments of ivory rods, and a nearby mammoth skull which has since been lost. Only long bones of the left side survive with a few ribs and partial pelvis, the rest was lost by wave erosion. At the time of burial the coast was 70 km away, but now the cave is at sea level. There must be many such important sites under the sea as coastal living was common in Palaeolithic times, as it is now, but sea levels today are the highest for tens of millennia whereas they were up to 100 m lower in the geologically recent past.

3000 km east of Paviland, on a mammoth migratory path, the Sungir site in Russia has five burials from 28 kya. Four had quantities of red ochre and three were richly decorated with ivory and animal teeth. The full importance of this site is detailed later.

The remains of a habitation site at Krems-Wachtberg, lower Austria, was largely destroyed by a road in the 1930s but fortunately the double burial of a pair of infants, dating to 27 kya, was still intact and discovered in 2005. They were covered with a large amount of red ochre, given ivory beads, and then placed under a mammoth's shoulder blade (scapula). A third infant nearby was discovered similarly treated.

An important permanent hunter-gatherer settlement spanning four thousand years is represented by a complex of seven sites in Moravia, Czech Republic. The triple burial which made this site famous is near the village of Dolni Vestonice, and dates to 26.6 kya. Two males and a female, "The Fox Lady", were laid out with red ochre sprinkled on the female's pelvis and the male heads had fox canines, charcoal and ivory present in the grave. A separate male burial was found with ochre on the head and pelvis dated to 26 kya. Nearby, the Pavlov sites have many artefacts of habitation, decorative items and evidence of ochre processing, but human remains are few and fragmentary.

In Italy, at the Grimaldi Caves, Ventimiglia, Liguria, several burials were discovered the 1870s with red ochre present, and have been dated to about 25 kya. These included adults and children, some richly endowed with grave goods of shells, teeth and ochre. One male was wearing a cap of shells with a border of 22 deer teeth, ochre around the face and a bone awl at the side. Also, further on the Ligurian coast, the Arene Candide Cave was excavated in the 1940s. At a deep layer, dated 23.5 kya, the skeleton of a boy was found. He died aged about 15. Archaeologists named him il Giovane Principe, the Little Prince, due to his large number of grave goods: red and yellow ochre, a cap of dozens of snail shells, some seashells, mammoth ivory and a stone knife. [110]

In Cueva Morin, Santander, Spain there are a pair of graves where the bodies have decomposed completely leaving a just an impression. Red ochre was used and a small deer placed with the burial known as Morin 2. This layer dates about 26 to 21 kya but the reality of this burial is disputed by some authorities.

A burial of a young male at El Miron Cave, Cantabria, north-east Spain, has ochre staining of bones and dates to 15.4 kya evidencing that the ROT was still practised in Iberia ten thousand years after the last Neanderthal disappeared there. Ochre traces are seen at the Muge Middens in Portugal at 8000 BCE.

At Grotta di San Teodoro in northeast Sicily the earliest of seven burials date to 14 kya and were covered in a thick layer of red ochre. Recognized as the first inhabitants of Sicily they must have brought the ROT from the mainland. The Grotta dell'Uzzo, also in Sicily, had ochre present in some graves from 7400 to 6200 BCE, evidencing a long continuation of the tradition.

An early burial of three people, a young adult and two children, was found at a site near Irlich, Rheinland-Pfalz in Germany. These date from the very end of the last glaciation, some 12.5 to 11.2 kya. The burials were covered in red ochre and a few grave goods – antler point, flint and a perforated deer incisor were found. [100]

In Britain, at Aveline's Hole, in a cave used as a Mesolithic cemetery at about 7000 BCE, the skeletons of between 50 and 100 individuals were found in 1797, many reported to be laid in repose and in articulated condition. Because of the early date of the find the remains are now very fragmentary. Red ochre was found with the last complete burial excavated, in 1925, and traces reported on loose bones.

At Ofnet Cave in Bavaria, Germany, red ochre was used on 38 individuals in two burial pits as well as shells and deer teeth dating to 6500 BCE.

In the Eastern Baltic states of Estonia, Lithuania and Latvia, while the Mesolithic traditions of hunting, foraging and fishing prevailed, red ochre was used in burials. The island site of Spiginas at Biržulis Lake in western Lithuania's Samogitian Highland has yielded four burials, including the oldest known in the country. Spiginas 3, a woman in her early thirties was buried with ochre, a projectile point, pendants of elk, red deer and boar teeth, and dated to 7500 BCE. Spiginas 1 was a 35 to 45-year-old male with lots of ochre present and teeth pendants, but dated much later, perhaps 5100 BCE.

In the Late Mesolithic, as soon as the development of large cemeteries appears in the archaeological record, there is a parallel institutionalization of red ochre in funerary ritual.

A truly exceptional site is the cemetery of Zvejnieki at Lake Burtnieks in northern Latvia where about 300 graves were discovered dating from ca. 7200 to 2750 BCE, a span of more than four thousand years. Yellow ochre was dehydrated to red by firing and used in 56 per cent of the graves, the remainder had no ochre. Many burials used substantial quantities, and often the grave was sprinkled before use, the whole body covered, but sometimes just the head, pelvis and feet.

The mysterious "Island of the Dead", Oleniy (Reindeer) Island, in Onega Lake, in the Russian Karelia, was reserved as a cemetery from 6300 to 5600 BCE. A third of the original 500 burials were excavated in the 1930s and most were found to contain red ochre. [103]

The Hamangia were a settled culture, relying on hunting and foraging as well as some domestication of animals. They lived on the western coast of the Black Sea, Bulgaria, between 6000 and 5000 BCE. A number of burial sites are attributed to them, but the largest is Durankuluk where about 1200 burials are known. These show funerary evidence of red ochre by way of small lumps in many graves, but this had become only part of a much more complex set of ritual beliefs, including animal renewal traditions.

A pair of shell-midden cemeteries, Teviec and Hoedic on the coast of Brittany, France, dating from about 5500 BCE, have red ochre common in burials.

The Late Mesolithic Ertebølle culture occupied Denmark, northern Germany and southern Sweden, from about 5400 to 3900 BCE and had a cultural emphasis on powerful funerary rituals. An important site in Sweden is a pair of cemeteries on two islands, known as Skateholm I and II, with nearly a hundred burials in total, many with red ochre present. A site assumed to be for preparation of funerals has evidence of large quantities of ochre still staining the earth.

Excavations at another Ertebølle cemetery, Vedbaek at Bøgebakken, Denmark are summarized by Svend Albrethsen and Erik Peterson:

> *Carbon 14 dating of this site was 4100 B.C. The burials were laid out in regular rows with most of the skeletons oriented east-west. Most of the pit graves contained only one individual, except one in which three skeletons were found. Almost all of the graves contained red ochre.* [105]

The double grave of two hunter-gatherer women covered in red ochre was found at Dragsholm, west Zealand, Denmark, dated to about 3800 BCE. This was the end of the Mesolithic and the Ertebølle culture and, so it seems, the Red Ochre Tradition itself, as a European-wide religious belief. An unrelated, slightly younger, grave of a farmer close to them had quite different funerary goods because spiritual afterlife radically transformed the Natural Rebirth Traditions. This is discussed in Chapter Six.

Northern Africa

The Iberomaurusian peoples occupied parts of Maghreb in northwest Africa during the latter phase of the last Ice Age, when the northern Sahara was forested with pine and oak. The earliest ritual burials found there date from between 12 and 11 kya at Taforalt Cave complex in Morocco, where 40 individuals were found in 28 multiple burials. Red ochre was present in many cases although this is a complex site with disarticulated remains. [101]

The subsequent Capsian culture is responsible for a number of sites in Algeria. An early cemetery exists at Columnata, used from 6300 to 5300 BCE, where some burials had red ochre, perforated shells and bovine horns present. "Site 12", a midden 100 km south-east of Constantine, yielded ochre in several burials from a similar period, with a burial containing ochre also being been found at Ain Misteheyia.

David Lubell, anthropologist, researches the important Pleistocene to Holocene transition sites of the Maghreb and shows in a summary typical of many academic authors that he is not recognizing the significance of archaeological evidence which is screaming to be heard:

> *Other than mortuary practices that imply some belief in an afterlife there is no direct evidence for religion or religious practices. Decorative art is extensive at Capsian sites as is the use of red ochre on both human remains and stone tools.* [111]

Similarly Lionel Balout, former director at the National Museum of Natural History in Paris, also writes about prehistoric northern Africa from the period 7000 to 5000 BCE:

> *Capsian man practised a variety of burial rites, and the corpses were often found lying on their side in a foetal position. The frequent use of ochre remains a mystery.* [112]

The GMR holds that not only is afterlife the very essence of religious belief but application of red ochre representing blood is the essence of the earliest belief system. The Capsian peoples were clearly part of the global ROT and Balout's further evidence of foetal positioning buttresses the inference that afterlife by rebirth was the Capsian belief.

In the western desert of Egypt the cemetery of Gebel Ramlah was excavated to reveal seven graves with multiple burials dating to 3600 BCE. Red ochre had been sprinkled in several graves which had many other grave goods of shell, animal teeth and pottery, coloured powder in horns, rounded stones and semi-precious stone pendants. This site is just at the cusp of the paradigm shift to a spiritual worldview which is evidenced in Egypt only two centuries later.

Southern Africa

> *In the majority of MSA2a assemblages, ochre is absent, or only present at very low frequencies; but in two sites there are significantly larger quantities than in any previous context worldwide. We can infer that among some groups, at least, ochre was now in regular use. But the explosion in the use of red ochre with the MSA2b is remarkable, an increase greater than an order*

of magnitude. From this point on, copious amounts of ochre are ubiquitous in cave/rockshelter sites. [113]

– Chris Knight

Knight writes about ochre usage south of the Limpopo River. In this region Middle Stone Age 2a was ca. 130 to 110 kya and Middle Stone Age 2b was 110 to 75 kya, which is also the period from which the ochre mine at Lion Cavern, Swaziland was opened up and shows that as soon as large quantities of ochre became available it was enthusiastically used.

South Africa boasts what is arguably the second oldest example of early modern human remains at between 90 to 66 kya, earlier than all except Qazfeh. This pit burial of an infant only a few months old was at the Border Cave site close to the boundary of South Africa and Swaziland. It is notable that red ochre stains appear on the bones and a shell was present – both indicating belief in rebirth.

Most Stone Age burial in South Africa is relatively recent, from 8000 BCE and was limited to rockshelters and the coast but, just the same, the ROT was strongly persistent where burial was a regular practice. In the Eastern Cape region of South Africa an analysis of 500 burials across many caves and rockshelters shows that red ochre was commonly used. Ray Inskeep, archaeologist, mentions 40 per cent of the Albany period from 10,000 to 6000 BCE, 28 per cent of the Wilton period from 6000 BCE to 2000 BCE, and 14 per cent of post-Wilton from 2000 BCE to the start of the Current Era, were burials with red ochre present.

It is possible that the ROT persisted very late, and even until the arrival of Christianity, as two Late Stone Age burials found below Cobern Street, Cape Town, date to about 1000 CE and had grave goods of ochre, shells, animal remains and some utility items.

Levant and West Asia

The earliest recognizable cemetery in the Levant is at Uyun al-Hammam, northern Jordan, and contains the remains of eleven pre-Natufian individuals dating to about 16.5 kya. Several were buried with red ochre present and animal grave goods of fox, deer and aurochs parts. Prior to the Natufian period, 10,500 to 8500 BCE, burials in the Levant were rare, but many hundreds of this period have been found, and ochre is seen in context with burials at the Early Natufian site of Mallaha and the later site of Nahal Oren.

In the village of Ali Kosh, western Iran, several burials, dated 7100 to 6750 BCE, where the deceased were covered in ochre, are known,

Brian Peasnell, historian, comments on burial sites elsewhere in Iran, from about 5000 BCE, in the *Encyclopedia of Prehistory*:

> *Even the burials appear to involve very little formal ritual. All of the burials came from deposits associated with the Early Chalcolithic. Burials from Tepe Yahya and Tal-I Iblis were interred among midden deposits and do not appear to have contained any associated burial offerings beyond a few beads and red ochre. These consisted of both children and adults. Those that were well preserved were tightly flexed.* [114]

Even this brief description resonates with an established tradition of belief in rebirth afterlife. Further, not all ritual is tangible. In the remote future, from which we now look back, all the formal ritual of fire and smoke, procession, wailing in grief and chanting in ancient times are forever silenced, blown away by the passage of time. What are left are sometimes only bones, beads and red dust.

East Asia

The usage of red ochre was as culturally embedded in East Asia as we have seen in Europe and Africa. The Zhoukoudian cave complex in northeast China yielded the famous "Peking Man" remains of *Homo erectus* which were found in the 1920s – but which were sadly lost during World War II. Further research has illuminated the much later occupation layers of modern humans. A joint US and Chinese group has uncovered the earliest evidence of red ochre funerary ritual in China. The skeletal remains of eight people, including three skulls, were found in a burial pit dated to 19 kya. Disturbance of the site could indicate a later secondary burial, although the nearby ground was also ochre stained. [99] Even if a reburial, this shows that the meme of red ochre aiding rebirth was present in Upper Palaeolithic China.

East Asia is an important region, it was a branching point for the human migrations which led south to Australia, north-east across the Bering Strait into North America and south-east over the Pacific. In the remote central area of the Kamchatka Peninsula, eastern Russia, we find, at Ushki Lake, the traces of a small settlement dating from about 14 to 13 kya. Their burial pits have red ochre present although even the bones have all but rotted away. [115] This is close to the Bering Strait migrations in both time and space. So it supports the hypothesis that the first Native Americans carried the Red Ochre Tradition with them from Asia, although these peoples would have been distant ancestors of the Ushki.

Ancient land-bridges connected Kamchatka southwards through the Kuril island chain to Hokkaido, and from Korea to Kyushu, during glacial maximums through which humans migrated and a few verified artefacts indicate their presence as early as 30 kya. The incipient Jomon became the first recognized culture to inhabit the islands of Japan from about 14.5 kya until 300 BCE and red ochre usage probably came with them as, in Hokkaido, it is evidenced by staining of the bottom of graves in a multiple burial site known as Yunosato 4 which dates to about 12 kya. Additionally, a couple of ritual assemblages of ochre-stained dolphin skulls have been discovered from the same period. Nelly Naumann, a professor in oriental studies at the University of Freiberg, noted:

> *In this connection we should again mention the Higashi-Kushiro Shellmound where red iron oxide was scattered on the well-arranged dolphin-skulls and also on the human bodies buried in the same shellmound. The identical treatment of animals and human beings can but suggest that the identical belief, the identical expectation of a rebirth in this world formed the basis of burial customs as well.* [116]

Then the fragmentary practice of red ochre usage in funerary ritual seems to disappear until the Late Jomon period about 2400 BCE, perhaps because of the invention of ritual pottery and abundance of seashells which were an alternative symbolism in funerals. For millennia babies and infants who died were buried inside pottery jars – which may have been symbolic wombs to help ensure they would be reborn successfully.

Because the Late Jomon performed secondary burials the evidence is that the spiritual worldview had reached Japan at this period.

The Hoabinhian hunter-gatherer culture was widespread in South East Asia, occupying the areas now known as South China, Vietnam, Laos, Cambodia, Thailand, and Sumatra, through a long period ca. 20 kya to 2000 BCE. In Vietnam, where the culture was first identified and named after the Hoa Binh province, there are about 120 sites with 19 having remains of human burials. Nguyen Viet, director of the Centre for Southeast Asian Prehistory in Hanoi, reports that 90 per cent of the Hoabinhian burials are in a sleeping or crouched position, that red ochre and shells are frequent grave goods and that it seems prehistoric people thought of death as an especially long sleep. Red ochre stains on stone tools are frequently evidenced at Hoabinhian sites so it was culturally significant to them. [117]

At the Coc Phuong National Park, south of Hanoi, Vietnam, is the Dong Nguoi Xua Cave where three burials dated 5500 BCE were found in a seated position, covered in red ochre and celandine flowers. At Khuoi Nang Cave, also in North Vietnam, are two burials – an adult and a child. These burials are dated 5000 to 2000 BCE. Both are rare in the respect of the formalized stonework entombing the remains, and had funerary goods covered with a significant amount of red "powder", certainly ochre.

Cultures identified as separate and later to the Hoabinhian also maintained the ROT. The Bacsonian culture (which may have been a contemporary branch of the Hoabinhian) left 80 to 100 burials with red ochre and shells at Lang Cuom cave. The later Dabutian culture, primarily 4500 to 3000 BCE, also used this tradition as evidenced at Con Co Ngua where 100 burials were found, many with red ochre present.

Further south in Thailand, the large settlement of Khak Phnom Di, 20 km inland of the east coast of the northernmost point of the Gulf of Thailand shows the ROT was vigorous there between about 2000 and 1400 BCE, declining some time before then. The archaeologist Charles Higham reports on the early work at this huge site. Habitation evidence reveals a culture using a mixture of hunting, foraging, fishing and early cultivation of rice. Excavation of just a 10 m by 10 m section of the 5 ha site reveals three layers, the first layer with very few burials, not all with grave goods, but the main layer shows dozens of adult burials, all with red ochre, and many infant burials, mostly with ochre. Higham summarizes the first and main layers:

> *The essential burial ritual however was similar in both zones, the*
> *same orientation to the east was employed, ochre was used to*
> *cover the corpse, pots and shell beads were commonly placed with*
> *the dead and graves were located in clusters.* [118]

When considering these diverse East Asian cultures and the commonality of red ochre burial practices it is obvious that they share an ancient belief, persisting until recent millennia and most likely spread by diffusion with early human migrations. Arguably, they held to a universal rebirth belief system: the Red Ochre Tradition.

Australia

> *Systematic use of red ochre as a colouring agent has been employed by humans in Africa for hundreds of thousands of years (McBreaty and Brooks 2000; Barham 2002) and is undoubtedly a symbolic behaviour that was brought to Australia with the first humans to arrive.* [119]

> – Peter Hiscock

Red ochre is the signature colouring material for the Australian Aboriginal culture and is used decoratively, artistically and practically. This is not a homogenous culture, about 500 different peoples and 200 distinct religious traditions and variations exist. Technology use also varied, and Australian Aboriginal languages, although from the same root, are often as unintelligible to each other as English and Italian.

Burial practices are complex, but there is evidence of red ochre usage from first occupation of the continent. The earliest known burial is Lake Mungo 3, an ochre-sprinkled skeleton at 41 kya. The ROT endured, as burials at Kow Swamp are dated 22 to 19 kya. At least 40 individuals, with early modern characteristics, had ochre as well as shells and teeth grave goods. At Lake Nitchie on the lower Darling River, New South Wales, a male burial dated about 4800 BCE had been sprinkled with ochre and had grave goods of 178 perforated Tasmanian devil teeth. This is a very late ochre burial when there is circumstantial evidence that spiritual afterlife had emerged before Tasmania separated from the mainland about 10,000 BCE but the disparate and numerous locations of Aboriginal culture means that it is possible that the naturalistic animism and spiritual worldviews prevailed concurrently for thousands of years before fusing into a stable paradigm.

As previously described, their Dreamtime belief is best considered an amalgam of the two worldviews. The Aboriginal religious traditions are explored in more detail in Chapter Six on Spiritual Afterlife.

North America

> *It seems apparent that the prehistoric use of ochre, especially in mortuary contexts, was a global phenomenon. Its use in the New World seems to have likely coincided with the arrival of the first people to its shores.* [104]

> – Rebecca Morris

Red ochre was of primary importance in funerary rituals to many native cultures in North America, and originates from the earliest occupation of the continent. Evidence of the ROT on the migration route from Asia is indicated by the floor-print and remains of a hut discovered near the Tanama River in central Alaska, dating to 9500 BCE. The mostly cremated skeletal remains of a three-year-old were present in a burial pit just below the floor. Significantly, two pieces of red ochre were found with these remains. The Clovis culture continued this early tradition; in 1968 the Anzick site in Montana yielded a juvenile skull dating to 8700 BCE, and it was heavily ochre-stained.

At a similar time, about 8000 BCE, but much further south, the Pericu people of the southernmost point of Baja California Sur, Mexico, conducted primary burials utilizing red ochre. Its usage was so ubiquitous that burials where it is missing have become significant. George Weber observes:

> *However, one skeleton found at Los Martires was that of a crippled person - it had not been painted with ochre. It seems that young (and female?) and handicapped people were not given the normal ochre treatment before burial.* [120]

Weber does not speculate why ochre is omitted from some funerary rituals but the reason in the context of the ROT may be apparent. This might be an unusual cultural interpretation of rebirth afterlife where the unfit are not selected for future survival. Ochre is withheld so that the deceased does not have a rebirth afterlife in case they carry their disability or "disadvantage" into the next life. It is only when ochre becomes the norm in burials that its absence can be considered as preventing rebirth. The withholding of proper funeral ritual, not for judgmental reasons, but for selective reasons of breeding tribal fitness, is conceptually the same as eugenics.

Another early site is at Lobo Canyon, on the north-east of Santa Rosa Island, near Los Angeles, California. Ochre-stained shells are present and this is seen in a global context and discussed at the end of this chapter. Fragments of a burial were found, subsequently dated to 7600 BCE, but at the time of discovery erosion was destroying the remains. Near the thorax location were five modified shell beads, likely a funerary offering. Four were identified as *Olivella biplicata* of which two had a reddish brown colour, seemingly of red ochre. [121]

The anthropologist Dean Snow writes about the archaic hunter-gatherer cultures of the Eastern seaboard and specifically here the L'Anse Amour site in Labrador from 5,500 BCE:

> *This Middle Archaic site presaged the development of the Maritime Archaic burial complex later found from this area southward to Maine. There was an emphasis on the use of red ocher pigment in the burials of this complex, a trait that has led to the use of the name "Red Paint" to describe it. Curiously, similar burial complex are found in maritime contexts in Europe around the same time. But this was more likely an example of parallel cultural evolution than evidence of contact.* [122]

In the GMR, diffusion is certain for archaic red ochre usage seen on both sides of the Atlantic due to its hundred thousand year history in burials and trail of sites through and from Eurasia. Here, the proposal of parallel cultural evolution is rejected and considered unnecessary.

Rebecca Morris' work *A Shroud of Ochre* has the first cross-cultural analysis of red ochre usage in mortuary ritual. She examines the burial characteristics from ten Native American peoples across the continent (the Moorehead Burial Tradition, Weeden Island Culture, Chumash, WIABC, Adena, Red Ochre, Hopewell, Meadowood, Northwest Coast and STMT) in order to draw conclusions by way of comparison. They all used ochre in burials:

> *In addition to this common characteristic, there are several additional traits which are frequently found among groups who practiced mortuary ochre usage. One obvious feature that these groups hold in common is that all were primarily hunter-gatherers. Though some groups had developed the technology and practice of cultivation, the focus of their economy continued to be hunting and gathering.*

Morris observes that ochre was widely used, but also that there was a bias to the hunter-gatherer cultures. This is in concordance with the GMR hypothesis that naturalistic animism and its rebirth afterlife paradigm were common to all hunter-gatherer cultures globally at the time North America was first populated.

The life-force worldview prevailed very late in western parts of the United States. An Archaic burial of a female aged about 30, in Yoakum County, west Texas, is dated to about 990 BCE. She was set in a foetal position with red ochre sprinkled on her pelvis. [123]

South America

The most important Palaeolithic culture in Brazil, the extinct Mongoloid peoples, left shellmounds along the length of the Brazilian coast dating from about 6000 BCE to the final pre-European contact era. About one thousand are known and many burials were made within them, some involving red ochre. From a similar date the Toca do Enoque rockshelter in Serra das Andorinhas, near Guaribas, has burials with red ochre, teeth and shells present dating to about 6500 BCE.

The burial of an infant in the Traful I cave, on the Traful River, Patagonia, Argentina, dated about 7000 to 6000 BCE, has red stains on the bones. Analysis of which shows that it is ochre and sourced from 50 km away, across a major river, showing considerable effort required to obtain it. [124] Central Argentina has burial grounds, such as the Liguna Chillbué sites, showing red ochre present and dating to the first century CE. Similarly, the Tapera Moreira I site on the Curacó River, which was used from 2500 BCE until 1500 CE has ochre in burials.

As with all sites in recent millennia, they need to be assessed individually to determine whether the life-force worldview or the spiritual worldview was prevailing.

Stone Breathing Traditions (SBT)

The ROT harnessed functional representations of blood for rebirth afterlife on a global scale. The second major Palaeolithic belief system harnessed the life-giving properties of breathing. These are more obscure beliefs which developed over hundreds of thousands of years and are grouped in the GMR as Stone Breathing Traditions as rock art was the principal medium of its representation.

Funerary Cupules

> *It has been abundantly proved that our stone circles, whatever other purposes they may have served, were undoubtedly places used for the burial of the dead. From the frequency, therefore, with which cup-marks are found on or near the recumbent stones of these circles, it seems a fair deduction to suppose that the marks must have had some connection with the dead lying within the circles, or with their burial ceremonies. [...] The conclusion, therefore, appears to be that the Aberdeenshire cup-marks, in several instances, and perhaps in all, are older than the circles in which they are carved, and had in all probability a religious significance.* [62]

– James Ritchie

There is at least one Neanderthal burial where cupules form part of the grave goods. At La Ferrassie rockshelter in France a limestone slab with 18 cupules present was found to have been laid upon the remains of a three to five-year-old child, dated about 74 to 68 kya. Jean Clottes, an archaeologist specializing in rock art, interprets this burial as evidence of spirituality in the Neanderthal:

> *In this case, evidence of complex thoughts exist at three levels: the will to protect the body by burying it; the deposit of a worked stone; and the nature of the work on the stone itself, as the cupules are organized in four or five small groups, which might have had a symbolic meaning. This would be enough to establish the existence and conditions of these people's spirituality, but we have other clues too.* [125]

At a minimum Clottes determines that this is general evidence of the Neanderthal capacity for religious belief.

However, the Geologic Model holds that the spiritual worldview emerged long after the Neanderthal was extinct so these humans never knew of spirituality. It also identifies the presence of landscape cupules at Palaeolithic sites as general evidence for belief in naturalistic animism with its stone-breathing representations. At this site we have an example of funerary cupules from the life-force worldview, a separate type originating at locations of excarnations and later used in burials.

What is very interesting is that La Ferrassie cupules are in pairs, and therefore likely to represent nostrils, and were part of a funerary ensemble in order to help the rebirth afterlife process by ensuring that the deceased breathes again. This interpretation is strengthened by noting that the slab was laid with the depressions facing *downwards* so that the rock "breathes" directly onto the deceased remains.

Another Neanderthal child burial, at Dederiyeh Cave in Syria, dated to a contemporary period, 70 to 50 Kya, may have similar symbolism. [75] There appear to be pits and dots on the edge of a stone next to the child's skull. This interpretation requires further analysis.

Funerary cupules are defined by the "breathing holes hypothesis" as functional representations issuing life-giving air. Unlike the other NRT their use in bedrock is location oriented, part of the monumental architecture within which religious practices and ritual took place.

A remarkable modern human burial site is Raqefet Cave of the Late Natufian culture at the eastern side of Mt. Carmel, Israel. Here, at least 77 holes exist, mostly large cupules 10 to 30 cm across but, including a few smaller ones, cylindrical holes and basins. Two mortars were also buried up to the rim, one with bones near the base. Some cupules are clearly associated with burials as described by Dani Nadel, archaeologist, and colleagues:

> *We believe that the concentrations of HBH [human-made bedrock holes] near the graves at Raqefet are not random, and are rather an integral part of the burial complex at the site. Furthermore, many of them do not appear to have been used for food production (Belfer-Cohen and Hovers 2005; Nadel and Lengyel n.d.), or flint quarrying; there is no flint in the local limestone, but see Grosman and Goren-Inbar (2007) for an example of the use of small "cup-marks" for extracting flints at an early Neolithic site west of Jerusalem. It is our notion that at least some of the bedrock installations are symbolic in their context, specifically carved to be used during burial ceremonies.* [126]

Human-made bedrock holes can be considered here as a sub-class of funerary cupules. Of note, one burial had three *Dentalium* shell beads found near the skull's nasal cavity. Cupules are also reported in context with a few, probably late, Natufian burials at the nearby coastal Hayonim Cave, dated about 9000 BCE. This find is described by the archaeologist Anna Belfer-Cohen:

> *Though no graves had been marked by 'stone-pipes' as in Nahal Oren or on the Hayonim Terrace, some had small cup marks made in one of stones above or beside them. [...] Several cup marks were incorporated in the stone circle of Grave VI. Another small cup mark occurred on a block of stone, on the edge of Grave V.* [127]

The cupules at Hayonim were about 9 to 10 cm wide, similar to many at Raqefet Cave. Here, the suggestion of grave markers is rejected. The interpretation in the GMR is that of breathing holes to make the bedrock alive, consistent with the naturalistic animism worldview. Stone-pipes were also used. Those at Nahal Oren are actually large and deep mortars, probably for grinding food, and had become holed after long usage, then adapted for a funerary context, similar to those at Raqefet Cave. Instead of marking a grave, the holed mortars could also have been associated with breathing: as airway representations.

An earlier variation of this tradition is seen at the nearby Neve David site where a male Kebaran burial, dated 13.5 to 12.3 kya, predating the Natufians, had a broken mortar placed over his head, a broken bowl by his head, and a grinding stone at his thighs. The first two items considered as a breathing hole representation and the grinding stone an egg representation. All were to facilitate rebirth.

Funerary cupules and airway grooves are seen in the anthropomorphic pillar tops and portal edges at Göbekli Tepe, Turkey, which is discussed in Chapter Four, Enhanced Rebirth Afterlife.

Richard Bradley writes about prehistoric rock art in northern England and, commenting on the different usage of carvings – mainly cupules, circular motifs, ring marks and lines – says:

> *One common process underlies virtually all these cases. Where the rock carvings in the natural landscape often commanded a view over the surrounding area, those found inside these cairns were turned inwards towards the burial. The funeral rites required the inversion of normal procedures.* [128]

Cupules hammered into earth-fast boulders and glacial erratics in the open landscape were simply to make the environment more alive in sympathy with the life-force worldview. The inversion is done in burials, with funerary cupules facing inwards, in order to breathe new life into the deceased remains. Bradley is describing a crucial period in northern England and Scotland, during the fourth millennium BCE. It is when the paradigm shift occurred between the life-force and spiritual worldviews – rebirth afterlife belief gave way to the ancestor worship of spiritual afterlife belief. This happened at the earliest phase of the megalithic building tradition in the British Isles and may well have caused this tradition, as megaliths became the dwelling place for the newly conceived ancestor spirits. Once the life-force worldview disappeared no more cupules were made on stones in the open environment unless they were part of a funerary complex.

The breathing hole representations of cupules were to make burial places and religious temples more powerful for ensuring afterlife for the deceased. In Europe, Levant and Anatolia, India, Australia and North America, cupules are seen in memorial stones associated with burial sites but rarely so obviously, within the life-force worldview, associated to a single burial as at La Ferrassie 6 and at Raqefet Cave. It appears that Kebarans and Early Natufians in the Levant adhered to belief in SBT. It is also interesting that modern humans, widely separated (Levant and northern Britain), are seen sharing a descendant belief of a belief system held by the Neanderthal in France some 60,000 years earlier.

Charcoal

There is firm evidence for the Palaeolithic belief that charcoal, from the remains of fires, was thought to have great significance in a funerary context. When wood is burnt the smoke and flames were considered as visible air, and charcoal was the source of it. Funerary charcoal was therefore thought to be a special type of breathing "stone". Consequently, charcoal pieces or charred bone were laid in burials in order that their air-giving properties would breathe new life into the deceased. Full cremations have a spiritual context so charcoal left over from fuel to conduct these is not considered here. Funerary charcoal in the Palaeolithic is used especially for its breathing symbolism ensuring afterlife renewal.

It is likely that charcoal in context with many burials has not been considered part of funerary ritual by archaeologists, but rather that it is accidentally present from nearby hearth fires, but some sites are unequivocal.

Burnt bone was reportedly found by the skull of the Neanderthal buried at Le Moustier, dated 50 to 40 kya. Charcoal was laid below the Sungir 1 burial in Russia at 28 kya. A burnt Scots pine branch was laid beneath the Neanderthal and modern human hybrid child burial at Lagar Velho, Portugal, dated to 24.5 kya. Near this same period several charcoal pieces were strategically laid about the triple burial at Dolni Vestonice and directly associated with burials at other Moravian sites: Vysoka Lesnice, Nizka Lesnice and Pod Zubem. [129]

Just like red ochre, funerary charcoal is seen in burials from the remotest parts of the European subcontinent and indicates a widespread religious tradition. Blood renewal and breathing symbolism were essential elements in funerary ritual to assist with the rebirth afterlife process. Cremations seen before the Neolithic are therefore certain to have had a quite different purpose than that of spiritual release which is general to today. What is interpreted as a cremation in the Palaeolithic would instead be an attempt to associate the deceased with the breathing properties of charcoal while it was smoking and burning. The earliest cremation known, Lake Mungo I, in Australia, is dated to about 40 kya. It is, however, a full cremation leaving only the skull and bone fragments which may even have been burned twice. Its unusual nature, where a corpse was excessively exposed to charcoal at this early date, is suggestive of an extreme attempt to ensure rebirth afterlife by association with life-giving air.

Charcoal in burials is seen in North America as described by Robert Cartier, archaeologist. He writes of a Native American burial, dating to 3590 BCE at Sunnyvale, California, with large amounts of red ochre, and some shells:

> *Another characteristic in the grave of the Red Burial was the clear presence of a fire in the base of the grave pit. Charcoal particles up to 15 mm in size were found in the soil under the skeletal remains and adhering to bones, particularly those lying on the base of the grave. Thermal scorching on portions of the bones was evident. From these data, it appears that the body was placed on the fire or embers of a fire as part of the funeral ceremony. This use of fire has been noted in archaeological investigations of regional Native American cemeteries, and it seems to extend chronologically*

> *throughout the range of the recognized prehistoric past of the area.*
> [130]

Cultures where primary burials and elements of the NRT, for example red ochre and shells, are predominant in their funerary rituals are very likely adhering to rebirth afterlife belief. So the use of fire during the funeral is an attempt to use charcoal at its most powerful – emitting smoke and flames, visible air, to ensure the deceased later breathes again via rebirth.

Perforations and Fossil Ammonites

> *What was described as a "ceremonial burial" was found, with a skeleton apparently placed in a disused hearth, together with red ochre, abundant animal teeth, some of which were perforated, and a set of fossil ammonites (Davies, 1925). The latter show no traces of being modified but were all roughly semicircular with smoothed ends, suggesting that they were intentionally selected. More tellingly, the fossil ammonites apparently could not have come from Aveline's Hole itself as lie nearest source is over 20 km distant (Donovan, 1968).* [131]

– Rick Schulting and Mick Wysocki

Associated with SBT, and probably developed in parallel with the concept of cupules in rocks as breathing holes, was the practice of perforating objects. This was widespread in the Palaeolithic and Mesolithic. Many stones, shells, teeth, beads and antler batons which are found in burial sites are deliberately holed. Different shells in the Skhul burials at 90 kya were also holed.

It is generally assumed that this was done so that objects could be strung on cords and worn decoratively. Evidence of microscopic striations supports the theory that cords were used in some cases, but this is the exception. An alternative explanation is that usually they were holed in order to make them "breathe", becoming alive, consistent with naturalistic animism and very effective as grave goods for rebirth.

The Mesolithic cemetery of Aveline's Hole, western England, at 7000 BCE shows many elements of NRT including breathing symbolism. The "hearth" mentioned by Schulting and Wysocki may well have been a bed of charcoal brought in for funerary ritual, as this cave was unlikely to have been used for habitation when it was a tomb for the deceased.

The nearby Mendips, a range of limestone hills and escarpments, is rich in fossil ammonites, spiral-shaped shellfish ancestral to the modern nautilus. To the Mesolithic mind these coiled fossils were very significant. Fossil ammonites were selected for their shape as this was representative of air, visualized from spiralling smoke, which was believed to breathe rebirth afterlife into human remains. Spiral symbolism was later re-used widely by the Atlantic coastal megalithic cultures in a spiritual context.

A burial of a child at Malta in Siberia, dating to 14.7 kya, had a necklace with 120 mammoth ivory beads present and seven pendants with numerous pit-marks or "mini-cupule" depressions on them. [132]

Breathing symbolism is present at this site in the form of a rectangular ivory plaque with a central hole surrounded by spirals made from pit-marks. The reverse side has three snakes. Both breathing and egg representations are present in this one object. The use of spirals within the NRT in Mesolithic funerary ritual thousands of kilometres apart indicates both cultures lived in the same worldview paradigm.

Animal Renewal Traditions (ART)

The third major Palaeolithic belief system harnessed the life-giving properties of eggs and antler renewal. Egg representation is by far the most varied ancient tradition in its many forms and materials used in funerary ritual, where the power of eggs could ensure physical rebirth.

Egg Renewal and Egg Representation

> *Egg. "Few simple natural objects have such self-explanatory yet profound meaning." Tresidder writes. Egg-laying creatures occupy an iconographic niche, from prehistory onward, connected with the primordial condition, creation, birth, fertility, and rebirth / regeneration.* [133]

> – Hope B. Werness

Werness, an art professor, is on the right track. She has pointed her finger at the beating heart of the world's most prolific prehistoric belief system, exceeding in scale even that of red ochre. The GMR goes further and characterises eggs in a Palaeolithic funerary context, not as simply symbolic, but as a functional tool within naturalistic animism to facilitate rebirth afterlife for the deceased.

Just as prehistoric peoples recognized blood and breathing as essential for life they also took great notice of how eggs can hatch into new life as birds and reptiles – although they were normally eaten on the spot. Chimpanzees eat bird eggs, whole, and this must have remained a staple part of the Palaeolithic diet for hominins of Australopithecus and Homo. Eventually, when personal mortality concerns led to the afterlife belief of rebirth and finally intervention by funeral ritual the ancient knowledge of eggs as life-giving was a concept easily associated with rebirth afterlife.

The power of "like-for-like", sympathetic magic, means that the presence of real eggs in a grave has a strongly beneficial effect upon the rebirth afterlife process for the deceased. The egg as a facilitator of rebirth afterlife is the largest belief complex within the Animal Renewal Traditions (ART).

However, any eggs associated with burials will have quickly decayed completely, leaving no evidence, as they have a very recent taphonomic threshold. Fortunately for decoding the past, eggs were symbolically represented from even the earliest burials with two egg-like classes of grave goods which are strongly persistent in the ground: shells and teeth. Egg representation is a further inferred concept and also spread as a meme, one that is conceptually fluid, so this meme evolved over tens of thousands of years in various forms.

How ancient are the Animal Renewal Traditions? The burial known as Skhul 5 at the Skhul cave site, which has a connection with red ochre and perforations, also shows that ART is at least one hundred thousand years old. Skhul 5 had the mandible of a wild boar placed on his chest. This is a relatively advanced form of ART because it demonstrates two later developments.

First, teeth only became associated with eggs over time. Their oval shape and hard, white substance made them into obvious egg representations for funerary ritual.

Secondly, the number of teeth present in a whole jaw is evidence of the meme of numerical strength. Two eggs are more powerful than one. A jaw with many teeth is more powerful than a single tooth.

The result is that the ART belief system had become branched and abstracted and is manifest in numerous forms in human burials as grave goods. Unlike the ROT, where red ochre is the principal representation for blood with haematite sometimes seen, there are a number of viable substitutes for eggs in funerary ritual. The preference for them depends upon cultural factors led by what was available in the environment.

The spectrum of egg artefacts for ensuring rebirth afterlife includes bird and reptile eggs, seashells, teeth – single or embedded in mandibles and maxillae, ivory beads, turtle, tortoise and snail shells. It also includes inorganic and functional representations of oval stones or fossils, moulded clay, egg and symbolic shell imagery in art and perhaps the hatching egg symbolism of a cross within a circle, the sun-cross, although this may be Neolithic.

Many burials contain multiple egg representations such as the Dolni Vestonice triple burial where wolf and fox canines, shells and ivory were all present.

A fractured and hatched egg was often considered unhelpful for assisting with the afterlife process, because its renewal properties were "spent", so unbroken eggs were strongly preferred. This applies especially with bivalve seashells. Also, larger "eggs" were more magically powerful; hence, ostrich eggs and large beaver and carnivore teeth are preferred in early burials.

Erik Trinkaus, a physical anthropologist, has studied Palaeolithic ivory objects and sees a correspondence in the raised dot patterns of the shell of *Pirenella plicata* with those found of worked ivory. So it was more likely a shell-likeness was being created in ivory instead of Marshak's calendar notation – for example. Also, some of the most preferred species of shells seem to have been selected for symbolic use because of resemblance to deer incisors. Bone has also been found worked into a deer incisor shape, as a tooth-like egg substitute object.

In the GMR this series of associations are different expressions of the ART functional representations within naturalistic animism and they appear to have influenced the emergence of sculptural artistry itself.

Bird and Reptile Eggs

Although these are at the root of the major ART belief sub-system, unsurprisingly, I have been unable to find any evidence in the literature of eggs used in prehistoric burial; they would have decomposed completely. However, absence of evidence is not evidence of absence, and perhaps eggs were used in burials or even placed with corpses left for excarnation before burial practices started. From the earliest burials at 100 kya, teeth and shells were used, meaning that a very early cultural preference for egg substitutes had already developed.

It is teleological to imply that shells and teeth were selected for grave goods because of their capacity to remain intact for a long time, let alone until archaeologists could find them in the remote future. The preference would simply be due to the sheer hardness of teeth and shells making them a stronger and better form of "egg" for facilitating afterlife by rebirth. Bird and reptile eggs can be symbolically represented with bird and reptile imagery in funerary ritual and this does occur within the domain of rebirth afterlife belief and this is explored later in Temples of Rebirth.

Whole bird eggs were often interred in human burials in the eastern Mediterranean and Levant region during Classical Antiquity. Because this was done within the spiritual worldview this usage is discussed only in Chapter Six on Spiritual Afterlife.

Seashells

Marine creatures populated the ocean shores but where did they come from? The conclusion to the prehistoric mind was obvious. Seashells are the eggs of marine animals! Broken shells on a beach were left after fish and other marine life had hatched out. Inside, raw shellfish were like raw bird eggs confirming this view.

Archaeologists find the presence of shells associated with prehistoric burials puzzling, especially when they are of an inedible variety. Yet, they are present because shells are important egg substitutes prehistorically believed to be life-giving in a worldview of naturalistic animism. Shells are seen directly associated with two of the three earliest burial sites, the Qafzeh and Skhul Caves in Israel from about 100 kya. They are also associated with the remotest; an Australian Aboriginal

Kow Swamp burial dated around 22 to 19 kya has the deceased laid upon a bed of mussel shells. At the Grimaldi caves one male was buried at about 25 kya wearing a net cap of 200 whelk *Nassarius* shells. So this tradition stretches through tens of millennia and on a global scale.

Many authors observe the importance of shells as symbolic of life-giving but then struggle to identify the reason why. Mircea Eliade was a professor of history, philosophy and religion. He wrote:

> *We have seen how exactly the sea-shell and the oyster express the symbolism of birth and rebirth. The initiation ceremonies include a symbolic death and resurrection: the shell can signalise the act of spiritual rebirth (resurrection) as effectively as it assures and facilitates carnal birth.* [134]

Eliade determined that shell symbolism as life-giving was driven by their shape as a metaphor for female reproductive anatomy: womb, vulva. Unfortunately any similarity there is just tangential if not coincidence. He also assumes that spiritual afterlife was the goal, and this is only true in recent millennia.

Nick Ashton, curator of the British Museum, and colleagues, consider the pierced periwinkle shells found in the Paviland burial as perhaps "worry" or prayer beads. [135]

That seems unlikely. The piercing of shells, commonly seen, implies that they were strung and may have been worn decoratively and it is possible that the shells were thought to have beneficial properties for the wearer. But these are also syncretic amulets with both egg symbolism and breathing symbolism. They would be considered very powerful when placed into a burial context, assuming their primary role as conducive to rebirth afterlife.

During the early Neolithic, shells were important to many cultures and were one of a select few goods (along with obsidian, copper and turquoise) that were traded long distances. Jaques Cauvin notes that Mediterranean and Red Sea *Dentalium* and basket shells penetrated the whole of the Levant with a significance that was more than symbolic. [136]

Trinkaus also points out:

> *Reciprocal exchange networks are highly selective and usually involve greatly valued objects. [...] These objects, which are frequently shells, take on an increased value not because of their scarcity alone, but because of their social importance.* [70]

Spondylus and *Dentalium* shells became very popular grave goods from 5000 BCE in the Varna and Durankuluk cemeteries, and their appearance in more Central European sites may reflect the opening up of trade routes, whereas they were long known in Aegean coastal burials. In contrast, the Mesolithic burial ground at Khartoum, Sudan, has some burials about 5500 BCE with shells sourced from the Nile River the only grave goods present.

Care is required differentiating between shell midden debris piled from years of food waste and shells deliberately associated with nearby human burials. Nowhere is this more complicated than the Jomon sites in Japan. There are at least 1100 shell middens, although these are not evenly distributed (perhaps because many have been destroyed during sea level changes), most are in the Kanto Plain which includes the Tokyo region. Some of them can reach a huge size, up to 170 m long, over 4 m deep and reaching several thousand cubic metres in volume. Later, intrusive burials occurred into shell middens and perhaps the whole midden was thought to be conducive for rebirth afterlife.

Some shells were prized by the Jomon as the subtropical species of cone shell and cowrie has been found in sites as far north as Hokkaido. Shell bracelets are commonly found on the skeletal wrists of Jomon female burials, such as at Tsukomo, Okayama Prefecture, but they are so fragile that they would break in normal use, preventing any manual labour during life, and so small that archaeologists theorize that they were worn from childhood. [137]

However, the more straightforward explanation is that they were part of dressing the corpse during funerary ritual, and intended to assist the rebirth process.

There is also the preference for intact or paired shells in some shell mounds and burials. This is seen at Native North American sites such as the Vaughn site in Mississippi, dated to 4500 BCE. The anthropologist Cheryl Claassen describes puzzling evidence:

> *A few observers have noted a high incidence of paired valves in these mounds. At the Deweese shell mound a single column sample (35 x 35 cm) taken from the center of the mound by the author had 15+ layers, each of which contained a minimum of 30 percent paired valves and several had 100 percent of the valves paired. Village or camp activities - walking, digging, running, sculling, tossing, dumping – are not conducive to maintaining*

> *bivalve pairs. While the quantification of this phenomenon is poorly developed, pairing this extensive suggests that this mound, and others with pairing, were not villages or camps.* [138]

Paired bivalves are also present at the Muge Middens in Portugal where some burials were clearly associated with unopened clamshells of *Scrobicularia plana* and *Tapes decussata*. The conventional hypothesis is that whole shellfish were thought to be food offerings for the dead. This can only be the case in cultures which believed in spiritual afterlife, and even then shells were normally empty. Shell offerings as spiritual food does not fit the life-force worldview.

In the GMR shells as egg representations in ART implies that paired shells were not food offerings to the dead but were instead considered to be "un-hatched" eggs of the sea. Therefore, they were more powerful for conveying the life-giving properties of eggs to the rebirth process.

The most lavish shell burial found is at the important site of Khak Phnom Di, Thailand, where a female was buried with 120,000 shell beads as well as being covered in a large quantity of red ochre. Such a lavish funeral directly echoes the desperate loss which the people must have felt at the Grimaldi caves thousands of years earlier and thousands of kilometres west. The people change but the grief, traditions, and fundamental symbolisms endure.

Teeth, Mandibles and Maxillae

> *In the angle formed by the left forearm and right humerus was the mandible of a very large pig. [....] There can be no doubt, from its position, and from the fact that the left forearm rests upon the broken, hinder ends of the mandible, that its inclusion in the grave was deliberate.* [139]

– T.D. McCown

The earliest known example of teeth as grave goods was described by McCown when it was found in 1937. A jaw of a boar was placed in the Skhul 5 burial dated between 100 and 90 kya.

After more than 80,000 years, this religious tradition endures to the time of Neolithic settlements. An echo of Skhul 5 is seen when a boar's jaw with tusks still present was carefully laid upon a double burial in the "cell buildings area" in Çayönü, Turkey about 6000 BCE.

The sheer resilience of teeth as opposed to egg-shell seems to have created an early preference for them in funerary ritual as an egg substitute. Further, it is evident that whole jaws were placed upon the dead to impart the power of multiple eggs for renewal. These are the upper, maxilla, or the lower, mandible preferred as they have many teeth embedded in them. The aforementioned Aboriginal Kow Swamp burial, where the deceased was laid upon mussel shells, also has a band of kangaroo teeth around his skull.

Near Dubbo, New South Wales a double burial was discovered containing a pair of lower left kangaroo incisors and a pair of freshwater mussel shells. [140] For cultural reasons this find is undated but the presence of the same grave goods seen at Kow Swamp, 600 km away, is striking and, for the GMR, evidence that Natural Rebirth Traditions, when practiced by the Aboriginals, are consistent long-term.

The presence of teeth as grave goods has long been perplexing and some authorities attempt to understand it by making a case for the animal's mouth being significant as a powerful orifice. Christopher Tilley, anthropologist and archaeologist, writes:

> *Red ochre was obviously a deeply important symbolic medium and I have noted that it is usually concentrated on two areas of the body – around the head and thorax and the pelvic regions. One explanation for this is that the head and pelvis contain the orifices – entrances to and exits from the body. [..] They are also in some cases decorated with strings of animal teeth, particularly those of red deer. With regard to the head decorations there is an obvious symbolic link between the teeth of red deer marking one of the orifices (the mouth) of this animal and the orifices of the human head.* [141]

Unfortunately for this interpretation, the mouth of the animal and the orifices of the human head are not relevant at all with teeth symbolism. The GMR holds that the believed power of teeth was in their shape and colour as an egg substitute. Animal strength and the size and number of teeth, and perhaps the "power" of animal remains only serve to make teeth a more powerful egg substitute. Deer teeth were commonly favoured because of an extra association with the power of antler renewal, described later.

In the Levant, gazelle mandibles were in context with the Ohalo II burial dating to 19.2 kya. Nine thousand years later a Late Natufian burial at Raqefet Cave, Mount Carmel, was found with two canine teeth from a wolf or a fox, evidencing a continuing belief system.

At the Grotta dell'Uzzo in Sicily, from between 7400 and 6200 BCE, the burial known as Uzzo 5, had a red deer jaw in his right hand as well as a shell nearby. Single shells and a whole necklace were found as burial goods at this site.

In Britain's Aveline's Hole, which was used as a Mesolithic cemetery around 7000 BCE, parts of a bear's jaw and a large deer's jaw, possibly elk, were interred with the skeletons there.

In the Mesolithic burial ground at Vedbaek Bøgebakken, Denmark, one of the most elaborate graves was of a woman and infant. She wore a necklace of more than 200 boar teeth pendants. At this burial site, and the red ochre site of Skateholm, the presence of teeth from several different animals have intrigued archaeologist Nick Thorpe:

> *The shark teeth found at Skateholm were nearly all used as grave goods, leading Jonsson to conclude that they had special meaning and might have been exchanged from elsewhere as gifts. [...] The ability to obtain tooth pendants belonging to these exotic and powerful animals may well have been highly significant, especially if something of the strength of the animal itself was thought to reside in its remains.* [142]

Thorpe has observed that some of these grave offerings were from the brown bear, shark, aurochs and elk – animals which were highly unusual or non-existent locally. So these imply trade routes or long-distance exchange of marriage partners. Either way, the strings of rarer teeth were status items.

It follows that when status items are chosen as grave goods they are more likely to be symbolic. One particularly illustrative burial at Vedbaek is that of a woman with an elk tooth (as part of a pendant string) placed below her pelvis. It is a demonstration of the like-for-like association of teeth with eggs to facilitate physical rebirth afterlife by reproduction.

Animal teeth are seen as grave goods in the other major Mesolithic cemeteries already described evidencing the ROT belief system. At Oleniy Island in Russia the hunter and fisher culture there used teeth extensively, often placing them over the eyes and head before burial. The reported figures are impressive: 4372 incisors of elks in 84 graves of some 739 individuals; 1155 beaver teeth in 70 graves of some 574 individuals; 230 canines of bears in 78 burials. [143]

Teviec and Hoedic cemeteries in France have pig and deer mandibles placed in most burials. Douglass Bailey, anthropologist, writes about the prehistoric Balkans and describes many burial sites between 6000 and 2000 BCE. The usage of teeth as primary grave goods is extremely common. Jaws of boar, deer, and even dogs and humans are seen. Individual fish teeth are also present.

Human teeth have been used elsewhere in funerary ritual. One was found associated with a burial at Skateholm, and many human teeth formed funerary ornaments at Vedbaek. Perhaps because they are relatively small, human teeth were considered less powerful and not often selected for offerings. The difficulty also exists that some will not be recognized because they may be assumed as displaced from the skeleton under investigation, or another burial nearby.

The Mesolithic Iron Gates burial grounds, at the Serbian-Romanian border region, dated at about 6000 BCE, has two adult female burials at Vlasac, each with a male human mandible as a grave good. Similarly, an example at nearby Lepenski Vir also exists.

Burials from the Mahgreb cultures at Taforalt in Morocco and Columnata in Algeria reveal skulls and jaws with a pattern of deliberate tooth removal (evulsion) during life. This evulsion was often found in females, some wretches losing as many as eight teeth. Perhaps the practice was done during mourning or funerary rituals and a tooth included with a deceased relative. Notably, at Columnata, human body parts are also seen as grave goods.

Ivory Beads

Ivory was certainly important for making the funerary beads, as egg representations, which occur in some burials. The early site at Sungir, Russia, has several burials with a total overall of 13,000 ivory beads, far too many for any decorative purpose.

At Krems, Austria, an infant burial has 31 ivory beads present and nearby twin infants had pieces of mammoth tusk supporting a scapula. The Dolni Vestonice triple burial had ivory pendants present. Tusks may have been seen as a further derivative from mere teeth. They grow large and have long been worked for making objects in the Upper Palaeolithic. Very likely it was thought the power of mammoths would magically persist in ivory objects, passing to the deceased after rebirth.

Turtle and Tortoise Shells

The practice of human burial with turtle or tortoise shells is likely an expression of ART, because an intact shell (carapace and plastron) is egg-shaped, as is a pair of carapaces facing together. Therefore, these shells are suitable as egg representations in burials for ensuring rebirth. There are examples found in different cultures.

Körtik Tepe is a 12,000 year old archaeological site with the oldest graves in Eastern Anatolia. These were from a pre-pottery fishing people who lived at the confluence of the Batman and Tigris rivers. Many graves had tortoise shells present and were not limited to a particular age group or to whether other grave goods had been interred. Many also had ochre and gastropod beads. As a group, these burial goods were within the NRT belief systems intended to facilitate rebirth.

At the same period a 45-year-old Natufian woman was buried at the Hilazon Tachtit Cave in Israel with 50 complete tortoise shells as grave goods.

The remarkable Horn Shelter burial, in Texas, United States, reveals the detailed funerary rituals of Paleoindians. At 9000 BCE an adult and a juvenile were buried together below a habitation layer. Turtle carapaces were set with concave faces inward to form an egg-shaped box. A piece of red ochre was placed behind the head of the adult and other items interred: 80 nerite seashells, antler fragments and coyote teeth. A large olive shell was present which must have originated in the Gulf of Mexico, some 300 km away! It appears snail shells may have been interred too. [144]

The Paleoindians who performed the double burial did all they could to ensure that the like-for-like sympathetic magic of blood and egg representations was as strong as possible to ensure rebirth afterlife for their loved ones. The similarities of ART seen on both sides of the Atlantic are compelling evidence that this belief system spread with the global dispersal of modern humans.

Snail Shells

Snail shells are egg representations also seen in grave goods but much less often than seashells. There are, however, striking examples which show they were part of an early religious belief system. The Arene Candide Cave burial of the "Little Prince" had a cap of dozens of snail shells. Each shell in the cap contributed, by virtue of numerical strength, to the whole making it powerfully harness egg renewal.

At the Muge Middens, Tagus Valley in Portugal, several early Neolithic sites exist, of which one, Moita do Sebastião, was excavated in the 1950s and yielded 34 skeletons subsequently dated to about 8000 BCE. Strings of snail shells, *Theodoxus fluviatilis*, are the main grave goods, sometimes around the neck or waist. David Lubell observes that land snails were present at this site, and at Gruto do Caldeirão but were not eaten. [145]

There is a complication in that some snails are carnivorous and may have been attracted to a poorly buried corpse, and not deliberately interred. More taphological analysis is needed by archaeologists in these cases to be clearer as to whether snails were grave goods or arrived later. Seashells are seen associated with human burial on a global basis where the populations lived at the margins of continents. Populations far from the sea may have found snail shells more accessible.

Stones and Fossil Sea Urchins

Spherical stones are known in very ancient human sites although only in the Upper Palaeolithic are they found in a funerary context. Their purpose is puzzling for archaeologists as they do not seem to have a utilitarian value, except possibly as bolas, stones roped together for hunting. Bolas seems an unlikely explanation and a better one is that they were egg substitutes, symbolic objects.

Oval stones as an egg-substitute are seen at the Ohalo II site between Tiberias and the River Jordan, in the Galilee region, Israel. A burial, dating to 19.2 kya, of a male aged between 35 and 40 was found. He was laid on his back in a semi-flexed position in a shallow pit, with three small stones under his head and a large round hammer-stone between his legs near the pelvis. Several gazelle mandibles were found in the vicinity of the grave as well as a 2.5 cm length of bone with decorative cut marks. [146] The placing of the hammer-stone, about 15 cm long, was deliberate and, in the location of the pelvis, is considered here to be an egg representation to facilitate rebirth afterlife. The stones under the head may have similar significance.

The Villabruna 1 burial at Ripari Villabruna rock shelter in northeast Italy, dated to 14 kya, had several limestone pebbles with markings painted in red ochre, laid on top. Grave goods included flint tools and a piece of ochre. [147]

Very interesting finds of round and oval fossils are reported in burials including sea urchins and echinoids, which are also egg representations, perhaps eggs of the earth because they are a rock-like form. The archaeologist Håkon Glørstad considers these fossils:

> *From the Mesolithic cemetery Skateholm in Scania two graves are known where petrified sea urchins were found at the hips of the deceased (Larsson 1983: 26). The fossils are interpreted as grave gifts.* [148]

However, placement at the hips must be symbolically associated with reproduction and therefore means that these were not mere gifts but egg representations to facilitate rebirth afterlife.

In North America there is a Late Archaic burial at the Thursday Site on the northern shore of Sevier Dry Lake in Utah. The flexed skeleton of a male aged about 45, dated between 70 and 220 CE, had the singular grave good of a white kaolin clay ball by his jaw which is probable ART egg symbolism. [149] The practice of placing round stones with burials is frequently seen through the Neolithic to Classical Antiquity and, like the placement of real eggs, is discussed in Chapter Six on Spiritual Afterlife.

Antler Renewal

> *The fact that antlers could be shed and replaced every year makes them a potent source of symbolism. The mature stag offers a powerful metaphor for fertility, as we know from later rock art, and the annual growth of its antlers provides an ideal symbol of regeneration. That may be why they occur in Mesolithic graves over such a wide area.* [87]

> – Richard Bradley

Deer antlers are the fastest growing tissue of any mammal, developing over one centimetre per day. Each year they become large bony structures, from pedicules which are located above the eye sockets. Antlers are cartilaginous when growing and then calcify into bone. Normally antlers are only present on males although in reindeer females have them too. In Eurasia, during Palaeolithic times, reindeer were by far the most prolific large hunting game, travelling in herds of thousands, and much further south than they do today.

Humans must have long been aware that antlers grow rapidly after being fully discarded each year and this became a significant symbol of renewal. The practice of offering deer antlers as grave goods to facilitate rebirth afterlife is an extremely ancient tradition seen in one of the earliest burials known. At Qafzeh Cave the burial, from ca. 95 kya, of an early modern human adolescent aged about 13, known as Qafzeh 11, had the antlers of a deer set upon his chest. This was certainly intended to facilitate his rebirth though the properties of antler renewal. Antler renewal is a separate belief sub-system within ART that's not related to the major belief sub-system of egg renewal.

There are two good examples of Neanderthal burial with antlers as a grave good; Le Regourdou from about 70 to 65 kya, and the previously discussed hybrid at Lagar Velho.

The "Little Prince" burial had four reindeer antler batons, each with a hole near one end. Their presence wouldn't be purely decorative and probably links breathing symbolism to antler renewal, creating a magically powerful combination in one syncretic amulet.

At the Saint-Germain-la-Rivière Mesolithic burial in south-west France, dating to 15.5 kya, a halved reindeer antler was interred, as well as bison skull-cap painted with ochre and hundreds of deer teeth.

The Teviec and Hoedic cemeteries, which used ROT and ART symbolism, have antlers placed in the graves of adult burials. Deer skulls and antlers were sometimes placed within graves at Lepenski Vir. The anthropologist Peter Bogucki observes that antlers are significant in burials at the Northern European Ertebølle cemeteries:

> *[At Skateholm] many of the burials are accompanied by grave goods. As at Vedbaek, red deer antlers figure prominently in the burial rite, with full racks often placed over the deceased as if to restrain them in the grave.* [150]

One Skateholm burial, for example, has several large deer antlers placed over his legs, which superficially appears to imply restraint. The opposite is certainly the case where this is a powerful symbol of animal renewal intended to make the dead *walk again* by way of rebirth.

Plant Renewal Traditions (PRT)

The fourth and last of the NRT is seemingly a much more recent belief system originating only from the Late Mesolithic. The reason may be taphological because plant materials will decay completely, unlike red ochre, shells, teeth and antler which are evidenced to 100 kya, as they are persistent in the ground and maintain their context with human remains.

Likely, it was before agriculture that people paid careful attention to the cyclic renewal of plants. The renewal of perennials must have been particularly visible through the seasons. Many plants die completely away each winter, yet in spring young leaves renew and push out from the bare ground. Within a worldview of naturalistic animism plant renewal could be harnessed to ensure afterlife. When the deceased are committed to the earth then they too could take advantage of the process of plant "rebirth" demonstrated by nature every year.

There is evidence of green symbolism in many cultures: grove worship, jade masks, the tree of life and pinecones, but all are related to plant renewal within the spiritual worldview, so are detailed in Chapter Six on Spiritual Afterlife. The symbolism examined here is only where plant renewal was for facilitating a physical rebirth for the newly dead.

Greenstone Symbolism

Archaeologist Barbara Barich describes usage of greenstone symbolism seen at Kadero in Nubia, Egypt between 5000 and 4000 BCE:

> *Only 14% have yielded grave-goods: these are quite varied and can be differentiated according to sex. Porphyry mace-heads, pottery painted with ochre, bone and precious stone necklaces, and bivalve shells were reserved for men. Pottery, personal*

ornaments (cornelian and marine-shell beads), amazonite and malachite lumps, were given to women. [151]

Three NRT belief systems are evident in this description, ROT (by ochre), ART (by shells) and the PRT through funerary use of green-coloured stones. This site also shows a rare ethnographic split in NRT based upon sex and status.

Malachite is probably the commonest green mineral known in prehistoric times and regularly used in a funerary context.

Flower Renewal

Flowers are strongly symbolic of plant renewal because they are annuals, so their presence in graves could well be intended to assist the deceased with attaining rebirth afterlife.

The Shanidar Cave in the Zagros Mountains of northern Iraq contained ten Neanderthal burials, four of which may be accidental from rock falls. One flexed male burial in particular, dating to 60 kya, has become famous as unusual amounts of pollen, from at least eight different wildflower types, were found in context, prompting even a book on the Shanidar flower people. [152] Alas, it seems to be wishful thinking that flowers were interred deliberately as grave goods here. Jeffrey Sommer convincingly argues that the pollen remains could have been introduced by the Persian Jird, which is a type of gerbil. [153] These industrious rodents store flowers for food in their burrows and their remains were found close to the Neanderthal skeletons.

The Nguoi Xua Cave in Vietnam, exhibits the ROT, and has three burials with a covering of celandine flowers dated to 5500 BCE, almost certainly representing one of the earliest examples of the PRT, utilizing flowers.

At Gobero, in Niger, the Sahara desert has yielded a large cemetery, some 200 burials, from the early Holocene 8000 to 6200 BCE. It was used by two distinct cultures, the second from 5200 BCE. Common to both the corpses were hyper-flexed, excessively folded or curled into a foetal position. One unusual three-body burial from the latter culture known as the "Stone Age Embrace" was found with a woman buried facing her two children, their hands raised and entwined. Discovery of pollen remains shows they were laid on a bed of wool flowers (*Celosia*) – this at a time, all those thousands of years ago, when the Sahara was still green and fertile. Four arrowheads were included, possibly for rebirth enhancement, a concept which is explored in detail in the next chapter.

Flowers present during funeral rituals and placed upon graves is still conventional in most cultures, even today, although always in a spiritual context.

Syncretic Amulets

Syncretism is the merging of two different religious beliefs and we see this from the Middle Palaeolithic. At several sites there is convergence of symbolism from the Animal Renewal Traditions with the Red Ochre Tradition and Stone Breathing Traditions (when such objects are holed). To capture the syncretic nature of this type of prehistoric artefact in the GMR these items are referred to as "Rot-Art".

Rot-Art

An interesting worked piece, one of the oldest decorative artefacts known, was found at the Neanderthal site in Tata, 70 km north-west of Budapest, Hungary. It is a slice, or plaque, of mammoth tooth just over 2 cm wide which has been artificially shaped and bevelled into an oval and then acquired a red ochre stain. Dating was difficult but has been settled at 100 kya. [154]

With respect to the NRT, this amulet is one of the earliest known syncretic tokens combining the renewal properties of blood representation (ochre) and an egg representation (tooth). This is Rot-Art. Assuming that the staining was deliberate, in the life-force worldview of the Neanderthal, this amulet would then be the most powerful type for functional use in rituals as "life-giving".

A discovery in 2009 of red ochre stained *Nassarius* shell beads from the Grotte des Pigeons site in Taforalt, Morocco, is significant as these are also syncretic tokens associated with symbolic thinking, if not NRT life-giving functional representations as well. They are taken from Aterian layers – 110 to 82 kya – which is very early for modern humans, and also outside the Neanderthal range of habitation. It is significant that the shells were sourced from the sea 40 km away. They were perforated and this is more likely to be breathing symbolism than that they were worn on a cord. The same red ochre staining of a *Nassarius* shell is seen at other sites in Morocco and also at the Blombos Cave site in South Africa! It is not possible to travel a greater distance through Africa so the convergence of human thinking to the same symbolism is remarkable.

These *Nassarius* examples defy explanation by conventional diffusion theories of palaeoanthropology because of the communication distances involved. Remote peoples independently developed an identical artistic practice. However, the theory of universal NRT belief systems, within a consistent worldview of naturalistic animism, makes this improbable convergence in thinking much more likely.

At a Neanderthal cave site, Cueva Anton, in Spain, a few examples of scallops and cockleshells were found to have been partially painted with an orange mixture containing red ochre.

Perforated cone shells with some ochre staining, dated to 37 kya, were found at Mandu Mandu Creek, Australia showing symbolism of three NRT remotely from Europe and Africa.

An intriguing reindeer antler baton found in Gough's Cave, England, dates 14 to 12 kya and has a large hole with spiral markings around it. The suggestion of a primitive pulley is unlikely as it would have suffered circular marks. Here, it is instead certainly a syncretic amulet with both antler renewal and breathing symbolism, where the spirals were air-flows to make the object alive.

Was the idea of the decorative body adornments first derived from pre-existing symbolic life-giving concepts related to red ochre as a blood representation and shells as egg representations? The earliest syncretic finds are not accompanied by human remains so they can only be categorized as evidence of advancing symbolic thinking. It is, however, from burials that the evidence for origin of religion is abundant. This evidence has led to rediscovering the afterlife paradigm of physical rebirth and the NRT as ubiquitous belief systems of all the hunter-gatherers before the Neolithic.

4 ◆ OUTER CORE RELIGION: ENHANCED REBIRTH

Enhanced Rebirth Afterlife (ERA)

Outer Core Religion (OCR) is differentiated from Inner Core Religion (ICR) as OCR comprises the belief systems associated with *improving* the next life after rebirth, or *interpreting evidence* of it, whereas ICR comprises belief systems associated with making certain that rebirth actually happens in the first place, or making it happen faster. Enhanced Rebirth Afterlife is the fifth major Palaeolithic belief system.

Skills and Strength in the Life-Force Worldview

The presence of stone hand-axes, knives, arrow-heads, spears, awls and other tools, meat offerings, and even ornaments: such as rods and statuettes in Palaeolithic and Mesolithic burials are now perplexing as these all appear incompatible with the idea of simple rebirth. The long-held modern explanation has been to consider them as tools, food or ornaments for use in a spiritual afterlife. This creates a serious conflict as to what type of afterlife belief really existed for these people.

However, the GMR holds that naturalistic animism, the life-force worldview, once prevailed everywhere. It is evidenced by primary burial and predominant ROT, SBT and ART representations indicating rebirth belief. So, the tools, offerings and ornaments have another purpose. This purpose is enhancement of personal capabilities when growing up and reaching adulthood *after* rebirth. This is especially so for strength and hunting skills. Therefore, in the life-force worldview, if someone is buried with a spear, then it is purely to ensure that they will be a better spear thrower in their next life. There is no intended spiritual afterlife for the person or the spear.

Common Palaeolithic grave goods are lithics – knapped stone axes, arrow-heads, blades or knives. Where they are deliberately placed in a grave they would be to ensure that the deceased, after rebirth, would be skilful at making and using lithics, the most essential class of implement required in adulthood: sharp stone tools for bringing down animals and cutting their meat. Lithics were as important to prehistoric people as reading and writing is today. All the extinct sub-species of *Homo sapiens* were skilled at knapping stone and spent years improving their technique at making such tools.

Table 4.1 illustrates the two main classes of rebirth enhancement which can exist, and both are represented in the archaeological record.

GMR:4.1   ENHANCED REBIRTH AFTERLIFE (ERA)

ENHANCEMENT	ORIGIN	FUNERARY ARTEFACTS
Physical: Strength & Repair	H. sapiens neanderthalensis 70 kya	Animal skulls, long bones and leg parts
	H. sapiens sapiens 30 kya	*Above and* scapulae, horns, prosthetics and sculptures
Mental: Skills & Learning	H. heidelbergensis 350 kya	Hand-axe
	H. sapiens neanderthalensis 70 kya	Hand-axes & flints
	H. sapiens sapiens 30 kya	*Above and* arrowheads, awls, rods, spears and sculptures

ERA takes rebirth, as assumed, and looks beyond that to the qualities of adulthood in the next life and how to influence and improve it. Very often evidence from Neanderthal burials show grave goods which are logically part of ERA, such as flints and meat joints, at a much earlier time than those seen with modern humans.

In general, the earliest burials of modern humans were NRT-oriented, whereas those of the Neanderthal were ERA-oriented.

The belief in ERA may even have begun before the Neanderthal became evolutionarily distinct. The quartzite hand-axe as the only artefact found in a cache of 32 *Homo heidelbergensis* skeletons, in Spain, was clearly thrown into the deep pit with them. This just may have been done for rebirth enhancement – so that the deceased would be skilled at making hand-axes in their next life. If so, then this pushes the evidence for religious belief systems to 350 kya! It would be the closest thing to a birth certificate of religion itself. The fact that the hand-axe was a rare pink one implies red colour symbolism is present as well. Blood symbolism is also evidenced with worked ochre in Kabwe, Zambia, about 300 kya; further, breathing symbolism of cupules is seen in Bhimbetka, India before 200 kya. Both these sites are probably associated with *Homo heidelbergensis*. Their brain size was only slightly smaller than the average modern human so it is entirely feasible that they had early belief systems associated with the concept of afterlife.

Neanderthal and ERA

We believe that there is enough evidence to suggest a well organized and very ancient funerary tradition among Near Eastern and European Neandertals. [85]

> – Francesco d'Errico, Christopher Henshilwood, Graeme Lawson, Marian Vanhaeren, Anne-Marie Tillier, Marie Soressi, Frederique Bresson, Bruno Maureille, April Nowell, Joseba Lakarra, Lucinda Backwell and Michele Julien

In the GMR the long and ancient burial tradition of the Neanderthal is also fully recognized so agreement, in that respect, exists with d'Errico and colleagues. However, they continue with an assessment of an example burial:

> *Careful reading of Peyrony's publications (1921, 1930, 1934) and notes indicate that several individuals were buried at La Ferrassie rockshelter, including a foetus. This last skeleton was found in a pit, with three flint flakes, possibly a gift, at the surface of the pit.*

The disagreement from the GMR is in the interpretation of the three flakes. These are not considered to be a gift, but are instead ERA symbolism for enhancing the next life after rebirth. The flakes are to make sure the individual will be skilled at making and using lithics. It was likely here that the foetus was interpreted by the Neanderthal, as the failed rebirth of a recently deceased adult. So the flint flakes were interred with the recent life of an adult in mind.

The overall burial evidence suggests that ERA was the principal belief system of the Neanderthal because they focused their energies on grave goods to provide rebirth enhancement rather than using ochre, antler or shells simply to ensure that rebirth actually occurred. Perhaps it was because they had culturally accepted that rebirth was always a given in the first instance. Although they were aware of functional representations from ROT, SBT and ART, occasionally using them, these belief systems were not their principal focus.

Two Neanderthal burials, one at La Ferrassie, France, and another at Kebara Cave, Israel, had knapped stone hand-axes in close context, which are possible examples of rebirth enhancement belief. Although some archaeologists assume that rubble backfill into the graves may have accidently included them. While rubble infill might argue the case for accidental burial of lithics, it is not an explanation for burial of an uneaten leg of meat.

Two other Neanderthal sites in France, discovered in 1908, have grave goods of lithics and animal bones, including ochre, at one of the sites, La Chapelle-aux-Saints. These are described in an early paper by Oliver Farrington and Henry Field of the Field Museum of Natural History in Chicago:

> *Over the head were several long bones lying flat, and one of them still in connection with some of the smaller bones of the foot and toes, suggesting that it was clothed with flesh at the time it was placed in this position. Here was apparently then a ceremonial interment accompanied by offerings of food and implements for the use of the deceased in the spirit world.* [155]

At La Chapelle-aux-Saints the "offering" of bovid leg bones is far more likely to be for imparting the strength of an antelope to the deceased, or making the deceased walk strongly, in either case after being reborn. It was very unlikely a spiritual meal, which is not contextual of burials from 60 kya, and is an idea not even first conceived of until a long time after the Neanderthal was extinct. Farrington and Field continue:

> *The second instance is that of the skeleton already mentioned as having been found at Le Moustier. This lay on a carefully arranged pavement of flint implements. It was resting on its right side, with the right arm bent under the head and the left arm extended. Burnt bones and Mousterian implements were disposed about the skull and a large implement, beautifully dressed on both sides, lay just within reach of the left hand.*

At Le Moustier the large implement was a worked hand-axe, likely present to ensure that the deceased would be skilled at making them in his next life. Various lithics were laid around the deceased at both sites.

A fifth Neanderthal burial, this from Le Regourdou, also in France, is certain to be deliberate and dates from 70 to 65 kya. In a pit, lined with flat stones, an adult was placed with both hands together near his head and two leg bones from a bear placed under his body. A huge limestone slab had been placed over him and grave goods of bear bones and deer antler were laid on top. Twenty caches of bear bones surrounded the burial. The surviving Neanderthal bones are in anatomical position indicating his body was protected from scavengers by a quick burial. Deer antler ART symbolism is strongly indicative of promoting rebirth and the presence of so many bear bones are for improved strength and walking in the next life. These items together are conceptually a single "tool", both to ensure successful rebirth and enhancement afterwards.

At a sixth burial site, Sima de las Palomas in south-eastern Spain, parts of three Neanderthal skeletons were found in a cave which has strong indications of intentional burial: anatomical position of bones, absence of any scavenger marks and placement of rocks over the graves. The burials of two adults and a juvenile date to about 50 kya and the best preserved, a female, had both arms deliberately folded toward her skull, as at Le Regourdou. Most significant, however, is the presence of bones from two paws of a panther which were slightly below one burial and close to the two others. The rest of the panther is *"conspicuous by its absence"*. [156]

Panthers are powerful animals and, like bears, the paws and legs would be suitable remains as grave goods for giving the newly deceased strength in walking and running after rebirth in the next life. These burials are 10,000 years apart and yet exhibit the same long and continuous tradition of ERA.

This hypothesis is a much more parsimonious explanation for animal remains in graves than the suggested Neanderthal "bear cults" which fuels vigorous debate both for and against. It has been suggested that a Neanderthal "shrine" of cave bear skulls was found at Drachenloch in the Swiss Alps, although no human remains were present and there is a good argument that the remains can be explained by long-term cave bear habitation. [33] Though, the existence of several other sites, like Petershohle Cave in Bavaria, with arranged bones may indicate belief that early humans could control or harness the power of these animals by magic.

ERA belief is seen at the late Neanderthal and modern human hybrid child burial at Lagar Velho, Portugal. Parts of a deer were laid at the head and feet and a *rabbit across the legs*, the latter is clearly symbolic of the belief that this would help make the deceased *fleet of foot* after rebirth.

Furthermore, if the Neanderthal conceived and practiced a belief system which may be classed here as ERA then it is difficult to see how modern humans were intellectually superior. At the same time moderns were doing nothing more complex, so this supports the Assimilation Model of human evolution, where some integration occurred, instead of outright replacement.

Modern Humans and ERA

The early modern human male burial of Nazlet Khater 2 found in the Egyptian desert dates from 38 kya and evidences rebirth enhancement, as an adze was placed adjacent to his head before burial. This adze associates him with a community which mined chert locally and valued such tools but, more importantly, it was very likely placed to ensure that he would be skilled at making adzes after rebirth. The idea that the tool was left as a memento or symbol of veneration is a weak interpretation from modern thinking where it is not possible to see past the concept of spiritual afterlife.

The ERA belief system of modern humans is beautifully illustrated by the spectacular early multiple burial site of five people at Sungir, near Vladimir, 150 km east of Moscow, Russia, dated about 28 kya. A single grave contained two adolescents, possibly a boy aged about thirteen and possibly a girl aged about eight, laid head-to-head. They had a large number of artefacts and red ochre present. He had 4900 ivory beads, a belt with over 250 arctic fox teeth, a cap with fox teeth, ivory lances and a sculpture of a mammoth positioned under his shoulder. She also had 5200 beads, ivory lances and parts of deer antlers. They shared a 2.4 m-long straightened ivory lance which weighed 20 kg – definitely not for normal use.

Thomas Wynn, anthropologist, and Frederick Coolidge, psychologist, discuss this burial:

> *But what strikes us as the most interesting features of the Sungir burial are the ivory hunting spears. Because ivory is soft, such spears were unlikely to have ever been intended for real hunting; thus these were truly ceremonial spears. This implies that these*

Homo sapiens sapiens were thinking about a life after death, and perhaps hunting in the afterlife. [157]

Wynn and Coolidge recognize the spears as symbolic but then interpret this as indicating a highly developed spiritual afterlife for the two adolescents. They go further by using this as an example of a supposed conceptual chasm between modern humans and the Neanderthal.

It is a chasm which is narrowed to a crack when considering instead that the ivory spears were intended to make the adolescents powerful hunters when they grow up after simple rebirth. The mammoth sculpture was to make the boy grow to be very strong in his future adulthood. That's why it was under his shoulder. Strong shoulder muscles are essential for successful spear-throwing! That rebirth was intended is made abundantly clear by the red ochre, teeth, and vast number of ivory beads present. Each bead took about an hour to make, so many hours went into these egg representations. The whole burial was designed to give two children the best possible future when reborn into a new physical life. Interestingly, the head-to-head feature of the Sungir burial is unusual but also seen in a Neanderthal burial in France. La Ferrassie 1 and 2 were laid head-to-head, at 75 to 60 kya – far earlier than Sungir. This position at Sungir may have been simply to accommodate the huge spear across two burials, although some interpretations make much more of this feature.

The Dolni Vestonice triple burial has a clear functional representation from ERA. One male has a mammoth ivory stake through the pelvis, which is relevant to reproduction, very likely to enhance virility when reaching adulthood after rebirth.

In a Mesolithic cemetery at La Vergne, western France, four burials dated about 8200 BCE were found with elements of ochre, shells, perforated wolves' teeth and stone tools. [158] However, unusually, the anklebones of aurochs were found in two burials and deer ankle bones in a third. [159]

In the GMR, ochre, shells and teeth are all representative of beliefs in the NRT, but three graves are showing ERA symbolism as well. The stone tools were again for improved skills after rebirth, but more interestingly here, the addition of these particular animal ankle parts would have been to ensure the deceased could walk further or run faster in their next life.

The first inhabitants of North America, before 8000 BCE, are known as Early Paleoindian. Their burials have common features as described by Peter Peregrine and Melvin Ember in the *Encyclopedia of Prehistory*:

> *Although rarely found, Early Paleoindian burials tend to contain only one or two very decomposed skeletons. They are usually associated with complete tool-kits covered with red ocher. These burial goods may be the dead person's possessions or tools to be used in the afterlife.* [160]

Here, the ochre is evidence of the ROT belief system which ensures rebirth occurs, and the "tool-kits" are lithics and hunting items interred for rebirth enhancement, ensuring the deceased will grow up to be skilled in the use of these items in their next physical life.

The prehistorians Pablo Arias and Juan Fernandez-Tresguerres, and colleagues write about the earliest Azilian burial of Cantabria, Spain, at Los Azules Cave, dated to about 7500 BCE:

> *Several items that might be considered grave offerings were found close to the corpse: some Azilian painted cobbles, ochre, atypical animal remains, such as the skull of a badger (Meles meles) and shells of the bearded mussel (Modiolus barbatus), and various artefacts — harpoons, endscrapers, burins, as well as remains of different phases leading to the fabrication of such artefacts. The hypothesis that the deceased had been symbolically furnished with an everyday tool-kit, rough materials, and tools for making new implements seems very likely.* [161]

Reading a complex burial like this Azilian example becomes straightforward when it is realized that the grave goods are in several groups. The painted cobbles, ochre and shell are to ensure rebirth happens, the skull is for strength in the next life, and the tools and artefacts are to ensure that after rebirth the deceased is skilled at making and using them. That is especially why artefacts are supplied in various phases of completion – so they assist in ensuring the deceased is good at learning after rebirth. Spiritual afterlife was not considered anywhere in Iberia at this period. Another important burial with ERA symbolism is at the Neolithic village site of Shillourokambos, near Limassol, Cyprus, dating to about 7300 BCE.

A 30 year old male buried with red ochre and shells also had stone axes, and the skeleton of a nine-month-old cat in a separate pit.

The archaeologist Stuart Swiny writes:

> *Thirty centimeters from his grave, buried at the same level in the same sediment, was the cat. This proximity strongly suggests that man and animal were buried together. Moreover, because there were no butchery marks on the cat skeleton, it is likely that the cat was interred with the man to accompany him to the afterlife, not as a meal but as a companion.* [162]

This burial received substantial press as it is the earliest indication of the domestication of cats and has been interpreted as a "pet", over 4000 years before any similar example in Egypt. Unfortunately, this sentimental explanation is unlikely, as ochre and shells are both NRT representations for rebirth. So the cat was most likely included as part of ERA symbolism in order to make the deceased a better hunter in his next life, just as the lithics were to make him more skilled with stone tools.

Skulls impart Power

Animal skulls are reported with diverse human burials from Palaeolithic times. However, the interpretation of skulls within burials is not as clear-cut as, say, red ochre. Considering ERA and ART three possibilities arise:

1) Skulls are for imparting the power of the animal to the deceased becoming a symbol of rebirth enhancement, particularly if the animal had horns and these are still present. This is ERA only. If teeth are still present then the belief may be that they will additionally act as egg substitutes to ensure rebirth happens, or ERA with ART.

2) Skulls are a large-sized egg representation and therefore more powerfully symbolic for ensuring rebirth happens. This is ART only.

3) Skulls are incidental, a container for the egg representations of teeth, without the effort of extracting the upper mandibles for funerary use, to ensure rebirth happens. This is also ART only.

The likelihood is that all three are legitimate descriptions of belief at different times and places where skulls were used in funerary ritual, with the first case being predominant.

A mammoth skull found adjacent to the Paviland cave burial, at 34 kya, was described by Buckland, and it would seem most likely for imparting the strength of a mammoth for enhanced rebirth. Here, the mammoth skull would imbue the deceased with great physical strength when growing into adulthood in the next life. Ivory rods were also present with the Paviland burial, which represent unfinished artefacts likely to be for imparting learning skills after rebirth. Paviland was truly an exceptionally powerful rebirth burial.

The picture of a mammoth was engraved on an ivory plaque in Malta, Siberia, close to a child burial at 14.7 kya. Much earlier is the ivory carving of a mammoth present at Sungir, yet both can be considered in the same way: as abstractions of the concept of interring animal parts with a burial, but still being within the ERA belief system.

A fox skull was present in one burial in Uyun al-Hammam, Jordan, at 16.5 kya, and other burials there contained tortoise shell, leading to the hypothesis that these were semi-domesticated animals or "pets". [163] However, the alternative hypothesis of the GMR is that these animal parts were placed in graves for facilitating rebirth (shell), and rebirth enhancement (skull). The fox skull may have been believed to impart speed and cunning in hunting for the next life.

Pigs were the principal domesticated animal in Neolithic China and a tradition of pig skulls as grave goods is seen at the large and well preserved Dawenkou cemetery. Anne Underhill, of the Field Museum, discusses the hypothesis that pig skulls were status items:

> *If elites were competing by using pigs (or pork) to enhance exchange systems, the differences among graves should be higher, especially by the Late Period. Also, one would expect that pig skulls (and greater quantities of them) would be found primarily in burials with log tombs; Figure 6 shows that this is not the case. Kim (1994) argues that rich graves tend to have pig skulls at Dawenkou and other sites from Shandong. [...] My assessment of display of status differentiation at Dawenkou, emphasizing the above criteria, does not show that richer burials have greater quantities of pig skulls, a pattern also noted by Lee (1994).* [164]

The status item hypothesis fails because the pig skulls were intended to facilitate rebirth afterlife and probably to imbue strength afterwards. It proves that no ethnographic analysis of burials can be safe without deferring to religious belief systems.

Human skulls sometimes appear loose in an otherwise normal burial and these may be interpreted by archaeologists as unrelated or a later intrusion, when they may actually be examples of rebirth enhancement of future physical strength for the deceased.

Horn Strength

Horns grow and persist for life, but after the death of the animal the core which is made of bone outlasts the surface layer of keratin. Horn found in burials at first appears to be a branch of ART egg renewal because of its visual appearance similar to the largest carnivore canines or small tusks. On balance, research shows it to be a relatively recent development in funerary ritual, within the last 15,000 years, and the purpose of it seems more oriented to capture the strength of horned animals, and therefore makes it part of the ERA belief system.

Whether the burial of a Neanderthal at Teshik-Tash Cave in Uzbekistan was deliberate and whether the goat horns close-by were grave goods remains controversial and is not generally accepted. The most significant horned animal in the Palaeolithic was the aurochs but evidence of burial with aurochs remains seems absent, and this is the case until the late Mesolithic in Europe, slightly earlier in Africa.

At Tushka in Nubia, southern Egypt, an early Qadan hunter-gatherer cemetery has three burials with bovine horns placed by the heads. In *Egypt's Legacy* Michael Rice, writer and historian, notes the similarity of this cultural practice with those of later times:

> *There, a number of graves of cattle were found and with them a human burial surmounted by two wild bull skulls; it is dated to the fourteenth millennium before the present and was the work of the hunters who followed the herds of wild cattle. The use of the bull heads to mark the site of the burial and, presumably, to give protection to it, is remarkable evidence for the survival of ritual and cultic practices in Egypt, for nine thousand years later wild bull heads were mounted around high-status burials at Saqqara and a wild bull's skull is buried in the southern court of the Step Pyramid complex, also at Saqqara.* [165]

The bull skulls in Qadan graves is to give strength in the next physical life, not spiritual protection which was the later belief.

At Taforalt in northern Morocco the rear of Grotte des Pigeons has yielded many pit-burials with horn cores present. Also, Hattab II Cave has a horn core, shell, and bone points in a late Iberomaurusian burial of a male aged about 30, dated at 7000 BCE.

At Lepenski Vir a burial dating to 6000 BCE the head of an aurochs with horns present was placed upon the grave. Another grave had an aurochs skull, with deer antlers and an additional human skull. The presence of antlers to facilitate physical rebirth and horned and human skulls to provide strength when growing up after rebirth means the two complement rather than overlap in purpose.

It was the spiritual worldview paradigm shift that destroyed or transformed ERA beliefs into a context consistent with spirituality. In some cultures the prehistoric association of bovine horns and funerary ritual will have led to bucrania shrines and bull cults of ancestral or fertility significance. The Neolithic domestication of cattle has left a rich tradition of bull worship throughout Europe, the Near East and North Africa. Their development originates from the eclipsing of rebirth belief and the rise and spread of spiritual religions.

Scapula and Clavicle Strength

The situation is clearer here, with shoulder blades and collarbones, than other animal parts. These are not easily interpreted as egg representations, and teeth are not associated. So the practice, seen in a number of cultures, of placing an animal scapula with human remains, was simply to imbue the deceased with strength after rebirth.

Shoulder blades were often chosen as this best represents the strength of an animal. Mammoths were the strongest of all and their bones appear in a number of burials in Eastern Europe. At the Moravian complex there was a tradition of burials under or near mammoth scapulae. In Predmostí, a multiple grave site, about ten burials were framed with three scapulae. Nearby, the Brno II burial and several at Vestonice and at Pavlov were interred under a scapula. These were all certainly intended to imbue strength in the next life for the deceased.

Mammoth scapulae have been described in archaeological literature as "protective" in burials – but protective against what? Prehistoric peoples were at one with nature and did not have the spiritual fears which are embedded in modern thinking. Radovanovic describes the Lepenski Vir site, where a female was buried accompanied a male's skull and clavicles of a child, dated to ca. 7270 BP. [166] The clavicles would have been to make the woman strong after rebirth, as well as drawing strength, and possibly wisdom, from the male skull.

A Neolithic burial site at Columnata in Algeria provides a suggestion of ERA as some examples of human body parts are seen as grave goods there.

Disability and Prosthetics

In the Upper Palaeolithic there seems to be a selective emphasis for NRT practices, such as ochre and shell usage, devoted to children and the disabled. For most people a healthy new life after rebirth could be assumed. However, special funerary treatment was needed to help the disadvantaged live a better life next time. It shows compassion and sense of fairness were qualities of prehistoric peoples, especially within their own family groups.

Selected animal parts as grave goods, which are intended to ensure that a disabled person has an able-bodied life after rebirth, invites imaginative speculation to be explained any other way. Leore Grosman, archaeologist, and colleagues, describe a 12,000-year-old Natufian burial at the Hilazon Tachtit Cave in Israel. It is a 45-year-old disabled woman who was laid to rest with very unusual items:

> *The grave goods comprised 50 complete tortoise shells and select body-parts of a wild boar, an eagle, a cow, a leopard, and two martens, as well as a complete human foot. The interment rituals and the method used to construct and seal the grave suggest that this is the burial of a shaman, one of the earliest known from the archaeological record. Several attributes of this burial later become central in the spiritual arena of human cultures worldwide.* [167]

The presence of an extra human foot in her grave is wholly bizarre to the modern mind, but it makes perfect sense if it was laid in place with the belief that it would enable her to walk properly after rebirth – especially when she was badly crippled in life! All the odd animal parts become clear. The foreleg of a boar was to make her stronger at walking. The wing from a golden eagle was to make her lighter on her feet, and the tail of an aurochs was to make her very supple, all after rebirth. The egg symbolism of 50 tortoise shells, to ensure the rebirth process itself, shows how sadly she was missed and the strong desire by her family to see her live again, and live well. The shamanistic and feast hypotheses both fail because their associated spiritualism does not hold as the spiritual worldview and afterlife had not yet been conceived of by this date.

Occasionally the burial of a disabled person will include prosthetics which were intended to make them whole after rebirth. The "Little Prince" red ochre burial in Italy, dating to 23.5 kya, had a single quantity of yellow ochre present in his jaw area which was badly damaged and crippled during life. The yellow ochre was likely intended as substitute flesh to make sure he would be reborn as a whole person.

Red ochre has long been linked to blood but there has been a parallel interest in yellow ochre at some Palaeolithic sites. While often viewed as decorative, this is not always true. Some cultures clearly had a religious interpretation for yellow ochre and perhaps this was for "flesh substitution". The prehistoric burials of two dogs in Kamchatka were sprinkled with yellow ochre. Several burials of babies at Çatal Höyük, Turkey, were reportedly accompanied by a yellow substance – considered to be ochre, but this would have been interpreted spiritually by them.

Jay Enoch, an optometrist, writes about two burials; one at "The Burnt City" in Eastern Iran and a second at Cingle del Mas Nou i Cava Fosca in Spain, both where an artificial eye had been made and inserted before burial. [168]

The Spanish example, at 5000 BCE, was crude and made of red ochre, inserted post-mortem and certainly intended to ensure that the individual could see with both eyes when reborn. In the Iranian example, at 3000 BCE, the eye was quite sophisticated, being made of bitumen, and had gold threads indicating it was cosmetic and worn in life. So although these are two ancient examples of prosthetic eyeballs, only one had a religious motive.

The conclusion is that humans quickly advanced beyond just rebirth as an antidote for personal mortality and were thinking about the next life. They believed they could intervene in the process to improve it for the newly deceased, and if someone was disabled they thought they could be restored to full function.

Rebirth Feedback Belief (RFB)

If the rebirth belief systems were being practiced for more than a hundred thousand years then it begs the question: How did the same motifs of the Natural Rebirth Traditions and Enhanced Rebirth Afterlife belief remain persistent for so long? Rebirth Feedback Belief (RFB) answers this question. It is the sixth and yet only Palaeolithic belief system indirectly evidenced. It is proposed, however, not only because of the question above, but more importantly, because modern humans have evolved significantly from all humans known to be living only 50,000 years ago.

Robust, Semi-Robust, Early Modern and Gracile

By 700 kya our ancestors had diverged from the *Homo erectus* lineage but were archaic, fully robust. For several hundred thousand years change was slow. *Homo heidelbergensis* at 350 kya was physically much closer to *erectus* than modern humans and may have evolved into the still fully robust Neanderthal in Europe, separately from parallel developments in Africa. However, evolution seems to have recently run both in fast forward and tangential directions for the *Homo sapiens sapiens* sub-species, which are modern humans.

One explanation for this unusual burst of evolution is self-selection. We can see how natural selection can become self-selection because of the influence of intelligence. Natural selection requires a process to work. And that process is an endless cycle of competition resulting in biological changes: everything from colour vision to the opposable thumb. Evolutionary change works incrementally, and until the era of *erectus* all challenges to living things, which drive evolution, were environmental: the natural landscape and its components, such as predators, bacteria and weather. The mastering of fire and simple tool use, like knapping flints, gave a survival advantage, so humans which practised these were naturally selected.

What is less often appreciated is that natural selection also responds to behavioural changes caused by the use of imagination.

Humans have advanced capability in symbolic and abstract thinking, together known as conceptual thinking. It is conceptual thinking which makes theoretical problems of the future become apparent, most importantly the worrisome discovery of personal mortality. It is also only conceptual thinking which can resolve such problems of the future.

It seems human evolution became influenced by the most basic environmental consequences of our own intelligence: individuals changing their behaviour due to their own abstract thoughts. Natural selection would then be applying a fitness level to the response to abstract thinking – this is only where abstract thinking made a physical difference to individual survival. If the same abstract idea influenced most or all members of the species, and would not subside, and individuals all reacted differently from before, then there exists an environmental change wrought by imagination alone. It was a new phenomenon in the history of evolution. Mindlessly, evolution accommodated this change of mental environment, just as it accommodates climate change or the advent of new diseases, plants and predators.

Since the most powerful abstract concept in humans is awareness of personal mortality, then the primary response to this awareness – rebirth afterlife – has potentially modified human behaviour, long-term. Natural selection of the responses to abstract thinking then becomes self-selection. Belief systems in the form of the NRT may have had a significant impact on human evolution by driving self-selection.

There was, at one time, robust and gracile members of *Homo sapiens*. All modern humans are gracile. Robust humans were the norm for hundreds of thousands of years and had many characteristics that we have lost: a thicker and stronger skeleton and muscle structure, perhaps twice as powerful as modern humans, full body hair and a thick skull. A robust skull has an occipital bun (possibly related to larger brain size), supraorbital tori (bony ridges behind the eyebrows), prognathism (projecting upper and lower jaw) and numerous smaller differences from modern skulls and jaws. The strength of robust humans was incredible. The Neanderthal burial at Le Regourdou had a stone slab on top weighing 850 kg, as heavy as a small car! Several of them must have carried or dragged it into place.

Conversely, gracile modern humans have a much thinner and weaker musculoskeletal structure, fine or missing body hair, a thin globular skull with flattened face, thin jaw and vestigial occipital bun, and missing bony eyebrow ridges. Another way of describing gracilization is neoteny, the tendency to express juvenile features into adulthood.

Semi-robust and early modern types are partway between the extremes of robust and fully modern graciles. It is very interesting that even the final migration from Africa seems to have been early modern humans, if the Nazlet Khater 2 burial in Egypt, at 38 kya, is any indication. The racial differences seen today and the punctuated and confusing fossil record of the last hundred thousand years are accounted for by Robert Bednarik's Self-Domestication Hypothesis which is outlined in his work *The Human Condition*.

Human Self-Domestication Hypothesis

The scenario remains that there is a significant change in the physiology of humans during the last 50,000 years in Europe, and modern Europeans differ genetically from robust Europeans 50 Ka ago. The same change from Robusts to Graciles occurs in other continents. Not only do these changes need to be explained, there is another issue which, oddly enough, the [recent Out of Africa] replacement advocates are silent on: the changes that did occur contradict all canons of Darwinian evolution. [169]

– Robert Bednarik

Since the time of Darwin, when he was caricatured as an ape, people have had conceptual difficulty with human evolution from an ape-like ancestor because of the gut impression that chimpanzees, gorillas, bonobos and orang-utans are so much more alike than they are to modern humans (leaving aside the religious objection). These similarities are as much an impression of the robustness seen in apes. The Neanderthal was also robust at 50 kya, but since then modern humans have become distanced still further by gracilization, the tendency to neoteny. Bednarik rejects the idea that there are evolutionary pressures for gracilization. Natural selection is unlikely to favour weaker bodies, expressing many new congenital disorders as a consequence, and brain shrinkage by about 11 per cent from the Neanderthal average.

Within the Multi-Regional Continuity Model Bednarik has in his thought-provoking work proposed the hypothesis of human unintentional self-domestication to explain the robust to gracile progression of our species. It is that anatomically modern humans are the outcome of robust human's own breeding choices.

Bednarik coined the phrase "mythical moderns" to emphasise that the skeletal evidence of gracile, anatomically modern humans is not in evidence anywhere until a sudden appearance between 30 and 28 kya. If modern humans exited Africa at 100 kya and overran, or assimilated into archaic humans everywhere else, then we would expect fossil evidence showing this progression. Yet there are difficulties from the outset. In Africa the potential source populations of modern humans, Omo Kibish (195 kya) and Herto (160 kya), both in Ethiopia, are considered semi-robust and could be ancestral to the first modern human graciles – but where are these graciles?

For such a successful group there should be some fully modern skulls found in north-east Africa dating to 100 kya. Bednarik regards the skeletal remains, evidenced at Qafzeh and Skhul in the Levant, the usual crossing point from Africa, as semi-robust, not gracile. The Australian Museum pulls no punches and calls the Qafzeh burials "Neanderthal". 170

Furthermore, fully modern skulls and skeletons in the fossil record are extremely hard to find anywhere before 30 kya. Some, like the Niah Cave specimen in Sarawak, Borneo have disputed dates, and the earliest known other modern human remains in Asia are from China, perhaps 40 to 30 kya. For such a successful world-conquering species modern humans did not leave a fossil record earlier than the point when their migrations through archaic human lands should have been completed.

The robust to gracile changes took place on four continents: Africa, Europe, Asia and Australia although it was a punctuated process which favours the explanation of cultural impetus rather than evolution by environmental natural selection. In Europe most change happened between 50 and 30 kya where the Mousterian was the end of the Neanderthal era and the Aurignacian the start of the modern human era. What is interesting is that there was no clean break in culture, technology or dietary change. For example, analysis of teeth wear of Neanderthals and early *Homo sapiens sapiens* does not show any significant difference. 171

What if the Neanderthal and other robust humans had instead eliminated themselves? Evidence from skulls at the Mladeç site in the Czech Republic, dated 30 kya, shows transitional features suggesting that gracilization begins in females with males following thousands of years behind. The process may not yet have stopped. The face, jaw and teeth of people today are 10 per cent less robust than those at the start of the Neolithic revolution, 10 kya. [169]

Beginning in the Neolithic, many animals and plants have been domesticated by humans and are vastly different as a result. Dogs are descended from wolves, but breeding has created dozens of very different forms unrecognizable from their recent ancestors. The breeding of ovines and bovines has created new high-yield forms, similarly for plants like wheat and corn which are far more productive, and genetically distinct from their ancestral wild types. All are the result of human selection, season after season, not the much slower natural selection. The "elephant in the room" of animal and plant domestication is human self-domestication by self-selection. What we humans did to other species we may well have done to ourselves, and far earlier, yet this is largely ignored in scientific literature.

Bednarik suggests that the principle reason for gracilization is mating selection preferences, physical attractiveness, which is a cultural reason from the subjective mind.

Self-Selection by Rebirth Feedback Belief

The GMR has an important contribution to make to Bednarik's hypothesis, but has an important caveat. Bednarik holds to the Multi-Regional Continuity Model of human evolution. Personally, I find it unconvincing and accept the Assimilation Model variation of the Out of Africa Replacement Hypothesis, and this is a common view. It is where the last migration from Africa, about 100 kya swamped, but did not quite eradicate, the genes of the local robust humans in Eurasia. However, the GMR can remain agnostic in this dispute as described shortly.

In the GMR the long evidence of the NRT belief systems in *Homo sapiens* leads to a separate reason for Bednarik's gracilization process, that it was not mating selection for attractiveness, but from choices made arising from afterlife beliefs, i.e. religious reasons.

Certainly the prevailing life-force worldview would have the effect of "locking-in" rebirth belief, as there was no real alternative until the paradigm shift to a spiritual worldview, which only began about 11 kya.

The very early and widespread usage of the NRT and ERA was the rebirth afterlife meme expressed in a practical application of ensuring rebirth and improving the next life. It is likely that the conceptual thinking performed by early humans was fairly rigid, literal and outcome based. So the implication is that early humans must have had feedback that rebirth funerary ritual actually worked! Humans must have been looking at their young for proof that a recently deceased loved one was actually reborn, that the NRT and ERA were effective.

What if they found the evidence they needed?

In a tribe adhering primarily to NRT belief systems, individuals that subsequently reached puberty and were more slender, younger-looking – gracile than their peers could have been interpreted by the group as proof of a "successful" rebirth.

Associations would then have to have been made back to the ritual funeral of a family member from, perhaps, 15 or 20 years earlier. There might even have been a determination made as to which deceased person had been reborn, especially in the event of there being a large family group. Either way, such a special individual may then be looked after better by the group, given more meat and fruit and preferentially selected for a mate. The self-selection process would be underway.

If there was a bias to NRT in *Homo sapiens sapiens* populations then this could mean that the extreme gracile form of fully modern humans is from accidental, unintentional, self-selection. It is because, for some periods at least, people were breeding for the youngest looking adults each generation. This also implies that the evolved humans who last dispersed from Africa need not have been fully modern. Perhaps they were really the early modern type seen in some Qafzeh remains, but also the Nazlet Khater 2 burial in Egypt, near the main Africa/Asia crossing point. The evidence certainly agrees with Bednarik that fully modern gracile humans did not exist until after 30 kya.

In the event of a tribe adhering primarily to ERA belief, individuals that subsequently reached puberty and were stronger – more robust than their peers could have been interpreted as proof of a "successful" rebirth.

If there was a bias to ERA in *Homo sapiens neanderthalensis* populations then this implies that the Neanderthal accidentally self-selected robust characteristics trending to an ever stronger physiology.

This lasted until they were genetically swamped by numerically superior African early moderns between 35 and 25 kya.

Considering Bednarik's "mythical moderns", is clear only the gracile fully moderns are mythical before 30 kya. Half of the Qafzeh remains at 100 kya are in fact early modern, as are the remains at the Border Cave burial from South Africa between 90 and 66 kya, the Lake Mungo 3 skeleton in Australia at 41 kya, and possibly the Paviland burial remains in Wales at 34 kya (although the skull was eroded away by the sea).

There is also something remarkable about these sites – they are as remote from each other as it is possible to get and most involve red ochre, two of them with copious amounts, three with shells. It seems early modern humans everywhere fervently practised the NRT.

The Taramsa Hill early modern child burial in the Nile Valley, Egypt, at about 55 kya, is normally assumed to have had no grave goods even as dozens of lithics, flakes and cores were found. These are generally in a "fresh condition" and many had a "slightly red patina." [172] It is arguable that lithics as grave goods were selected in this burial with ERA and ROT beliefs in mind, though it's difficult to determine rubble infill.

Red ochre and shells, contextual with early modern remains at Qafzeh indicate ROT and ART belief at 100 kya. This is dated close to the window when the conventional Recent Out Of Africa theory has fully modern, gracile *Homo sapiens* migrating from Africa via the Levant. The fossil record on this is non-supportive, as Bednarik points out. It does however support the migration of early moderns.

Both Taramsa Hill and Nazlet Khater 2 are on the primary migration route from Africa to Eurasia and it is incomprehensible how they are early modern, and not fully modern, if the last migration from Africa were fully modern humans.

Across the world in Australia the Aboriginals are an early Caucasoid type of people, yet an inconsistency exists where the Kow Swamp burials seem to be an even earlier type than the Lake Mungo skeleton at 41 kya, 20,000 years before. The Kow Swamp group may be an aberration due to local self-selection for robustness. The Aboriginals may also have arrested their self-domestication because they were no longer selecting for juvenile features as evidence that rebirth worked. The reason for that is the possible early adoption of spiritual religious beliefs. Perhaps they were ahead of the world and the first people anywhere to embrace spirituality. This is explored in Chapter Six on Spiritual Afterlife.

Robust Neanderthal occupied all of Europe, until about 35 kya, which should have been an early arrival point for modern humans although, to be fair, moderns would have had a hard time out-competing Neanderthal, who were much stronger and had larger brains and were adapted to the European environment better as they had been there for 300,000 years. Importantly nowhere is there an obvious modern human layer atop a Neanderthal layer where the tools and objects of habitation show a step-change in technology. Modern humans could only displace older robust forms violently through better technology as they certainly were physically weaker than the Neanderthal and seemingly, no more intelligent.

This standoff favours the theory that a process of assimilation of moderns from Africa through interbreeding took place. Transitional forms are evidenced at Mladeç in the Czech Republic at 30 kya. If the modern human and Neanderthal hybrids also practised the NRT, as seen at Lagar Velho, Portugal, the hybrids were now losing on two fronts:

1) Disappearing genetically through numerical swamping.

2) Disappearing through self-selection for neotenous traits.

When considering the sites at Paviland and Sungir, it is remarkable how two powerful rebirth burials are seen at the opposite ends of Europe, implying a European-wide tradition, at precisely the same 5000-year-window when the Neanderthal suffered their catastrophic decline. These sites exhibit both NRT and ERA, but NRT is predominant.

In conclusion, an amendment is suggested to Bednarik's Human Self-Domestication hypothesis. That it is by Rebirth Feedback Belief the process of *Homo sapiens* gracilization and self-domestication occurred. This was a positive feedback cycle of self-selection of neotenous forms and features due to an enduring religious belief in the success of rebirth afterlife and the funerary rituals to attain it.

The hypothesis of Rebirth Feedback Belief, as a prehistoric belief system, can explain either of the following:

1) Within the Assimilation Model, the cultural process which transformed the last dispersal of early modern humans from Africa into the fully modern type we are today with racial differences. It may have even driven the robust to early modern change inside Africa first.

2) Within the Multi-Regional Continuity Model, RFB explains the cultural process which transformed robust humans everywhere,

locally, into the fully modern type we are today with racial differences.

The perceived success of the rituals for rebirth afterlife driving gracilization would then have produced the modern human form in many places around the world, but in parallel, with local variations. A 1 per cent selection bias over tens of thousands of years would have been sufficient for major physical changes to occur. The RFB hypothesis can apply in either the recent Out of Africa or the Multiregional models.

Further, in the paradigm shift to the spiritual worldview it seems the old Palaeolithic RFB belief system may have been transformed into selection based upon physical attractiveness. This "gracile meme" is still with us today, firmly established in cultural memory. Models airbrushed to perfection on the cover of magazines are a tangible expression of the tendency in the modern mind to prefer gracile characteristics and, as Bednarik points out, the gracilization process has continued since the Neolithic.

Temples of Rebirth

The culmination of tens of thousands of years of rebirth afterlife belief was a remarkable phase of monumental architecture built before the Neolithic revolution. Great temples were constructed but carried the seeds of their own destruction. This was by changing the lifestyle of its builders from hunting and gathering to settlement and agriculture, but also changing the fundamental basis of their afterlife beliefs.

Göbekli Tepe

"Who are the T-Shapes?" may be a little easier when these non-stylized statues are taken into account. The more or less naturalistically depicted statues seem to represent members of our world, powerful and important, but inferior to the T-Shapes, who remain in mysterious, faceless anonymity. [173]

– Klaus Schmidt

On a ridge overlooking the plains of Eastern Anatolia and the region below the Taurus Mountains, about 12,000 years ago, different hunter-gatherer bands had observed natural cupules on stretches of exposed limestone and long considered it a good place for excarnation. Their dead could be left for consumption by vultures and hyenas with the expectation that rebirth would later occur. Perhaps they hammered out their own cupules to help make the rock breathe more, and be more alive, to improve the process, and also found out that the limestone could be worked into shapes. What we do know is that they had started to seriously consider the most fundamental question about rebirth afterlife:

What happens to people between the time when they die and are reborn?

They not only answered this question but wanted to go further and improve and control the whole process. Perhaps a chief had just died and they were concerned with how he, and indeed everyone else, might potentially be lost unless something is done to memorialize and provide continuity through the process of death, decay and rebirth. The answer to this problem could only be practically implemented through religion. At this time, even before settled society began and the Neolithic revolution occurred, the Temples of Rebirth were started to make certain the process of transition between death and rebirth.

Since 1995, Klaus Schmidt, of the German Archaeological Institute in Berlin, has been excavating what is absolutely the most important archaeological site in the world. Göbekli Tepe was constructed as the last Ice Age waned. The plains of South-eastern Anatolia were lush with green forests and marshlands full of hunting and fishing game when the temple complex of T-shaped monoliths and rubble stone walls was constructed over hundreds of years. It quickly became a spooky place of the dead, protected by the smell of decomposition. No one ever lived there.

Many of the T-shaped monumental pillars excavated by Schmidt's team are anthropomorphic; they physically resemble abstract humans bearing long, curved arms with hands and fingers. Pillars 18 and 31 in enclosure D have belts and pelt loincloths marking the waist, but they are all deliberately incomplete. One monument has a large cupule suggestive of a nostril, again capturing the essence of air as life-giving, while many pillars such as in enclosures B and D have the top surface peppered with cupules. Pillar 43 has three large vertebrae representing a stylized human backbone, horizontal and lifeless. It appears that every few decades hunter-gatherer bands would work together to erect more sets of monuments in a new part of the complex, for the processing of the deceased. Clearly there was organizational effort to coordinate up to 500 people to extract and drag up to 20-tonne limestone slabs, and skilled carvers needed to work them with granite adzes hafted with wood. There is even a double portal, several metres wide, with two rectangular entrance holes, relief animals, and cupules. That alone is a truly staggering artefact carved 6500 years earlier than the construction of the Giza pyramids in Egypt.

The monument that is Göbekli Tepe is a fusion of two of the NRT with ERA, richly symbolized in stone. The power of sympathetic, like-for-like magic meant the symbolism was not passive but was believed to be actively functional.

First, ART egg symbolism is represented. The many motifs of ducks, storks, vultures and snakes are intended to facilitate rebirth, for they are all reborn from eggs. Vultures also consume the dead and pillar 43 has the image of a vulture carrying a large egg at the end of its wing beneath the vertebrae of the aforementioned lifeless backbone. This is a visual of the conceptual link between death, decay, and regeneration into new life. Loose carvings exist, including a cameo of two dancing figures with a turtle between them – turtle eggs facilitated their rebirth, no wonder they are happy.

Secondly, stone breathing symbolism of the SBT is present. The Breathing Holes Hypothesis identifies cupules on the top surface of the T-shapes as breathing hole representations, imparting the pillars with life-giving air, maintaining the existence of the deceased while awaiting physical rebirth. Channels in the T-Shape tops are airways. Cupules on the edge of rectangular stone portals breathe air to whole chambers behind them, ensuring renewal of those excarnated inside.

Thirdly, ERA strength and skills symbolism is represented. Enhanced rebirth means the attributes of the carved animals present are transferred to those growing up after rebirth; so, a carved lion is to give great strength and ferocity to the reborn; a carved scorpion is to give the ability to strike hard and fast. A spider imparts patience to wait for the kill in hunting and a fox imparts speed and elusiveness. This is the reason why many of the animals are not ones which are hunted or eaten, but are themselves dangerous and carnivorous. Some animals have the ribs showing. An example is the magnificent carving of a leopard, vertical on a pillar, which is likely symbolic of its ferocity and strength being drained out of it *into* the stone monument.

Schmidt asks: Who are the T-shapes? The answer is they were no one in particular. The larger central pillars were probably reserved for deceased chieftains or high-ranking members of the hunter-gatherer bands awaiting rebirth. Therefore, the smaller encircling area and pillars were for ordinary, lesser members of these groups. Each newly deceased person had their body carefully placed next to an appropriate monument for excarnation and it was believed that they temporarily became that monument as their remains disintegrated. Finally, rejuvenated by the cupules and egg symbolism, drawing future strength from the carnivores, they were restored by rebirth as a newborn to one of the hunter-gatherer bands.

Multiple bands may have long cooperated in the arrangement of marriages and working together. This allows for the possibility that newborns in any band could be interpreted as rebirths from deaths at any of the other bands. Even so, the belt symbols on some monuments may be band totems to help the newborn regenerate in the same band as they lived in before.

Archaeologists suggest that the site is for ancestor worship, but this is a hypothesis formed within modern spiritual beliefs. Göbekli Tepe was created and developed as a "rebirth machine" for the newly deceased. It was not built for remote ancestors, and not for ancestral spirits, and the dead were not worshipped, and there were no gods. It was designed as a tool to take the newly deceased and maintain them in stone – halfway between old death and new life, where they could draw the strength to be reborn, with enhanced personal capabilities as faster and better hunters. The monuments are anonymous as they became a succession of many people over time, all while awaiting rebirth.

There was never any roof over the pillars as this would have covered the cupules and stalled the process of excarnation. The chronology of the site implies that some of the best construction was done early on and after one circle of stones was used for a while then it was partially buried and another circle constructed, used, and then filled in, until finally, about 8200 BCE the great Temple of Rebirth lay beneath hundreds of cubic metres of rubble. It was abandoned.

While Inner and Outer Core Religion of the GMR can explain the mysterious and ancient religious beliefs at Göbekli Tepe, it can't explain the social changes, but enough is indicated. Perhaps as generations passed, people did not want the dead they no longer knew to be reborn, and felt they had to start fresh. Burying old stone circles stopped them from functioning! With new, unused, stone they could ensure that only excarnations of recently deceased family members became reborn into their band. This thinking may have eventually split the culture so that there were several sites with rebirth temples, all guaranteeing that rebirths would be from their own local group. The splitting of construction teams was a factor causing later temples to be inferior efforts compared to the early ones.

Schmidt theorizes that religion came first and settlement came second, and he is certainly correct. The main temple served a wide area, then eventually permanent settlements were built, and their own singular rebirth temples were constructed. Religion had brought together large numbers of people cooperatively, which gave them time to develop settled communities. Finally it gave them reason to branch out independently on a road that ultimately led to civilization.

Decline and Fall of the Temples

Nevali Cori is a small settlement site which dates from about 8400 to 8000 BCE lying 20 km north-west of Göbekli Tepe in a valley originally 3 km from the upper Euphrates River. Among the residential structures is a square temple building in three phases, incorporating monuments of the earlier T-shaped style. It seems rebirth religion continued here for a while but the presence of eight skulls under a house indicates the emergence of spirituality and ancestorhood. Their settlement faded away and now the site is flooded under the lake behind Ataturk Dam, although many artefacts were saved. Also flooded is the site of Jerf el-Ahmar, with even earlier indications of proto-spiritual beliefs, which is discussed in the next chapter.

Other rebirth temples appear to have existed at Çayönü Tepesi, Sanliurfa (now beneath the modern Yeni Yol Street), Hamzan Tepe and Karahan Tepe and, perhaps, near Arsameia. [174] Of these sites, Çayönü Tepesi, located 100 km from Göbekli Tepe, is a complex settlement, and revealingly excavated, with residential and religious buildings which spanned the important end of the rebirth temple period. The main building phase of occupation started about 8000 BCE and evidence of the early grid phase shows the religious Flagstone building similar to that of

Nevali Cori's rebirth temple and the Terrazzo building, possibly, associated with rebirth religion too.

The archaeologist Mehmet Ozdogan led some excavation campaigns at Çayönü Tepesi and describes a literal break in the style of monumental architecture which is very significant:

> *The two rows of standing stone that were set into the plaza are also of interest. At least one of them had traces of red paint, and another had indications of some modelling. The standing stone varied greatly in size and shape, the largest one exceeded 2 m in height and the smallest one was about a meter high. The only other places where standing stones have been encountered are in the special buildings, in the flagstone building and in the skull building. It is also of interest to note that some of the standing stones were intentionally broken and then buried under the subsequent reflooring of the plaza.* [175]

Red paint on standing stones, holding funerary remains, and linked to buildings with the architectural style of rebirth temples is symbolism within the ROT. This appears to be the case here. The breaking up of the standing stones in the plaza, probably related to rebirth afterlife belief systems, indicates the end of that paradigm. Why did that occur? Perhaps the question which rebirth afterlife could never answer was finally posed: If rebirth happens then how can the personal identity of the newly deceased ever be preserved into the afterlife?

In settlements, a fundamentally new religion was needed where the identities of the ruling class were preserved indefinitely. The spiritual worldview allows this and the memes of this template and spiritual afterlife was already established in nearby northern Syria and the Levant.

Perhaps some changes came about through violence and social turmoil. Certainly the main religious focus in Çayönü was the Skull building where blood rituals were practiced. The Skull building was named as it yielded the partial skeletal remains of up to 450 individuals. Additionally, there is a large, shaped, "sacrificial" or "altar" stone, and even a flint knife, both of which had sufficient traces of blood for scientific analysis. Sheep, aurochs and human blood were present dating to 7000 BCE. It is speculation whether the human blood was from pre-mortem human sacrifice or post-mortem funerary ritual. In any case this religion was now different from anything seen before.

It seems Göbekli Tepe was not only the first rebirth temple, but one of the last surviving, along with the unexcavated Karahan Tepe where 266 pillars are known, as the tops still exit the surface. Clearly other temples are now destroyed, so hopefully these surviving sites will all gain World Heritage status and be given due protection.

The rebirth temples of Eastern Anatolia are the pinnacle of the prehistoric belief systems within NRT and ERA. After perhaps 350,000 years since *Homo heidelbergensis* threw a pink hand-axe into a cache of the skeletal remains of his people, and 90,000 years since the Qafzeh and Skhul burials, in the eighth millennium BCE the curtain was closing. The last phase of the Temples of Rebirth had ended with the coming invention of a stranger, more complex form of religious belief which swiftly spread and has dominated the world ever since.

5 ◆ MANTLE RELIGION: SPIRITUAL WORLDVIEW

The First Great Paradigm Shift

Spirituality is a Neolithic phenomenon! It was conceived of in Eurasia at the start of the ninth millennium BCE as it is evidenced then at Jerf-al-Ahmar, Syria. The First Great Paradigm Shift, from life-force to spirituality, is a hypothetical, but temporary, quasi-worldview for Eurasia and the Americas. This paradigm shift was largely complete in Eurasia and North Africa by 3500 BCE. It also occurred in the Americas sometime after 3000 BCE and was not complete until the first centuries of the Current Era. There is at least one culture where spirituality independently developed, but the paradigm shift froze and became permanent: it is described by the Australian Aboriginals as Dreamtime. They may have conceived of spirituality before any other culture but retained some of the life-force worldview in their beliefs.

Emergence of Spiritual Afterlife

> *But, like all men and women, ancestors at death are ushered through an underworld from which, once they have accounted for their lives and been helped by the prayers and sacrifices of their kin on earth, they pass on by reincarnation to a world of anonymity. [...] The screen of anonymity may be pierced soon after death to allow the living a glimpse of the new identity of their late kinsman, but it is an identity that has no direct connection with them and in which they will take no continuing interest.* [176]
>
> – Maurice Freedman

The GMR holds that Palaeolithic humans had a literal view of rebirth and believed in a "life-force", as evidenced by the NRT. Rebirth with the slate wiped clean of all trace of a previous life is the simplest religious answer to personal mortality. However, it contains a fatal flaw which has extinguished it: the destruction of individual identity.

This is resolved with the invention of the spiritual template which enables the spiritual worldview. The spread of spiritual afterlife belief, which is an inferred concept from the template, is tightly coupled with the development of settled societies and ultimately civilization itself. Religion played a critical role in the stability and success of the whole process. The premise of spiritual afterlife is that an intangible, ethereal double of each person exists during life. It separates from the physical body after death to a continued existence as a disembodied identity.

The GMR also holds that spiritual afterlife was developed only in settled societies, except for the Australian Aboriginal peoples, and spread with the Neolithic revolution, in the last 11,000 years.

The paradigm shift from the life-force worldview, where the environment itself was alive, to the spiritual worldview, meant that all existing worldview concepts were transformed or destroyed. It was only when this happened did the concept of ancestral spirits become established.

As the spiritual worldview paradigm spread, each culture accepted that the environment was no longer considered alive, but could be inhabited by human or nature spirits. Those spirits could be ancestors or legendary people involved in cultural myths.

All the Natural Rebirth Traditions (NRT) of Inner Core Religion became transformed into facilitating the transition to and from spiritual afterlife. The old NRT which are transformed into the spiritual worldview are grouped in the GMR as Natural Spiritual Traditions (NST) and are discussed in Chapter Six on Spiritual Afterlife. So a grave with red ochre present in a spiritual culture is no longer evidence of the Red Ochre Tradition, but just the symbolism borrowed from it and used in a spiritual sense: transmigration. Painting ancestral bones with ochre was for assisting in their partial reincarnation.

Most religions of ancestor worship allow for partial reincarnation where ancestral spirits can be reborn as infants but their previous identity fades away after a few years. Partial reincarnation is described by Norman McClelland. He is referring to African traditional religions, although this applies in ancestor worship everywhere:

> *Partial reincarnation occurs when only some of the characteristics*
> *of a deceased ancestor are reborn into one or more descendants.*
> *The main part of the deceased, however, retains a separate*

existence in the world of the ancestors, at least until the memory
of that ancestor fades away among his or her descendants; and at
which point the deceased goes through a second and final death.
177

This is not the same as full reincarnation as envisaged by the
Dharmic religions, which are part of Upper Mantle Religion (UMR) as
these religions hold to permanent preservation of identity in a spiritual
form, particularly that the spirit inhabits each new body for life with no
separate existence at the same time. Spiritual religions which consider
partial reincarnation are all within Lower Mantle Religion (LMR).
Maurice Freedman, anthropologist, in writing about Chinese traditional
religion, describes partial reincarnation belief, which was seen in most
cultures around the world when ancestor worship first prevailed in the
spiritual worldview.

In the new worldview, naturalistic animism or life-force belief has
disappeared and spiritual animism and totemism prevail. Adherence to
the spiritual worldview paradigm implies that discrete environmental
objects, such as animals, trees and mountains, are possessed by their
own spirits: spiritual animism, or ancestral spirits: totemism. These
spirits may become powerful deities. Chris Fowler comments:

Totemic relations are connections with places containing
ancestral energies. The ancestry of humans and certain animals
can both be traced from the land, and so they each contain the
same energies associated with specific places, specific ancestral
beings (Ingold 2000b:113). [25]

The spectrum of belief in ancestral power ranges from respect and
honour to worship and divinity. All cultures found a natural comfort in
the memory of their forefathers and believed that they offered guidance
and protection from the spiritual realm, as they had done years earlier
when physically alive.

Spiritual afterlife was first conceived as existence in the earthly
world. This is most often seen in ancestor worship and totemism. The
Australian Aboriginal traditional religion, early Megalithic traditions of
the Atlantic seaboard, Oriental beliefs, Native American and African
tribal religions all have a strong tradition of ancestral spirits in earthly
places.

After a few thousand years, spiritual afterlife developed to represent existence in a world of the dead – one that is roughly an image of the physical world, but on a spiritual plane. It is a place variously called afterworld, netherworld, otherworld or underworld. Cultures with this belief were Mesopotamia, Ancient Egypt, Scandinavia and the Greco-Roman sphere of Classical Antiquity. This also includes later Chinese traditional religion, Shinto (non-Buddhist beliefs) and Polynesian religions. In spiritual religions with a spirit world it is believed that after someone dies the whole person is transmigrated into it, always in the same state as when they died. Royalty remain as royals, children remain children, lepers remain lepers, and so it goes. This is preservation of identity and the expression of adulthood in afterlife which replaces the old tabula rasa belief in rebirth from infancy.

Spiritual afterlife has been confused with renewed physical life, resurrection, which is what the Abrahamic religions promise. Wallis Budge in his 1911 work *Osiris or the Egyptian Religion of Resurrection* mixes terminology which has continued until the present day. It is only possible to decompose religious belief by being precise about the believed outcomes possible in afterlife. The resurrection paradigm of the UMR, however, always begins by a phase of spiritual progression towards physical resurrection.

Breathing Air as Essence of Spirit

> *It pleased the Greeks, as well as other nations, to give the name of wind, breath – "pneuma," – to that which they vaguely understand by respiration, life, soul. So that, among the ancients, soul and wind were, in one sense, the same thing; and if we were to say that man is a pneumatic machine, we should only translate the language of the Greeks. The Latins imitated them, and used the word "spiritus," spirit, breath "Anima" and "spiritus" were the same thing.* [178]

– Voltaire

Spirituality is a template for beliefs associated with air because people need to breathe to stay alive. Many inferred concepts or memes have developed such that this template has branched into an entire worldview.

Air, the essence of breathing, is a mundane substance to modern people fully comfortable with scientific explanations of the gaseous phase of matter. Yet, it was only in the 1770s that scientists Priestly, Scheele and Lavoisier, all working independently, identified oxygen and how it is consumed by animals and released by plants. For thousands of years everyone's mindset was completely different – air was closely associated with a spiritual essence as life-giving. It was a mystery how a cupped hand over a person's mouth quickly renders them lifeless, even if they were in perfect health. Furthermore, early people were well aware that not all babies live after birth. There can be plenty of life-giving blood present but sometimes that is just not enough. A stillborn baby, not breathing, proves that the spark of life has not entered the new body.

The mystical importance of air endured. Feng Shui literally means nature's breath. Its defining principle is that all of nature is a breathing organism which must be harmonised with. Although this is a philosophy, not a religion (because Feng Shui has no afterlife belief), it is proto-spiritual akin to the SBT in the life-force worldview paradigm. It is instructive upon how the Chinese have long regarded nature and their place in it.

The Neolithic paradigm shift to the spiritual worldview assumes that life is from "spirit" which must be breathed into each new person by moving air or wind, to animate them. Spirit must then remain with that person to keep them animate. The spark of life, the entry of spirit, is synonymous with first breath.

The association of invisible air, which could be felt on the skin and supported life, with an invisible spiritual essence drove the conceptual transformation of afterlife belief in this new worldview paradigm. Spirits of individuals can then transition to a separate spiritual existence after physical death.

The atmosphere itself was considered a spiritual essence. The wind was thought to be divine because it appeared to be a physical manifestation of the spirit essence, and is much stronger than the human breath alone. Leaves moving on trees and bushes, a field of wheat rippling in the breeze, were constant proof of the spiritual envelope which penetrated all places in the world, from forests to seas to caves. It was this medium that made possible the intellectual leap of imagining afterlife as a transition to a spiritual state.

Surviving texts from the earliest civilizations: Mesopotamia, Egypt, China and Mesoamerica, all show a convergence of views on the association of spirit with breath. A diffusionist explanation is partially acceptable as memes will have spread in the ancient world through migration and trade, perhaps as far as China. Though, the remote Mesoamericans may have independently developed the concept of spirit.

In Mesopotamia the importance of breathing influenced which gods were senior when their pantheon was established in the fourth millennium BCE. Lil is the Sumerian word for air, and signifies breath, wind or spirit. Their creator god, Enlil, was lord of the earth and Underworld – all living things, wind and storms. En, (later becoming El in Babylonian times) meant lord. So the high god of the Sumerians was the Lord of the Air and his wife, Ninlil, Lady of the Air.

It can be inferred that storms and weather are closely allied to air, and so it proved that the major Semitic gods, which waxed and waned with each subsequent invasion, retained these roles. Around 1700 BCE, Marduk, originally a storm god and then the city god of Babylon, assumed the roles held by Enlil as Babylon spread its empire wider. Baal was a generic name of any senior god of the Levant, but was often associated with Hadad, also another Semitic storm god, and it was an early title assumed by the new storm god, Yahweh of Judaism and later Christianity.

The Hebrew word ruach and the Greek pneuma used in early Christian scripture mean "breath" or "wind" and imply that spirit has entered a person's body to animate it, bringing it alive. The Holy Spirit, part of the Christian Trinity, is also closely associated with air as a spiritual medium. Pneumatology, the study of the Holy Spirit, grapples with the codification of the spiritual world in its relationship with the church and Christians. It is the Holy Spirit which is breathed into those who are resurrected to new life. The Holy Spirit as the personified breath of God may have evolved from ancient Egyptian beliefs about the concept of ka.

The Egyptian ka was considered a separate essence of both humans and gods. At birth, ka was breathed into khet, the inert human body, sparking life into it. After physical death and during translation to the Netherworld (in the West beyond the sunset) spiritual afterlife was "breathed" into the dead as described by the second millennium BCE *Book of the Dead*, with translation by James Wasserman:

> *The First One, Osiris, Lord of All, mysterious of body, gives*
> *command, and puts breath into those frightened ones who are in*
> *the midst of the West.* [179]

The *Rig Veda* is the oldest of the sacred texts of the Hindu religion, dating to the second millennium BCE, containing some inherited traditions passed down from the Indus Valley civilization. In this translation by Robert Van Voorst it has a clear representation of the equivalence of breathing and spirituality:

> *When he goes on the path that lead away the breath of life,*
> *Then he will be led by the will of the gods.*
> *May your eye go to the sun, you life's breath to the wind.*
> *Go to the sky or the earth, as is your nature.*
> *Or go to the waters, if that is your fate.*
> *Take root in the plants with your limbs* [180]

The path is the direction for a person's spirit (breath of life, known in Hindu as prana) determined by their karma, which is the process of self-judgment, an internal weighing of deeds and thoughts. The gods are the Hindu pantheon. The third line is an echo of the importance of the sun god, but also a representation of the spiritual realm, felt as the wind, who is able to take the breath of life after death as well as give it at birth. Despite Van Voorst's comment that there is no explicit reference to reincarnation, there are hints in the last three lines to a type of thinking which later emerged as reincarnation in Hindu religion.

The Shang culture is recognized as having the earliest civilization in China from about 1200 BCE. As Loewe and Shaughnessy indicate, they had a high god, Di, which was above even their ancestors:

> *That Di was virtually the only Power who could directly order*
> *the Rain, or the Thunder, as well as the only Power who had the*
> *Wind Powers under his control set him apart from all the other*
> *Powers, natural, predynastic, or ancestral.* [181]

We see once more the importance of air associated with the senior deity. The god of wind certainly controlled the spirit world where ancestors existed.

Ch'i (also qi) in Chinese literally means breath or air and is an important element of Chinese religions. In recent centuries it has become abstracted until Ch'i is thought to be an invisible component of everything. Shi is aspiration. Shen also is associated with spirit and spirituality and is ubiquitous in Chinese folk religion (also called Shenism).

In North America the same association was made by the Hopi, as described by Ferguson and colleagues:

> *Bradfield 1973:41-42) and Geertz (1984:228) described some aspects of Hopi burial customs that relate to the afterlife. The hiqwsi (spirit breath) of a person is immortal and at death leaves the body through the mouth. [...] Bradfield (1973:42) remarks, "The underlying idea behind each of these ritual elements is the same: namely, that the 'breath body' may be light, not 'heavy' . . . and so be enabled to go on its way to the land of the dead."* [182]

In Mesoamerica the Popol Vuh is a surviving fragment of Mayan creation mythology which describes the origin of the world and people. Allen Christenson's literal translation of the Quiché version sets out the personal deities of the first men:

> *They speak first*
> *The Tohil, Auilix, Hacavitz.*
> *Great their day,*
> *Great also their breath,*
> *Their spirit,*

The connection between breath and spirit is evident in an original source and has also long been recognized as part of Mayan culture. Ik' is a day name in the Maize Life Cycle described as:

> *Wind, breath, spirit, life – when the breath of life has entered the maize, the spirit of maize has entered the kernel.* [183]

Perhaps the most popular of the Aztec high gods was Topiltzin-Quetzalcoatl and he had different guises – one of which, Ehecatl, was the Lord of the Winds.

In the Congo region of Central Africa, the Lugbara tribe have an indirect association of air and breathing with the concept of spirit. John Middleton in *Lugbara Religion* describes their belief. Although breath is only a sign of life, not its essence, it is closely associated with the heartbeat which equates to spirit:

> *When alive the body contains breath (ava). [...] Breath is sometimes equated with the concept of orindi, but they are usually*

distinct. Breath is in the lungs, orindi is in the heart, and it makes the heart swell and contract. Ava and orindi leave the body together at death, but are distinct. I translate orindi as "soul". It is not an impermanent thing, but survives after death and can affect and contact living men. It is not thought to enter the body at birth, but "just comes". It cannot be seen and is "like the wind". It is said to go to God in the sky after death. [184]

The concept of air and breathing as an essential feature of the life-force worldview is arguably via hyper-diffusion – it originated with humans in Africa and spread around the world. The much later Neolithic association of air with the concept of spirit may have had several origins but also spread by diffusion as the primary element in the wave-front of the spiritual worldview paradigm shift.

It is only in recent centuries that spirit has lost its relationship with air and become imagined as a pseudoscientific energy or force. This transformation is a result of the scientific explanation of human respiration and the atmosphere. Spirit as energy or force is therefore an example of Tectonic Religion in the GMR.

Transition to Spirituality in Funerary Evidence

Some burial rituals such as cremation or the use of colorants, especially ochre, have old roots to the preceding Mesolithic and even in the Palaeolithic. The evidence for these old rituals is more dense in central or western Europe than in south east Europe, whence most of the new Neolithic ideas came. [185]

– Eva Lenneis

There is substantial archaeological evidence in burials for the decline of rebirth and rise of spiritual afterlife belief. In some places, such as the Balkans, the paradigm shift was slow, in others, such as, north-west Europe there was a rapid transition. A temporary, merged Dreamtime-like worldview may have existed in places where the transition was slow, but hardly existed where it was rapid.

Numerous aspects need to be considered to build a complete picture. Rebirth religion was generally peaceful; it is with spiritual religion that we see elements of violence, sacrifice and blood rituals involving the living. This is not a direct consequence of spiritual afterlife but the result of pressures from the templates of adulthood in afterlife, judgment and quality of afterlife.

The signatures of burials conducted within the life-force worldview are primary burials, single burials, corpses curled in a foetal manner, partial cremation, unfinished objects in graves, or strong emphasis on ERA and the NRT (red ochre, teeth, shells, stone tools or animal parts).

The signatures of burials conducted within the spiritual worldview are secondary burial, multiple burials, corpses set in repose, day-to-day utility grave goods, like drinking cups and food pots, full cremation, or weak emphasis on NRT symbolism (transformed into the Natural Spiritual Traditions, described shortly). The presence of human sacrifices in graves is a definite signature of belief in spiritual afterlife, so is the presence of deliberately broken objects as grave goods.

Obviously, the variations actually seen are determined culturally.

The spiritual template may have first developed, but remained in isolation in Australia as an incomplete transition. There is a major conceptual difference between rebirth with life from infancy and spirituality with preservation of adulthood. However, the first bridging of this gap in Eurasia may have taken less than a thousand years.

The first evidence for a proto-spiritual belief anywhere in Europe, Africa or Asia is the systematic skull removal at Jerf-al-Ahmar, by 9000 BCE, in Syria. This is only about 40 km south of Göbekli Tepe and the Rebirth Temple tradition in Anatolia. The pillars of Göbekli Tepe, where stone monuments temporarily represented the deceased during the rebirth process, must have been the trigger for the concept of a disembodied spirit. A headless skeleton under a floor and loose skulls found in post holes at Jerf el Ahmar show the beginnings of secondary funerary practices. It seems that the belief where the deceased persisted in stone pillars quickly inspired the idea that the dead could persist in their lifeless skulls. It was the birth of spirituality!

The rebirth temples endured a little longer in Anatolia with sites showing gradual changes. A late phase has life-sized human statues at Urfa performing the same function of maintaining the deceased – perhaps with even more emphasis on preservation of previous identity. Nevali Cori started with a rebirth temple but later shows skull removal by 8000 BCE.

This practise spread fairly quickly southwards into the Levant where skull removal is also seen around 9000 to 8500 BCE. The Late Natufians in that region and period are categorized as *Pre-Pottery Neolithic A*. Some of these peoples left evidence of the new belief, such as those at Hayonim Cave on Mount Carmel in Israel. Yet nearby, and during the same period, Raqefet Cave is unusual for the number of shells associated with burials, compared to other Late Natufian sites, and also for the heavy use of cupules of the SBT. So, this site held to the NRT while the rest of their culture began to embrace a new and very different religion: spiritual afterlife.

Indeed, the difference in funerary tradition at these two sites has been seen and commented upon by Dani Nadel and colleagues:

> *The Raqefet 2006 finds corroborate the finds and interpretations of previously published inhumations (Lengyel and Bocquentin 2005), namely that single primary burials dominate. This is not typical for the Late Natufian. Most of the contemporaneous graves belong to Hayonim cave and Eynan, where plural burials, simultaneous or successive, dominate. The Raqefet burial area may attest to the continuation of the earlier tradition. A wider understanding of the diversity and norms of burial customs during the Late Natufian is necessary for further interpretation.* [126]

The GMR holds that the wider understanding of these sites has the Raqefet Cave people clinging to their Palaeolithic rebirth afterlife belief in the life-force worldview, whereas the Hayonim Cave people had adopted proto-spiritual beliefs. In reality, the antiquity of these sites means that the main phases of activity could be hundreds of years apart.

The break in funerary practices by the Natufians is noted by Tobias Richter and colleagues:

> *Secondary burials, more common in the Late Natufian, reflect even more elaborate processes of re-opening graves and involving dead bodies in likely ceremonial practices. [...] In contrast, the lack of such practices in the Early Epipalaeolithic could be understood as a more fluid and flexible structure of how the living perceived their dead.* [186]

In the GMR the Early Epipalaeolithic burials in the Levant would be excarnations or primary burials conducted by Natufians living within the life-force worldview. It was the paradigm shift to the spiritual worldview that made secondary burials more common, as new rituals emerged around deceased remains for ancestor worship.

Further south-east in Jericho the later ochred skulls with shell eyes were reportedly set "in conference", indicating persistence of identity of the deceased. However, this interpretation is disputed and it is suggested that they were thrown aside instead. Of course, ancestors may have sometimes been seen as failures (perhaps during a drought) and we only see the result of their demise before final burial. Half a dozen sites exist in the Levant with a tradition of skull plastering or painting between 7200 and 5500 BCE.

By the time of the last phase of Çayönü Tepesi and the first settlement of Çatal Höyük the concept of preservation of identity after death, where the deceased is resident in stones, statues or skulls, was well advanced. Belief in a following partial reincarnation for the deceased is indicated by ancestral bones beneath sleeping benches. Spirituality and ancestorhood had fully emerged at Çatal Höyük.

The human and cat burial at Shillourokambos, Cyprus, about 7300 BCE, was clearly performed within the life-force worldview paradigm and shows that the memes of spirituality and spiritual afterlife had not reached the island, 40 km from the Anatolian coast, at this time. However, Khirokitia, a large village of up to 600 people, occupied 6000 to 5000 BCE, had complex burial practices which included deliberately broken stone bowls as grave goods. The reason funerary items are deliberately broken it is to send them into the spiritual afterlife with the deceased.

In western Iran, the transition from Neolithic to Early Chalcolithic was about 6000 BCE when farmers replaced the hunter-gatherers. One of the earliest settlements there is the agricultural community of Zagheh on the southern Qazvin Plain which was present from 6000 to 5000 BCE. A complex of mud-brick houses and a central religious temple has been identified. Infants were buried under floors within the houses without any grave goods but adult burials were in a courtyard within the village near the temple. Grave goods were pottery and ornaments and, significantly, all skeletal remains are found to have been stained with red ochre. [187]

The collection of remains at a central point near a temple indicates it was a shrine for ancestor worship. The belief in the power of red ochre had then been transformed to assist with spiritual progression, possibly subsequent partial reincarnation.

Brian Peasnell describes the later changes in funerary ritual:

The Middle Chalcolithic is better represented with several burials coming from a number of sites including Jaffarabad, Jowi, Bendebal, Chogha Mish and Qabr Sheykeyn. All had come from deposits associated with the late phases of the Middle Chalcolithic. Most of these consisted of adults laid on their backs in an extended position. Each were accompanied by a beaker or cup and a small jar, and most were interred in tombs made of mud-brick. [114]

Clearly the concept of progression into afterlife had changed further. The purpose of the containers with these burials is likely to provide the deceased with the essential of a drinking vessel for use in the spirit world of the dead.

Further east towards Sialk, the old ROT and rebirth belief lasted longer. In the fifth millennium BCE, the practice of red ochre burials was now waning. Richard Dibon-Smith describes this transition:

By contrast, in the sixth millennium village of Tepe Sagheh every one of the eighteen burials was treated with red ochre. At nearby Sialk skeletons were ochred throughout the Sixth Millennium, then only the head for some time, and finally by mid-Fifth Millennium, the use of ochre died out entirely. This general tendency to use ochre less and less in burial rituals may also be the reason no trace of the material has been found either at the Fifth Millennium necropolis of Tepe Giran, central Iran, or at the very large Fourth Millennium necropolis of Tepe Hissar, in northern Iran. Its abandonment was a significant transformation of ancient cultural practice and may have arisen out of newer ideas associated with the Neolithic Revolution. [188]

In the GMR the "newer ideas associated with the Neolithic Revolution" are those of the spiritual worldview paradigm. The paradigm shift travelled west to east across Iran during the sixth to fifth millennia BCE.

In Egypt, at 4000 BCE, the Badarians were including naked female figurines in burials, and the deceased were in a foetal position and often had malachite, symbolic of plant renewal, present – all signatures of a continuation of rebirth belief. It is during the subsequent Amratian period that the complexity and choice of grave goods swings towards consistency with the spiritual, rather than a rebirth afterlife paradigm.

The western desert site of Gebel Ramlah has a strong NRT emphasis in burials, evidencing rebirth afterlife belief at 3600 BCE. Yet a Qustul (Nubian culture) incense burner is dated, at the latest, to 3400 BCE and has a royal procession depicted. This places the spiritual worldview early in Nubia, but only a few hundred years before the earliest Egyptian kings and pharaohs during the First Dynasty at 3100 to 2890 BCE. The evidence is that a transition from rebirth to spiritual afterlife belief took place in Egypt in the mid-fourth millennium BCE, and was abrupt, like a phase change. As it spread from the Fertile Crescent it swiftly displaced the older rebirth religion, well within a 500-year period.

The very widespread practice of the ROT in Europe faded away at the start of the Neolithic. Mound burials in east and south-central Bulgaria from 4000 BCE frequently had red ochre spread on the deceased. However, of eleven graves in the north-central area, of Batin, from about 3000 BCE, only one piece of red ochre was found in one grave, whereas four burials had ceramic pots. The importance of ochre was disappearing. [189]

Two unrelated graves were found close together at Dragsholm, West Zealand, Denmark. One was a Mesolithic Ertebølle burial of two hunter-gatherer women covered in red ochre with grave goods of a flaying knife of bone, a bone awl and an arrowhead. The other was a Neolithic grave of a male farmer with pendants made of pig and deer teeth, a stone knife, awl and teeth beads, but no ochre. Because they are quite different it was thought that they were from very different times, but recent dating shows them only 200 years apart, ca. 3800 BCE and ca. 3600 BCE. It appears that the Neolithic revolution swept quickly through northern Europe after 4000 BCE. [190] Ideas which are well advanced take root more quickly and powerfully. In the GMR this is also the wave front of the paradigm shift, indicating that spirituality came to Denmark around 3700 BCE.

Neolithic Ireland, at the remote west of Europe might be considered the final receiver for the important social changes which rippled through Europe, but his was not the case for spirituality. Farming in Ireland dates from 4200 BCE, rapidly followed by the construction phase of the Boyne monumental tombs: Knowth, Dowth and Newgrange between 3900 and 3500 BCE. The Boyne was now a place of spiritual religion and ancestor worship, where the dead were cremated to release their spirits.

Ilga Zagorska writes about waning red ochre funerary usage in the eastern Baltic by the end of the Stone Age (about 1500 BCE):

The graves dated to the Late Neolithic did not contain ochre. In this period, crouched burials without ochre predominate. This has been observed not only at the Zvejnieki burial ground, but also in burials from Late Neolithic settlement sites: Abora I and Kvapani II in south-eastern Latvia (Loze 1995:33–42) and Tamula in Estonia (Jaanits 1957:80–100). It appears that in the East Baltic the tradition of using ochre in burials had disappeared completely by the end of the Stone Age. This same development has been observed in Finland (Purhonen 1984:43–44). [90]

In Latvia, the Late Neolithic is described as the period between about 2450 and 1500 BCE. Because of its remoteness, the transition is seen very late in the Baltic region of Northern Europe.

In Japan, the Jomon originally had rebirth afterlife beliefs with the ROT in evidence, then a long tradition of egg renewal through shell symbolism. This was changing by the Middle Jomon where collective burials occurred in the centre of settlements, about 3500 BCE. John Whitney Hall, historian, writes about the Japanese Late Jomon development of cemeteries, at about 2400 BCE, as evidenced at Ebijima in Iwate Prefecture:

This development is undoubtedly related in some way to an increasingly large number of skeletons painted with red ochre (evidence of secondary burials) and to a trend toward burial in a flexed position, Whether the paint was seen as a preservative or a simulation of blood (the substance of life), whether flexed positions suggested the completion of a life cycle, or whether a corpse was wrapped in order to prevent a return to life, considerable religious evolution is indicated. [191]

Hall advances several explanations about the ochre and flexing, but in the worldwide context of blood symbolism or representation, because these were secondary burials, it appears the Jomon were performing ancestor worship consistent with spiritual afterlife at this period. The flexed positioning of the deceased was believed to be conducive to their partial reincarnation.

We have seen how the burial practices of early cultures in Vietnam: the Hoabinhian, Dabutian and Bacsonian, commonly involved dusting flexed and crouched burials with ochre and shells.

A cemetery at Man Bac, Ninh Binh province, Northern Vietnam is dated to a short period around 1500 BCE. Eighty-four burials by a culture similar to, or part of, the Phung Nguyen agrarian peoples have new features. Adults and children were treated similarly, they were laid straight in repose, usually with a pot or two nearby. None have red ochre present, although shells are still common. [192]

Man Bac contrasts with the earlier cultures and clearly shows that there is a new phase where even the shell usage is different, as the shells are very often placed in the hands of the deceased, a position that suggests a utility use or even payment for entry to the spirit realm.

In Richland County, south-west Wisconsin, United States, archaeology reveals the time when rebirth afterlife gave way to spiritual afterlife in a single site, dated between 1710 and 1280 BCE. Feature 25 at the Price III site is a large multilevel burial pit containing the remains of 88 people and described by Theron D. Price, professor of religion:

> *A series of radiocarbon determinations indicate that the maximum use-life of Feature 25 was likely no more than 500 years. The nature of this burial feature at Price III suggests intermittent use by the same population through time. Depositional conditions in the burial pit are generally constant with little change in soils or moisture. Some changes in the contents of the burials, position of the body, and form of burial can be observed from earlier to later graves. Red ochre is present only in the lower levels; rock mantle occur only on graves in the upper portion; cremations are more common in the upper levels.*
> 193

Over a period of 500 years there was a profound change in burial signatures which the GMR holds is the acceptance of spiritual afterlife and rejection of simple rebirth. Red ochre was seen with a few cremations at the Price III site and this is likely part of NST, where the ochre was reinterpreted to assist with spiritual progression. Limestone and sandstone slabs directly on the remains of those without ochre may be an attempt to keep the dead in place, to ensure only the spirit moves on. It is a practice seen in many parts of the world.

The first cremation burials evidenced by the Mixtec culture of Mexico date to about 1100 BCE. They occur at the village site of Tayata, in a period where social structures were forming as a precursor to the development of the Mixtec civilization.

The spiritual worldview paradigm shift and the decline and transformation of the NRT into the NST originated between Anatolia and the Levant, spread westward throughout Europe and eastward throughout Asia in a chronologically consistent manner. This was followed in the second millennium BCE in the Americas which may have been by diffusion from late migrations from north-east Asia, or independently developed in either of the Eastern Woodlands of the United States, or Mesoamerica.

Society and Civilization

The spiritual worldview developed from the spiritual template which was the mental paradigm that disembodied identities can exist. We shall see how this development became essential for large stable societies. A critical and fundamental cognitive limit in human brains expressed by Dunbar's Number which limits the size of societies, was finally overcome by the conception and social acceptance of the spiritual worldview.

Dunbar's Number

> *It is of interest to note that estimates of the size of Neolithic villages in Mesopotamia are of about the same magnitude. Oates (1977), for example, gives a figure of 150-200, based on the fact that 20-25 dwellings seem to be the typical size of a number of village sites dated to around 6500-5500 BCE.* [194]

– Richard Dunbar

A large society is one which exceeds 150 people. We are so used to modern civilization that we might think only of a city of one million people as "large". A society of 150 people seems pitifully small. How can this be significant? Research by the anthropologist Richard Dunbar in the 1990s, referenced above, showed that there are cognitive limits in human brains as to how many separate individuals we can know on a personal basis. Dunbar studied 36 primate species to obtain mean group size and neocortex size and extrapolated for humans giving 148 individuals possible for interpersonal relationships. Statistically, there is a 95 per cent confidence of the maximum number being between 108 and 189. This does not mean that people can't have relationships with more than 189 people, instead it sets a critical level where having 100 relationships means they can be stable long-term but at, say 200, would mean that new connections are unstable unless old ones are diminished and ejected. Dunbar's number is often cited as 150, but it is not hard and fast. Two hundred is a practical upper limit.

Dunbar's number might appear abstract but that is because society has evolved so that it is not necessary to have a personal relationship with everyone for it to function. However, it was very important in the past, when people lived in small villages. The importance of the limit is that competition for resources occurs between those who lack a personal relationship or a cooperative strategy. For smaller groups, people will tend to cooperate and share because they all know each other. This level of cooperation declines as group size grows. Once a group, or settlement, expands to exceed 150 members then the pressures of fission will overcome natural cohesion, causing the group to split. Dunbar has collated many examples of successful groups, from Roman army units to the Hutterites in the United States. Typically, they reach approximately 150 people when they are most efficient and then suffer from splitting or stalling. Between 150 and 200 individuals is the threshold where society must acquire a hierarchical or authoritarian structure in order to maintain long-term stability.

Dunbar's number as a measure of the physical limits of the human mind was recently given support by researchers who examined interpersonal relationships arising within a twenty-first century phenomenon. On Twitter two-way social activity reaches a maximum between 150 and 200 contacts and is saturated beyond that. [195]

Tribal living was the norm for the *Homo sapiens* species since their first appearance about 700 kya, only changing with the Neolithic revolution from 10 kya. In a hunter-gatherer model, whether completely nomadic, semi-nomadic or fixed (e.g. operating long-term from caves), it was the case that individuals always knew everyone else. It just didn't happen in a tribal society, as an adult, that you might bump into another member of the tribe you had not interacted with or recognized before.

The human brain has not evolved much in the past 10,000 years. People had the same cognitive capacity when villages first became towns as people have now.

After the first villages of settled cultures became common, Dunbar's number prevailed as the maximum settlement size for several thousand years. In many areas successful hierarchical structures could not be maintained at a large size. However, in a few exceptional cases, settlements did grow into the hundreds and low thousands. Jericho and Çatal Höyük had overcome the normal limit around 7000 BCE – and we begin to see why shortly.

Moral Imperative via Afterlife Judgment

> *At some point, probably still in the Neolithic, the commemoration of the dead - a feature common to many early cultures, including the Greek and Mesopotamian - probably became more orderly and articulated in China, taking on an ideological and juridical power of its own.* [196]

> – David Keightley

Arthur C. Clarke, a science fiction writer and theorist, expressed a common, but profoundly misguided, view still prevalent in non-religious thinkers: that it is a tragedy that morality has been hijacked by religion. He recognized that morality is reflected by religion, globally, but not it seems how cognitive limits expressed by Dunbar's Number limit the size of human groups. Religious cohesion was critical to the development of large societies. There is a good reason for the development of religiously enforced moral behaviour, but first a review of the driving forces and motivation for morality in societies.

Durkheim considered religion tightly bound with society, and although religion flowed from it, the rules of society were religious ones, and that the main purpose of religion was to support the moral order. This is sociological, as the main purpose of religion is the defence against personal mortality, predating society. However, its purpose expanded greatly as a buttress for formalized societies when they evolved later.

Charles Moore, an editor at the Daily Telegraph newspaper, in 2010 writes about trust exists between many people and how it underpins civilization:

> *But what is fascinating about the history of economic collapse is that it brings one back to the basis of civilisation. Government and civil society itself depend for their existence on an infinitely complicated web of trust. Money is a prime expression of this. If money cannot be trusted, nor can any but the most primitive exchanges between human beings. You cannot plan, build, save, borrow, bequeath. Your values, both material and moral, radically deteriorate. In extreme cases, only your next meal matters.* [197]

We now ask, what underpins trust itself?

Humans alone make the distinction between good and evil and, furthermore, all share an instinctive awareness that good is superior to evil. The innate benefits of good behaviour in a family group is a template for good behaviour capable of producing an improved society. To discover how religious cohesion harnesses this predisposition and works in societies we begin by considering how moral behaviour develops in individuals.

Psychologists Dennis Krebs and Maria Janicki cite research that young children view morality primarily in terms of obedience to authority, the avoidance of punishment and superior power of authorities. This is called morality of constraint. Because children are weakest, their deference to adults is an adaptive strategy. As children grow older and interact with peers, their basis for morality changes to become morality of cooperation, instrumental exchange, where norms of reciprocity prevail. They will trade and take turns. Over time a number of necessary relationship strategies have evolved. However, all strategies must contain methods to catch and punish those cheating, and contain antidotes to strategies which exploit them. For example, selfish behaviour has an antidote with tit-for-tat behaviour. [198]

The Morality of Cooperation model normally remains with adults throughout their lives. It also follows that people must continue to learn and remember the expected behaviour of whom they are dealing with for the next occasion. This is what makes Dunbar's number effective, as a limit upon how a growing society can function with a Morality of Cooperation model. The flaw with antidotes for selfish behaviour is that people cannot learn and remember the behaviour of thousands of others, nor can they form friendships or have kinship ties with them all. The alternative Alpha Male or Alpha Female model alone is also insufficient to enforce social cohesion beyond Dunbar's Number.

The GMR holds the following key theoretical assertion: *The morality of constraint seen in children is reintroduced in adulthood by the inferred concepts arising from the template of judgment in afterlife and is a cultural feature in all settled societies comprising more than 150 people, Dunbar's Number.*

Adults recognize the superior power of their ancestral spirits, nature spirits or gods which may intervene in their progression through afterlife, or directly affect their current life. Deference to spiritual judgment becomes an adaptive strategy, especially when such judgment is based upon a moral code when alive. The evidence is overwhelming that afterlife judgment is closely tied to the moral code of societies. All large societies would then be a complex mixture of both models of morality: co-operation *and* constraint. Religious doctrine is ubiquitous in stressing moral codes which buttress society.

So Morality of Constraint ties together the moral imperative in religion with how it facilitates cooperation within large groups overcoming the Dunbar's number. So, just what is this vague idea of "religious cohesion"?

In their groundbreaking work on how human culture is significantly driven by natural selection Richerson and Boyd show how norms and values become selected traits within cultures:

> *Natural selection acting on culture is an ultimate cause of human behaviour, just like natural selection acting on genes. [...] Much cultural variation exists at the group level. Different human groups have different norms and values, and the cultural transmission of these traits can cause such differences to persist for long periods of time. Now the norms and values that predominate in a group plausibly affect whether that group is successful, whether it survives, and whether it expands. For the purposes of illustration, suppose that groups having norms that promote group solidarity are more likely to survive than groups lacking this sentiment. This creates a selective process that leads to the spread of solidarity.* [199]

The influential norms and values also include moral behaviour. David Sloan Wilson, whose important contribution to the emergence of civilization is discussed shortly, observes:

> *Darwin proposed group selection to explain the evolution of human moral virtues, but by his own account these virtues are*

practiced within groups and against other groups. Even within groups, the so-called moral virtues are often enforced by coercive mechanisms. [200]

Judgment in afterlife is the ultimate coercive mechanism. It is the essence of religion reinforcing within-group morality, intensifying it, and raising the fitness level of groups with this paradigm far higher than would otherwise be the case. Wilson continues:

> *One of the beauties of multilevel selection theory is that it employs the same principles at all levels of the biological hierarchy. Within-group selection by itself creates a world without morality in which individuals merely use each other to maximize their relative fitness. Group selection creates a moral world within groups but doesn't touch the world of between-group interactions.*
> [200]

In other words: a man can be pious, respecting his elders and family-oriented *within* his group but capable of viciously beheading his enemy during a battle *between* groups.

Furthermore, there is one more conclusion which can be drawn from all the analysis above, with striking implications. If judgment is the coercive force driving religious cohesion in societies and the moral basis for society, and societies undergo natural selection, then this implies that afterlife belief in individuals is itself strongly selected for in competing societies.

In practice this means that strong memes of afterlife belief, which themselves undergo Darwinian processes, will thrive in societies which are successful, or if these memes are poor ones, will be slowly eliminated in failed societies. It is time to look again at the origins of village society.

Settled Societies and the Neolithic Revolution

> *When we study religion as it is actually practiced, we see group selection contending with, and not always prevailing against, other strong forces. When we study religion as it is idealized, we see something much closer to the expression of what would evolve by pure group-level selection.* [200]

> – David Sloan Wilson

The Fertile Crescent of the Middle East stretches from Upper Egypt through the Levant, Syria and southern Turkey, then south through Mesopotamia. It had vast tracts of lush landscape. perfect for the fumbling and inefficient first attempts at agriculture.

The Temples of Rebirth in eastern Anatolia and upper Euphrates from 9500 BCE show a convincing catalyst for the development of settled society and it was in that region the emergence of agriculture and domestication of animals first took place, becoming known as the Neolithic Revolution. This knowledge spread westward to the Levant and then Egypt, and eastward to Mesopotamia and the Indus Valley, where civilizations later appeared.

The earliest known agricultural settlement is Abu Hureyra in northern Syria, on the right bank of the Euphrates River, about 36km, downstream from Mureybat, although its remains are now flooded under a modern reservoir. It was occupied from about 9500 to 5000 BCE in three phases which are important because the first two straddle the development of agriculture, (the latter two are divided by the transition from pre-pottery to a pottery-using culture). When Abu Hureyra was first settled it was a hunting and foraging community which relied upon migrating gazelle for food, supplemented with fish and edible plants and berries.

These peoples used wild rye initially and later developed harvesting and grinding skills, then transitioned fully to planting their own crops. Human selection of rye and wheat soon produced higher-yielding varieties than the original wild type.

Many settlements followed elsewhere and, interestingly, some of them significantly exceeded Dunbar's Number in size. The GMR supports the hypothesis of a two-phase development within the spiritual worldview paradigm which is critical to supporting large societies. It requires ancestor worship evolving into god-worship. This is an old idea, but not framed in terms of the importance of judgment and multilevel natural selection.

The first phase of the spiritual worldview is the belief that the dead become ancestors and persist at special places in the landscape or at shrines; this is ancestor worship and totemism. Judgment is visited upon the living by watchful ancestors and this reintroduces the morality of constraint within adults as the primary moral model. Judgment of the dead may also occur where spirits of the newly deceased are accepted into the ancestral realm based upon morality in life. It is these concepts which enabled large societies to develop and is evidenced by secondary burials and skull painting at Jericho and Çatal Höyük in the eighth and seventh millennia BCE. Ancestor worship and belief of their intervention in day-to-day life was sufficient buttress for some early societies, allowing them to exceed Dunbar's Number in size for the first time. However, early towns lacked any central infrastructure.

The second phase after ancestor worship, which was always a family affair, came several thousand years later. It was god-belief. This emerged and became a unifying form of worship for the whole of society. Judgment of the living and the dead was now performed by gods. This enabled very large towns to develop, probably the first one being Eridu in Mesopotamia from about 4500 BCE. Eridu was built by the Ubaid culture and had the first signature of a central infrastructure with its own paramount religious temple. The GMR has the hypothesis that *it was only afterlife judgment executed by gods which enabled the first true cities to develop.* Ancestor worship is flawed because people are only accountable to their own ancestors, not those of other families. With the concept of deity came the accountability of all people in a society to a single spiritual being. This is strongly seen in Shang China where the high god Di spoke for all the ancestors in the oracle bones.

What was the process driving the replacement of ancestors by gods?

The answer lies in multilevel natural selection. The early villages competed against each other for hundreds of years until one of them developed a model for society which allowed it to grow to an enormous size, perhaps it was Eridu, then all the others nearby succumbed. This new model spread throughout Mesopotamia and far beyond.

Multilevel Natural Selection

Natural selection is a multilevel process that operates among groups in addition to among individuals within groups. Any unit becomes endowed with the properties inherent in the word organism to the degree that it is a unit of selection. The history of life on earth has been marked by many transitions from groups of organisms to groups as organisms. Organismic groups achieve their unity with mechanisms that suppress selection within without themselves being overtly altruistic. Human evolution falls within the paradigm of multilevel selection and the major

> *transitions of life. Moral systems provide many of the mechanisms that enable human groups to function as adaptive units.* [200]
>
> – David Sloan Wilson

Individual natural selection is recognized as the engine of evolution, but this is more appearance than reality. The whole process is better considered as multiple layers of multilevel natural selection which act upon groups of individuals. It is this that played the biggest part in the development of both religion and civilization.

Multilevel or group-level selection has long been a poor cousin of individual natural selection. The torchbearer for it is David Sloan Wilson, biologist and anthropologist, who has done much to roll back the tide of bias. Of particular interest here is his seminal work *Darwin's Cathedral*, where multilevel natural selection explains the fundamental importance of religion in human society and the moral imperative that is closely woven into them.

There is a grey-scale spectrum across the range of individual animals, where multilevel natural selection at the group-level is virtually absent at one end and strongest at the other. For polar bears, a solitary life is all they know. Anthills, termite mounds and beehives are all group structures of thousands of individuals which strongly react to the relative density of their neighbours. Multilevel natural selection has had a profound influence upon the evolution of these insects, such that any individuals cut off from their hive will quickly die. In their hives, individuals do better than they would alone, but at the great price of surviving only as part of a group-level organism. Wilson also uses the example of insects to explain that hiving benefits the hive directly and the individuals indirectly. Therefore individualism weakens as group cohesion strengthens.

Humans have moved the furthest in the shortest time across the spectrum, from a region of low to high multilevel selection. It is the price of civilization. No other organism has made such a large transition in such short time: 10,000 years. This process is still underway. The year 2009 marked the moment when the world's most populous country, China, transitioned to having more people in cities than in the countryside. The "hiving" of humanity is irreversible without a horrendous population crash. A whole generation of city-dwellers are now only vaguely aware of self-sufficiency. They are dependent for food, water, fuel and shelter via the industrial arteries of civilization, like a body-cell is dependent on arterial blood supply.

Similarly, in a strict sense, the biological individual is a cell colony, and competition between individuals is multilevel natural selection from the perspective of DNA in the cells. The larger the animal or organism is, then the greater the number of cell-types exist in it. Similarly, the larger human society becomes, the greater specialization of work is done by people within them. There is no denying that multilevel natural selection is a subtle yet fundamental force in evolution. Kathleen Donohue, a professor of evolution, writes about it as seen in plants:

> *The ecological conditions that influence the strength of different levels of selection are poorly known empirically. One of the factors most likely to influence the relative strength of individual and group selection is density. If density determines the intensity of interactions among neighbours, one expects that individual selection may be strong at low density but that group selection would be strongest at high density.* [201]

Density is the key factor. The denser a population of individuals is, the more powerful group-level selection becomes over that population. Density applies to human populations as well. In the case of separate but nearby Neolithic groups or settlements, there will be competition at the settlement level, between settlements, not just at the individual, human level. The larger each settlement is, the more competition there is at the group-level, and the less overall influence there is by competition between individuals.

Why are large societies successful? Division of labour and task specialization leads to expertise, technology, efficiency and ultimately science. So there is an improved fitness level associated with increased settlement size. This is because many secondary products, for example metalworking, require a skilled infrastructure and market beyond the capability of just 150 people (who have to do everything else to survive as well). The measure of success of competition at the settlement level is therefore improved reproductive environment and improved living standards for individuals within the stronger settlement. The better a settlement does, the better everyone and their families will do personally. Competition between settlements is usually economic via trade (wealth creation), or military (outright force to seize land and resources).

In practice, when we talk about density of settlements, there was a specific type of place which was needed to allow many settlements to co-exist near each other and the best was along fertile riverbanks, and adjoining plains.

In ancient Egypt the Nile would flood every year covering the riverbanks in a thick layer of black silt several kilometres inland. Settlements had been on the riverbanks since the Palaeolithic but it was only in the fourth millennium BCE that the change to civilization occurred. There were many communities interacting with each other and, significantly, the site of Merimda Beni Salama in the southwest Delta shows pottery and artefacts consistent of a culture within emergent civilization.

A true civilization emerged by 3200 BCE. It was 700 years later that the great pyramids were being built, involving an organized workforce of 20,000 men, supported by a similar number of women. Such a large number of people constitute many networks of networks.

Much further east, the Indus River Valley of Pakistan also had excellent soils as every spring there is flooding from snow melt in the mountains. Similarly to Egypt this allowed many agrarian settlements to develop. Kenneth Pletcher in *The History of India* describes the emergence of the Indus Valley civilization:

> *At a somewhat later date, probably toward the middle of the 4th millennium BCE, agricultural settlements began to spread more widely in the Indus valley itself. The earliest of these provide clear links with the cultures along or beyond the western margins of the Indus valley. In the course of time, a remarkable change took place in the form of the Indus settlements, suggesting that some kind of closer interaction was developing, often over considerable distances, and that a process of convergence was under way. This continued for approximately 500 years and can now be identified as marking a transition toward the full urban society that emerged at Harappa and similar sites about 2600 BCE.* [202]

The population of the city of Harappa itself may have once surpassed 40,000, although this culture was to be overrun by 1500 BCE. The same environmental conditions which existed in the Indus Valley also existed in Mesopotamia, Egypt and the Yellow River, with its tributaries for the Shang in China.

The Olmec in Central America are mysterious as they thrived in a swampy forested region, but maize itself is a phenomenal crop and was an important factor. David Drew, archaeologist, considers the problem of how the Olmec civilization first coalesced:

> *In the Olmec case, maize cultivation in this lowland environment would have proved highly successful. The alluvial soils of the Gulf Coast are very fertile and two crops a year could have been harvested with ease. Growing villages and the creation of new settlements may have led groups of these to aggregate under new forms of organization and managerial authority of a more coercive nature, to ensure the kind of social stability that benefited the bulk of the population within the larger territorial unit.* [203]

Drew also describes ideal conditions where it is obvious that multilevel natural selection could thrive as a process.

It is also a hypothesis of the GMR that *the emergence of a specific type of religious belief at any one of a set of competing settlements would quickly allow it to out-compete its neighbours, seeding the development of a ruling class and explosive growth.* This applied at least once in each of the above-mentioned foundation civilizations of the world.

Civilization via Judgment by Gods

> *Animism was the "groundwork" which was found in all religion past and present. From animism developed ancestor worship, with departed spirits surviving as disembodied entities capable of possessing the bodies of the living. Belief in spirits as gods who controlled the elements then followed. This polytheism was ultimately joined by monotheism, the belief in a single god which characterized Christianity, Judaism and Islam.* [204]

> – Mike Parker Pearson

The region of Mesopotamia is instructive. Melt-waters of the last Ice Age had raised sea levels such that the Persian Gulf extended 200 kilometres further into the area now known as southern Iraq, than it does today. Large areas which are dry or desert today were wet and green for several thousands of years. Then, sedimentation from the Tigris and Euphrates Rivers were to later build up and reclaim the land from the sea, leaving large areas of very fertile soils. The first peoples into the new area were Samarrans from the north that developed into the Ubaid culture. Villages flourished.

The region of all Ubaid culture was vast, extending through Iraq, into Syria and southern Turkey. We are particularly interested in the same area of southern Iraq where early settlements subsequently became overlaid by the Sumerian civilization, which became the Mesopotamian civilization. The Ubaid period of pre-Sumerian civilization was from about 5600 to 4000 BCE but it is not known to what degree the Sumerians are represented by migration from externally to the area.

At 5000 BCE small settlements existed where everyone would have known everyone else on a personal basis. Nowhere else in the world were so many separate settlements operating independently, yet in close proximity. They were typically 10 to 20 km apart and, it appears, all small in size. One of the largest sites, Tell Abada, evidences a population of just 70 to 120 people. [205] They had mastered growing cereal crops, domesticating early sheep, goats and cattle and importantly, introducing irrigation, which is the major cooperative development for increasing food production.

Eventually the society, which first evolved a mechanism for making large numbers of self-interested strangers begin to harmonise, live and work together, beyond simple ancestor worship, would prevail and absorb its neighbours. And, indeed something remarkable was happening. By 4500 BCE the town of Eridu had developed with a population as high as 5000 and had a central temple which was copied many times over, while it endured for about 1700 years. By 3000 BCE, in the Sumerian era, there were many such towns. One properly called a city, Uruk, was by far the largest in the world with a population of some 50,000, requiring 200 to 600 square kilometres of nearby irrigated land. Commerce was boosted through a sound judicial system, standard measurement of goods and standard time periods of hours, minutes and seconds, still essential today. Uruk rang with the sounds of carpentry, leather-working, brick-making, markets, domesticated animals and the babble of thousands of voices.

Sumeria developed the world's earliest written language, progressing from an early pictographic form to wedge-shaped sequences representing syllables. Thousands of their clay tablets, first translated in the 1840s, survive, and their cuneiform script gives us a window into their culture – and god belief.

Their religion is described by Jean Bottéro and colleagues:

> *In Mesopotamia religious feeling was in no way mystical. [...] One finds only signs of respect, veneration, deference, submission, and admiration, a feeling of the greatness of the gods and of the uncrossable distance that separated them from humans, at the very most servants to their awe-inspiring masters. There is not a single impulse of attraction, of fervor, of the desire to approach them, of tenderness or of love, of an impression of finding in them something like an indispensable part of oneself. As the myth of the Super-sage emphasizes well, humans were created by the gods to serve them.* [206]

This is a culture unlike any seen before where its people were clearly under a self-constructed morality of constraint deferring to judgment by gods.

We are interested to know more of the Sumerian view of afterlife, how strongly they believed in judgment after death and had an established judgmental mechanism. The *Code of Hammurabi*, dating to 1772 BCE, which sets out the tenets of civil law and conduct, had moral force from the gods through the king. Percy Hancock, a curator at the British Museum, concludes his translation with an epilogue:

> *The king, who is pre-eminent among city kings, am I. My words are precious, my wisdom is unrivalled. By the command of Shamash, the great judge of heaven and earth, may I make righteousness to shine forth in the land. By the order of Marduk, my lord, may no one efface my statues, may my name be remembered with favour in Esagila for ever.* [207]

Shamash is the god of afterlife judgment and Marduk the high god. There was a meme in the cities of Mesopotamia that the sun god, was all-seeing, all-powerful and dispensed justice upon criminals, both in life and in death.

Written language is often considered a fundamental development necessary to civilization, more so than metalworking. However, it is evident that judgment by gods is earlier and more fundamental to civilization than even writing.

Writing itself does become critical in maintaining civilizations long-term. Prior to writing, all information had to be memorised and passed through the generations as oral tradition. Oral tradition requires proximity between the speaker and listeners as members of a society. Therefore, oral tradition is subject to the constraints on the cohesion of society imposed by physical association. The invention of writing overcomes this problem. It enables the same information to be disseminated to all parts of a civilization, to people who will never meet. It also enables information to be passed from the dead to the living. We can read the *Epic of Gilgamesh*, the world's oldest story, from copies of copies of clay tablets which were first inscribed 4000 years before anyone living today was born. So, writing is the perfect vehicle to maintain religious cohesion across a civilization. Many groups of people within a civilization can absorb the same religious teachings, even if there is little contact between the groups. Scripture also improves the authority of priesthoods, as they can directly evidence higher thought in their arguments.

All of the five foundation civilizations had a written language, three of which are extremely well deciphered: Mesopotamian cuneiform, Egyptian hieroglyphics and Shang Chinese pictograms. The Indus Valley script is abundant but undeciphered. Finally, the Olmec script is both extremely rare and also undeciphered. Of the first three, the deciphered material has substantial evidence for the moral basis of society buttressed by religion.

The anthropologist Gregory Possehl coined the term "Middle Asian Interaction Sphere" to describe the trade and cultural links between several ancient civilizations in the period 3000 to 2000 BCE. These are Mesopotamia (Modern Iraq and southern Turkey), Elam (Iran), Magan (Oman) and Meluhha (India). As well as beads, bronze, cloth and other trade goods, they would have exchanged memes, ideas, particularly those concerning religion. Conceptual memes about judgment in afterlife through gods would have continued to spread at this time.

In Egypt, the *Instruction of Ptahhotep* is a series of common-sense and wise advice, first written approximately 2400 BCE during the reign of Djedkare Isesi during the Old Kingdom, which illustrates how moral behaviour is backed by religious authority. Since Egypt had a multitude of gods, the text is written to be independent of which one is the reader's personal god. It does not matter who is your god, the instruction is still relevant. Battiscombe Gunn, Egyptologist, wrote in his translation:

> *Be not covetous as touching shares, in seizing that which is not thine own property. Be not covetous toward thy neighbors; for with a gentleman praise availeth more than might. He [that is covetous] cometh empty from among his neighbours, being void of the persuasion of speech.* [208]

The obtuse terminology about being "void of the persuasion of speech" is an allusion to the importance of being able to speak one's name to the gods after death. Failure to do so guaranteed oblivion.

The Shang culture was the first recognizable civilization in Eastern Asia. It was located in the Yellow River valley, Honan, China and survived to form the basis of the Imperial dynasties. The previous and first Chinese dynasty, Xia, was little more than a series of Neolithic settlements.

Bovine scapula (cattle shoulder blades) and turtle shell were the much preferred "oracle bones" used for divination. The process involved using bronze needles to scratch messages on the bone, and heating them in a fire and then interpreting the resulting cracks which intersected the logograms in meaningful ways. Sometimes the messages were written in cinnabar, symbolic blood, and other materials which have not survived, so the oracle bones appear blank. About 150,000 are known and many are deciphered. Analysis has been done to see if they are representative and random enough to give a perspective on the Shang culture. David Keightley, Sinologist and historian, makes this point:

> *The indications we have – archaeological, traditional, and ethnographic, as well as inscriptional – present a consistent and convincing picture of a theocratic polity in which matters of state were equally, and perhaps by definition, matters of religion.* [196]

The earliest divinations during Wu Ting's reign, the first Shang king, ca. 1200 to 1180 BCE, were often related to determining the curses of ancestors, so this indicates a deep respect by the king and society for the perceived directives and wishes of ancestors. The ancestors were represented by a weather god who was the high god, known as Di. This is described by the sinologists Michael Loewe and Edward Shaughnessy:

> *Where weather was concerned, Di's most important function was his control of the rain. Typical charges are "from today, gengzi (day 37) down to jiachen (day 41), Di will order rain", and "Di,*

when it comes to the fourth moon, will order rain". One may note the parallels between the worlds of religion and politics; just as no other Power but Di ever issued orders in the world of the inscriptions, neither did any other person but the king. [181]

It is not explicit, but enough of the picture emerges to how spiritual concerns directed day-to-day affairs in the Shang civilization. Individuals were responsible to their king and to their ancestors and their representative high god. They were obligated to follow orders from the king who had religious authority. Therefore, physical sanctions arose from the spirit realm against those who disobeyed. From a cultural perspective there would not need to be a complex religious basis to royal orders if physical force was sufficient to control society.

The Deuteronomic Code enshrined in the *Book of Deuteronomy*, common to the Jewish Pentateuch and Christian Old Testament, is fundamental to orderly society and was heavily influenced by the Code of Hammurabi. Once the Jews reached the Promised Land after years of wandering, this code was in place as the legal framework for their new society. The Ten Commandments delivered by God are central to the code and the theme of afterlife judgment. The first four are concerned with individual recognition of the authority of God. The remainder express the required moral code of a stable society concluding in Deuteronomy 5:20-21 with:

Neither shall thou bear false witness against your neighbour. Neither shall thou desire thy neighbour's wife, neither shalt thou covet thy neighbour's house, his field, or his manservant, or his maidservant, his ox, or his ass, or any thing that is thy neighbour's.

When the Jews were finally dispersed by Nebuchadnezzar in 587 BCE they could have been destroyed as a potential society forever. They had lost their homes and property and were living as servants and slaves. One thing still held them together: the written word. They carried with them religious texts which sustained their cohesion through exile. Eventually, when the opportunity came, they returned to their homeland and reformed their society. Only written religion was capable of this feat.

For Christianity, the Bible in its current form coalesced through a series of priestly decisions until the compendium of 66 earlier works was largely finalised by the third century CE. Copying the Bible, word for word, where accuracy was paramount, was an important activity until the invention of printing. Its divine authority has endured, from monks in cold stone monasteries carefully copying each word, to pioneers in mid-western wooden plank huts earnestly reading each word.

The Vedas of India, after 1500 BCE, were similarly important to the origin maintenance of the Hindu religion in large Indian societies. Religious morality is a common theme throughout the Vedas.

The Inca civilization of South America did not have writing. They did have quipu, complex collections of knotted cords, which carried symbolic information, certainly for accountancy purposes, but also to represent religious beliefs. Perhaps the largely undeciphered quipu also has elements of religious morality present.

All the major civilizations were buttressed by belief in judgment by gods, and used written language to codify this throughout their lands.

Self-Importance reinforces Adulthood in Afterlife

The signature effect of self-importance in religion is self-preservation which is expressed as adulthood in afterlife, and this requires the spiritual worldview in order to support it. In LMR, purely spiritual religions, the preservation of an individual may be poorly defined as in the Australian Aboriginal tradition religions, or it may be well defined as in the Greco-Roman pre-Christian religion.

Individual self-importance was only weakly expressed before the Neolithic Revolution and settled societies, as the evidence presented in Core Religion is that rebirth afterlife was a satisfactory belief for an extremely long time. Small hunter-gatherer family units within bands did not foster the same level of self-importance which is seen in large societies. This changed with settled society and the Neolithic revolution.

The concept of self-importance has slowly gained within the past 10,000 years until it has become a major element of human civilization. This has occurred for several reasons, and an early driver comes from division of labour which accelerated with the Neolithic revolution. The more specialized a job is, the fewer people in a local community will be able to perform it, so there is recognition of individual uniqueness. Secondly is the effect of kingship, where the larger a society is the greater the ego of the ruler and also the ruling class. Thirdly, self-importance may also be a reaction against the pressures of social cohesion which tries to diminish individuality within society – as the most effective society acts as a single unit in competition with other societies. Perhaps the fourth and most subtle pressure for self-importance comes from judgment in afterlife and multilevel natural selection. As we have seen, this is a key element of the GMR.

The term "Cult of the Individual" was coined by one of the world's greatest sociologists, Emile Durkheim, and perhaps "cult" is a loaded word, but it does convey the strength of this idea. It is a concept that we all happily accept as much as we spread to one other. The primacy of the individual recognizes that every person is unique, has their own potential, their own life to lead as they see fit. It is the ultimate celebration of diversity, of the right to an education, to own personal property, to desire physical and spiritual progression, to gain respect and recognition and to assert independence. It demands recognition of all this by the state. Eventually the concept was formalized into law as human rights.

Stephen Turner, a professor of philosophy, writes about Emile Durkheim's theories on sociology and how, particularly over the last few hundred years, the individual has continually gained in primacy:

> *Together with this controlling function, the State has integrative functions. It is the "protector of the collective ideal". In traditional society, it stood guard over the "cult of the state". Under archaic collectivism in which the individual counted for little the State was everything. In modern societies the relation between the State and the individual is reversed and the individual becomes sacrosanct. Yet without the State thereby losing any of its functions.* [209]

For centuries it was only the chiefs, pharaohs, kings and generals who knew self-importance and fame. The Cult of Individualism applied first at the level of kingship, then diffused slowly downwards into the general population. The ancient viewpoint of rulers being spiritually superior is also unacceptable to educated people today. Today, anyone can aspire to self-importance, fame and celebrity, and be admired for it. Even unborn babies have rights as individuals enshrined in modern culture. After death, there is a great social pressure for belief that the individual endures. Hence, afterlife belief has progressed to reflect improved preservation of identity due to enhanced self-importance, first for the rulers, then for everyone else. It's because eventually the idea of self-importance spreads from the rulers to the ruled, via memes and imitation.

Religion has developed to reflect self-importance and it gives rise to the two major divisions of Mantle Religion:

1) LMR beliefs preserves the individual spiritually, but that is where it ends, in a spiritual state. Where partial reincarnation is considered to happen, preservation of previous identity is soon lost.

2) UMR beliefs preserve the individual spiritually but also promise renewed physical existence, effectively promising a form of personal immortality.

Immortality is the ultimate expression of self-preservation and self-importance.

Judgmental Templates

Nothing angers God so much as division of the Church. Even if we have done ten thousand good deeds, those of us who cut up the fullness of the Church will be punished no less than those who cut His [Christ's] body [on the cross]. Not even martyrdom can wipe that crime. [210]

– Saint John Chrysostom

Saint John Chrysostom, Bishop of Constantinople from 398 to 404 CE, is noted as one of the earliest, most prolific, authors of sermons and homilies. He is honoured by Catholic, Orthodox and Anglican Christians alike. You can almost feel the quill bending to breaking point as he scratched the passage above striving to emphasise: *not even martyrdom* can save, from eternal damnation, those who cause break-up, schism, of the church.

Chrysostom's words resonate within Christianity even today. His intention was to prevent schism and heresy, but the cultural meme behind this fragment of homily is about the protection of society against individuals. Established churches formalize religion within society, and structured society nurtures established churches. They are in symbiosis. A crime against your neighbour may be a crime with limited social impact, but a crime against the established church cuts at the very fabric of society itself. Chrysostom's statement sets clear that an individual who has failed established religion, and ergo society, is permanently doomed no matter what he or she does to redress the failing. It is an effective warning against all others who might make the same error. It also makes clear that individuals are subordinate to religious society, even in afterlife.

Having established that judgment in afterlife exists as a basis for the morality of constraint upon adult individual behaviour within society, it follows that several templates have evolved from the social condition which are then expressed with inferred concepts for judgment-related beliefs. Judgment during afterlife, especially where the church and state are combined, is not to be confused with judicial judgment by any religious hierarchy which is judgment of the living by the living.

Table 5.1 (next page) is a summary of the templates within religious judgment.

In the life-force worldview of Core Religion judgment from the afterlife did not exist. The life-force worldview did, however, permit judgment of the dead by the living. Judgment by funerary ritual is arguably present, but sporadic, throughout the Upper Palaeolithic and is the prototype inferred concept, or paradigm, using a judgmental template. However, because the level of judgment was elementary – simply people deciding whether or not to assist with the rebirth process by providing funerary items within NRT or ERA belief – the spectrum of religious judgment was limited.

The overwhelming application of religious judgment is within the context of belief in a spiritual afterlife and therefore falls within Mantle Religion.

In the spiritual worldview there may be judgment in afterlife of the dead, or judgment of the living from the afterlife realm. Judgment will, and always, has existed in large societies above Dunbar's Number in size. In small societies this is not a requirement to enforce moral standards, as the networks of personal relationships are enough for stability.

There are several different mechanisms for afterlife judgment to operate. Which judgmental mechanism is selected and realized in each different spiritual religion is a result of cultural development. The judgmental mechanisms are discussed in turn in the next section.

GMR:5.1   DRIVERS AND JUDGMENTAL TEMPLATES

SOCIAL CONDITION	JUDGMENTAL TEMPLATE
Social Cohesion	Judgment *in* Afterlife. Judgment *from* the Afterlife
Reward or Penalty for Behaviour in Society	Quality of Afterlife
Social Cohesion *in extremis*	Self-sacrifice of Individuals. Martyrdom

Judgment leads to a variable *quality of afterlife*, or judgment from afterlife leads to a variable *quality of earthly life*. The former is most common but the latter exists particularly with ancestor worship, where propitiation to ancestors is important within a society. The case where judgment is not associated with spiritual afterlife is almost unknown. Even the isolated Australian Aboriginal traditional religions have a form of it.

Afterlife judgment must have a sanction, so quality of afterlife developed, most famously, for example, the places known as Heaven and Hell in Christianity, although there are many variations. Oblivion is frequently considered as the sanction applied to those who fail afterlife judgment in spiritual religions.

End of life judgment is essential to human civilization as this is the most powerful mechanism natural selection has found to generate the fittest individuals functioning within the fittest societies. The evidence is not only clear and present but positively fizzing in front of our faces. The Abrahamic religions promise an eternity of punishment for just a few unrepented transgressions!

Martyrdom is self-sacrifice for religion, but mostly seen as a defence for a religious society. Multilevel natural selection between societies would favour those where individuals would perform self-sacrifice, *in extremis*, as this would be a raised fitness factor. There is a balance. In the case of the citadel at Masada, where Jewish Zealots known as Sicarii were besieged by Romans in 73 CE, hundreds of the Sicarii reportedly committed mass suicide when the walls were breached. If it occurred, this was martyrdom, but the price to their society was so high it was terminal.

Four Judgmental Paradigms

Judgment in afterlife is a template because it is filled in before it can be used. No religion will employ the empty template as a formal belief. Cultures will develop inferred religious concepts or mechanisms which slowly evolve through generations.

Afterlife Judgment

> *Perhaps the most frequently repeated constructionist generalization is that the concept of afterlife judgment was invented by the elite as a tool of social control, to ensure good conduct through the promise of heaven and the threat of hell (e.g. Weber 1922: 140-1; Brandon 1967: 193). This theory is problematic in that the earliest afterlife texts were usually written and read by the elite, but still contains references to judgment. It is clearly the case, however, that the concept was manipulated by the elite.* [211]

– Gregory Shushan

As a researcher of religion, Gregory Shushan observes that afterlife judgment was not invented by the ruling class as a method of social control, but developed organically in society and applied to the rulers as well as the ruled.

There are four discernible separate paradigms which are religious beliefs arising from this template.

Table 5.2 (next page) lists them with a description of their context in major religions.

In the GMR, these classes of judgment are: *ritual, external, internal, and fatalist.* They are known as judgmental paradigms. These will be found in all spiritual religions of large societies and optionally in small ones. Physical judgment after resurrection developed from spirituality.

The judgmental paradigms themselves are concepts which have been adopted variously through differing paths of cultural development, historical accident, and decisions taken by generations of priesthoods.

GMR:5.2   PARADIGMS OF JUDGMENT IN AFTERLIFE

JUDGMENTAL PARADIGM	RELIGIONS AND AFTERLIFE PARADIGM
Ritual *Quality of Funeral*	**Palaeolithic tribes within the life-force worldview**: Neolithic societies. Religions with spiritual afterlife. Aboriginal, native & tribal societies throughout the world. A proper funeral is important to successful afterlife.
External *Ancestor / God*	**Ancestor worship:** Spiritual judgment upon the living or dead. Spiritual religions e.g. Mesopotamia, Ancient Egypt, Greco-Roman, Scandinavian: Spiritual judgment of the dead. Abrahamic religions and Zoroastrianism: Physical judgment after resurrection
Internal *Karma*	**Dharmic religions:** Self-judgment by accumulated good and evil actions and thoughts through physical life are a direct influence on spiritual judgment and the spiritual path through reincarnation cycles determining quality of personal afterlife.
Fatalist *Pre-ordination / Destiny*	**Mesoamerican religions:** Role in society and chance determines quality of afterlife. Roles which benefit the stability of society, e.g. warriors, are strongly favoured.

In some religions there is an amount of crossover, particularly with funerary ritual. In Islam it is regarded as important to bury the newly dead before sunset on the day of death and to orient the body to face the Kaaba at Mecca. Correct funerary practices are believed to reduce the spiritual "pain" of the deceased even before external, supernatural judgment.

Ritual Judgment

Burial is conducted by the living, and, consequently, the corpse is a resource or ritual display manipulated in a contextually strategic way that may invest power and draw attention to the interests of living individuals or communities. [212]

– Simon Hall

The first development of judgment in afterlife, in the life-force worldview, is post-mortem judgment by the surviving tribe and family members. This is a natural progression from the early funerary practices of NRT and ERA, intended simply to assist the rebirth afterlife process. As soon as funerary ritual was formalized in cultures where the dead were laid out properly, given grave goods and interred with ceremony, then the roots of afterlife judgment are present. People then expect a proper funeral to help them with their own afterlife. This expectancy creates the potential for the *withholding* of proper funerary ritual. It becomes a potential punishment for wrongdoers. This is afterlife judgment by funerary ritual. Absence of grave goods and mistreatment of the corpse are the critical elements of a negative ritual judgment.

Within the life-force worldview there is a possible candidate for ritual judgment, dating to at least 25 kya. In 1873, the amateur archaeologist Emile-Valere Riverie de Precourt had excavated what was to become known as the Grimaldi Caves at Ventimiglia, Liguria in Italy. He uncovered several burials with grave goods: red ochre, shells, flints and deer bone. In the sixth cave next to two adult burials with shell, flint and bone grave goods he found a third skeleton, aged about 15 at death, *"face-down with no grave goods"*. [213]

Unfortunately, with such an early discovery, the taphonomic context is lost. Yet, the description is clear enough to consider it a disrespectful burial, absent of ritual, in order to ensure that the deceased did not achieve rebirth. Perhaps this young man had committed a serious crime against his group and was ritually punished after death.

In the emerging spiritual worldview with ancestor worship, secondary burial and skull removal developed as cultural concepts. Partly, this was because they imply a continuation of control by society in a deceased's afterlife. Similarly, this was the case with cremation which was believed in some cultures to be a necessary ritual for releasing the spirit of the dead:

The first Neolithic farming communities in Europe are seen in Greece, from about 7000 BCE. Catherine Perlès, ethnologist, writes about their burial practices:

> *The majority of burials that we can observe, the intramurous pit burials, are actually the exceptions. That they correspond to individuals who were denied 'normal' funerary rituals (sensu stricto), the latter being exemplified by the small cremation burial*

> *ground from Soufli Magoula. This reversal of perspective leads to*
> *the conclusion that funerary rituals, far from been "simple", were*
> *in fact highly invested and demanding in terms of labour, time*
> *and energy.* [214]

Perlès mentions cremation sites and burning pits at Soufli Magouda so perhaps cremation was the normal funeral rite, leaving little evidence. In which case individuals denied cremation funerals were being ritually punished to prevent a spiritual progression.

If so, then this is further evidence that the paradigm shift to a spiritual worldview travelled closely with the Neolithic revolution. The lifestyle change to settled and agricultural communities was carried from the Levant and Anatolia into Greece and on to Europe and with it the meme of spirituality. These earliest settled cultures quickly developed more sophisticated traditions of funerary ritual and must have benefited in terms of social cohesion.

The view in *Merriam-Webster's Encyclopedia of World Religions* is that proper funeral rites were to help the deceased progress spiritually:

> *Indeed, the proper performance of funerary rites was deemed*
> *essential by many peoples to enable the dead to depart to the place*
> *and condition in which they properly belonged. Failure to expedite*
> *their departure could have dangerous consequences.* [215]

Universally, in early settled cultures there was, and often still is, the belief that funerary ritual has some direct effect on quality of afterlife. Enhanced moral behaviour is improved when people think the quality of their own afterlife depends upon the quality of their own funeral. So judgment by funerary ritual is a widespread foundation of early settled societies.

Quality of funerary ritual is the only judgmental paradigm within human control and not the supernatural. It is an imperfect form of afterlife judgment because it has two important drawbacks:

1) Incomplete knowledge of wrongdoings done by the deceased, which is *incomplete access to strategic information.*

2) Difficulty of punishment by funerary ritual because family and society leave themselves at *risk from unsettled or vengeful spirits of the dead.*

Quality of afterlife, depending upon the quality of treatment of the corpse, creates a dilemma. Corpses must be treated with utmost respect, tending, washing or other preparation. It is commonly thought that if a dead person is not disposed of properly, then they will have an unsettled, disturbed spirit which may even return to haunt the living.

Most cultures accepted the memes of supernatural judgment in religious belief which overcame these flaws, solving the problem of incomplete knowledge and deflecting vengeance from the dead.

External Judgment

> *Let them bear, on the Day*
> *Of Judgment, their own burdens*
> *In full, and also (something)*
> *Of the burdens of those*
> *Without knowledge, whom they*
> *Misled. Alas, how grievous*
> *The burdens they will bear!*

> – *The Holy Quran*, 16:25, Trans. by Yusuf Ali, 1934

The Holy Quran of Islam is clear about external judgment. God will perform this on the day of final judgment.

External judgment is supernatural, performed by ancestor spirits or gods. Ancestral judgment of the living certainly dates from the origin of spiritual afterlife itself, which is identified in the GMR to 9000 BCE, at the beginning of the Neolithic revolution. Supernatural judgment by gods is later, unlikely seen anywhere before 5000 BCE.

In ancestor worship, actions in life are thought to be perpetually judged by the ancestors and bad fortune: toothache, failed crops, any afflictions, are the subject of divination to determine which ancestors were displeased. Care and respect for the elderly is important as they may take retribution after death to those failing them. The oracle bone writing of the Shang shows that ancestor worship was an important part of their culture as they strived to divine ancestral opinions and actions through burnt bone. The Shang interpreted the results as delivering judgment upon them while alive and this tradition echoes through 5000 years of Chinese traditional religion.

Supernatural judgment is superior to judgment by funerary ritual for the reason that spirits and gods are assumed to be all-knowing; no criminal deed is secret to the supernatural. Pascal Boyer categorizes this as full access to strategic information. So, criminal behaviour which might escape detection, for example a murder perpetrated away from the society, may never get taken into account by the time the criminal has died. However, spirits and gods will presumably be aware of the deed and can take it into account when judging for quality of afterlife. It goes further than physical actions. Even evil thoughts can be assumed as weighed and taken into account by supernatural forces. Supernatural judgment is the ultimate method of thought control. With supernatural, external judgment angels, gatekeepers, demons and gods all become inserted between the deceased spirit and a joyous final afterlife.

For religions with external judgment it is also the case that priesthoods claim to be able to advance the cause of believers with respect to successfully navigating judgment.

In the Old Kingdom of ancient Egypt, judgment was against any perceived transgression and people could never be fully prepared, by way of funeral ritual, because they could never be fully sure of which charges are to be levelled by the gods. By the time of the New Kingdom, judgment was highly structured. There was a known list of about 40 possible crimes and the deceased in his or her funerary texts would deny all listed crimes and undergo the weighing of the heart. The heart, not the brain, was thought to hold memories and could even give away secrets during the weighing process.

In many cultures ritual judgment works side by side with the more intellectually advanced paradigms of supernatural judgment. The Egyptian mummification ritual was essential to reaching the point of judgment by gods. External judgment developed after ritual judgment but in their culture did not supersede it entirely.

The Australian Aboriginals living a traditional life still believe in pre-Christian judgment. Their spiritual judgment is delivered upon the living not the dead, as Jack David Eller describes:

> *Two recognizably political institutions – agents of social control – outside of the family unit were Kurdaitja and the Red Ochre Men, Kurdaitja or "feather feet" were men who, as supernatural beings, would walk among camps without leaving footprints and punish other men for transgressions, particularly ritual improprieties like showing sacred objects to women or uninitiated men. The Red Ochre Men were another association of powerful ritual leaders to patrolled society and administered similar*

punishments, largely through fear. I watched people run in every direction when they heard the Red Ochre Men were coming. [216]

The Red Ochre Men, rarely seen but reported in central Australia, deliver judgment upon wrongdoers and are believed to be able to "kill" the spirit of an individual, a fate worse even than death.

Judgment was always performed spiritually up until the resurrection religions developed. This new paradigm has a final judgment performed upon living people who have recently been raised from the dead. External judgment is by far the most highly successful interpretation of judgment which is geographically the most widespread in human civilization today.

Internal Judgment

Essentially, the laws of karma state that every action, thought, word, or deed produces a physical or mental effect. It also produces an invisible intention or inclination. This proclivity is stored in your soul (the memory track of your spirit). [217]

– Lynn Anderson

Internal or self-judgment is the measuring of oneself in the afterlife against an invisible all-knowing yardstick. Effectively, it is by karma although other examples exist, which imitate this idea. Anderson describes karma as it is believed in the Dharmic religions, although dispute exists between Dharmic theologians as to whether progressive self-judgment advances by way of deeds and actions alone, or whether thoughts are included. Purity of thoughts raises the bar for successful judgment and achieving the ultimate goal of escaping the reincarnation cycle of samsara.

Karma is not itself considered an act of judgment; it is the accumulation of "evidence" which, in the spiritual afterlife between death and reincarnation, has two results. The first is that karma determines an immediate spiritual reward or punishment for the previous life. After this is finished, of which the duration is also determined by karma, it also sets the path or next direction for the spirit. The next direction is being reincarnated as a greater or lesser person, or even an animal or insect. The result is effectively afterlife judgment spiritually, then physically.

McClelland summarizes:

> *For all practical purposes karma replaces the judging, sentencing, and rewarding power of a Western style personal God.* [177]

In non-Dharmic religions parallels to karma exist. There is a school of thought in modern Wicca and Paganism that the Law of Three (also Threefold Return) should be interpreted as good and evil deeds in one life having repercussions in the *current* life. These repercussions are magnified threefold.

The processes of internal judgment, within religious belief, moderate behaviour in society.

Fatalist Judgment

> *The sign of the day of his birth will govern him until the day of his death – it will even decide his death and so his after-life: it will decide whether he is to die as a sacrifice and thus join the splendid retinue of the sun, or to be drowned and so inhabit the unendingly happy Tlalocan, or to be consigned to the void in the shadowy hereafter of Mictlan. His whole fate is subjected to the strictest predestination.* [218]

– Jacques Soustelle

Least common in society anywhere is *fatalist* judgment by destiny or chance. This is successful afterlife judgment by virtue of a person's role or rank in society, mode of physical death, or even a chance event.

On the face of it, fate-based judgment appears to be unworkable and have no benefit to social cohesion. Why should individuals show moral behaviour, in a large society, when they are destined for a gloomy afterlife? At least with external judgment by God or self-judgment by karma it is feasible to have influence over one's afterlife. Improved behaviour is rewarded by improved probability of a quality afterlife.

Even in a model of fatalist judgment, social cohesion is still possible and this is evident by examining the largest centre for this belief: Mesoamerica.

Seemingly, the Aztec belief in afterlife was strongly fated and destiny driven. People were prejudged by roles in physical life instead of by actions and thoughts of good and evil behaviour. Significantly, warriors were destined for pleasurable afterlife. This becomes important to the religious foundation of Aztec society. Afterlife for warriors meant that they were always "on-side" with established society. When individuals of the establishment, protecting society, are favoured for afterlife, then society itself is buttressed, even by force of arms authorised by religious doctrine. It will encourage young men to become warriors in such numbers that force itself is social cohesion. Aztec society is recognized as one of the most violent in all of human history. Perhaps this is because fated judgment is inferior to external and internal judgment as many people are automatically excluded from pleasant afterlife. Like a pressure cooker, it is inherently dangerous. Is this really correct?

Miguel León Portilla, an anthropologist and historian, disputes the degree of fatalism:

> *This leads us to an evaluation of the popular opinion of Aztec "fatalism." Although the Nahuas certainly believed in the strong influence of the various signs and dates of the tonalpohualli [sacred calendar], it is also true that they considered self-control an important force in overcoming a destiny. This idea is far from what is normally understood as absolute fatalism or blind belief in Predestination.* [219]

The implication is that true fatalism is weakly observed as people had influence over their fate as it was modifiable by individual actions, and amounts to a form of internal judgment.

There is uncertainty over the scope of fatalism when discussing the Mayans. Charles Phillips critiques the common view of Mayan religion, that most people were fated for a gloomy afterlife and only the nobility enjoyed the chance to escape it:

> *According to some scholars the Maya believed that only the noble elite would proceed to the afterlife by way of the tests in the underworld. Other authorities argue that such a religion would not have been generally sustainable and that people at all levels of society must have believed that their ancestors had somehow*

> *triumphed over death and that they themselves might do the same.*
> 220

The implication is that true fatalism was weakly observed if ordinary people could aspire to a quality afterlife.

Shushan describes yet another alternative:

> *It is possible that one's conditions and social status in life are determined by the gods according to one's behaviour, amounting to a form of pre-mortem judgment which has consequences in the afterlife. This was the case in Mesoamerica despite (similarly) concurrent underworld judgment.* [211]

This paradigm has fatalism as a secondary effect arising because supernatural judgment of the living was taking place. Fatalist judgment was actually an indirect form of external judgment. So people might have control over their afterlife by being virtuous which then is rewarded with the appropriate destiny during life, ultimately leading to a better afterlife.

Fatalist judgment buttressed Aztec and Mayan society whether it was interpreted literally, was reduced in scope or degree, or was in the masked form of external judgment.

Christianity wrestles with the implications of fatalist judgment. Many Christians assume that newborns are "innocents" and cannot be considered punishable in afterlife. They are too young to have committed any wrong. Still, the conventional Catholic doctrine includes "original sin", where all humans are born unholy unless they are "saved", at least by baptism. This is an implementation of fated judgment within an external judgmental tradition.

Quality of Afterlife

Quality of afterlife developed synchronously with judgment, as it is not possible to imagine afterlife judgment without some consequences for the deceased. And, further, both could only properly function in the spiritual worldview with adulthood in afterlife. It is only by preservation of identity that the punishment or reward in afterlife makes sense and therefore contributes to the magnification of self-importance seen in all civilized societies.

Quality of Afterlife Paradigms

They also believe that souls have an immortal vigour in them, and that under the earth there will be rewards and punishments, according as they have lived virtuously or viciously in this life; and the latter are to be detained in an everlasting prison, but that the former shall have the power to revive and live again; on account of which doctrines, they are able greatly to persuade the body of the people. [221]

– Flavius Josephus

The Roman era historian, Josephus, writes about the varied resurrection beliefs of the Jews, but this was simply an advancement of much earlier spiritual concepts.

Quality of afterlife is also a mental template, so each religion must develop inferred concepts or paradigms of how successful judgment is rewarded and failed judgment is punished. This is completely dependent upon which afterlife paradigm applies in the religion in question.

Table 5.3 shows in context the different quality of afterlife paradigms seen in spiritual religions.

GMR:5.3   **QUALITY OF AFTERLIFE PARADIGMS**

AFTERLIFE PARADIGM	AWAITING JUDGMENT	SUCCESSFUL JUDGMENT	FAILED JUDGMENT
Spiritual	Spiritual journey	Existence in a spiritual world with ancestors or divinity	a) Exile, hopelessness or spiritual torment b) Oblivion
Reincarnation	Spiritual Bardo	Spiritual reward then physical life as higher person or achieving Brahma / Nirvana	Spiritual punishment then physical life as a lesser person or becoming animal or plant
Resurrection	Spiritual life in Purgatory / Sheol / Hell, or temporary oblivion	Spiritual reward then physical life on earth after final judgment	Spiritual punishment a) Physical life in Hell b) Oblivion

Some competing Neolithic societies had populations most saturated with the memes of all three strands of belief: spiritual preservation of identity, spiritual judgment and differences in quality of spiritual afterlife.

Multilevel natural selection of competing societies ensured that the memes persisted, as they clearly produced fitter societies leading to civilization. All these concepts are deeply embedded in the major religions of today.

Quality of Spiritual Afterlife

In Manianga thought, moral and upright people go to Mpemba, the world of the ancestors. Evil people are prevented from entering Mpemba and are barred from meeting and staying with ancestors. 222

– Elias Bongma

A varying quality of spiritual afterlife is found in all of the spiritual worldview. It began with the origin of ancestor worship and totemism, where the ancestors dwelt at special places in the landscape and in shrines. The effect of judgment on the newly dead spirits was that they could be accepted or rejected by the ancestors. If rejected then exile or oblivion (a "second" death) would follow.

The modern example described by Bongma, concerning the Manianga of the Kongo Kingdom, Central Africa, is quality of afterlife by permission of ancestors. This was common in cultures with ancestor worship.

A further advancement is the belief in a spiritual world, much like the earthly one, and this is known as the sky, earth and underworld, (SEU) paradigm described in the next section. Acceptance or rejection of the dead entering into spiritual worlds is usually at the hands of deities. In ancient Egypt the deity Anubis tested individuals before the afterlife reward of tending the Fields of Osiris. Those failing judgment met oblivion by the monstrous hippo-like Ammut.

The final advancement is spiritual punishment, which is seen in all the higher reincarnation and resurrection religions.

An Islamic belief, still current, is that spirits of the newly dead are cross-examined by two black angels, Munkar and Nakir, and those failing examination are gnawed and flung by 99 dragons with seven heads each – until Judgment Day. [223]

A Tibetan Buddhist belief is that spirits of the newly dead who fail karmic judgment are pierced in the hands, feet and torso with red-hot irons and are progressively cut with hatchets and razors. [224]

Quality of Physical Afterlife

> *If one believes in reincarnation, however, the next world promises to be at best a relative improvement on the current situation, and at worst an unimaginable horror. [...] Waiting for the afterlife will simply plunge you into samsara again, so one had better attain moksha now, in this life, for there is no telling when birth as a human will be in the cards again. This is true for the high-born as well as the low-born, for they are both equally caught in the mesh of Maya and the spokes of samsara.* [225]

– Manish Soni

Imagine that you are thin, tired and poor, hoeing a rocky field under the hot sun, seeing flies circling your hungry children – what is the one thing that you have left? What is the one thing that cannot be taken from you? It is the promise of a better life by reincarnation or resurrection.

In the Dharmic reincarnation religions the result of karma, internal judgment, is subtle. Quality of physical afterlife in the reincarnation religions is by way of becoming different *types* of human, animal or plant in the next life.

Success in acquiring good karma leads to spiritual progression through the wheel of samsara, death and reincarnation, in a better human form until, eventually, *Moksha* is achieved, escape from the life-and-death cycle to a state of spiritual bliss and full enlightenment. Failure to acquire good karma leads not only spiritual pain in afterlife but physical reincarnation as a lesser human, possibly even a rat, or a worm. As Soni writes, seizing one's chance of achieving moksha in the current life is a wise action.

In practice, this belief fosters enhanced moral behaviour leading to social cohesion.

In the Abrahamic religions the final quality of afterlife involves reward or torment *after* physical resurrection. This is after the second or final judgment: on Judgment Day. First judgment is a temporary, spiritual process which may result in time spent in purgatory until the final judgment.

The resurrection religions do not leave choice beyond Heaven and Hell. Accepting Christianity may be seen as a Faustian bargain because although the clarity and quality of afterlife on offer is excellent, there is the high price of failing judgment by God. Arguably, it is better to be reborn with complete loss of identity, like the simple Neanderthal, or reborn as a lesser animal, like the failed Buddhist, than to be perfectly resurrected into an afterlife of burning Hell, tortured for eternity, as a failed Christian. Furthermore, the dice are loaded against the aspiring Christian, as all humans are deemed by their very nature to be sinful (the Original Sin) and would fail judgment even if they did nothing! Christians must actively worship and behave themselves to have any chance of passing judgment. Why?

This situation exists because multilevel natural selection of competing societies has run amok until it has stalled at a local maxima, a plateau. It was after Zoroastrianism and Judaism developed the paradigm of only a single physical life before afterlife, with an eternity of punishment for transgressions against society. This paradigm spread as a meme through the Near East and reached a plateau in the apocalyptic doctrine of newly established Christianity at 100 CE. This is explored in Chapter Seven on Physical Afterlife.

Genetic algorithms are a type of computer software used to find optimal solutions to problems where the combination of variables is too great to be examined sequentially. An important aspect of these is that they will discover improved results only for a period of time until they stall at local maxima. Small, genetic changes in the variables then fail to produce a better result. Only a paradigm shift, a change in the set of variables itself and the way they interact, will allow escape from the local maxima.

Natural selection in the real world is of course far more complex than genetic algorithms which simplify reality. However, we can plainly see the local maxima of quality of afterlife in competing human societies: infinite punishment for just a few unrepented transgressions in a lifetime.

This model of ultimate judgment during afterlife is so successful at controlling individual behaviour that societies with this tradition have come to dominate much of the world today. It will only last until the next paradigm shift is completed, a subject which is explored in the epilogue.

Martyrdom

Martyrdom is a template for the by-passing of judgment to a good quality afterlife. Therefore, culturally specific religious concepts fill the martyrdom template. These define the events and actions to represent an act of martyrdom.

Self-Sacrifice of Individuals

> *Through their sufferings, the martyrs were purified and drew closer to Christ, who, they thought, suffered with them in their trials and carried them to heaven. In their deaths, they were joined with Jesus Christ, the supreme martyr, who delivered them from the pains of this world into heaven. It is noteworthy that the martyrs believed they would be delivered into heaven immediately upon their deaths.* [226]

– Terence Nichols

Such an act is the most powerful meme for group-level benefit at the heart of religious cohesion. This is self-sacrifice, suicide or fatal defence for the cause. These individuals put religious and social considerations above their physical selves, comforted by spiritual gain.

In the first few centuries of the Christian era martyrdom was very common throughout the Roman Empire. It may have been the stoning to death of Saint Stephen, in about 35 CE, which led to the word "martyr" being given new meaning from the original Greek for "witness", as Saint Stephen was thought to have witnessed God. Early Christians believed that they witnessed God – and were killed for it. The witnesses were martyrs.

Paul Middleton presents a study of martyrdom in the Abrahamic religions and makes it clear that the definition of martyrdom is elusive and depends on the viewpoint of the observer. Some martyrs commit suicide, some are murdered, some commit murder and therefore one man's martyr can be another man's terrorist:

> *Above all, I have argued that martyrdom is not a category that can be defined. Martyrdom is essentially created when a narrative about a death is told in a particular way. The central character is not the most important element in the creation of martyrdom; it is the narrator.* [227]

In the mind of the narrator, if he or she sees martyrdom, then the narrator is also making an assumption about afterlife for the martyr – that the martyr has achieved a shortcut through successful judgment. Likewise, no martyr has ever died believing in oblivion. Further, through their deeds they are considered by fellow believers to have attained a glorious afterlife.

Martyrdom is first recognized in Classical Antiquity but the roots of self-sacrifice go much further back.

Queen Puabi of Sumeria lived between 2600 and 2500 BCE, but it is not her life which is remarkable, but her death, or to be more specific, the death of 21 servants interred in her tomb. These sacrifices, mostly women, were effectively grave goods, servants for the afterlife. As the tomb was found intact by archaeologists it is credible from the position of the skeletons that they went willingly to their doom, or were poisoned first.

In the pre-civilization era, 2500 years earlier, when Mesopotamia was sprinkled with simple villages, no group would ever accept the premature death of so many people. It would make no sense. There was a profound change during the transition to civilization. Multilevel natural selection relentlessly rewarded larger, more powerful and fitter societies while the individual diminished in proportion. The spiritual worldview, enabling spiritual afterlife, adulthood in afterlife and afterlife judgment had created the conditions where it made sense for an individual to die for society and religion. Guaranteed quality of afterlife meant that individuals firmly believed that they earned a place in Paradise for their total commitment to the success of their culture. This was, and still is today, a measure of the fittest societies within the religious spiritual worldview.

Aspects of the Spiritual Worldview

Spiritual afterlife drove the development of the overarching spiritual worldview which replaced the Palaeolithic overarching conception that the environment was alive. Instead, the environment became passive or inert but inhabited by spirits. Many aspects of spiritual religion are the completion of this worldview, outside of the direct and primary concern of eschatology.

Sky, Earth and Underworld Paradigm (SEU)

In the spiritual worldview ancestors were originally considered to dwell in shrines, temples and the landscape – on earth, close to the living. This is seen, for example, at Jericho and Çatal Höyük around 7000 BCE, and the early phase of the megalithic cultures on the Atlantic seaboard until about 3200 BCE.

The sky, earth and underworld (SEU) paradigm is often described as primordial, but this is incorrect, as it developed at the end of the Neolithic, and may have contributed to its demise and succession by the Bronze Age. The SEU developed in the formative period of Sumeria in Mesopotamia in the fourth millennium BCE and spread to the emerging Old Kingdom of Egypt before 3000 BCE. The first belief may have just been of a sky realm for ancestors. The earliest Pharaonic afterlife in Egypt was passage to the "undying" stars, those which stayed above the horizon all night. The underworld may first have developed from graves into an underground world, then considered similar to earth, as was the Duat of Egypt and Netherworld of Mesopotamia.

The SEU paradigm was invented in many cultures around the world and had general features. The sky was an upper world over the earth. The sun and moon rode in boats and chariots across the fabric of a dome-shaped sky. Stars were thought to be fixed points of light, lanterns or deities hung far above. Planets were wandering stars. The sky was another land inhabited by gods who cast down lightning, thunder, rain and even meteorites at will. The galactic disk, now only clearly seen when far away from the lights of modern civilization, was known as the backbone of night by African tribes. The earth was a plate or disk, rarely a sphere. The oceans poured over the edge, or met the sky at a mystical boundary. As the paradigm aged, the sky world became open for all who were virtuous and the underworld became progressively gloomier, with caves, black stone walls and dark rivers becoming a prison for the non-virtuous, populated by the tormented dead.

In many cultures the SEU paradigm became layered so that there were multiple sky realms and multiple netherworlds which often coped with granulation in judgment. Only the most virtuous or noble reached the uppermost realms and the most unworthy reached the lowest.

Obviously, the Abrahamic resurrection religions inherited the concept of Heaven or Paradise from the sky realm, and Hell from the underworld of the spiritual worldview. This has led to a complex mesh of ideas seen today, where Heaven and Hell are the spiritual realms *transformed* into tangible physical places. This transformation, evolution of concepts, occurred to support physical resurrection afterlife. Physical afterlife usually involves the earth – so there is the concept of a Kingdom of God, which is to be constituted on the earth itself as well. Variations of these ideas exist between sects in all major religions.

So the Sky and Underworld were always considered spiritual realms only, until the more recent advent of resurrection religion, when they came to be considered as physical realms. The earth was also seen as an exception, where not only the living but spirits of the dead could both exist.

During the Neolithic, isolated stones in the landscape gained a special significance as places for spirits of ancestors, which is explored in more detail in the section on Atlantic Megalithic Religions. Subsequently, in the Bronze Age when god belief largely superseded ancestor worship, standing stones in many locations were considered places for deities and gods. There is a clear reference to this in the Judeo-Christian Book of Genesis 28:18-22:

> *And Jacob rose up early in the morning, and took the stone that he had put for his pillows, and set it up for a pillar, and poured oil upon the top of it. And he called the name of that place Bethel: but the name of that city was called Luz at the first. And Jacob vowed a vow, saying, If God will be with me, and will keep me in this way that I go, and will give me bread to eat, and raiment to put on, So that I come again to my father's house in peace; then shall the LORD be my God: And this stone, which I have set for a pillar, shall be God's house: and of all that thou shalt give me I will surely give the tenth unto thee.*

Travellers in the Middle East viewed isolated stones as inhabited by gods which may assist them on their journey. This biblical passage is very much written with that perspective of the spiritual worldview in mind.

Religion as a Framework for Society

A creation myth conveys a society's sense of its particular identity; it reveals the way the society sees itself in relation to the cosmos. It becomes, in effect, a symbolic model for the society's way of life, its world view – a model that is reflected in such other areas of experience as ritual, culture heroes, ethics, and even art and architecture. [228]

– David Adams Leeming and Margaret Adams Leeming

It is unknown what myths existed in the Palaeolithic before the spiritual worldview but people must have had ancient oral traditions. It is reported that at least 600 flood myths exist in cultures around the world, which suggests that some of them do indeed stretch back to passed down memories of sea level rises during the early Holocene, when the ice sheets melted.

Since the Neolithic, at least, the importance of explaining the origins and history of the world, humans and society has become essential in all cultures, as David and Margaret Adams Leeming describe. Until the science worldview paradigm shift started, religion was fully interwoven into the "ritual, culture heroes, ethics, and even art and architecture" of every society. In *A Dictionary of Creation Myths*, the Adams Leemings frame much of the results of their investigation into divisions by religion.

Early peoples had logical thinking long before science, so creation and historical myths are a logical attempt to make sense of the world. This might be considered naïve today but it certainly cannot be considered irrational. Additionally, religion was never separate from the worldview in which people lived until the modern era and, because religion had to resolve personal mortality – the one question larger than any creation or historical myth – it inevitably had to resolve lesser questions of origins as well.

Where creation myths involve gods, there will typically be a genealogy of the gods explaining their origins and roles. Some will cross over into afterlife beliefs where they facilitate external judgment. In resurrection religions, the creator god will facilitate the physical afterlife process itself.

Once religious cohesion made possible cities and whole civilizations, religious restrictions and duties became embedded in many aspects of domestic and personal life. This was at several levels. At the social level, by backing the authority of the elite and the judicial system itself; domestically by marriage rituals, choice of school, and other formal events; personally by food restrictions, clothing norms, forms of worship: the examples are legion. The specific areas under religious control are not so important. From the perspective of multilevel natural selection, religion buttressing stable society, it simply does not matter which of hundreds of different memes of control are accepted by individuals. The whole affects a positive feedback to group-level cohesion.

For most of recorded history there has been a close association between the ruling hierarchy and religious hierarchy, implying joint judicial authority.

In ancient Egypt the pharaoh was considered a living god, king and an honorary if not active chief priest. The emperors of classical Rome and dynastic China assumed divine authority and title of chief priest. Similarly, the kings of Sumeria, Babylonia and Assyria all had the title of chief priest. In medieval Europe the kings assumed a divine right and ruled with the auspices of the pope whose monasteries usually delivered local justice. These examples of religious judicial authority were not in themselves sufficient for a large society to be stable in the long-term – it is the facade of religious order. But the real force behind religious order is the universal belief in afterlife judgment.

Until recent centuries anyone who had profound doubt about the truth of the prevailing religion of their society, and voiced it, were risking their neck. They would be exiled if they were lucky or horribly tortured and killed if they were not. Strong belief in religion was often shown by 100 per cent of the population, an incredibly high percentage compared to today. By making outcasts of non-believers, early rot in the structural integrity of society is cut out. The most rebellious people would go no further than rejecting some small aspects of their prevailing religion. For example, Martin Luther was primarily concerned with ecclesiastical corruption. For a protestant to reject all of Christianity was inconceivable.

Fairness in judicial systems is also secular. A judicial system enshrining religious principles can be incomprehensible from the perspective of individuals. The Shari'ah Law penalty of stoning and imprisonment for rape victims only makes sense where individuals are wholly subordinate to society. This becomes a collective constraint upon the individualism of all women in a society.

Arguably, the secular common law and inquisitorial legal systems are framed by the science worldview, which is why there is a separation of church and state and subsequent dichotomy between secular and religious legal systems. Nevertheless, religion is still an invisible buttress to law as described by Mark Juergensmeyer:

> *These four aspects of law – its reliance on ritual, on tradition, on authority, and on universality – give law a sacred quality and link law with religion as matters of faith.* [229]

Religion is like the buffers on the end of a railway track, if the runaway train of social collapse is underway, then complete disaster may yet be averted.

6 ◆ LOWER MANTLE RELIGION: SPIRITUAL AFTERLIFE

Spiritual Progression

Lower Mantle Religion includes all religions where a spiritual existence is the final state after death. It also includes religions where ancestral spirits might be reborn but their prior identity fades and there is no concept of a further physical life as an adult with prior spiritual identity preserved.

Nature Spirits and Gods

> *People do not invent gods and spirits; they receive information that leads them to build such concepts. Particular systems in the brain specialize in particular aspects of objects around us and produce specific kinds of inferences about them. Now we may wonder what 'pushes' the systems to pay attention to particular cues in our surroundings and produce inferences. Part of the answer is that such mental systems are driven by relevance.* [5]

– Pascal Boyer

Boyer comments on the question: What is the motivation of having gods and spirits?

There was never an organized motivation to create them. Multilevel natural selection amongst the earliest competing societies meant that those which became saturated with the template meme of the spiritual worldview were fittest; those which adhered to the old life-force worldview were weakest.

The belief in spirit and spirituality is inference from the existence of the invisible atmosphere and that it is highly relevant to people because people need this invisible medium to stay alive. A further inference made about the invisible life-giving spiritual medium is that it becomes life-taking when people die. The idea of people existing in a spirit-form is highly relevant because it is fundamentally driven by self-importance, requiring the preservation of individual identity.

The spiritual worldview solved the problem of preservation of personal identity in afterlife and also allowed for the concept of judgment in afterlife to work – critical to large societies bigger than Dunbar's Number in size. While these beliefs became established as ancestor-worship and totemism, there was a parallel establishment of belief in nature spirits, spiritual animism. These have innumerable forms representing streams, trees, mountains, the sky, and so on.

A volcano erupts because the mountain spirit is angry. A mountain can be thought of as having a stronger spirit than a tree because it is much more massive. Often the sky was the strongest spirit of all as it even overreaches mountains. Spiritual personification of the environment is the root of polytheism, the belief in many gods.

Gods developed from nature spirits and some legendary ancestors primarily because they are communally significant and can be venerated throughout a whole culture or civilization. Gods are also highly relevant to the SEU paradigm of the spiritual worldview. In the SEU, where spirit realms exist as analogous to the earthly realm, the rulers of them are by definition gods. In ancient Greece the earth became personified as Gaia, a mother goddess. The sky became personified as Zeus, a father god, and the underworld personified as Hades.

In many cultures the earth was strongly associated with a mother goddess, while storm and weather gods were associated with a father god. These gods were to maintain a particular importance, and the evolution of them are explored in the next section.

Gods evolved by representing abstract concepts as well, particularly matters relating to life and death. Anubis, the jackal-headed god of ancient Egypt, was originally thought to be the god of the dead, as jackals scavenge like hyenas, and then over centuries became more concerned with the process of dying itself. The Classical Greeks interpreted Anubis as Hermes, a messenger god, and similarly the Roman god of travellers, Mercury; both due to their earlier roles facilitating the spiritual journey of the dead.

Gods even came to represent the abstract matter of human lifespan. Each of the three Fates or Moirai would have part of the task of spinning the thread of life, measuring it and cutting it.

Fertility gods are strongly associated with Demeter, a harvest goddess, as a bountiful harvest was of utmost importance to settled societies. Rain from the male sky fertilising mother earth was considered like-for-like sympathetic magic with human reproduction. At the same time, people observed the cyclical nature of the process of growing crops through the seasons, and associated the scything of crops with dying, winter as death and spring as rebirth. The Grim Reaper, popularly known in Europe, with a sickle and sometimes an hourglass, representing lifespan, came to symbolize death, and developed from the harvest symbolism.

Storm gods from Breathing Symbolism

This Storm-god concept has been one of the most potent forces in the evolution of the religious experience of early man. To a certain degree, it has evolved into the mythical foundation of the modern conception of God. [230]

– Alberto Ravinell Whitney Green

In the year 1658, working by flickering candlelight as the winds swept in from the North Atlantic, the Archbishop of Armagh, James Ussher, extracted the ages of Adam's descendants from the Christian Bible and computed the date of Creation as Sunday, October 23, 4004 BCE. This is now a quaint side note in historical thought but, it seems, with a slight modification, he might have hit the nail on the head: *4004 BCE approximates the birthdate of the Abrahamic God himself.*

Before this time the only human-like spirits were ancestors. It was in the fifth millennium BCE that superhuman spirits, the first gods, were conceived. This belief enabled cities to develop.

Alberto Green's work, *The storm-god in the ancient Near East*, details the development of the long and deep European and Middle Eastern tradition of storm gods. He traces their history culminating in God:

Anthropological and archaeological evidence relative to the meaning of the Storm-god motif within the Anatolian heartland dating as early as 7000 BCE traces the theme of a Storm-god from his zoomorphic antecedent in Çatal Höyük through his anthropomorphic appearance in the cultural assemblages of the historic period at the turn of the second millennium BCE. [230]

He also pinpoints the emergence of the concept at the dawning of Mesopotamian civilization and its importance due weather extremes and floods:

> *The most dreaded peril, which had menaced the inhabitants of this area since prehistoric times, were the raging and destructive floods. This was metaphorically the "violent storm" of the early mythical accounts. This was constantly evident in the threatening dark clouds, the vicious streaks of lightning, and the crashing thunder that periodically menaced the region. They presaged the wrath of an angry Storm-god.* [230]

Green conjectures that the reason the principal god in some many cultures was the storm god stems from the violent and destructive power of storms, lightning and thunder preceding heavy rain. Such rains were often welcome as the climate grew steadily drier and dependence upon crops remained absolute. So the storm god was associated with fertility as well as destruction. There were many storm gods including even a desert storm god, Ilumer, who was never benevolent.

However, in the GMR the principal reason for the supreme importance of storm gods is breathing symbolism due to air being essential to life and storms are violent masses of moving air. When a man can barely blow away a feather, and yet that breath is essential to his life, then how much more powerful must a storm god be when it can uproot whole trees? The fact that storms are accompanied by rain reinforces this symbolism, as water is the third essential for life (after blood and air).

The three principal gods of Mesopotamia at the time of Eridu, the first ever city, were of sky, air and water. Storm gods were usually the high god of Semitic, Middle Eastern cultures – and this continued until all gods were subsumed into the single Abrahamic God.

The Hattian culture which ruled most of Anatolia from 2500 BCE for 500 years had a storm god as their high god. Archaeologist Piotr Taracha summarizes:

> *The fact that the pantheon in Hattusa is headed by the Storm god and Sun-goddess comes as no surprise, considering that the situation is the same in the case of many local pantheons in central and northern Anatolia. The Hattian name Taru, like Hittite Tarhuna and Luwian Tarhunt(a), refers to the whole category of storm-gods who were worshiped outside the capital under a variety of local names or nicknames. The Palaic Storm-god also*

> *bears the Haitian name or epithet Zaparwa/Ziparwa (c.f. a similar*
> *epithet of the Storm-god of Hatti, Taparwasu).* [231]

The Aramaeans, also known as Chaldeans, were a dis-unified and relatively short-lived culture, mostly in Syria, which is most famous for its widespread language Aramaic, probably spoken in Judea at the time of Christ. The scholar of Semitic peoples Edward Lipinski examines Aramaean religion:

> *Our knowledge of the religion and the social organization of the*
> *early Aramaeans is very limited, but we know for sure that their*
> *main god was the Storm-god Hadad and that this god is often*
> *represented in the Syro-Hittite art of the 10th-8th centuries B.C.*
> *standing on the back of a bull. Although this iconographic pattern*
> *was inspired by the Hittite religious art, it expresses the belief that*
> *the wild bull, that became the visible support of the*
> *anthropomorphic Storm-god, assists the "Aramaean" totemic*
> *group.* [232]

The Phoenicians were an eastern Mediterranean maritime trading culture of Canaanite origin. They occupied the coastal Levant and Sinai from about 2300 BCE until decline and conquest by the Persians in 539 BCE.

Baal is known as their high god, but this name simply means "Lord" and there were several manifestations of him. Mark Smith in *The Early History of God* presents the context of the Phoenician high gods:

> *That the biblical baal was a Phoenician god with power over the*
> *storm may be deduced from extrabiblical texts. The baal is*
> *identified either with Melqart or Baal Shamem. Nothing in the*
> *meagre Phoenician sources bearing on this god directly*
> *contradicts an identification with Melqart. [...] The evidence for*
> *Baal Shamem is manifestly meteorological. Attested in*
> *Phoenician inscriptions at Byblos [...] Baal Shamem had power*
> *over the storm, which is mentioned in a curse in the treaty*
> *between Esarhaddon and Baal II of Tyre.* [233]

Melqart was probably the city god of Tyre and of uncertain attributes.

The Canaanite storm god Baal, described in Ugarit clay tablets as a rider of the clouds, was clearly from a long tradition of similar high gods in many Near East cultures. His principal temple was atop Mount Zaphon, north-west Syria, and this was the same location as the earlier Hittite storm god Tarhuna.

Storm gods symbolic of the powerful forces of moving air never lost their seniority in polytheism: Enlil, Hadad, Ashur, Adad, Taru, Tarhuna and Baal Shamem endured, just changing in name with each new culture. Zeus in Greece, adopted as Jupiter in Rome, capriciously wielded thunder and lightning bolts and is most accurately described as a storm god too.

Baal proved to be the second-to-last of the line of storm gods in this veritable backbone of the spiritual worldview. Yahweh was the last of all.

Birds, Psychopomps and "Killed" Objects

Among all the peoples of the eastern Mediterranean basin the idea was anciently spread that the essence or the spirit which animates man escapes from the body in the shape of a bird, especially a bird of prey, for in order not to perish this soul must feed on blood, the principle of life. The gravestones and funeral vases of Greece give us a large number of representations of the bird-soul. [234]

– Franz Cumont

Birds have a long association with afterlife because of the triple link with egg symbolism, air as a spiritual essence and carrion eating during excarnation. During the life-force worldview, when rebirth belief prevailed, an elaborate burial at Vedbaek had an infant laid upon a swan's wing, which may have been syncretic of air (breathing) and egg symbolisms. Bird imagery was very important in the Temples of Rebirth for its egg symbolism, however, this was just before the paradigm shift to spirituality.

A psychopomp is a spiritual being who guides a newly deceased person's spirit to the place of judgment or ancestral realm. With the advent of spiritual afterlife bird symbolism never faded but became transformed into a progression of the spirit, as described by the archaeologist Franz Cumont. His own passing in 1947 meant he never saw the powerful bird symbolism at Çatal Höyük, where there are wall paintings of the headless deceased below giant swooping vultures. This vulture art, dating to the seventh millennium BCE, looks like the pitiful dead are being harassed. Instead, the birds could well be the earliest known psychopomps signifying a spiritual transition of the dead. Spirits becoming birds, taking to the air for the journey to join the ancestors, was a belief which ultimately spread through Syria, to Greece and Rome, and eastwards to the Mongols of Central Asia.

The vulture goddess was very significant in ancient Egypt for its link with motherhood, regeneration and rebirth. The Egyptians developed a complex view of the human person, which was believed to have numerous spirit-like forms with different characteristics. A very early spiritual concept from the Old Kingdom was the ba which represented the identity and personality of a person. This left the body after death and was imagined as a bird, and so was its hieroglyphic symbol.

In China, the crane has long been thought to fly the spirits of the dead to the afterlife, and a statuette of a crane was often laid upon a coffin during a funeral. They have since become symbolic of longevity and happiness. The immortals of Taoism are also represented by cranes.

Charon ferrying the dead to Hades across the River Styx is a well-known psychopomp from Classical Antiquity, and clearly this echoes the Mesopotamian ferryman of the dead, Urshanabi, some 2000 years earlier. In ancient Egypt, Amentet was the goddess who represented the netherworld and welcomed the dead to it with spiritual bread and water before they went for judgment.

Belief in psychopomps is entirely within LMR as they are not required in the rebirth belief of Core Religion, and they are omitted from the Upper Mantle Abrahamic and Dharmic religions. For example, the Grim Reaper has long been the personification of death and a guide for deceased spirits, but he has never been part of Christianity.

It was the ERA belief of the life-force worldview which was mostly destroyed and the most radically transformed in the spiritual paradigm shift. Rather than grave goods being included for ensuring strength and skills in the next physical life after rebirth a new concept developed. It was that of sending burial goods into the spiritual afterlife with the deceased person. So, pots and weapons were considered for use in the spiritual realm. It is the understanding of this spiritual belief which is confused with ERA in the interpretation of Palaeolithic graves.

Sometimes, just including grave goods for spiritual use was not enough. Families of the deceased were very concerned that earthly goods should actually reach the spirit realm and took a further step to ensure it happened. The Etruscans, which preceded the Romans in central Italy, left significant evidence of this. Nancy De Grummond, archaeologist, writes of their burial practices:

> *Also in the tomb were two crushed shin guards and a shield of bronze, broken and folded. Again from Bomarzo, but dating considerably earlier (6th—5th century BCE) is a shield in the Vatican (Buranelli 1992, 100), covered with cuts and gouges and folded in three and deposited in the burial. This kind of practice is regularly referred to as "killing" the object, so that it can accompany the deceased to the afterlife. [...] Of course the very act of cremating was intended to make the human body undergo a transformation releasing the spirit to another world. Similarly burning grave goods on a pyre meant that they were destined for another kind of existence.* [235]

The deliberate breaking of funerary objects is like-for-like sympathetic magic. It is a worldwide tradition and was certainly intended to "kill" items, thereby sending them into the afterlife with the deceased. It is the best signature of the belief in spiritual worldview and afterlife; therefore this practice is wholly within LMR.

Full cremation began in the Neolithic and was seen in Greece at 7000 BCE. It continues today with the belief of spiritual release undiminished. This was also the fate of the old Palaeolithic charcoal breathing tradition, transformed within the spiritual paradigm.

Natural Spiritual Traditions (NST)

All of the Natural Rebirth Traditions within the life-force worldview were inherited and transformed within the spiritual worldview. The main transformation was to change their focus from physical rebirth to assisting with spiritual progression in the afterlife. Therefore, these new beliefs are defined as a separate group within the GMR known as Natural Spiritual Traditions (NST).

Unlike the NRT for rebirth which comprised all of Palaeolithic religion, the NST were secondary, or supporting of afterlife beliefs within the larger formalized spiritual religions prevailing in settled cultures. For example, shell motifs on pre-Christian Roman coffins were to assist spiritual progression but were peripheral to the whole Greco-Roman religion itself.

Due to the importance of agriculture in the Neolithic revolution, the late arriving beliefs within PRT, inspired by observations of plant renewal in the life-force worldview, developed further into many different forms. All these forms were integral to spiritual afterlife belief: greenstone symbolism, the Green Man, pinecone symbolism as well as Grove Worship and the concept of a "Tree of Life".

Blood Symbolism – Spiritual

> *The human burials, as noticed at Burzahom, reveal striking parallels with those obtained in comparable times at Çatal Höyük. Some similarities can also be noticed in those from Tepe Hissar and Sialk. The use of red ochre seems to have been prevalent in Russia also.* [236]

> – Amalananda Ghosh

The ROT was a major part of the NRT of the life-force worldview and was global in reach. It was inevitable that the believed renewal powers of ochre would be preserved into the emerging spiritual worldview, and indeed there is a clear, but not absolute, distinction present in the archaeological record for this transformation.

In the Palaeolithic, ochre was applied to primary burials. As previously described, this procedure magically harnessed the power of blood in the belief it would ensure rebirth occurred. It often happened, as at Paviland, Sungir and Skateholm, that the large quantity of ochre was used causing the bones to become stained over many years, as the ochre dispersed through the flesh as it decayed.

In the Neolithic, ochre was applied to secondary burials. First beginning in the Levant, this is usually after excarnation or a temporary burial when the skull and major bones were later recovered and ochre painted. This procedure also magically harnessed the power of blood – either in the belief that it would assist in maintaining the ancestor in the totemic place of spiritual afterlife, or for facilitating partial reincarnation.

The religious practice of secondary burial of painted bones is seen throughout the Neolithic in Europe and the Levant, but less frequently by the Bronze Age due to the fading of ancestor worship. Some primary ochre burials did still occur for a while. Although this practice has disappeared completely, secondary burial persists even to the present day in a few remote cultures such as the Aboriginals of Arnhem Land.

At the Natufian settlement of Abu Hureyra, about 9000 BCE, many of the stone artefacts, grinding dishes and querns from the earliest Phase One pre-agricultural, wild rye harvesting period show traces of red ochre. The first phase of this culture may have held the life-force worldview and developed concepts of spirituality by Phase Two when cinnabar occurred in burials. Traces were found in two: a child's skull and the front teeth and jaw of an adult. Cinnabar is not found locally and may have come from Anatolia through trade routes.

Cinnabar is mercury sulphide ore and a more rarely seen alternative to ochre, also seen sprinkled upon the deceased and in graves. Harder than ochre, it can still be crushed to a powder and mixed with water to make vermilion for ritual blood with a fresh look, whereas ochre always has the hue of drying blood. Cinnabar was used in funerary ritual only from the Neolithic and appears to be a good signature of spiritual beliefs. Jasper necklaces and beads are commonly seen in burials from this time, and may similarly represent the power of blood.

At Çatal Höyük, ochre and cinnabar stained skulls and skeletons were found from several layers. However, only a small number of them compared to the approximately 500 burials known at this site. Unfortunately, confusion in record keeping in the 1960s means that the exact number and position of the ochre specimens is unknown.

Painted skulls are seen in the Levant, Jordan and Syria, but more rarely in Anatolia. The settlement of Hajji Firuz, in Iran, dating to about 5500 BCE, shows significant ochre usage in secondary burials, applied most heavily on skulls. Ochre was also used on some primary burials and the mass grave of victims of a massacre.

At the settlement of Sialk on the Iranian plateau, ochre is found on the bones of many burials, some of which were flexed or buried under houses.

The transformation of red ochre use in the spiritual paradigm shift is seen in predynastic Egypt in the fourth millennium BCE. Ochre was still present in a burial context right up to the time their sophisticated spiritual religion prevailed. At Tell el-Farkha necropolis in Memphis, in the First Dynasty, niches for corpses were painted with ochre, clearly symbolism associated with spirituality.

Kashmir in India was home to the Neolithic Burzahom people who lived in huts, made pottery, domesticated animals, and survived by hunting, fishing and foraging. At 2000 BCE they were performing secondary burials. Red ochre was applied directly to limbs of articulated corpses which were often flexed and then placed in pits or under house floors.

Ochre is seen in an Olmec burial at Fabrica San Jose, Oaxaca, Mexico, about 600 BCE and clearly the spiritual significance of the colour red endured there. Twelve hundred years later, powdered cinnabar was important in the funerary rituals of Mayan nobles. David Drew describes the tomb of Yax K'uk Mo at Copain:

> *The burial and the whole chamber had also been plastered with an enormous amount of bright red cinnabar or mercury sulphide, a compound so poisonous that it had initially delayed entry into the tomb, but which to the Maya represented sacred blood and resurrection.* [203]

The burial of a fifth century royal at Calakmul was copiously covered. Similarly, the famous burial tomb of Lord Pakal under the Temple of Inscriptions, Palenque, had cinnabar spread throughout just before it was finally sealed about 685 CE.

Ochre painting in secondary burials continued until the Renaissance period when European exploration and colonization overran many cultures. The native peoples of the Americas, Australian Aboriginals, New Guinea tribesmen and Polynesians modified their funerary practices under the influence of Christianity. Also, ochre painting became abstracted from funerary ritual itself, and religious temples became coloured with it instead, as seen in Japan and Crete.

Breathing Symbolism – Spiritual

Throughout the Upper Palaeolithic and certainly much earlier, when the life-force worldview prevailed, early humans hammered cupules in prominent rocks to make them "breathe" and interpreted them as "alive" in sympathy with everything else in the environment. However, when the spiritual worldview emerged landscape cupules lost their importance. Ritchie describes the fate of cupules when megalithic stone circles were first being built in Scotland:

> *The evidence rather points to the conclusion that the cups were made while the stones lay flat on the ground, before they were erected as members of their respective circles. [...] The recumbent stone at Braehead of Leslie rests upon another stone, which has four cup-marks on its upper surface. These marks are so placed, right underneath the recumbent stone that they could not possibly have been made while that stone occupied the present site, which is evidently its original position in the circle. Indeed, the use of a cup-marked stone as a support for the recumbent stone rather indicates that the cups had become obsolete before the circle was erected.* [62]

The spiritual worldview did not make cupules completely obsolete; they maintained a useful existence in tombs, temples, cairns, barrows and other funerary places. These funerary cupules were transformed within spiritual beliefs and had a continued association with breathing air, now in the context of maintaining ancestor spirits.

The interpretation of ammonite spirals, seen during the life-force worldview Mesolithic cemetery at Aveline's Hole, was similarly transformed. Cupules, spirals and ring-mark designs on tombs all capture the essence of *moving* air. These facilitated the spiritual existence of ancestors or ensured they achieved partial reincarnation.

Charcoal beliefs were also transformed within spiritual religion. Christopher Daniell, archaeologist, investigated the practice of including charcoal in medieval graves in England, primarily between 800 and 1200 CE, and summarizes:

> *It is possible that the use of and reasons for charcoal in graves changed over time, for two different phases of charcoal burial were discovered during the Castle Green excavations, being probably dated to the tenth and eleventh centuries (Shoesmith 1980: 25-8). Whatever the reason for the grave linings, they are all found in Christian settings and only a minority of graves had them. Their significance is probably therefore a combination of social status and religious belief.* [237]

The use of charcoal so recently, halfway into the Christian era, is puzzling, but there are several theories: that it was a preservative for the body protecting it from the ground, a vivid marker, symbolic of cremation, symbolic of penance or a status item.

In the GMR the original Palaeolithic association of charcoal with visible air (smoke) as breathing symbolism may have persisted, or it may have been "rediscovered" in medieval times. Charcoal is seen in Isle of Wight Bronze Age barrows, which is equally curious when the skeleton itself is missing! In the Lofkend Iron Age cemetery, Albania, dated 1000 to 600 BCE, the skeleton of Tomb 50 has deliberate staining with bitumen – a charcoal proxy. Charcoal burial is also reported in Scandinavia, and in France, including St Martin of Tours. If it is a sporadic and dimly remembered tradition from prehistory then during the Christian era, it may have been believed by some in medieval times that charcoal facilitated the process of spiritual progression into the afterlife. Many charcoal burials are in cathedrals, so the believed powers of charcoal, could have been a secret known only to senior clergy.

Egg Symbolism – Spiritual

> *Eggs are represented on Roman sarcophagi, and funerary offerings of eggs, whether real or made of clay or stone, were common in early Greece, perhaps with the wish that the spirit of the departed may have a renewal of life. Such associations are found widely across Europe.* [238]

> – Frederick Simoons

Ostrich eggs are the largest type of egg and these were regularly placed in high-status graves and tombs in both predynastic Egypt and early Mesopotamia. Sometimes there were whole or part eggs or ones made into containers. Richard Zettler, anthropologist, and colleagues comment:

> *They might have been intended as food offerings for the dead, yet all the eggs were pierced at the end, indicating that the contents had been removed before the eggs were buried.* [239]

The important observation that the eggs were empty very much undermines the theory that these were spiritual meals. In the GMR it is the egg symbolism itself which is important and this became transformed from the ART beliefs of the Palaeolithic to magically assist with spiritual progression of the dead.

Kenneth McNamara writes about the history of fossilized sea urchins (echinoids) in various cultures and notes their importance as thunderstones, amulets to protect against lightning, but also their long use in funerary traditions:

> *Arguments for fossil sea urchins having a similar ritual significance in earlier Neolithic times are supported by the discovery at La Motte St. Jean, Safine-et-Loire in France of a polished axe and three fossil sea urchins. Likewise, late first to third century remains of Gallo-Roman dwellings, temples, and wells at the Fort de Rouvray, near Rouen in France, contained a cache of twenty small Neolithic axes, along with twenty-two fossil sea urchins.* [240]

In the GMR the evidence of fossilized sea urchins as egg symbolism ensuring rebirth afterlife in the Mesolithic enables us to interpret the presence of these fossils in later Bronze Age burial mounds across Europe. When the spiritual worldview came to prevail in Europe the belief in the magical power of egg-shaped stones, including fossil sea urchins, also underwent a transformation into a spiritual tradition. They also now ensured spiritual progression for the deceased into afterlife.

As examples of funerary goods, fossil sea urchins were to attain afterlife and the axes were to be used as a tool or weapon when arriving there.

Ostrich eggs were most desirable but often expensive and difficult to obtain, so smaller bird and reptile eggs were also used. A plate of unbroken hen eggs was found in a Roman tomb on the island of Cyprus and is now in the Palaipafos Museum. However, egg substitutes in stone were most commonly used. Graziano Baccolini, chemist, identifies egg symbolism present in virtually all Etruscan tombs:

> *These connections between Montovolo, an Etruscan oracular center, Delphi and the egg as symbol of all the archaic civilizations, brought me to realize that the stones with egg shape on the Tombs of the Etruscan necropolis of Marzabotto were not simple cippis, tomb's segnacolum (signal) as reported by all the Academic and the most famous Etruscologists, as Pallottino, but these oval stones were Etruscan important religious symbols, indicating the egg, symbol of rebirth, and that therefore they can be connected to the symbol of the presumed oval stone...* [241]

Baccolini is dismayed at the lack of recognition of eggs as funerary objects directly facilitating afterlife and at the number of egg representations in stone at archaeological sites that have not been recognized in context, and subsequently lost.

Although he uses the term "rebirth", in the GMR, within the spiritual worldview paradigm, egg symbolism facilitated spiritual progression or partial reincarnation. Stone eggs are seen in tombs in many Mediterranean cultures. On Malta there are regular findings of "slingstones" which are biconical or ellipsoidal and are assumed to be for hunting. However, generally they are too large for this purpose, and the amount of game present in Malta was always minimal in any case. Unless they were for warfare in the afterlife there is no other reasonable explanation than egg symbolism.

It is possible the veneration given to snake gods by Native Americans and to the rainbow serpent of Australian Aboriginals stems from the association of reptiles with the life-giving power of eggs. A goddess found in an Etruscan tomb had snakes wrapping each arm. Similarly, the strongly negative depiction of a serpent (and all snakes) in the Judeo-Christian *Book of Genesis* is a mythological rejection of pre-Abrahamic serpent and egg-facilitated afterlife beliefs, but this has not been completely successful.

Christianity has inherited and reinterpreted egg renewal. Easter, celebrating the resurrection of Christ, has long been associated with eggs. The Bible does not associate them with the resurrection directly but several extra-biblical traditions have arisen concerning eggs and the women followers of Christ, particularly in the Eastern Church.

Eggs painted and illustrated on Etruscan tomb walls, such as at the Tomb of the Lioness and Tomb of the Leopards, was an idea later adopted by the Romans. In art, a deity is often holding out an egg for a deceased person which may represent an invocation to the gods to offer afterlife to those entombed. A further derivative of egg symbolism is the cross within a circle, or sun-cross. This is sometimes seen on funerary stones and may originally represent an egg symbolically hatching. Perhaps this was interpreted to have stronger magical renewal properties than a dormant unhatched egg. The four-armed sun-cross is the world's oldest religious symbol but in its most abstracted form can mean almost anything.

Shells and shell symbolism are extremely common in burials within the spiritual paradigm and there is an uninterrupted usage in many cultures throughout the Neolithic. These are however, now commonly considered by anthropologists to represent an afterlife journey through a watery part of a spirit world. By way of example, James Fitzsimmons, anthropologist, writes of the funerary practices of the Mayan royals and observes their grave goods of arranged shells:

> *Despite their limited distribution, these practices clearly represent specialized versions of broader lowland beliefs; the large quantities of Spondylus and other shells found throughout lowland royal – and elite – burials probably represent similar ideas. The lord is physically, if not iconographically, set within the surface of the watery Underworld.* [242]

However, in the GMR, shells were originally believed to be egg substitutes to magically harness the like-for-like rebirth power of eggs. Where they are used in the context of burials within the spiritual worldview the essence of the earlier belief is still present but instead they ensure a spiritual progression. Where they occur in bands about the head, feet or pelvis this is likely a symbolic hatching or simply a more powerful magical emphasis represented by numerical strength.

Scallop shell embossing is the most common motif on Roman coffins made of lead and has long been associated with belief in a spiritual journey into the afterlife. Again, this was not because of the journey over the waters of the River Styx, but spiritual progression instead. The goddess Venus being born in a shell is a mythical use of this religious symbolism. Scallop shells found their way into Christianity as a symbol of baptism from its first beginnings: spiritual awakening and admission to the church.

Plant Symbolism – Spiritual

> *Into the Song dynasty, jade objects were buried with the wealthy to confer immortality and happiness in the afterlife. A piece of jade in the mouth of the deceased was believed to prevent decomposition of the body.* [243]

> – Milton Walter Meyer

Green colour symbolism is seen in many cultures from the Neolithic period onward, and the best preserved evidence of this are grave goods in the form of greenstone artefacts. These are made from jadeite, malachite, serpentine, nephrite, or any green-hued crystal. The high number of greenstone and malachite beads as funerary items in the Levant suggest plant renewal beliefs originating in the Natufian period and persisting for thousands of years.

Anthropologist Manuel Aguilar-Moreno in *Handbook to Life in the Aztec World* describes greenstone symbolism in Aztec Mesoamerica:

> *The greenstones, such as jadeite, diorite, and serpentine, were the most important precious stones in Mesoamerica. Jade beads were placed on a corpse's mouth as payment for the trip of the soul of the dead through the underworld, a tradition also found in ancient China. The greenstone acted as an offering to protect the soul in its journey through the afterlife. Greenstones were also buried in the floor of the temples.* [244]

Within the GMR greenstone is more than an "offering to protect the soul", it is like-for-like magic harnessing plant renewal to ensure progress to a spiritual afterlife more akin to Meyers' conferring of immortality upon the deceased. This is closer to the jade symbolism described by archaeologist Thomas Guderjan:

> *Michael Coe has linked the Classic Maya burial practice of placing jade in the mouth with a funerary ritual described by Landa in the sixteenth century. Further, Karl Taube indicates that such jade beads were regarded as the breath spirit essence of the deceased.* [245]

The historian Lynn Foster and archaeologist Peter Mathews also identify jade with breathing symbolism:

> *A standard custom for all burials, regardless of position in the class hierarchy, was to place a jade bead in the mouth to symbolize life, or breath – just such a jade bead was recovered from the jaw of Hanab Pakal in Palenque and from skeletal remains in Preclassic burials at Kaminaljuyu.* [246]

Funerary jade in China seems more heavily oriented to preservation of the corpse, especially the use orifice plugs and expensively produced entire suits. It was thought that the corpse was required for a while until spiritual progression was complete.

In contrast, in Mesoamerica jade seems more oriented to harnessing the magical power of plant renewal to ensure spiritual progression. In Mayan culture jade was associated with vegetation, crops (particularly maize) and water. Burial of high status people with jade masks (or jade substitute stone) was also for spiritual regeneration.

Insect Metamorphosis Symbolism

> *The multiple forms assumed by the cicada during its lifecycle are analogous to the renewal of the spirit in the afterlife. The Chinese belief that the physical body must be kept intact until such time as its spiritual element is prepared to make the journey to explains the significance of jade shrouds, body plugs and tongue amulets: by preserving the body...* [247]
>
> – Mary Gardner Neill

Butterfly beads are named because they are of an oval or triangular shape, ground very thin and often have two convex carved incisions back-to-back. "Butterfly" is a name given by archaeologists to a class of pendant which may or may not have been considered symbolic of the butterfly in Neolithic times. The style of these carvings is very suggestive and some, such as a soapstone example in the British Museum from Tell Halaf, north-east Syria, dated between 6000 and 5000 BCE, is very clear in its design. Often they have a hole bored through and importantly they are usually made of serpentine, sometimes obsidian, and at Abu Hureyra, almost always found in a funerary context. Interestingly, no insect undergoes a greater transformation than the butterfly.

Butterfly beads were common in Natufian graves throughout the Levant and this may have derived from a particular Neolithic pre-occupation: metamorphosis. Many cultures were intrigued by the process where a caterpillar transforms into a chrysalis which in turn transforms into a butterfly. They associated the radical change of these transformations with how the deceased might transform in the afterlife: from a corpse to a spiritual existence.

Green beads, particularly in an agricultural settlement, are likely to be symbolic of plant renewal and there could be syncretism between plant renewal and insect metamorphosis into an afterlife belief which interprets these amulets as powerful for funerary use.

As indicated earlier, the settlement of Abu Hureyra in northern Syria may have straddled the paradigm shift to a spiritual worldview. The hunter-gatherer pre-agricultural Phase One was characterized by NRT rebirth belief with red ochre usage. However, this had changed significantly during the agricultural Phase Two when ochre use diminished, cinnabar is seen, and the practice grew of including beads as grave goods. Early examples of butterfly beads were from two Abu Hureyra graves between 7600 and 6000 BCE, one a male the other a female.

The scarab is a small beetle which had an enduring significance to the ancient Egyptians, such that they carved many stone amulets of them and used them widely in tombs and mummies. They were also found in a domestic context and, by 1600 BCE, Egypt exported them throughout the Levant where they also were used in burials. William Ward, archaeologist, comments:

> *In origin, the scarab is a purely Egyptian object that had meaning only in an Egyptian religious context. The scarab-beetle itself is associated with the sun god Re and with Atum, the divine force of the primeval hill of creation, both deities being concerned with rebirth and resurrection.* [248]

The cicada, a large, winged insect common in temperate and tropical climates, has long been part of folklore. In China and Japan they symbolise rebirth and immortality, especially as these insects can be seen emerging from the ground. Their green to greenish-black colour has led to associations with plant renewal and to jade in particular – a stone which itself has a long association with immortality. The cicada, as a carved symbol, is seen in burials and this practice is a spiritual interpretation of animal renewal. There is a conceptual link to the insect as life-giving, as the immature nymph insect will shed its first exoskeleton after emerging, this is considered similar to how a spirit sheds its failed body.

The significance of metamorphosis in the cicada is observed in Classical Antiquity in Europe as well. Rory Egan, professor of Classical Tradition at the University of Manitoba comments:

> *The cicada is also one of several insects widely known as symbols of resurrection, immortality, metempsychosis or renewable youth.*

Greek literature and material culture offer several testimonia to such beliefs in the preternatural attributes of the insect. [249]

Images and statuettes of butterflies, scarabs and cicadas, as forms of jewellery in a funerary context, were more than symbols but had like-for-like magical power, effecting the spiritual transmigration required for the afterlife.

Pinecone Symbolism

Nothing would be more natural than definitely to represent the emblem of generation by means of the cognate shape of the fruit which from time immemorial had itself been regarded as an instrument of fertility. Then, again, this primitive symbol becomes, by the purifying influence of religion, the visible pledge of a spiritual resurrection. [250]

– Eugénie Strong

Eugénie Strong, archaeologist and art historian, reported that throughout the Greco-Roman burial grounds the pinecone was a funerary symbol, not just an ornamental stone, but significant for the process of attaining spiritual afterlife. It is seen in cemeteries as diversely located as Italy, Libya, Britain and Dacia. Her view is echoed by that of her husband and fellow art historian, Sanford Arthur Strong:

So, too, his pine-cone, like the cross on a Christian grave, must be symbolical of the belief in life after death. No other explanation can adequately account for the universality of the symbol. [251]

Charred pinecones have been found with cremated remains in Roman burial grounds, and funerary urns of this shape are also seen. A female grave, possibly of a gladiator and dating to 70 CE, was found in London. It had the remains of several pinecones present.

The Green Man

The Green Man signifies irrepressible life. Once he has come into your awareness, you will find him speaking to you wherever you

> *go. He is an image from the depths of prehistory: he appears and*
> *seems to die and then comes again after long forgettings at many*
> *periods in the last two thousand years. In his origins he is much*
> *older than our Christian era. In all his appearances he is an image*
> *of renewal and rebirth...* [252]

– William Anderson

Perhaps the most mysterious European mythical figure is the Green Man, not just peering through leaves but a face actually sprouting vegetation. The Green Man is still commonly seen in stone and wooden carvings as a male face surrounded by and often disgorging vegetation from his mouth, sometimes ears and eyes too. He is also a foliate face, made of leaves. Images are found on ceiling bosses, arches, pillars and roofs in churches and abbeys throughout Northern Europe, particularly in Germany and England, with some also in France, Spain and Malta.

In the 1930s Lady Raglan was the first to research the phenomenon of foliate faces after seeing so many in churches and on the signs of public houses. She connected the two to assume they are both aspects of an ancient tradition. Yet it was unnamed, so she coined the term "Green Man". Her other conclusions were that Green Man carvings often represented real individuals, and erroneously, that the term should include fertility and woodland folklore figures.

Kathleen Basford, botanist, associates the origins of this tradition with leaf masks made by the Romans in the first century CE. [253] William Anderson, a poet and writer, goes much farther in also associating the tradition, in Britain at least, with agricultural deities current during the megalithic stone circle building period. This period being contemporary with the green-skinned god of dead, Osiris, in Egypt.

In the GMR the Green Man is an attempt to strongly associate progression to spiritual afterlife with the renewal of spring vegetation. Perhaps medieval church builders wanted to hedge their bets. Christianity would have seemed very distant and abstract to the illiterate serfdom of Old Europe. They lived close to the land. Life and death is defined by their relationship with nature and the changing seasons. So, these carvings represent the hope of spiritual progression of loved ones, sadly mourned, through a spring-like process of nature. The umbrella of Christianity makes the fabric of churches even more powerful in dispelling the corruption of death. In early churches pagan symbols of renewal were used to buttress and supplement the more sophisticated, abstract, resurrection afterlife promised by Christianity.

Sometime during the 1600s the Green Man ceased to be incorporated into churches. Those in London rebuilt after the great fire of 1666 do not have him present and he is unknown in the New World. It seems he was finally seen as pagan and no longer acceptable as Christian symbolism, and was replaced by cherubs and angels.

Antlered Deities

> *In many instances, deer appear in Celtic myths and legends in order to guide, lure or entice people away from the known world and bring them into contact with the realms of the supernatural. The hunting of magical deer also leads people into unexpected Otherworld encounters. Sometimes these deer undergo magical transformation in the tales and are associated with supernatural women.* [254]

– Sharon Plaice MacLeod

Antler renewal of the NRT was transformed within the spiritual worldview into the form of stag-horned nature gods and the mystical properties of deer. There may have been a European-wide tradition of these beliefs prior to the spread of the Roman Empire, as carvings and statue imagery of antlered gods has been found in Italy, France, Britain and Ireland. These are rare but unequivocally of religious significance.

A bronze model chariot was found with a seventh century BCE cremation burial at Strettweg, Austria, which has a group of figures with stag imagery headed by a goddess. The archaeologist Hilda Davidson concludes:

> *The fact that the model was placed beside ashes of the dead might indicate that it had some link for the mourners with the afterlife, possibly indicating a welcome by the goddess.* [255]

The chariot, with stag images, was arguably intended to assist the deceased journeying to the spirit world in the afterlife.

A carved and named antlered god, Cernunnos, from the first century CE, was found on the Pillar of the Boatmen, below the Notre Dame in Paris. This pillar was originally within a temple with a mixture of Roman and Gaulish deities. Since this discovery, Cernunnos has become eponymous for all antlered deities, both male and female.

Antler renewal seen adopted into spiritual belief is evidenced on the Gundestrap Cauldron made by Thracian smiths, in south-east Europe, from about 100 BCE, and found in pieces in a Danish swamp. A Cernunnos-like deity is pictured in a yogic position with animal attendants. Most significantly, the Gundestrap cauldron also has a scene of spiritual transmigration. Spirits of deceased soldiers are mournfully led to a deity who dips them in a cauldron (possibly symbolic of itself) which may contain waters of life, as a tree of life is nearby. Subsequently, the spirits ride off on horses into the afterlife.

Bull Symbolism

Indeed, Cauvin (1997) was the first to point out the important role played by the Near Eastern cattle cult of the Neolithic period (as reflected in his concept of "peuple du taureau") in the development of organized religion. Most notably, Bos is a common iconographic image appearing in clay figurines of this period... [256]

– Liora Horwitz and Nigel Goring-Morris

The large wild aurochs which became domesticated into cattle during the Neolithic were the natural focus for some beliefs deriving from animal strength. One of which was creating a powerful spiritual envelope for ancestral remains in burials and totemic shrines.

Kfar Hahoresh in Israel, east of Haifa, was the earliest southern Levant cemetery of the Pre-Pottery Neolithic B peoples which succeeded the Natufians, dating to about 6600 BCE. A mixture of 60 primary and secondary burials had a variety of animal parts present, particularly cattle. In one case a human skeleton was accompanied by eight headless cattle skeletons. In another, a cattle or carnivore shape was formed from human bones. Liora Horwitz and Nigel Goring-Morris, archaeologists, assess the various remains of funerary rituals and conclude:

Given the range of species represented and types of these associations, it seems unlikely that, as has commonly been conjectured, the faunal remains were solely intended as food items

*for the deceased or even as food offerings for the departed.
Moreover, the fact that the Kfar Hahoresh faunal ritual repertoire
is paralleled in other Neolithic sites, demonstrates that human-
animal burial and depiction of animals in sacred contexts were
widespread PPNB practices.* [256]

Horwitz and Goring-Morris assert that animal remains in burials
were unlikely to be spiritual food, and the perspective from the GMR
shows agreement. The transformation of the old Palaeolithic rebirth
beliefs of NRT and ERA within the spiritual paradigm, especially at this
early date, certainly retains the central principle of facilitating afterlife.
The animal remains were most likely believed to assist with spiritual
progression, aiding partial reincarnation, or maintaining ancestral spirits
in a totemic location.

Mary Boyce gives an insight into bull worship from the spiritual
worldview perspective. It was practiced in Iran until the advent of
Zoroastrianism in the second millennium BCE:

*Among the Iranians the belief grew up that the spirits of animals
which died a consecrated death became absorbed in a divine being
whom they venerated as Geush Urvan, the "Soul of the Bull"; and
they believed that the blood sacrifice strengthened this divinity,
who used for all useful animals on earth, and helped them to
flourish.* [257]

This tradition may have been descended from the bull symbolism
seen so powerfully at Çatal Höyük, further north and west, in the
seventh millennium BCE.

Bull worship became a widespread aspect of the spiritual worldview
in many cultures and bull symbolism maintained a place in funerary
ritual for thousands of years. In Classical Antiquity the religion of
Mithraism directly associated bull symbolism with afterlife progression.

Spiritual Religions

A purely spiritual religion does not offer a renewed physical afterlife
while preserving identity. Because of this fundamental drawback, many
of the world's spiritual religions are now extinct, and those which are
discussed in this section are marked with a dagger symbol. The

traditional Australian Aboriginal and Native American religions have been marginalized by Christianity into just a few locations. The African tribal religions are similarly marginalized by Christianity and Islam but are still viable in Central African regions. It is notable that Chinese traditional religion continues strongly in its homeland, Shinto has adopted full reincarnation from Buddhism, and the new religion of Baha'i is successful.

The following synopses of afterlife and judgment belief in spiritual religions cannot, of course, be fully comprehensive and is intended to give a perspective from the framework of the GMR on the global reach of the spiritual worldview and its interpretation by specific cultures, particularly observing where judgment buttresses society. Within them we also get further insight into how the NRT became transformed into the NST.

Australian Aboriginal Religion

Mungo did not behold unmoved our sacrilegious invasion of the solemn and silent repository of one of his countrymen, whom he described as a great warrior from the circumstances of his burial. When I asked Mungo the reason of the spear being struck into the tomb, he replied quietly, "To fight with when he is asleep". [258]

– Thomas Henry Braim

In Braim's history of New South Wales he describes a rockshelter burial near the west bank of the Shannon River, central Tasmania, which was opened in 1829 by a party led Jorgen Jorgenson and his guide Mungo. Jorgenson's account of the Aboriginal burial fits a people for whom death was a kind of sleep and the deceased continued in a spiritual existence. This early account, before widespread missionary interaction, gives a rare view, of what the Aboriginal peoples believed before the introduction of European spiritual concepts. The account is useful only though, if Jorgenson can be trusted, for he was an adventurer, a self-styled ruler of Iceland, imprisoned in London, then transported to Australia, finally pardoned, becoming a constable in Tasmania.

The Australian continent was joined to New Guinea during the major glaciations, as the Arafura Sea is shallow enough to become mostly dry land. This greater landmass has been named Sahul. However, Sahul has always been separated from the Indonesian islands off Bali and was not reached by *Homo erectus*. It required modern humans to make the final sea journey, most likely between 60 and 50 kya. With the end of the last Ice Age, the Torres Strait Islanders and Tasmanian Aboriginals were all cut off from the mainland by about 9000 BCE.

Such an early date for the isolation of Tasmania, and the report suggesting a well-developed spiritual religious tradition for the relatively small population of Aboriginals there, implies that spiritual afterlife developed on the Australian mainland before Tasmania became separated for the last time, the terminus ante quem for spiritual beliefs. This would then imply that traditional Aboriginal religion was arguably the most advanced and complex in the world by at least 11.5 kya, when the Temples of Rebirth were just being started in Anatolia. If the extreme physiology of the Kow Swamp people at about 20 kya is due to local self-selection for robust characteristics, then this is indicative of Rebirth Feedback Belief (RFB), which implies a terminus post quem for the emergence of spiritual beliefs. So the life-force to spiritual paradigm shift in Aboriginal Australia probably began between 20 and 11 kya, bearing in mind, of course, that prehistoric memes took several thousand years to traverse continental-sized land areas.

The conclusion that Aboriginals had early spiritual traditions also supports the hypotheses of gracilization for the remainder of modern humans by RFB. The Aboriginals stopped looking for evidence of rebirth in their young, and stopped self-selecting based upon it before anyone else; hence they retain more of their early Caucasian physiology than anyone else.

To the Aboriginals, the landscape is subject to special reverence, as part of life itself, and tightly linked to the concept of Dreamtime. This is a relic of the primordial life-force worldview. Because these peoples developed in isolation, they had no external pressure to prevent a normally transitional phase becoming permanent. Dreamtime emerged from an amalgam, retaining the life-force of the landscape but overlaid with spiritual concepts associated with humans and animals. Because spirituality has long been the major component of Aboriginal religion, Dreamtime is properly included as part of LMR.

The Dreamtime-like phase elsewhere in the world was only temporary, probably because of external competitive pressures resulting in the establishment of a fully spiritual worldview. The Aborigines did not undergo the Neolithic revolution, so their religious thought was not modified by the effects of multilevel natural selection between large sedentary societies, which is fundamental to the emergence of strong afterlife judgment. Although, there are spiritual sanctions available against the living and some spirits of the newly deceased are tested as they journey on. In Aboriginal religions there is no differentiation in the quality of afterlife based upon personal behaviour during life.

This is a complex culture, with many varying religious traditions and languages, which makes further generalisation difficult beyond the recognition that spirits exist in traditional Aboriginal belief and that there is partial reincarnation where the identity of the individual is not preserved spiritually at the same time. Anthropologist Jack Eller writes on Aboriginal afterlife belief:

> At death, a person's "spirit" returned to the earth, to be reborn into another human in the future. Death, however, except for the very old and young, was not considered a "natural" event but a supernatural one (or both) and was often the occasion for angry duels and real bloodshed. It was also a time for "sorry business", which included funeral rituals, self-mutilation (such as bashing one's head or cutting one's face), and restrictions on the name or image of the dead. [216]

Perhaps the unhappiness which surrounds death in this account is the very problem which the paradigm of spiritual afterlife solves – loss of personal identity of the newly deceased. The anguish of the Aboriginal is anguish at the loss of an individual as, for them, unlike other modern cultures, spiritual identity fades quickly or is absorbed into the ancestral spirit realm, never to return.

However, there is also the concept of a wandering spirit of the dead. For example, the Tiwi tribe imagine these and a spirit realm. [21] Indeed, most of the disparate Aboriginal tribes have a concept of the spirit realm known in English as the Land of the Dead.

Trevor Jacob, writing for the Australian Ministry of Education, interprets Aboriginal belief as a form of reincarnation:

> In traditional Aboriginal society death is not feared: it is the time when a person's spirit is released from the physical body to rejoin the unseen world. Death signifies a return of the spirit to the

Dreaming and the eternal life-stream. It is believed that upon death a person's spirit returns to its source - its sacred totem site - to await reincarnation. [259]

A more correct interpretation is that this is belief in partial reincarnation because prior identity is only briefly preserved, if at all. Where partial reincarnation occurs from a reservoir of spirits in a spirit world, but prior identity is believed lost – this is not yet an example of a fully-fledged spiritual reincarnation afterlife. Overall, we get a mixed picture of an early Lower Mantle religion transitioning towards a Dharmic-like Upper Mantle reincarnation belief with spiritual preservation of the individual's identity, but this may be thousands of years into the future. Further, the process has now been disrupted by the introduction of Christianity and resurrection afterlife belief.

Levantine and Anatolian Religion †

Skulls and long bones were removed for rituals in the forecourts or in distant earth and stone circles. Skulls were regarded as cages for the spirits and were used to carry spirit power to places that required sanctification. They were sometimes smashed to pieces, probably to release the spirit power where it was needed. [260]

– Rodney Castleden

Rodney Castleden in *The Stonehenge People* comments on skull removal in ancient Britain. However, this practice started some 4000 years earlier, in northern Syria, and spread south through the Levant, becoming common in the earliest settled societies there.

Interestingly, skull removal, indicating spiritual beliefs, seems to have originated nearby to the Temples of Rebirth in Anatolia, where rebirth afterlife belief continued later there, until about 8000 BCE.

Peter Akkermans and Glenn Schwartz, archaeologists, describe in *The Archaeology of Syria* how widespread the skull removal and decoration practices became:

The skull was often separated from the rest of the skeleton before final burial took place. This practice was first attested in Natufian contexts in the southern Levant but became very common in the Neolithic, occurring as far north as Nevali Cori in Anatolia and

Qermez Dere in Iraq, and as far south as Nahal Hemar cave near the Dead Sea. [...] At Tell Ramad, a pit ascribed to layer l contained six skulls, and two pits in layer II contained three and twelve skulls respectively. Nearly all were remodeled with plaster to produce at lifelike image of the human face, some with traces of red paint. Such plastering of skulls, occasionally with marine shells as eye-inlay, commonly occurred at sites in the southern Levant, such as Jericho, Beisamoun, Nahal Hemar, and Ain Ghazal, but it has rarely been reported from any of the settlements north of Ramad. [261]

These are descriptions of the earliest shrines, empowered by skulls decorated with red ochre and shells for eyes. The conclusion is that these practices were for bringing ancestors into the world of the living and ensuring they remained part of society. This helped regulate society and maintain social order.

Ofer Bar-Yosef also suggests that skull removal may relate to ancestor veneration:

Skull removal, a practice begun during the Late Natufian, was performed only on adults: child burials were left intact. The separated crania were sometimes found in domestic locales or special-purpose buildings. [...] The differentiation along age lines probably reflects changes in attitudes toward the dead within the Early Neolithic society and perhaps is evidence for the veneration of ancestors. [262]

Children were normally omitted from skull removal practices because they did not have descendants before they died, however, in some cultures children appear to have had the same funerary ritual as adults – and this reason is explored shortly.

Michael Parker Pearson, archaeologist, also observes the changes in funerary traditions within the Natufians, at a number of sites, in terms of emerging ancestor veneration:

Yet there is probably an altogether more significant aspect underlying the elaborate treatments, the digging of proper grave pits and the keeping of the dead beneath the community of the living. What we may be seeing for the first time in the human experience, is the explicit construction of ancestorhood. [204]

Skulls, as a container for the spirit, and their removal, imply the collection of them into a communal shrine where ancestors may have a spiritual afterlife or ancestorhood. Jericho is one of the oldest settlements exceeding Dunbar's Number in size, whose earliest inhabitants were descended from Natufians. Between 7200 and 6700 BCE skulls were removed from the deceased and re-fleshed with clay, sometimes ochre coloured, and had shells inserted for eyes. They may have been set in an arranged manner.

These practices were certainly attempts to facilitate spiritual afterlife for the deceased, often using shell and red ochre of the NST. The ancient NRT traditions, transformed in the spiritual paradigm shift now assisted with *living and seeing* in the spirit world. Decoration of skulls is firm evidence for the emergence of true spiritual religion, where the intellectual leap is made from belief in physical rebirth to belief in survival of adulthood in an intangible state, the birth of ancestorhood and therefore ancestor worship.

In 1958 archaeologist James Mellaart made the remarkable find of the ancient town of Çatal Höyük, in central modern Turkey. It is the world's largest known prehistoric settlement, established about 7400 BCE growing to have a peak population of between 5000 and 8000 people, but without any public buildings or central infrastructure. The inhabitants practised metalworking, pottery, textile making and painting. Despite being in a large settlement, life was tough and close to nature. Limited domestication of plants and animals meant that hunting was still vital to survival. Life expectancy was a little over 30 years. The evidence for religious cohesion in this culture is remarkable as Mellaart writes:

> *Out of 139 living rooms excavated, not less than forty appear to have served Neolithic religion. Such worship rooms or shrines are more elaborately decorated than houses and they are frequently the largest buildings.* [263]

It appears that many domestic houses had living rooms which effectively doubled as shrines. During the 1500 years that Çatal Höyük was occupied, spiritual afterlife became well advanced. Disposal of the dead was first by excarnation, on high wooden platforms which are seen illustrated on wall murals. Certainly the use of platforms was to prevent animal scavengers from removing the bones entirely, as these were required later. Once Griffon vultures had removed the meat, the clean bones were collected and interred as secondary burials under the floors or under sleeping benches of houses.

Ian Hodder, who excavated parts of the site in far more detail than in any previous campaign, writes about an unusual figurine which is a pregnant female at the front with a skeletal back:

> *Immediately on finding the figurine we were all taken aback by its very strange and unusual imagery. The front of the figurine looks very much like the small, squat, so called "mother goddess" figurines that are so well known (though rare) from Çatalhöyük. There are full breasts on which the hands rest, and the stomach is extended in the central part. There is a hole in the top for the head which is missing. As one turns the figurine around one notices that the arms are very thin, and then on the back of the figurine one sees a depiction of either a skeleton or the bones of a very thin and depleted human. The ribs and vertebrae are clear, as are the scapulae and the main pelvic bones. The figurine can be interpreted in a number of ways - as a woman turning into an ancestor, as a woman associated with death, or as death and life conjoined.* [264]

A fourth interpretation is that it shows an ancestor undergoing partial reincarnation, *spiritually entering a female* to become reborn as an infant. The figurine would most likely have been interred with ancestral bones which had undergone secondary burial within a house. Its presence is either like-for-like sympathetic magic to *assist* with the reincarnation process or a representation *instructing* the ancestor in making this transition. The remains of buried women sometimes had shells filled with red ochre which, in the context of the spiritual worldview, also implies belief in a form of partial reincarnation.

Patrick McNamara observes that treatment of the dead in Anatolia had changed markedly from the Palaeolithic and suggests human sacrifice had developed:

> *At Çatal Höyük, Jericho, and Ain Ghazal infants were buried beneath entrances to cult buildings and in the walls. In many cases the heads had been removed from these infants whose skeletons were otherwise intact (not decayed), again indicating sacrificial violence. It is important to underline the fact that human sacrifice was very likely an innovation of these peoples of*

the Near East Neolithic. The evidence for human sacrifice among peoples of the Upper Palaeolithic is slim or non-existent. [265]

The argument for human sacrifice here is possible because infant skulls would not normally be wanted for ancestor veneration. There is another interpretation arising from partial reincarnation; if births were sometimes believed to be ancestral spirits returned into the world then infant death by natural causes would be dismaying. An ancestor's desire to be reborn was thwarted, so by removing the infant's head and interring it into the building, they were preserving the ancestral spirit once again for another chance of rebirth.

Ancestor veneration is evidence that religion buttressed society through ritual judgment, because when people die they would be given a proper funeral and internment in the ancestral shrine. Those undeserving would have their remains scattered, consigning them to oblivion. As seen elsewhere, the living would also have interpreted misfortune as ancestral judgment delivered upon them for imagined transgressions and failings.

The hypothesis of a Mother Goddess cult at Çatal Höyük is discredited. These symbols are likely for partial reincarnation or simple fertility rituals. The suggestion of a vulture cult is likely just evidence of the belief in vultures as spiritual psychopomps and the vultures were not worshipped as gods in any modern sense.

Perhaps the most striking component of the dual religious and domestic buildings are the benches made with a series of aurochs (bull) skulls, or clay models, all with horns. The same bucrania was also inserted into walls. The common assumption that this is evidence of bull worship is understandable, but perhaps worship is the wrong word. By creating shrines of bull symbolism they may have been creating ancestral-bull shrines, where the spirits of many deceased bulls then dwelt. Red "paint", presumably ochre, is reported with the shrines, so bulls were expected to regenerate from them. This means people would have control over the population of an important animal which eventually became domesticated into the cattle of today. So the bull shrines were likely more about control of an important resource than simple worship.

There is, however, a truly bizarre form of religious symbolism which is described by David Warburton in *The Discovery of the Dawn of Consciousness:*

> *Sticking from the walls of some houses were sculpted pairs of
> human female breasts, containing lower jaws of boar, skulls of
> foxes and weasels, or of Griffon vultures — all animals associated
> with scavengers, hence death. Some of the "breasts" have open
> nipples, with the beaks of vultures, the teeth of foxes and weasels,
> as well as the tusks of wild boars sticking out of them.* [266]

Warburton calls this "ghastly and shocking" but much of the
symbolism is actually life-affirming and can be recognized as NST belief
transformed from the ART of the Palaeolithic. Jaws full of teeth, boar
tusks and small skulls are all egg symbolism. Embedding egg symbolism
into human female symbolism creates a fertility object for assisting the
process of partial reincarnation. This also applies for bull spirits where
the decorated breasts are found with bull symbolism. The use of vulture
beaks in a fertility symbol is not seen before so it is an advance in
symbolism invented by the people of Çatal Höyük that then went extinct
with their culture.

Mesopotamian Religion †

> *How, O how could I stay silent, how, O how could I keep quiet?*
> *My friend whom I love has turned to clay.*
> *Enkidu my friend whom I love has turned to clay.*
> *Am I not like him? Must I lie down too, never to rise again?*
>
> – Epic of Gilgamesh, Tablet X, ca. 2700 BCE

Mesopotamia is the place of the world's first civilization, Sumeria,
which succeeded the Ubaid culture, bringing cuneiform, the first written
language, seen as wedge-shaped markings in clay. It says much about
the priorities of humanity when the earliest written story to reach us is
about a heroic quest for *immortality*. The pathos in Gilgamesh's struggle
is worthy of Shakespeare.

This is the earliest human culture which can speak to us directly, and
immediately we hear their concerns about the worry of personal
mortality, which has already been silently expressed in a hundred
thousand years of funerary ritual.

Partial reincarnation would have been an early spiritual belief in
Mesopotamia but this developed into the paradigm where ancestors

remained in a spirit world. There were strong ancestor cults where regular tribute was paid to the deceased. They were buried under the floors of houses and sometimes had a feeding tube where libations were poured. The wealthy might have separate rooms for the dead. So they had a powerful tradition of funerary ritual. Burials in Eridu, the first town with central organization, were in repose, which is often a signature for the belief in continued spiritual life as an adult.

As time passed, cemeteries were increasingly used until only children were buried below the floors of houses. Perhaps it was thought children who died needed another chance to be reborn and live a full life before they could become a spirit ancestor.

The Sumerians also had a dualistic view of the world: a realm of the living and a separate parallel existence for the dead. There was a transition in progress to the beginning of the sky, earth and underworld (SEU) paradigm which came to dominate many later cultures. When people died their ghosts had a continued existence carrying on largely how they lived while alive. The dusty and barren underworld (often known as netherworld) described in Gilgamesh would seem to discourage belief in an afterlife with such apparent injustice. Yet, there was a behavioural feedback taking effect upon the living. The dead depended on the living for ritual food and this makes such obligations personal to everyone, as they will eventually be depending upon ritual meals from their own descendants.

Unlike most cultures, where it is believed that a spirit inhabits a living body and is released at death, the Mesopotamians believed that the spirit was *created* at the time of death. So technically speaking, their underworld was peopled by ghosts. Andrew Cohen, an archaeologist specializing in the Near East, writes about Mesopotamian veneration of the dead and their association with providence as seen in the city of Ur:

> *Mesopotamian concepts concerning the afterlife and the ghost's existence in the netherworld required the living to provide the dead with offerings of food and drink. [...] I suggest that, in choosing to make at least some of those offerings in the highly visible Royal Tombs Complex area, the elite publicly associated their dead with abundance.* [267]

As mentioned in the last chapter, it was only god belief which enabled large cities, like Eridu, to develop. All people were then accountable to a central deity and this vastly improves social cohesion.

Each city had a major temple and the god of the city resided there. Cohen continues:

> *The cult statue was not merely a portrait of the divinity — it was the god's very incarnation. [...] Rather a god was simultaneously immanent in a cult statue or statues (some gods having temples and statues in multiple cities) in those forces of nature with which they were associated (Enlil with air and the wind, for example).*

Anu was the Sumerian high god, their sky god, Ki, was god of the earth, and the god of the underworld was Erishkigal whose brother was Enki, a water god. Enki was also the city god of Eridu and this may have been due to the importance of irrigation, essential to the city when maintenance of it required the city-wide cooperation of its citizens.

When it was night in the world of the living, the sun was passing through the underworld. Utu means "sun" in ancient Sumerian and also their solar god. He travelled the sky during the day and traversed the underworld at night. Too bright to look at and higher than the mountains he was regarded as all-seeing and all-powerful, dispensing justice to gods, men and the dead. Many city states had sun gods of their own and as the Sumerian civilization absorbed each city by 3000 BCE the sun gods of these lesser cities became members of Utu's retinue. After the Akkadian invasion, about 2270 BCE he was renamed "Shamash". Cuneiform tablets mention him a number of times. Excerpts from *The Great Hymn to Shamash* show his acts of justice:

> *A man who covets his neighbour's wife*
> *Will [. . .] before his appointed day.*
> *A nasty snare is prepared for him. [. . .]*
> *Your weapon will strike at him, and there will be none to save him.*
> *[His] father will not stand for his defence,*
> *And at the judge's command his brothers will not plead.*
> *He will be caught in a copper trap that he did not foresee.*
> *You destroy the horns of a scheming villain,*
> *A zealous [. . .] his foundations are undermined.*
> *You give the unscrupulous judge experience of fetters,*
> *Him who accepts a present and yet lets justice miscarry you make bear his punishment.*
> *As for him who declines a present but nevertheless takes the part of the weak,*

It is pleasing to Shamash, and he will prolong his life. . . .
The progeny of evil-doers will [fail.]
Those whose mouth says 'No' - their case is before you.
In a moment you discern what they say;
You hear and examine them; you determine the lawsuit of the
wronged.
[. . .]
The prowling thief, the enemy of Shamash,
The marauder along the tracks of the steppe confronts you.
The roving dead, the vagrant soul,
They confront you, Shamash, and you hear all. [268]

Not everyone was judged. There is an allusion to horror of oblivion when Gilgamesh repeatedly questions Enkidu about what happens in the underworld:

Didn't you see him who was set on fire?" "Why, my friend, did
not you spare this question?" "I asked it, my friend!" "His spirit
is .... from the nether world, it went up to the sky with the smoke
(?). [269]

Despite the usually dusty and gloomy existence in the underworld it seems that, like in ancient Egypt, oblivion was a fate worse than death.

Spiritual judgment remained the glue of social cohesion for the Sumerian civilization, even through successive invasions, until their culture faded within a century after it was temporarily overrun by the Elamites from the east in 2004 BCE.

Atlantic Megalithic Religion †

The construction of large earthen mounds or barrows and
megalithic tombs helped integrate small dispersed populations
into new and larger social groupings and more permanent
settlements. The highly visible and elaborate burial and
ceremonial structures defined their physical place in the world by
linking notable ancestors to these places. [270]

– Robert A. Birmingham

From about 4700 BCE megalithic tombs, dolmen and monuments started appearing on the Atlantic coast of Europe, from Portugal in the south to as far north as southern Sweden. France alone has 6000 sites dating from about 4600 BCE and Denmark has 5000 sites from 3800 BCE. The megalithic tradition was particularly concentrated in the British Isles with thousands of sites of all types. Sites are also seen across northern Germany, southern France and a strong tradition of megalithic monument building existed in Malta. "Atlantic Megalithic" is used here, as translated from the French term, which best captures the scope and type of cultures under discussion.

Prior to the megalithic building traditions rebirth afterlife belief prevailed, but the template of spiritual afterlife spread with farming, and the Neolithic revolution, as a meme, westward from the Levant. It washed across Europe in a slow 4000 year-long wave, sometimes faster with territorial conquests. This belief may have first *caused* the megaliths to be erected – as a totemic place for ancestors where the dead would persist spiritually.

If the megalithic monuments are split according to the predominant religious belief which prevailed at the time then there are two separate classes. The first Atlantic Megalithic spiritual religion was ancestor worship.

The monuments consistent with this belief are single upright stones, obelisks, and dolmen which are single-chambered with several uprights and a capping slab. They are often on prominent sites and certainly places of excarnation which created a link between ancestral spirits and the megaliths. Tombs contemporary with them were single or multi-chambered barrows which are stone-walled and covered with earth, and stone-lined cairns, for the usual secondary burial of bones.

When life expectancy was between 30 and 40 years many people did not know their grandparents as they usually do today. Family bones in a tomb or cairn were the only evidence of former generations who quickly faded into an abstract concept of "ancestors". When space was needed in a tomb, rearrangement took place and older bones were finally disposed of. If, by then, the oldest ancestors had not yet had partial reincarnation to the world of the living they presumably would never do so.

The Stoney Littleton long barrow, in western England, is an earth-covered multi-chambered megalithic tomb from about 3500 BCE with human remains present when found in 1760. One entrance slab has a fossil ammonite embedded, which is certainly a continuation of the SBT belief system within the life-force, seen earlier at the Mesolithic cemetery of Aveline's Hole, where at least seven fossil ammonites were found as grave goods. When transformed within spiritual beliefs, natural and carved spirals were symbolic of moving air and now represented like-for-like magic to ensure continued spiritual afterlife for the deceased at these sites. Carved spirals are at the entrance to the contemporary Newgrange tomb in Ireland. Further, the masterfully carved Knowth mace-head resembles an ancestor spiritually alive by immersion in spiralling air.

Remarkable similarities exist in megalithic tomb entrance decoration over long distances. Newgrange in Ireland and Tarxien in Malta have large slabs with many cupules and circular spiral motifs. This is a set of breathing symbolisms: cupules for air holes, concentric rings and spirals representing moving air. These motifs, when situated at the entrances of tombs, make the whole tomb spiritually alive, a literal home for the ancestors. The uncommon triple spiral motif may also represent air flow through a mouth and a pair of nostrils. Lozenges and wedge-shaped motifs may represent the stones, and even a tomb itself, submerged in its spiritual ether.

Karsten Wentink, archaeologist, investigates the deposits of ceremonial Neolithic flint axes of the Middle Neolithic Funnel Beaker Culture. These people were also responsible for megalithic sites in the northern Netherlands and he observes what these tombs meant to them:

> *The tombs were places that had been built to last. They formed permanent locations where human remains were accumulated and objects were deposited. These were places that could be visited again and again. During each visit objects and human remains could be added while the artefacts and human remains deposited on earlier occasions could be rearranged. [..] This process might also be related to the fact that no more new tombs were built after 3200 BC. The period during which new tombs were erected only lasted 200 years after which no more megaliths were added. These were places that were associated with the histories of local communities whose use of the tombs led to a process of inalienation. The megaliths became meaningful not only as places to bury the dead, but as one the community's most treasured inalienable possessions. [271]*

The megaliths and tombs established a territorial link between the people and their land. It kept their ancestors in context. For the stability of society there is now an undeniable form of pre-mortem judgment of the living and post-mortem judgment in afterlife of the newly deceased – this judgment is either acceptance or rejection by ancestors who dwell in the tombs and landscape and are ever vigilant over the living.

The easternmost part of the Atlantic megalithic tradition was in Malta where a dozen significant temple complexes survive in good condition. Each, on their own, is a remarkable monument but one stands out as truly exceptional and unique: the Hal Saflieni Hypogeum, underground megalithic tomb complex. Discovered in 1902, it then suffered a century of depredations, including loss of the entrance and loss of 7000 human remains, and slow erosion of the walls and red ochre art by tens of thousands of visitors. Properly conserved now, it can still illuminate a dark period of religious history.

The tomb was first started in a natural cave about 4000 BCE and was later excavated to three levels with many separate chambers. They were carved out of the limestone bedrock with columns and windows reminiscent of above-ground temples such as nearby Tarxien. The Oracle Room, which would have seen a shaft of sunlight at the midwinter solstice, has its ceiling painted with red ochre spirals and dots, symbolic of air, ensuring spiritual afterlife.

In the main chamber a few statuettes were recovered, the most complete being the Sleeping Lady. It is a small terracotta figure of a large-hipped recumbent woman, clearly on a low bed, asleep. It seems very out of place in a dark tomb with the dead, and there was no other significant statuary present. Giulia Battiti Sorlini, archaeologist, gives a profound insight into this peaceful and enigmatic statuette:

> *The Hypogeum's main function was burial, probably of a minority group and associated with reverence for ancestors. Evidently there was also a cult of incubation, classically associated with healing. [...] As the Hypogeum was the context for the cult, incubation there appears linked with death and rebirth, possibly some "reincarnation". The Sleeping Lady could be an ex-voto terracotta given for a pregnancy posterior to an act of incubation.* [272]

Sorlini interprets the Sleeping Lady with partial reincarnation, which is certainly correct. The people who set this statuette in place over 4500 years ago were expecting it to assist, via like-for-like magic, with ancestors becoming reborn into the world of the living. The statue was probably instructive to the spirits of the ancestors, but unlikely to mean that women slept in the tomb expecting to become pregnant, or a post-facto offering after a pregnancy which was assumed to be a rebirth.

It is the second phase of the Atlantic Megalithic religion which develops so that gods assume precedence over ancestors.

Wentink reports the lack of new tombs built after 3200 BCE in the northern Netherlands and this is the time when the whole nature of the Atlantic megalithic sites changed. After the tomb-building period there was a stone circle building period, particularly with ever larger rings of monolithic stones culminating in the most famous: Stonehenge with its main construction phase at 2600 to 2400 BCE. More than 2000 stone circles still exist in the British Isles. The archaeologist and ceramics specialist, Aedeen Cremin, describes this change:

> *During the third millennium BCE profound changes were taking place among the farming communities in north-western Europe. Competition led some groups to become dominant and new ideologies emerged. The ancestors previously so powerfully invoked by the living, lost their importance and instead, new monuments emerged: stone and timber circles. The scale of some of these undertakings, the time, effort, and coordination required, speak strongly in favor of powerful leadership challenging the old traditions and creating a new order in which individual authority could be drawn from a special relationship with the gods.* [273]

Spiritual religion had evolved focus away from ancestor worship towards god worship: deified spirits of legendary leaders and powerful elements of the environment. Perhaps the dead were now thought to be in a spiritual realm separated from the affairs of the living. Stone circles, nature itself, and the lives of the people were now overseen by watchful gods. This transition is similar to that in many cultures such as the Shang in China and Ubaid in Mesopotamia.

Stonehenge may have developed in an era of god belief but this did not mean the newly dead had lost any importance. It was the centre of a funerary tradition where many cremations took place and also sky-burials – excarnations on high wooden platforms. The "death" of the landscape in winter is much more apparent in Northern Europe than in tropical latitudes, so it is significant that the primary orientation of the largest sarsen stones is made with the midwinter solstice. Because this is a funerary site it would be to synchronise the seasons with human death. Partial reincarnation may then have been the intended result as the circle itself was certainly considered not just symbolic of the cyclic passage of the seasons, but magically harnessing it. If so, then funerary rituals which took place at Stonehenge and other circles harnessed the godlike power of spring to enable deceased spirits to achieve a new physical life, even if it took several months or years to occur. So, the dead were brought from far and wide in the hope that they would achieve a partial reincarnation. Its reputation spread as isotopic evidence of human remains reveal a few people were distantly raised, and therefore originated, as far afield as Central Europe.

However, the influence of the stone circles was much faded by 1600 BCE and the subsequent emergence of the Iron Age. Perhaps it came to be believed that partial reincarnation would occur naturally, even without help from megalithic stones, or more likely that most ancestors remained permanently in the spirit world.

The investigation of a barrow at Pool Farm, Somerset, 50 km west of Stonehenge, yielded the cremated remains of an adult and a child dating to about 1850 BCE, with an impressive example of rock art. A two-metre-long slab of stone carved with six large human feet and ten cupules was set facing in towards the burial chamber. The presence of a single-horned square glyph on it is of uncertain meaning, but probably represents the tomb itself reopened – for a spiritual exit. Spiritual afterlife must be assumed because of the late date, the practice of full cremation, and the presence of feet carvings. So, the large slab with its funerary cupules of stone breathing symbolism is to powerfully ensure that the deceased achieved a spiritual existence. The feet are unusual like-for-like magic *instructive* to the spirit to walk, or to *compel* the spirit to walk away, presumably on to the ancestral realm.

The similar Calderstones Chambered Tomb in Liverpool, destroyed by workmen in the nineteenth century, was much larger, yielding a cartload of cremated bones. As well as cupules and feet carvings on surviving chamber stones there are the spirals and concentric ring marks symbolic of air and breathing in a spiritual context.

These sites invite comparison with the Neanderthal burial at La Ferrassie rockshelter, 65,000 years earlier, because they all have a slab of rock with funerary cupules facing the deceased. La Ferrassie 6 was a burial intended to achieve rebirth within the life-force worldview. The fundamental difference at Pool Farm and Calderstones is evidenced by the presence of feet carvings. These are consistent only with adult spiritual progression (newborns don't walk anywhere).

During the fourth millennium BCE the template memes of spiritual afterlife and worldview swept over the British Isles from continental Europe and transformed the meaning of funerary cupules. They now breathed ensuring spiritual afterlife with adulthood preserved instead of breathing for physical life as a newborn.

Spiritual religion was enduring in the megalithic cultures and used NST symbolism to ensure afterlife happened.

Egyptian Religion †

The most important transformations a deceased person would expect to make, however, were spiritual in nature. These were the aspects of the afterlife personality which correspond most closely so our concepts of a soul the akh, the ka, the ba, and the Shadow. [274]

– Raymond Faulkner, Ogden Goelet, Carol Andrews and James Wasserman

There is confusion of terminology at the heart of understanding the world's most famous and best studied ancient religion. The Egyptians believed in a spiritual afterlife but often resurrection is used to describe the process by which the spiritual transfiguration was meant to be achieved. It seems that interpretation of the "spirit-body" concept may suggest a partial or even full resurrection. This is an important matter as resurrection is clearly a superior form of afterlife than a spiritual existence. If the Egyptians held to it by the end of the Old Kingdom then this is about *2000* years earlier than the development of the resurrection paradigm first seen in Judaism and Zoroastrianism. It raises the question of why resurrection had not spread throughout Europe and the Middle East much earlier than the Christian era.

The long duration of Egyptian religion, from 3100 BCE to 200 CE, encompassed a reasonably consistent but very complex paradigm of afterlife. In order to understand this religion it is first necessary to understand their SEU paradigm.

The ancient Egyptians imagined the world as a disc with Upper and Lower Egypt in the centre and remote lands surrounding it. Libya was in the west, the Levant was north, Arabia was east, and Nubia to the south. All were surrounded by an encircling sea. Beneath the disc was the underworld, called Duat, which was a land with many similarities to the normal earthly realm, especially the Field of Reeds. In the Duat the dead lived as they did in life: farmed, raised animals and carried on trades, often with the help of shabti, servant statues. Differences existed with earth as Duat was where the gods lived, and there were places of afterlife punishment like a fiery wall and fiery lake. The Egyptians were greatly concerned with the problems of walking upside down, and that their bodily functions would still work correctly, so they had magical spells to ensure that the upside down nature of Duat was perceived normally. Tombs were thought of as entrances to the underworld.

Many theologians who research the Egyptian religion spend a lot of time determining the role and history of each god in the pantheon. There were hundreds, but almost all of them are window dressing in the religious worldview. The GMR holds that the only gods of importance are those who directly facilitate afterlife and judgment.

The sun god Ra (also Re) travelled in a solar boat, later a solar chariot, over the earth during the day, and crossed the western horizon at sunset so that it was then dawn in Duat. Daytime in Duat was night in the normal earth. This concept was the same as in Mesopotamia and likely originated there, spreading 1500 km to Egypt as a meme. Both cultures also imagined seven gates to their underworlds. The unique aspect of Egyptian religion, compared to Mesopotamia and Assyria, was that the king or pharaoh was destined to be a god in the underworld. These religions all held that the sun-god was directly associated with the judgment of the dead. However, in Egypt it remained the case only during the first dynasties. John Gwyn Griffiths, Egyptologist, asserted that in the Egyptian Old Kingdom:

> *The importance of Re in the early idea of posthumous judgment is undeniable.* [275]

During the Old Kingdom the god Osiris, first depicted in a tomb in the fifth dynasty, became the major deity and was to remain so until a few centuries BCE when his sister, Isis, superseded him. It was believed that Osiris, when living on earth, was killed by his brother Seth, dismembered and scattered. It was Isis who reassembled and mummified him. Other gods then gave him spiritual life and he became the god of the dead in Duat. Osiris was depicted with green skin and worshipped as the god of vegetation and of the annual flooding of the Nile so essential for crops. This is a clear link with the older PRT which facilitated human afterlife.

The death and afterlife of the pharaoh was closely tied to the myth of Osiris and his son Horus as described in pyramid texts and summarized by Griffiths:

> *Horus as the living Pharaoh and his father Osiris as the dead Pharaoh: these are the basic elements of the royal funerary cult. Osiris, per se, is king of the domain of the dead so that the dead Pharaoh is naturally regarded as aspiring to sovereignty in the afterworld in the form of Osiris. At the same time the royal burial rites adumbrate the birth of a new Horus in the son of the deceased. [..] As for the deceased King, he is urged to sit on the throne of Osiris (Pyr. 134bW); he inherits now the sovereignty of the dead.* [275]

Originally, only the Pharaoh could expect a spiritual afterlife in the solar boat or with the undying stars. Perhaps ordinary people still had to settle for partial reincarnation unless they were chosen as a human sacrifice! Sometimes dozens of servants and animals went sent to join the Pharaoh in spiritual afterlife, a practice seen also in Mesopotamia at the same time. It did not last – early in the Old Kingdom things changed and first the nobility, and then the general population, could expect a proper spiritual afterlife in the underworld, Duat.

Additionally, in the Egyptian worldview there were multiple components, essential elements, which were believed to make up each individual. During earthly life a person was made of the following: the body (khet), heart (ib), self and personality (ba), life-force (ka), shadow (sheut) and name (ren). All of these comprised the individual. The ka was the life-force or spark which entered the person at birth with their first breath, yet during life it was always linked to the remote gods and ancestors.

After physical death the life-force of ka had now exited the body, joining the ancestors, and the ba had also exited, joining the gods. In order for a person to experience afterlife by avoiding oblivion they needed their ba and ka reunited to form an "effective" spirit (akh). Even then, the akh could not enjoy a spiritual existence in the underworld without a spirit-body (sahu). The sahu was drawn from the continued existence and symbolic rebirth of the corpse, hence the importance of mummification, to preserve the corpse so that it could magically provide a spirit-body for the akh in the afterlife. A person's name was also essential to physical life – entering the afterlife, and continuing existence – so needed to be written down and spoken by the living as much as possible.

The most important funerary ritual was the "opening of the mouth" ceremony which could comprise up to 100 separate procedures. Performed by a priest or close relative, this was a symbolic rebirth by opening the mouth, eyes and other orifices, enabling the corpse to take up ritual food offerings which the ba and ka regularly required. Importantly, this ceremony was for bringing the ba, protected by the shadow, back so it could rejoin with the ka and begin the afterlife as an akh. This ceremony is a distant descendant echoing the Palaeolithic blood and breathing symbolisms, the two most important principles of life. At the height of the ceremony blood was given to the corpse, sometimes by way of the grisly removal of the foreleg of a live calf. A bloody leg had long been appropriate like-for-like magic to make the dead walk again. After the ceremony the mummy was deemed a whole individual and was thought to be divine as it became symbolic of the god Osiris who had also been dismembered and then made whole again. The deceased were called "Osiris" to symbolically link them with Osiris's proven ability to regenerate from scattered parts. The afterlife process had developed in sophistication to the point where it merited a board game known as senet for which to practise journeying after death.

At this point the journey to the afterlife was well underway, and it was a long and complicated process culminating in judgment: the famous "weighing of the heart" ceremony. The task of judgment was delegated to lesser gods: Anubis the jackal god, son of Osiris presided and Ma'at, the daughter of Ra, represented the principle of order in society. It was her feather used in the weighing of the heart ceremony.

Gary Stilwell, researcher of religious history, observes conduct and behaviour determining afterlife judgment and that it was relevant to everyone from the beginning of Egyptian civilization:

> *It remains that conduct and behavior counted very much from the earliest written records for both king and commoner. Thus, by the end of the Old Kingdom, both groups appear to have been subject*

not only to any judicial proceedings that may have arisen after death, but also a more fully-developed general judgment. [276]

Further, the concept of oblivion was seen as a fate worse than death. In Egypt, those failing judgment had their heart and akh immediately consumed by a hippopotamus-like monster, Ammut. Their afterlife was done. The Egyptologist John Taylor describes how treason, a crime against the integrity of society itself, met with denial of afterlife – oblivion:

Those who were executed for major crimes such as treason, however, were potentially denied the afterlife, as expressed in the phrase 'There is no tomb for the rebel'. Execution by burning was a punishment for serious offences, and since the corpse was destroyed in the process no afterlife was possible for those condemned to suffer this fate. [277]

So the complex and formal afterlife judgment in ancient Egypt evolved out of the desire for social order and preservation of society, not consciously or planned, of course, but organically by natural selection of memes, as was the case in other cultures.

Having successfully navigated judgment the deceased's akh finally entered the Field of Reeds in the underworld, but that was temporary. While Ra was the sun god, Osiris and Ra were seen as a duality, and the importance of Osiris's regeneration becomes apparent when it is realized that every spirit akh in the underworld separated into its ba and ka at sunset (which was dawn on earth). The ba returned to the tomb on earth each sunrise and had to be reunited into the akh at sunset, sent away by written spells in the tomb, for another day in Duat. Similarly, the sun was thought to regenerate through the power of Osiris in Duat before sunrise on earth each day. A large number of afterlife adventures, journeys and challenges were envisaged which could include ghostly visitations to earth.

Has physical resurrection taken place? Many authors consider it has, but the GMR accepts the considered view of Egyptologist Raymond Faulkner, and colleagues, who posthumously compiled his work, concluding that Egyptian afterlife beliefs were wholly spiritual. They point out that the funerary texts describe numerous places in the afterlife but not the normal earth, and include the exhortation that the dead should be worshipped by the living. If the Egyptians had a true resurrection religion so early then surely the concept would have spread widely before even Judaism and Zoroastrianism first codified it.

The spiritual afterlife tradition in Egypt lasted over three thousand years but fell out of favour during the Roman period. In the third century CE the physical resurrection model of Christianity quickly overran the old Egyptian religion forever.

Chinese Traditional Religion

Thus the 'po' soul of the deceased is also believed to descend into the Chinese underworld, or Hell, to be judged and tried for its sins by the infernal judiciary before being punished and, eventually, reincarnated. This is an ancient belief, well established before the coming of Buddhism to China in the first century CE. [278]

– Jennifer Oldstone-Moore

The Chinese civilization is the oldest continuously surviving and, perhaps because it has never been fully subjugated, still keeps its long and continuous traditional religion. This has about 400 million adherents today and as many again non-practicing who still retain some level of belief in it. Of all the spiritual religions, the Chinese traditional is the largest surviving.

Syncretism is tolerated in Chinese traditional religion as it is able to absorb many external ideas, sometimes contradictory, and still maintain its essential character. This religion, also known as Folk or Shenism, which is investigated here, excludes the influences of Buddhism and Christianity. While Folk religion has been influenced by the philosophy of Confucianism, it is Taoism which can be considered the "state" form of the traditional religion. It is characterized by ancestor worship including nature deities and legendary historical figures.

Often, it has been considered that in the first millennium BCE before China became united under one dynastic emperor, and before Buddhist influences, the concept of a person's dual spirit, hunpo, had developed. However, Kenneth Brashier, a professor of religious studies, calls the hunpo a scholastic model and summarizes:

Grave stele texts, which also never distinguish between a hun and a po, suggest a different dualism — that between the hun or po

> *with its corporeal associations on the one hand and the more
> rarefied shen on the other. This dualism may have found a
> practical expression in ancestral worship because the hunpo and
> body were generally confined to the cemetery but the mobile shen
> enjoyed its sacrifices at the lineage shrine.* [279]

This physical evidence supports the shen as the primary concept of a spirit. It is this which journeys to the afterlife realm, but there is no real consensus. The concept of kuei as a spirit form may have been for the poor and it was the wealthy that were honoured as a shen after death. The requirement for more than one spirit is also cited as an explanation as to how an ancestor can be existing in a shrine and also in a distant spirit world and, further, that the duality of spirit fits the Taoist principle of yin and yang.

Ancestor worship requires a small shrine, of which there are several millions in China, where names are recorded on scrolls or plaques, and offerings can be made. The writer Jonathan Chamberlain observes in *Chinese Gods*:

> *Ancestors were worshipped long before the Gods were born. [...]
> The dead continue to look after the welfare of the living just as the
> living continue to take care of the dead.* [280]

Chamberlain hints at the principle of external judgment. The Chinese ancestors are typically benevolent, but they can be provoked. Alan Barnard and Jonathan Spencer describe a delicately balanced relationship seen in both ancient Rome and China:

> *In these systems the ancestors are believed to exercise a moral
> guardianship over their descendants and they are particularly
> concerned that the group of descendants do not quarrel among
> themselves. This guardianship, although ultimately thought of as
> beneficial, is double-edged since the ancestors mainly manifest
> themselves through the punishment of their descendants; often by
> sending them diseases. In such a case ancestor worship often
> involves appeasement in ways such as sacrifice.* [281]

This was a two-way relationship. The ancestors passed judgment on the living and yet in the afterlife the ancestors depended upon continued veneration by them. The effect is a form of social control which seems to have been harnessed by the emerging state, particularly as graves slowly came to replace names written in shrines as the focal point of ancestral existence. Freedman describes an evolving process with the advent of imperial dynasties:

> *..the cult of the ancestors assumed a new character: 'it was a moral cult, completely symbolic, quite abstract'; whereas among the 'feudal' nobility there had been an intimate and emotionally charged communion with the ancestors.* [176]

We have a picture of a culture where spiritual afterlife leads directly to a feedback mechanism for the stability of society. From its earliest beginnings of the oracle-bone beliefs at 1500 BCE to the present day, religion has been instrumental in maintaining the fabric of the Chinese civilization.

Japanese Traditional Religion

It was during the Middle Jomon period when several significant changes occurred, strongly suggesting that the spiritual worldview had arrived by 3500 BCE. Cemeteries were being set up in the centre of settlements which must have been ancestral shrines, and the settlements themselves were expanding with populations of many hundreds. Burial mounds containing ritual artefacts such as clay statuettes and beads started appearing. Variation in the types of burials increased, and sometimes they were in pits under the uprights of stone circles.

Secondary burials with ochre-painted bones are seen by the start of the Late Jomon, about 2400 BCE, and ancestor worship continued to prevail throughout the Final Jomon.

The first and primary formal religion in Japan is known as Jinja Shinto, developing from a fusion of ancestor worship and varied traditional beliefs between 1000 and 500 BCE. The principal element is kami, spiritual beings which are ancestors, legendary or mythical figures and totemic nature spirits. Shinto shrines are always carefully sited near natural features such as streams, isolated rocks, trees and hills where a watchful kami dwells.

A realm of the dead known as Yomi, was considered. This was not a place of reward or punishment, but very gloomy in a similar respect to that imagined by the Mesopotamians. Judgment was delivered upon the living as ancestor worship remained a powerful control on moral behaviour in society, and this was supplemented by the Confucian moral code imported from China.

Buddhism also arrived in Japan in the middle of the sixth Century CE and came to supersede the old idea of afterlife in an ancestral realm. The earlier belief was replaced by the cycle of full reincarnation with physical afterlife, and this newer Dharmic religion is discussed separately in the next chapter.

Indus Valley (Harappan) Religion †

> *The religious and funerary beliefs and practices of the Harappans show great variety. While there are dangers in viewing these through the lens of later-day Hinduism, it is interesting to note that the Harappan civilization does display a few features reminiscent of later traditions, except, however, the important element of temple worship. Not a single structure found at any Harappan site can conclusively be identified as a temple.* [64]
>
> – Upinder Singh

The Indus Valley civilization is one of the five foundation civilizations of the world, starting about 3500 BCE, and then, between 2500 and 2000 BCE boasting great cities, Harappa and Mohenjo-Daro, with tens of thousands of people. Decline occurred until it was extinguished by invasion before 1500 BCE. All of its ruins are silent, unlike Egypt, Mesopotamia and China; its language, seen on clay and metal seals, has never been deciphered.

Debate rages over the meaning of the Indus Valley logographic script. Most sentences are very short, rarely more than five symbols, perhaps only proper names and titles. The frequency distribution of the symbols is unlike a spoken language, leading some epigraphists to suggest it is non-linguistic. Asko Parpola, Indologist, disagrees and convincingly argues that the script is a true spoken language. [282] The most important early function of writing was not just economic or political but its assistance in formalising religion across the whole of a civilized society, especially one as spread out as the Indus Valley which occupied numerous river valleys and stretched nearly a million square kilometres. However, until this script is deciphered it is necessary to consider the Indus Valley religion based upon archaeological remains and the pictorial representations on the seals. The most common image is a mythical unicorn with a perforated filter for extracting juices from a crushed plant, perhaps as a hallucinogenic for religious ceremonies.

Considering the number of people who lived in this civilization, even the burial evidence is meagre. No proper cemetery is yet known from the major site of Mohenjo-Daro. In Harappa, a large cemetery, R-37, reveals the wealthy were often buried in stone or brick-lined graves with wooden coffins, laid in repose with heads pointed north. They had daily possessions: bowls, pottery, weapons and ornaments. The poor were laid in simple graves. Many funerary urns with ashes have been found showing a parallel or later tradition of cremation. Grave goods representing the NST are mostly absent except for some shells and shell bangles. In one house two infants were found buried beneath the floor – this was the practice of rebirth belief transformed during the spiritual worldview paradigm shift into partial reincarnation belief in many cultures.

Iravatham Mahadevan, epigrapher and historian, describes a religion unlike that in the Hindu Vedas:

> *The Harappan religion, as far as we can make out from pictorial representations, included the worship of buffalo-horned male gods, mother goddesses, the pipal tree, serpents, and probably also phallic worship.* [283]

For the purpose of the GMR we are interested in the afterlife paradigm where the conclusion that this culture had a mature spiritual religion is undeniable. Additionally, we would fully expect afterlife judgment to have existed, underpinning society. There is clear evidence of funerary ritual in burials and this is, of course, the earliest form of afterlife judgment. In other civilizations ritual judgment was superseded by the external judgment of ancestors, then gods. There is certainly evidence of god belief but nothing can yet be concluded about external judgment or spirit realms.

The Indus Valley civilization had gods but they were not Hindu. It predates Hinduism and no Hindu figurines or artefacts have been found at their sites. The Rig Veda, the oldest Aryan literature, dates from 1500 BCE which is at the very end of the Indus Valley civilization and only once seems to mention Harrapa (Hariyupiyah), their major city. Some aspects of Indus Valley belief endured: a deity practising yoga, communal ceremonial baths, fire rituals, veneration of the pipal tree and north-pointing burials.

Greco-Roman Religion †

> *The Iliad in particular presents a very austere picture of the after-life as a total contrast with life on earth, and neither rewards nor punishments would have suited the poet's bleak conception of death as the common end for all men alike, whether good or bad, humble or great. Such was not, it seems, the universal belief of those times, as we can see from passing allusions to characters who do escape this common lot.* [284]

– Nicholas Richardson

Many authors look at Homer's *Iliad* and conclude that the Greeks had a gloomy belief in the realm of the dead and it did not matter how people behaved in life – they met the same end. Nicholas Richardson, tutor in classics at Oxford University, presents a different view. In *Greek Religion and Society* he concludes that judgment before afterlife, leading to a poor or good quality afterlife, is mentioned in many different sources and was the majority belief by the classical Greeks.

Crete, the island home of the Minoans had Elysium as a place of spiritual reward perhaps by 1800 BCE. Rodney Castleden writes of a late clay coffin, known as the Agia Triadha Sarcophagus, dated close to 1470 BCE, when the Minoan culture was badly crippled by the Thera volcanic eruption:

> *It is beautifully painted with scenes of the dead person's funeral along the sides, and scenes of Elysium, or the way to Elysium, on the ends; smiling goddesses in plumed head-dresses ride along in a chariot drawn by a griffin on one end, and by a goat on the other, presumably ready to convey the human soul to Elysium, to live ever after with the gods.* [285]

Elysium as a spirit world, was a belief later adopted by the Athenians and other classical period city-states on the Greek mainland.

Kaufmann Kohler, theologian, also notes the presence of the large number of charms which were placed in graves in classical Greece to ensure a good afterlife for the deceased:

> *Recent discoveries of hundreds of little gold plates belonging to the fourth and fifth pre-Christian centuries, which contain extracts of the Pythagorean system of belief in afterlife retribution, and which have apparently been deposited as charms for the dead in those tombs or coffins of South Italy (and also of Crete).* [286]

The Hellenistic period was from Alexander the Great's death in 323 BCE to Octavian's victory at Actium in 31 CE and was characterized by a situation of religious flux, when many new deities from the East came to be worshipped, including Isis from Egypt. By the end of this period the Roman Empire was in full control.

The Italian afterlife beliefs, first by the Etruscans and then by the Romans, were largely borrowed from Greek religious tradition. The pantheon of Greek gods was accepted wholesale: Elysium as a realm of the dead and judgment of deeds in life, and also the idea of spiritual transmigration with birds as psychopomps. A widely held belief in Roman times was that the spirit was carried from the deceased by an eagle, and this belief originated in Assyria.

Elysium was a place of reward and Tartarus a place of retribution. In later times Elysium and Tartarus were subsumed into separate regions of Hades (which has only since become analogous to Hell by the English-speaking Christian peoples). In the Greco-Roman spirit world two lakes or streams were believed to exist. Those who drank from the Lethe would "forget" and meet oblivion. Those who drank from Mnemosyne would remember their past. This is allegorical of the desire for preservation of identity in spiritual afterlife and an explanation of those who lost their identity after death.

The largest unconventional religion in the Roman Empire was the mystery cult of Mithraism which flourished in the first to fourth centuries CE. It was a popular religion with the military and government officials, conducted in caves or semi-buried temples. Ritual sacrifice of a bull was its central symbolism. The meaning of it is unclear but thought to be for facilitating the progress of spirits into the afterlife, perhaps by harnessing the blood and power of the bull.

Although a few exceptional Romans denied the existence of afterlife, like the Stoics in Greece, the majority by far, held to the mainstream belief of afterlife and judgment. Jocelyn Toynbee, classical archaeologist, writes on the situation in the first century BCE:

> *Nevertheless, it is clear that there was developing among the Romans the sense that the survival of the individual implies some kind of moral responsibility on his or her part as regards afterlife destiny; and that all men must expect a reckoning and judgment after death, when an earthly life well spent, with duties successfully performed and talents made the most of, would reap its reward.* [287]

The Greeks and Romans of Classical Antiquity had a rich tapestry of spiritual beliefs with the spirits of the deceased usually judged and treated accordingly. Most of the Olympian gods were part of the fabric of the religious worldview, which was used to explain how the world works and how it came about – but were tangential to the affairs of the dead. Eventually, the resurrection afterlife of Christianity swept aside the old beliefs when it finally won imperial support after the conversion of Constantine in the early fourth century CE, although many Greeks had been Christian for a long time already.

Celtic Druidism †

> *They wish to inculcate this as one of their leading tenets that souls do not become extinct, but pass after death from one body to another, and they think that men by this tenet are in a great degree excited to valour, the fear of death being disregarded.*

> – Julius Caesar, Book Six of the Gallic Wars

The pre-Roman Celts occupied a large swathe of Central Europe from the British Isles to the Black Sea coast in the seventh to first centuries BCE, then were largely overrun by the expanding Roman Empire. These peoples left no written evidence of their culture, relying instead on long oral histories committed to memory by a priestly caste known as the Druids. The religion of the Celts is considered as Druidism, which incorporated many nature deities and traditions of shamanistic magic.

Determining their afterlife belief comes from two sources. In Britain and France the burial evidence points to belief in a spiritual realm of the Norse Valhalla or Greco-Roman Hades type. Smashed pots, weapons, jewellery and wine containers are all found in Celtic graves, strongly indicative of immediate spiritual afterlife with adulthood preserved.

Written sources are less certain. Caesar, in his account, appears to be describing reincarnation, and it is commonly considered that Druidism was similar to the Dharmic religions in this respect. The Greek historian Diordus Siculus made a similar observation. The probability is that the Celts, in their Druidist beliefs held that afterlife was originally in a spiritual realm and that after a period there the deceased were partially reincarnated as a new-born, although losing previous identity soon afterwards. Further analysis of evidence in burials for the funerary rituals expressed would clarify the situation.

Scandinavian, Norse and Teutonic Religions †

> *All Nordic peoples possessed beliefs in further otherworlds, usually situated in a vertical array underground and open as destinations for the dead. In general, each was presided over by a deity or spirit. [..] In Sami tradition, a more or less generic land of the dead Jabme-ajmuo (Jabmeaimo) was ruled by the goddess Jabme-ahkka, while a deeper and darker Rut-ajmuo was reserved for the wicked and was presided over by the evil god of death, disease and calamity, Ruto.* [288]

– Thomas Andrew DuBois

When the Mesolithic Ertebølle culture disappears, the evidence for subsequent NRT and rebirth burials also disappears, and finally the spiritual worldview prevailed in north-west Europe. The concept came of ancestors permanently existing in the landscape and it sets the scene for the rise of ancestor worship.

DuBois in *Nordic religions in the Viking Age* describes ancestor worship as an early religion:

> *The closest and conceptually perhaps the oldest otherworld for Nordic dead merged with the grave itself. Forms of familiar ancestor worship occurred among all the Nordic groups to varying degrees and often took place on or near the grave. Balto-Finnic peoples practiced varieties of ancestor worship which had their roots deep in the Finno-Ugric past.* [288]

In Southern Sweden, Denmark and Northern Germany, ancestor veneration, just as in the Atlantic megalithic cultures, was a transitional belief, never fully disappearing but subsequently submerged into the pagan Norse and Teutonic mythologies with the rise of gods.

In the centuries before Christianity reached Scandinavia the pagan religious traditions prevailed. Grave goods were consistent with spiritual afterlife: weapons and day-to-day utility goods reflecting the occupations of the deceased, sacrificed animals, and even sacrificed men or women as servants in elite burials. Certainly these would have been of symbolic significance as they were intended for use in the afterlife. The Viking sagas recount Valhalla, which was reserved for warriors who would fight enemies and feast continually, and also many lesser halls of the dead. The Gundestrap Cauldron from Denmark, previously described, illustrates dead soldiers, revived by a deity, and then riding off to fight in a spiritual afterlife. These spirit realms where the dead were confined were thought to exist in many places and reduced the problem of wandering ghosts. Gods ruled these realms, but were initially not responsible for facilitating spiritual afterlife which was a natural process.

Images of the famous Norse gods are essentially absent from burials, except for Thor who is seen occasionally as a carving but most often simply by amulets of his hammer. Thor was a storm god and the association of storms with wind and breathing likely made his hammer the most powerful pagan amulet for ensuring spiritual afterlife. A soapstone mould from Trengarden, Denmark, dated to the 900s CE, was used by an amulet maker and had three impressions for pouring metal: one a hammer shape and two Christian crucifixes showing the importance and correlation of both symbols. Perhaps the cross symbolizing Christian resurrection generated the parallel meme of Thor's hammer symbolizing spiritual transmigration. Both of these were very popular, but rarely worn together, showing a separate coexistence, until finally Christianity replaced the pagan beliefs.

African Traditional Religions

Nyame is responsible for death. When a human dies, his soul stands before Nyame for judgment. If the soul is worthy it will pass into the spirit world, but if the human was bad his spirit

> *must return to haunt for a designated amount of time, and in*
> *some cases, forever.*

– Molefi Asante and Emeka Nwadiora

The Dark Continent hides its secrets well, including two important events in its history: the worldview paradigm shift from rebirth to spiritual afterlife, which certainly became ancestor worship for most African tribes, and then the influences from, or transition to, Christianity or Islam. These have both spread far into the continent and often elevated a pre-existing nature spirit to the position of high god. For determining the extent of LMR in Africa it is important to distinguish the traditional beliefs before they became overlaid with Abrahamic beliefs, and that is what is being attempted in this section.

For most of African history, during the Holocene, people were hunters and foragers. In some places where small-scale farming villages developed, there was sufficient density to allow true multilevel natural selection, by way of inter-settlement competition. This was, of course, most significant on the Nile, giving rise to Egyptian culture and religion, and the influence of it spread southwards. North and East Africa was also an early arrival point for Christianity, which is still strong in Ethiopia.

The Nuer and Dinka of Sudan both have a concept of the afterlife but it is very vague. Yet, the Dinka in particular are considered very religious people who believe in a high god and have equally high moral standards. Their perception of judgment is unusual in that the repercussions for morally poor behaviour are illness and misfortune during life. This is a form of internal, self-judgment.

The traditional religion of the Masai of Kenya and Tanzania has a high god belief but no clear afterlife belief; the deceased were left for the hyenas by way of excarnation and the only spirits were warring gods.

The anthropologist John Peel writes of the Yoruba people in Nigeria, West Africa, and he attempts to discern their religious traditions before the influence of Islam. It proves difficult as the Yoruba seem predisposed to accepting the principle of afterlife judgment:

> *So the idea of the afterlife as a site of punishment or reward, and*
> *not just as a staging-post between one earthly existence and*
> *another, was widespread in central and western Yorubaland.*
> *Townsend summed up attitudes in Badagry in 1845: "It is a*

common saying . . . that they shall meet their forefathers after death and they have some notions of a state of reward or punishment, but it is indistinct and seldom spoken of." [289]

This is echoed by Molefi Asante and Emeka Nwadiora, Professors of African American Studies, who are definite in their summary:

When the time for man's death comes he knows Olodumare will judge him. Yoruba fear this judgment at death most. [...] The acts one commits in present life determine his final destination, either Orun Rere (Good Orun) or Orun Apadi (Bad Orun). Naturally, people strive for eternal peace and happiness, therefore, "whatever is done in the present life, therefore, must be done with due regard to this great future" (Idowu, 1962. p. 189). [290]

Asante and Nwadiora are searching to identify a unified African religion and particularly the presence of a universal high god. Nyame is the high god of the Akan people who performs judgment. The Ibo tribes have similar traditional beliefs as described by the theologian Edmund Ilogu:

There is no clear concept of life after death in some bodily form. Although there is the general idea of a form of continuity after death within and outside reincarnation, [...] There is the belief in an "afterlife" reward for the good man, especially through the quick reincarnation that he is allowed to make. [291]

The concept of a high god is true in parts of West Africa, but not all of it. Edward Geoffrey Simons Parrinder, before becoming a Dean of Theology at King's College in London, spent many years as a Methodist missionary in West Africa. He describes the Ghanaian Ashanti afterlife beliefs:

Even with the best fortune in the after-world, the highest possible reward is to be allowed to return to this earth in a well-arranged reincarnation, in the same blood and totem clan. [...] In the future world the deceased one still depends on his family for sustenance, in the form of the offerings which are made at regular intervals: the adae ceremonies that play such a large part in Ashanti religion. [292]

The concept seemed undefined in the Ashanti until the Christian era, and is still often absent in Central Africa where even the prerequisite spiritual worldview can be vague.

Unlike the Yoruba and Akan, with their clear tradition of external judgment, the Ashanti show a tradition of ritual judgment, where quality of afterlife depends upon funerary practices performed by the living. This puts behavioural constraints on members of society who will then be concerned that they receive proper ritual funerals in due course.

Afterlife belief is weak or even non-existent throughout Central African tribes. In the south Congo, the Bushongo have some tradition of ancestor veneration but it is not strong and the primary belief is in nature spirits, fetishism and gods – as the chief is thought to be of divine origin. John Middleton, anthropologist, observes the absence of afterlife beliefs in the nearby Lugbara peoples:

> *There are no beliefs in heaven or hell, nor of any belief of award or punishment after death for the life lived on earth. Offences and sins are punished while the offender is still alive, or, if he has died, punishment falls on his living kin. There are no beliefs in reincarnation nor in any mystical connection between a certain ancestor and a certain descendant.* [184]

Despite this, they still had a concept of spirituality. There is also a clear implication of internal judgment similar to that of the Dinka.

The Bambuti peoples are Pygmy tribesmen of the Congo region and live a hunter-gatherer existence. They do not have significant afterlife beliefs either. Early Portuguese missionaries reported that the Thonga tribe of southern Mozambique did have a belief in an afterlife realm and deceased males were buried with weapons in their hands to prepare them for it. The Lozi peoples, primarily in Zambia, have strong afterlife beliefs. During a burial, broken ("killed") objects are interred and the spirit of the deceased first journeys to a place of proto-judgment by the high god Nyambe. After a trial by identification is performed, they continue on to an ancestral realm, but those failing judgment face oblivion.

Hilary and Janette Deacon, archaeologists, write in *Human Beginnings in South Africa* about the spiritual beliefs of the Khoisan people in South West Africa. /Xam is their almost extinct language which incorporates clicking sounds:

Where nineteenth-century beliefs about death and the afterlife have been recorded, as from the /Xam informants, it appears that the spirits of the dead were believed to have remained in the landscape and could be called upon for assistance with rain-making and controlling the game. [293]

Spirits in the landscape is a form of totemism, which might seem to be incredibly ancient throughout all of Africa, but evidence from burials suggests otherwise, particularly in South Africa. Red ochre and shells of NRT were the primary ritual elements of South African burials until only about two thousand years ago. This indicates that rebirth afterlife belief held sway there for longer than in most of Africa and Eurasia before the paradigm shift to a spiritual worldview occurred.

North American Native Religion

Here the good father and all who advocate a theory of borrowing are at variance with Master Thomas Heriot, 'that learned Mathematician' (1588). In Virginia 'there is one chiefe god, that has beene from all eternitie,' who 'made other gods of a principall order'. Near New Plymouth, Kiehtan was the chief god, and the souls of the just abode in his mansions. [294]

– Andrew Lang

Interpreting North American Native traditional religions presents the same difficulty as seen in Africa – identifying the transition between life-force and spiritual worldviews, and excluding the religious influences from Europeans. Andrew Lang, in 1887, mentions afterlife judgment in context with the glimpse of Native American religion provided by Elizabethan polymath Thomas Harriot at the time of the first contacts. Colonization of North and South America proceeded apace from 1500 and Native American burial traditions changed quickly. For example, in New England, burials before 1500 were without personal goods, but shortly after European interaction effects such as arm bands were being interred.

The Native American peoples are almost all descended from Asian migration across the Bering Strait. The journey across the far north would have been difficult and slow, likely via coastal migrations 16,000 years ago before the last Ice Ages had relinquished its grip. A reward of temperate virgin territory of vast size secured permanent human occupancy. By 13,000 years ago the whole of North and South America had been colonized with Paleoindian hunter-gatherers, but at a low population density.

Landscape cupules in exposed rock are widespread in North America and some are Palaeolithic, evidencing the life-force worldview of naturalistic animism. Red ochre, shells and lithics are seen in primary single burials evidencing the NRT and ERA. In the Americas rebirth afterlife beliefs were continued for thousands of years by descendants of those who crossed the Bering Strait.

Encompassing the transition from the first sedentary camps about 8000 BCE to fully fledged farming and agricultural lifestyles are the Early, Middle and Late Archaic Periods which are considered to end about 1000 BCE. However, this final date was earlier in the east and much later in the west. As settlements were being established and the density of populations continually increased throughout the Archaic Periods, group ranges reduced and interactions with other groups increased. The intensity of multilevel natural selection between groups also kept increasing. Farming first began in the Eastern Woodlands about 3000 BCE spreading across many of the eastern states of the USA by 2000 BCE.

Just like in the Fertile Crescent of the Middle East it was the settled cultures which first developed the spiritual worldview, allowing for ancestor worship, totemism and far larger societies. The remaining nomadic tribes, such as the Apache, certainly learned the spiritual memes through later interaction.

It seems that it was during the Late Archaic Period that spirituality emerged. Burials are much more elaborate at the end of it with NST as supporting symbolism. Clues exist as they do in the Old World.

The previously described cemetery at the Price III site, Wisconsin, suggests the spiritual worldview paradigm shift occurred there between 1710 and 1280 BCE. Clearly it was later in the west of the continent, as a burial in Yoakum County, West Texas, is dated to about 990 BCE and is of a classic ROT nature. The Thursday Site burial in Utah, dated between 70 and 220 CE, has probable ART egg symbolism, also for rebirth. This very late date shows that the paradigm shift took at least 2000 years to traverse North America and reach the remotest areas.

Mound building was prevalent in Native American cultures and this seems to be in two general groups: mounds in the shape of animals or geometric shapes, and burial mounds. Animal mounds may have been to help make the landscape alive, conceptually similar to the purpose of landscape cupules. The early Poverty Point mounds don't have burials and neither does the famous Serpent Mound in Ohio, possibly made by the Adena tribe.

The *burial* mounds are, however, a strong signature of spiritual afterlife belief. They were totemic locations, domains for ancestors who were venerated and in turn watched over the living. The Adena started burial mound construction around 1000 BCE and continued with them for some 800 years, with many richly endowed burials. Their successors, the Hopewell, carried on this tradition. High Plains mounds are seen from about 200 CE with multiple burials.

The Pueblo cultures of the south-west were notable for their permanent settlements. They had complex burials with grave goods, implying progression to a spiritual realm of the gods and ancestors, but also allowing for partial reincarnation – especially for children.

Stephanie Whittlesey and J. Jefferson Reid, anthropologists at the University of Arizona, describe the Grasshopper Pueblo site of the Mogollon culture in the central transition zone of central Arizona. It is regarded as the most thoroughly studied site in North America with the funerary remains of nearly 700 individuals found in the period 1300 to 1450 CE. They cite many references, observing:

> *Subadults were more likely than adults to be buried within rooms. The youngest infants and fetal burials often were placed in pits immediately below the floors of occupied rooms. This has been explained with reference to ethnographically documented Pueblo practices. By keeping the deceased child close to the mother, its spirit may be encouraged to return quickly in the form of another baby.* [295]

In an early spiritual worldview context this is certainly correct.

Evidence for judgment in afterlife exists but is almost impossible to disentangle from post-contact Christian influences. Tom Lowenstein, ethnographer, and Piers Vitebsky, anthropologist, relate a nineteenth century account of Hopi belief concerning spiritual progression:

> *On the path to the place where the Hopi emerged onto earth (sipapu) in the Grand Canyon (Oraibi), the "breath body" of the deceased traveller is met by a guardian called Tokonaka. If Tokonaka judges the traveller to be good, he lets him or her proceed*

> *to the town of the dead. Otherwise, a spirit traveller might have
> to journey on a forked trail leading to a series of up to four fire
> pits. If the spirit can be purified in the first pit, it can return to
> the trail of the good. The incorrigibly evil are burnt in the fourth
> fire pit.* [296]

The origin of spirituality in the Americas is uncertain. It is arguable that the Native North American peoples developed their own spiritual paradigm, as well as independently developing agriculture. However, the proximity with the Mesoamericans means that diffusion is very possible. The template meme of the spiritual worldview may have developed in the Eastern Woodlands and spread down to the emerging Olmec culture, or vice versa. A final diffusion of spiritual concepts from Asia cannot be ruled out either. Careful study of contemporary burial evidence may reveal the answer to this interesting question.

Mesoamerican Religion †

> *Life and death were not separate states for the peoples of
> Mesoamerica. The life-force was eternal, and one's brief "life" on
> earth was a moment in that eternity. Assimilation into that
> eternal force was not death; on the contrary, it was a movement
> into the essential nature of life. The funerary mask was the most
> fundamental metaphor created by the peoples of Mesoamerica for
> that conception.* [297]

– Peter Markman and Roberta Markman

The Olmec civilization flourished from 1500 BCE to about 400 BCE in the southern Gulf of Mexico coastal region with their main centre at San Lorenzo, west of the Yucatan. The religion of the Olmec is very obscure and needs to be inferred from burials and art, as remains of their written language are almost non-existent.

Because of the acidity of the soil, bones and even shells have dissolved, leaving only robust grave goods in burials. Those found include serpentine, jade, red ochre, cinnabar and pottery. The Olmec had special veneration for the jaguar and many half-human half-jaguar figurines exist, especially of infants. The latter are reminiscent of the Palaeolithic ERA belief system. These statues may have been made to capture the spiritual power of jaguars and transfer it into newborns – jaguar speed, strength and ferocity being attributes which Olmecs would want to see in their young who would grow up to inherit their civilization.

Many of the famous Olmec colossal heads, which depict rulers, are peppered with cupules. These are not sculpted as part of the original design but seem to have been added in antiquity all the same. Perhaps, as their civilization was fading, late descendants bored cupules into the stone heads as an attempt to "animate" them via breathing symbolism – to obtain ancestral assistance in the event of a major problem.

Christopher Pool, archaeologist, writes about the burials of nobles from cultures which followed the demise of the Olmecs:

> *During the Terminal Formative period, elites were buried with clam shells and jade ornaments. In one particularly sumptuous burial, the deceased was covered with red cinnabar and accompanied by ceramic vessels, an Olmec-style pottery figurine (undoubtedly an heirloom), a ball-game yoke, and a turtle shell elaborately carved with a profile head surrounded by two intertwined serpents.* [298]

From the perspective of the GMR we can see a range of funerary ritual artefacts consistent with the NST: shells (egg renewal), jade (plant renewal), cinnabar (blood renewal), turtle shell and serpents (egg renewal). Shells in particular are prevalent in burials in all the Mesoamerican cultures.

Eastwards of Olmec centres, the Maya were the main civilization in southern Mexico, Guatemala and Belize, with beginnings in about 1800 BCE and flowering after the Olmec in the Classical Period, from 250 to 900 CE. Their written language is well-represented in archaeology and also well understood by epigraphists. It is at once revealing and remarkable that the religious worldview which buttressed civilization in the Old World should be mirrored so similarly in the New World. The Mayans had spiritual afterlife, enabling ancestors to persist and be worshipped, and allowing external or fatalist judgment as a control over society. Lynn Foster, archaeologist and writer, with Peter Mathews, archaeologist, summarise the Mayan beliefs:

> *Maya funerary customs were based on a belief in rebirth and ancestor worship. These two beliefs combined into the foundations of Maya life from the earliest periods to the present. Powerful,*

> *semidivine ancestors were reborn as gods and acted for the benefit*
> *of descendants – if they were properly propitiated.* [246]

Ancestors were thought to have an active interest in the affairs of the living and mediated on behalf of the living with the multitude of nature and mythical deities. The anthropologist Arthur Demarest adds:

> *As Maya family groups were probably patrilinial and often patrilocal, the veneration of a prominent deceased male was often emphasized, sometimes with a small shrine within the household plaza group. [...] In many ways, the great stone temples of the Maya centers with splendid royal tombs within them were merely aggrandized versions of the household shrines. The great pageants of the ceremonial centers venerating the dead kings were simply ancestor worship writ large, the celebration of the dead kings as ancestors of the ruling lineage and as a collective ancestor of the entire community.* [299]

The Maya also conceived of their spiritual afterlife with regions of reward and punishment. Their heaven was Tamoanchan, with 13 levels, and hell was Xibalba, with 9 levels. Only a few such as the rulers and a few fated individuals went directly to Tamoanchan. Most Mayans had to journey through Xibalba and were tested by deities who inflicted disease and injury. Drew comments:

> *It is none too clear how Xibalba was truly conceived, nor how many could hope to escape from it. Apparently most were doomed to spend eternity within its rank halls, unless they could outwit the Lords of Death or unless they died in war, through sacrifice or in childbirth. Only then would they be given an easy birth within the Underworld itself or be resurrected and take an immortal place amongst the thirteen levels of the Heavens.* [203]

Caves were regarded as entrances to the underworld and were used for many burials, presumably to speed up the dead on their spiritual journey, although how this is reconciled with ancestors remaining near the living is indeed unclear. The Mesoamerican cultures were notorious for practices of human sacrifice and many burials contain skeletons of servants or captives. Pots and other items were deliberately broken to send them into the afterlife with the deceased for use in their passage though Xibalba.

The Aztec of central Mexico was the last of the Mesoamerican civilizations before European colonization. Like the Mayans, they conceived of afterlife with spirit realms of reward and of Mictlan, the place of gloomy punishment. Unlike most other cultures morality and behaviour did not count. The deceased were destined for a fated judgment. Who you were and how you died was all that mattered. Aguilar-Moreno describes how the 52-year-cycle of destruction applied to not only the earth but the realms of the dead:

> *This extended to the realm of Mictlan and weighed upon those destined to the underworld – a majority of the Aztec population, regardless of social position. Upon reaching Mictlan after a journey of four years, a person's essence would be completely eliminated in a dramatic fashion from any conscious memory of the Aztec nation. The prospect of this demise brought feelings of hopelessness and despair to many Aztecs.* [244]

As described in the previous chapter, fatalist judgment is still capable of enforcing social stability and this is illustrated by the pleasurable afterlife intended for warriors. The warriors that are guaranteed a good afterlife will uphold hold the ruling hierarchy and laws of their society by physical violence, if necessary.

Aguilar-Moreno continues by describing their afterworld:

> *They spent their sunlit time in mock battles and war songs. It can be inferred from such a blissful conclusion that this place of rest was a great motivation for soldiers, for if they died at war, they would be "chosen" to live in the house of the Sun. It demonstrates the strong ideological interaction between religion and politics and allows for the Aztec ideal of immortality and reincarnation.* [244]

There were others who were destined in a similar manner. The spirits of women who died giving birth also went to the sun-god's domain. Tradesmen who died travelling to work were considered favourably in the afterlife too. The stability and continuation of society are thereby guaranteed by the "fated" afterlife of those who are most important in maintaining it.

There is strong evidence of forms of spiritual judgment showing that religion buttressed all the Mesoamerican civilizations.

Polynesian Religion †

The Polynesian peoples of the central and eastern Pacific Islands had firm spiritual beliefs with many myths of the gods, nature spirits and also a continued spiritual existence for the deceased. These were often totemic beliefs, ancestors associated with places in the landscape and, additionally, a spirit world where the dead persisted. Sometimes there could be as many as 10 to 14 levels of spirit worlds with the lowest similar to earth, and higher ones like paradise. Robert Craig, historian, illustrates the concept:

> *Bulotu is on the western point of the island of Savai'i and ruled over by Saveasi'uleo. In this underworld, spirits carry on life much as they had on earth. To reach paradise, one's soul has to have a powerful guardian spirit ('aumakua in Hawai'i) as well as relatives (deceased as well as living) to assist it on its journey. Proper burial by the living is a necessity.* [300]

However, the anthropologist Douglas Oliver observes in his *Polynesia in Early Historic Times* that judgment in afterlife did not exist in the Polynesian cultures:

> *There was, however, widespread agreement that a person's ghost was not punished for his or her behavior during life. Indeed, in the view of one of their most perspicacious observers, the Maori were not only generally fatalistic but were little concerned with their fates and little interested in the nature of the afterlife — except for the behavior of those ghosts likely to affect them in the (current) world.* [301]

Craig mentions "proper burial" and this is of course a form of ritual judgment, so there is a strong element of afterlife judgment in Polynesian culture where funerary rites are important to the deceased spirit reaching the spirit world.

The Melanesians of New Guinea and the western Pacific were encountered by the missionary James Chalmers in the 1880s who recorded their description of a spirit world afterlife:

> *At Port Moresby the natives say that the spirit as soon as it leaves the body proceeds to Elema, where it for ever dwells in the midst of food and betel-nuts, and spends the days and nights in endless*

enjoyment — eating, chewing betel-nuts, and dancing." Even this crude eschatology contemplates a retributive judgment upon those who have misspent their lives. [302]

It is clear that an element of external judgment existed, although whether this arose from Christian or Islamic influence may remain uncertain.

The inhabitants of Easter Island were responsible for more than 600 monumental statues symbolic of ancestor veneration. They were also the first victims of a self-created ecological collapse in the seventeenth Century when all the trees on their island were cut down. During the subsequent population collapse the statues were felled. The missionary Hippolyte Roussel describes their afterlife and judgment belief which he learned from them in the 1860s:

After death the soul of a person went to a foreign country where the degree of his happiness depended upon the extent to which he had respected tapus during his life. [303]

Tapu, also taboo, is an important ritual aspect of social order in Polynesia where there are numerous forbidden objects, places and activities. The Maori of New Zealand considered tapu extremely important and it acted as a social control during life. Its importance persists even into the Christian era.

The Maori had traditional beliefs which also exclude an afterlife judgment, but did consider that gods could be angry with the living, delivering punishment, so people did what they could to appease them. Augustus Earle, travel artist, describes their afterlife beliefs in 1827, soon after European interaction:

I found that the natives had not formed the slightest idea of there being a state of future punishment. They refuse to believe that the good Spirit intends to make them miserable after their decease. They imagine all the actions of this life are punished here, and that every one when dead, good or bad, bondsman or free, is assembled on an island situated near the North Cape, where both the necessaries and comforts of life will be found in the greatest abundance, and all will enjoy a state of uninterrupted happiness.
304

The colour red was considered by the Polynesians to be significant to their gods and was high status. Although red ochre was unavailable on most Pacific islands it is present in New Zealand. Before European colonization the Maori had elaborate funeral rituals which involved dressing and sitting a corpse at a whare (house) for a mourning period. The face was sometimes painted with a mixture of red ochre and oil, and many white feathers were laid on the corpse. The chief mourners were also painted with ochre.

After a respectful period they interred the corpse in a cave for at least a year. [305] Secondary burial of the bones where they were painted with red ochre then wrapped in a red-stained mat for final entombment was occasionally performed. [89]

Partial reincarnation was believed possible when the gods allowed a spirit to be reborn on earth.

The Australian Aboriginals and New Zealand Maori are separated by 1800 km of sea and never communicated in the pre-Modern era. Yet, they shared beliefs descended from the ROT. The Maori and most Polynesians have genetic ancestry in the island of Taiwan from about 6000 BCE.

Since Aboriginals arrived in Australia between 60 and 50 kya, it is likely that they inherited this tradition from common South East Asian ancestors around 70,000 years ago. Traditions of blood renewal, subsequently transformed spiritually, must have been passed down from one generation to the next since time immemorial.

European missionaries converted the Polynesians to Christianity, but they retained cultural elements of their traditional beliefs within the spiritual worldview.

Baha'i

It is clear and evident that all men shall, after their physical death, estimate the worth of their deeds, and realize all that their hands have wrought.

– Baha'u'llah

Baha'i is an international religion with an estimated 6 to 8 million adherents today.

Its original doctrine was written by Bab (formerly Ali Muhammad) of Shiraz, Persia, in the 1840s. It was built upon by his successors, primarily Baha'u'llah (formerly Baha) whose efforts were instrumental in ensuring that new the religion was properly established. Effectively the Baha'i religion was formed by way of schism from Shia Islam but was, for a long time, considered just a sect of Islam.

Baha'i is firmly monotheistic, adhering to the single supreme God close to the idealised Abrahamic God, without the Christian concept of trinity. It is very unusual for a significant modern religion as it only promises a *purely spiritual existence* in the afterlife. Even the apocalyptic eschatology of the resurrection religions is firmly diminished, as described by William McElwee Miller, a Christian missionary in Persia:

> *The Bab says that the Day of Judgment is not different from any other day – it passes, and most men are unaware of its coming. According to the Bab, it was because people were looking for a literal fulfilment of prophecy that they always failed to recognize the new Manifestation when he appeared.* [306]

"Manifestation" refers to the presence on earth of each of the earlier significant religious leaders in world history, who are considered mortal prophets in Baha'i.

After death, it is believed that a deceased's spirit ascends to a heavenly sky realm to be close to God and that the result of judgment determines the distance that the spirits remain from God, so the most worthy are nearby and the most unworthy are very remote.

7 ◆ UPPER MANTLE RELIGION: PHYSICAL AFTERLIFE

Spirituality with Physical Afterlife

Upper Mantle Religion (UMR) is comprised of religions which offer two concepts which are most important to believers today: physical afterlife with preservation of personal identity. UMR includes the remaining two afterlife paradigms: reincarnation and resurrection, which are fundamental to modern religions. Three-quarters of the world's population hold to Christianity, Islam, Hinduism, Buddhism, Sikhism, Judaism or Jainism. [307] These great religions currently buttress global society, helping billions of people live in relative harmony.

Physical Afterlife

And many of them that sleep in the dust of the earth shall awake, some to everlasting life, and some to reproaches and everlasting abhorrence.

– Book of Daniel 12:2, Hebrew Bible

The GMR holds the hypothesis that *most of the spiritual Lower Mantle religions are extinct or severely diminished because they were outcompeted by Upper Mantle religions which offer physical afterlife.*

Rebirth in the prehistoric life-force worldview was always a physical process. It is the Upper Mantle religions, prevailing today, which have returned to this more satisfying form of afterlife with the critical improvement of preservation of identity. It can be argued that the purely spiritual afterlife of the Lower Mantle religions was an aberration. Although some theologians assert that spiritual purity unencumbered by flesh is the ideal in religion, in practice, for millions of people, it is physical afterlife which has the greatest attraction.

On a fine breezy day in the year 654 CE a small group were arriving at their new home amongst strangers. They had sailed down the coast of

England from Holy Island in the far north to live and work by the mouth of the River Blackwater in the south-east. At the thriving settlement flew a small, coloured pennant. They were expected. The Saxon ruler Sigbert had invited missionaries to teach his people Christianity.

Cedd (later a saint) saw the ruins of the Roman fort of Othona, abandoned two hundred years earlier, and decided it would provide shelter and much raw material to build a church. Today, it is one of the oldest churches in England – a simple rectangle with a round chancel long since eroded by the sea, but the greater part of the building still stands. The long walk to its medieval door is still like a pilgrimage of ages past, trodden by the feet of all those countless and nameless who have gone before.

Saint Cedd was part of a Europe-wide missionary operation following in the steps of Martin, Patrick, Augustine, Columbanus, and many others. Their example was followed earnestly in another wave by missionaries at the forefront of 500 years of European colonization ending in the twentieth century. Missionaries travelled the globe overturning the old religions in North and South America, much of Africa, South East Asia, Australasia and the Pacific Islands. Islam conquered the Middle East, large parts of Africa, Central Asia, Indonesia and Malaysia.

So, Christianity and Islam swept relentlessly over dozens of ancient pagan traditions. What did all these successful missionaries say or do? While they were preaching the word of God, what blazed the path for them was a subliminal message: *Afterlife as a resurrected adult with all your memories and personality intact is far superior to intangible spiritual afterlife, where death as an ancestor means fading away forever.*

This is why a Christian missionary can convert pagan tribespeople but ask the same person to convert a follower of Islam. The missionary would be more likely feel his own warm blood on the cold steel of a curved knife instead of feeling the success of such a difficult task of conversion. And the reason why? Because the missionary has no better afterlife on offer; he is offering what someone already has and does not need again. The quality of afterlife is the same. They both believe in preservation of identity; rejuvenated and immortal. The only reliable way to change a believer's religion is to describe a better afterlife. This wins the convert.

There was a missionary tradition by the followers of Buddhism which had much success in East and South East Asia. Yet, even

Buddhism found itself on the back foot against Christianity and Islam in the clash of reincarnation and resurrection afterlife, but the difference was not enough to be decisive.

Both reincarnation and resurrection are, however, built upon a foundation of spiritual afterlife, as this is the mechanism by which identity is preserved. In the Dharmic reincarnation religions there is a division of emphasis upon samsara, the cycle of death and being physically reborn. According to religious doctrine samsara is not itself the main goal, it is moksha, a release from the cycle. In terms of natural selection of competing memes, it is the physical afterlife offered by reincarnation which gives it a greater fitness value over purely spiritual afterlife. This is why, for most Hindus and Buddhists, acceptance of the inevitability of samsara is itself satisfactory and achieving moksha a remote ideal.

David Leeming examines the state of moksha and finds various interpretations:

> *For different sects of Buddhism, the paths to nirvana are different. For some it can be achieved through disciplines and asceticism in this life. For others it is synonymous with immortality. For those who see samsara as life itself, nirvana is, in fact, sometimes "the farther shore" or almost a physical afterlife.* [308]

The cycle of reincarnation may not always end in an intangible state – but could be almost physical.

An important principle of reincarnation belief is that individuals can be reborn in a different form, through transmogrification. A female may reincarnate as a male and vice versa. The concept of progression requires that a person with poor karma, and failing judgment, becomes a lesser being: an animal, plant, or even in some traditions, a mineral. As unpalatable as it may be to the modern western mind, it is still common in reincarnation belief to imagine that females are inferior to males. It is often considered that reaching Nirvana or Brahma, escaping from samsara, can only be achieved by males, therefore females require at least one more reincarnation as a male.

A permanent physical afterlife was always assured with resurrection which came with Zoroastrianism and the Abrahamic religions. This was a major change from the old afterlife of spirituality which was considered in Classical Antiquity a pure state free of the bounds of earth.

People required proof before they would convert to belief in resurrection. The resurrection of Christ is considered primary evidence by believers, but in antiquity other evidence was looked for. Roelof van den Broek, a professor of Christian history, investigated the origins of the myth of the phoenix and establishes its importance to afterlife belief:

> *It may be considered reasonable that the phoenix was related to the death of man and the life thereafter. It is in this sense that the bird believed to find new life by its death, was assigned a role in Classical funerary symbolism and was used symbolically on coins issued at the consecration of Roman Emperors. For the Christians the phoenix constituted a form of natural evidence of the resurrection of Christ as well as of the resurrection of the flesh in general.* [309]

Birds were long considered guides for dead spirits. This developed further with the new symbolism of the long-lived phoenix dying, burning, and then being reborn – further "proof" to the ancients that resurrection afterlife was possible.

An important change seen with the spreading of higher religions is the absence of utility grave goods, which were common in purely spiritual religions. The promise of a physical afterlife with all requirements met by the God of resurrection, or simple reincarnation in Hinduism and Buddhism, means that only clothing and personal effects are provided in burials or cremations, a practice which continues today.

Preservation of Identity

> *As a rule, it is not assumed that this life – even though it does not end with death – is eternal life. Rather, it is visualized as a gradual disappearance into twilight, a second death. Because descendants remember their ancestors only as long as the ancestors' living tradition is present among them, more genteel families sacrifice to more generations than do the common people, who seldom remember more than four or five generations.* [310]

> – Richard Wilhelm

In the spiritual worldview, originally, the spirits of the dead were considered to exist only in ancestral shrines or totemic landscape locations. In this model, individual ancestors are only distinct for a few generations. Wilhelm describes the belief in China which would have been representative of ancestor worship everywhere it was practised. Fading of individual identity was inevitable as the deceased became considered amorphous with each other in the ancestral realm.

This changed with the sky, earth and underworld (SEU) paradigm, because the earth was then only for the living and the ancestors dwelt in the sky or the underworld. Usually, these were conceptually more earth-like realms and the belief was then established that individuals would exist forever, achieving spiritual immortality.

The desire for spiritual immortality is a natural consequence of increasingly sophisticated human culture leading to increasingly sophisticated spiritual identities – for all people, not just rulers who have long considered themselves as having a divinely inspired spiritual identity.

Karin Klenke, psychologist, writes about the elements of authentic leadership and the important contribution made to it by the spiritual identity system, and comments:

> *Regardless of underlying philosophical foundations, most conceptions of spirituality embody notions of a path, a journey, a process, and a developmental sequence; they also include references to inner life, meaning and purpose, connectedness, and transcendence.* [311]

When people have invested so much into their spiritual self they will prefer afterlife concepts which ensure long-term preservation of identity. More important still is the social requirement that afterlife judgment is as effective as possible. The SEU paradigm is naturally selected as it is superior to ancestral totemism in this respect.

The major reincarnation and resurrection religions require identity to be preserved spiritually, but then promise a subsequent physical afterlife. Full preservation of a single identity only occurs in the resurrection afterlife model. In the Dharmic religions this is by way of a cycle of many physical lives. The drawback with reincarnation is that each new life will always dilute the integrity of prior spiritual identity. Sometimes it is considered that the quality of spiritual identity depends upon the physical state of the mind before death. A young person who dies will be more accurately represented spiritually than an aged person who has lost his or her mental faculties. Even Buddha is believed to have had 500 previous lives.

Reincarnation Religions

Hinduism

Hindu notions of samsara and endless ages of time, concepts of judgment, heaven, and hell survive in popular lore along with the more obvious reality of physical death. Body is only temporary, but the Spiritual self lives on and will be held accountable for all choices. When we pass on to the next world for judgment, Yama, lord of the nether regions, tallies the individual's record and assesses reward or punishment. Perfectly sinless individuals are led upward to the paradise of Brahma, there to remain eternally.
312

– John Renard

Hinduism is the third largest religion in the world with about 900 million adherents today, the vast majority being in India and Nepal. It originates from the time the Indus Valley civilization fell, about 1500 BCE which is when the oldest scripture of Hinduism, the Rig Veda, was written.

Originally, early Hinduism held to the SEU paradigm which was conventional in the older spiritual religions grouped as Lower Mantle religions in the GMR. The early belief was that people had a single physical life then a spiritual afterlife. This is implied in the Vedas which also make references to the underworld being ruled by Yama, an ancient king who became god of the dead. It is believed he was the first person who died and assumed the role as overseer, dispensing judgment on everyone as decreed by their karma. Yama's underworld domain is divided into regions where the deserving had a pleasurable existence and undeserving suffered punishment.

Around the eighth to seventh centuries BCE a significant development occurred in Indian religious thinking, mentioned in the Upanishad texts, which was the concept of new physical life for departed spirits by way of reincarnation, which could become an eternal cycle. Karma was further developed, although this was at first secret knowledge.

Hindus believe in a personal spirit, atman, which derives from the words to move and breathe. They consider that this spiritual representation of each individual is trapped within layers of mind inside physical bodies. Once freed after death, usually by a prompt cremation, the spirit will travel to the spiritual realm for karmic judgment. Temporary reward or punishment occurs for spirits according to their karma for the previous life only. All previous lives are acted upon in aggregate by karma when the spirit is finally sent back for reincarnation on earth.

It is believed that there is a universal atman or spirit which is a blissful state unified with Brahman, the highest god. Although Hinduism appears to be a strongly polytheistic religion with dozens of greater and lesser gods, many believers consider them to be different aspects of the single god, Brahman.

Escape from the cycle of reincarnation, moksha, and spiritual unity with Brahman, is achieved when in an enlightened state. This is variously attained by realising that reality is an illusion or by eliminating all desires and being pure of karma.

Jainism

> *Do not speak ill of anybody, nor feel jealous. Avoid strives and quarrels. Maintain mutual good-will and do not do evil to anybody. Be delighted at the, sight of virtuous. Be desirous of allaying the sufferings of the unhappy. Be friendly towards all living beings. By giving pain to others, one will have to experience bitter fruits.* [313]
>
> – Jayatilal S. Sanghvi

Jainism, with about four million adherents, developed by way of schism from Hinduism as early as the ninth century BCE. It has the standard SEU paradigm, with a sky world for the spirits of those who have achieved Nirvana and an underworld for those experiencing punishment before later reincarnation.

Although reincarnation was adopted from Hinduism, karma is considered differently in Jainism. Instead of an accumulation of intangible evidence it is thought to be material, like a form of dust which is attracted by bad actions and thoughts. The goal is to rid oneself of karma, the presence of which attracts one's spirit to matter and therefore maintains it trapped in the cycle of samsara.

William Uttal describes how Jains view the afterlife:

> *Jainism, perhaps reflecting a vestige of some earlier animism, as befits its ancient origins, asserts that everything, organic and Inorganic alike, has a soul or spirit. Furthermore, all humans who achieve the enlightenment (Kevalainana) that permits them to rise above their mortal constraints become Jinas (Tirthankaras) or god-like teachers themselves. [...] If a person has been particularly bad, there are hells to which they may be sent. Even worse is that the Jains believe that you can be reincarnated as a (much) lower animal ...* [314]

Jainism also rejected the concept of a supreme god but expects the sky realm to steadily become filled with spirits who have achieved Nirvana, progressing to a god-like state.

Buddhism

> *If you kill, lie or steal, commit adultery or drink, you dig up your own roots. And if you cannot master yourself, the harm you do turns against you, grievously.*

> – Buddha, from the *Dhammapada*

Buddhism is the fifth largest religion in the world with between 350 and 400 million adherents, mostly in East Asia.

Siddhartha Gautama, also known as Buddha (The Enlightened One), was born about 586 BCE in Kapilavastu, in the mountains of Hindu India, an area of Nepal. At age 29 he spent much of his time meditating and practising asceticism until he achieved enlightenment and had determined fundamental truths about the world. He then spent the next 45 years along the Ganges River preaching his new beliefs which ultimately became the religion of Buddhism after its schism from Hinduism.

Buddha's principal teachings were about the Four Noble Truths which pertain to recognizing and overcoming suffering, the Buddha Nature where any living thing can theoretically achieve enlightenment, and the Eightfold Path which defines moral and mental conduct to achieve wisdom. Buddha also rejected the concept of a supreme god (although, ironically, he is often regarded by believers today as a god). The cycle of reincarnation: samsara and the law of karma remain from Hinduism but serious dispute occurred over how the individual is meant to survive samsara. In Hinduism it had always been via spiritual progression but Buddha rejected this and concluded that it was the anatman, or "non-self" which survived death.

All of Buddhism firmly asserts that it does not accept oblivion or nihilism, in which case identity must still be preserved in some way after physical death. Sameer Grover provides a typical description of anatman by those who subscribe to this view:

> *According to the Buddha's teachings the only things that exist are momentary states called dharmas (dhamma in Pali), "a person is a temporary collection of constantly changing dharmas." In Buddhism there are five of these that constitute a person, these are also known as the five aggregates. According to this principle everything is made up of the five aggregates. These aggregates are form, sensation, perception, will or karmic predisposition, and consciousness. "The individual is in made up of a combination of the five components, which are never the same from one moment to the next, and therefore the individual's whole being is in a state of constant flux." The self is usually perceived as the permanent center linking these aggregates.* [315]

To reiterate, in the GMR the term spirit is used to group the various types of disembodied identity in religious belief. For the practical purpose of comparative religion the collections of dharmas of five aggregates, also known as skandhas, describe a disembodied identity, which is analogous to the concept of spirit in other religions.

Although Buddhism originated in India the strongholds of it are further east. There are two major denominations, or schools. The first is the Theravada school which is dominant in Sri Lanka and South East Asia where it spread through Burma, Cambodia, Laos and Thailand. The second is the Mahayana school which has mostly spread through Tibet, China, Vietnam, Mongolia, Korea, and Japan.

In these eastern countries, as both schools of Buddhism spread, they were heavily influenced by the older religions of ancestor worship and native deities which existed before, along with influences from Hinduism which are still strong as far afield as Bali. This has resulted in Folk Buddhism which is different from the canonical Buddhism of India. There is a disconnection between Buddhism as master theologians view it, and Buddhism as it is interpreted by the great majority of adherents.

McClelland observes that despite the official doctrine of anatman, believers in Folk Buddhism still regard spirit as the personal identity which undergoes samsara, the cycles of reincarnation and karmic judgment. [177]

Spiritual reward or punishment immediately after death was a concept inherited from Hinduism and has remained central to Folk Buddhism since. James Pratt, a lecturer in philosophy, in *The Pilgrimage of Buddhism and a Buddhist Pilgrimage*, describes the belief in afterlife judgment in Thailand:

> *As a fact, from very early times Buddhism has dwelt at length upon the rewards of heaven and the punishments of hell and has often made much more vivid use of them as sanctions of the moral life than of the pains and pleasures of rebirth. Hell is a very Buddhistic conception – as any one familiar with the frescoes on the walls of Buddhist temples ancient and modern, Southern or Northern, will realize.* [316]

The primary religious concern of most Buddhists is quality of afterlife based upon karma from the current life, with less concern about future reincarnation and even less about whether they will escape the great Wheel of Life and pass to Nirvana, a spiritually pure and blissful realm.

Manichaeism †

> *May you be blessed, for as you are now fortunate and honoured among men, so will you be fortunate and pleasing in the eyes of the gods on the last day of the soul (i.e. on the Judgment Day). And you will be eternally immortal among the gods and beneficent righteous ones.* [317]

– Prophet Mani

Manichaeism originated in Sassanian Persia in the third century CE. It spread westwards through North Africa, even into Spain, and eastwards into China. Within 100 years it had become the most widespread religion in the world.

The founder, Mani, was born in Babylon to a Judeo-Christian minor royal family. As a young man he had two separate visions inspiring his conceived of a new religion, and teaching it as a universal belief. It was an amalgam of elements from the contemporary major faiths, with Adam, Buddha, Zoroaster and Christ all considered important prophets. His royal connections gave him access to many courts when he preached his beliefs.

The dualism of good and evil, personified by the Lords of Light and Darkness, is fundamental to Manichaeism and a feature certainly inherited from Zoroastrianism. The writer Peter Novák comments:

> *Dualism was central to Manichaean teaching, as was reincarnation. Salvation was effected via an inner knowledge, or "gnosis," although actual liberation was only thought to take place when a person with gnosis dies.* [318]

Novák presents a thorough investigation of dualism in religion and links it to the split-brain aspect of neuropsychology which has some merit. However, in the GMR the principal cause of duality in religion is the critical importance of afterlife judgment to enforce the morality of constraint to buttress large societies. Duality in religion is naturally selected as it helps sustain the SEU paradigm which in turn sustains the believability in the extreme results of judgment itself.

Manfred Heuser and colleagues provide further insight:

> *Manichaeism teaches that the soul of the just person comes directly to redemption after death, while the remaining souls experience reincarnation of the soul which ends when the soul has lived as a just person or when the end of the world has come.* [317]

The early Christian texts contributed to Manichaeist doctrine to such an extent that it was considered by many as Gnosticism, a branch of Christianity. Indeed, Gnosticism has proven to be the most important source of extra-biblical texts. However, Manichaeism adhered to reincarnation afterlife, and had many other differences, such as not accepting that the god of judgment was also the creator of world. It was immediately considered unorthodox and rejected by mainstream Christians.

The essence of Gnosticism is achieving salvation through secret wisdom, of which Manichaeism had in abundance with a very complex eschatology. Nevertheless, it was a religion which could only promise a final spiritual afterlife for the righteous, and it was unable to compete with Christianity and Islam which overran most of its domains, except China, where Manichaeism continued until the sixteenth century.

Sikhism

In the hereafter one's words and deeds are scrutinized and one is brought to account for them.

– Adi Granth, Sikh Holy Scripture

Sikhism is a monotheistic religion with about 23 million adherents found mostly in the Punjab in India, but also in many communities with temples existing throughout English-speaking countries. It was founded about 1500 by Guru Nanak Dev who was succeeded by 10 gurus who maintained the new religion through Islamic Moghul repression.

Nanak conceived of a fusion of Islam and Hinduism which principally adopted the concept of a single supreme God with human life and death considered to follow the reincarnation cycle of samsara. Accumulated karma determines the nature of each reincarnation. The old SEU paradigm, with realms for spiritual reward and punishment, is rejected.

The Sikh writers K. Singh, Trilochan Singh and George Sutherland Fraser express the Sikh view of reincarnation:

Nanak and his followers believe in the doctrine of karma and rebirth. We are born with different temperaments. Some are greedy and possessive, others fretful and passionate. We come into the world bearing the impress of our past karma. Circumstances may stimulate these qualities. We may by our effort weaken the evil dispositions and strengthen the good ones. [...] We can be freed from the rotating wheel of samsara by union with God attained through devotion. [319]

Sikhism is less ascetic than Hinduism and Buddhism and much less so than Jainism. However, there is still a strong emphasis on personal discipline which is essential in acquiring good karma in order to obtain a spiritual escape from samsara and unite with God. The paradigm of afterlife judgment is a fundamental aspect of Sikhism, just like Hinduism, Jainism and Buddhism. Hence, the Dharmic religions are all essential to the cohesion and buttressing of the cultures they exist within.

Wicca

Death is not final. To most Wiccans, death is part of a cycle. This cycle is defined as birth/death/rebirth. The closest thing to heaven in Wiccan philosophy is Summerlands. This is the place where a person's soul goes to rest before it's ready to start its next life. In the Summerlands, people get the opportunity to reunite with their loved ones. [320]

– Geraldine Giordano

Wicca is a twentieth century religion found mostly in the United Kingdom and United States. It has a corpus of tradition which is an interpretation of how the ancient pagan religions of witchcraft and magic are believed to have existed. However, it dates from no earlier than the 1920s and was formalized in the 1950s.

Although there are already several denominations, commonality exists in afterlife belief, which was borrowed from the Dharmic reincarnation religions. Identity is preserved spiritually and the Summerlands is a spiritual world of the dead awaiting reincarnation. It is believed that spirits may occasionally visit the earth directly as ghosts, and when next physically incarnated the memories of previous lives are suppressed.

As a reinvention of Druidism it is certainly consistent with what is known of that religion. However, the essential difference which makes Wicca an Upper Mantle religion is the permanent preservation of adulthood in a spiritual identity progressing through many lives. Druidism, on the other hand, would only have had a single partial reincarnation before spiritual identity faded away. This is consistent with virtually all other ancient spiritual religions. At the time, even Hinduism had only just developed the idea of samsara, a reincarnation cycle, when Druidism was flourishing. Written scripture is essential in persisting very complex afterlife beliefs such as those seen in Dharmic religions – and Druidism was present in an illiterate culture.

There is no afterlife judgment in Wicca, instead internal or self-judgment is considered to operate in a karmic manner where the effects of good and bad deeds are visited back in the present world, a belief echoing that seen in the Nuer and Dinka cultures of Sudan, and some native Polynesian traditions.

A few concepts are borrowed from science, and this is universal in twentieth century religions. Some Wicca believers consider the Summerlands exist in another dimension and that spirits are pure energy. These ideas are consistent with the quasi-worldview of Tectonic Religion, detailed in the next chapter.

Monotheism: One Supreme God

The essence of the resurrection afterlife paradigm is the concept a single physical life, followed by a period of spiritual afterlife following death. The whole person is temporarily translated into a spirit world, the "intermediate state", awaiting resurrection to physical life. A process, requiring the existence of God, achieves reversion back to a physical life, reuniting the spirit with a new body – but this time as an immortal. Resurrection is all about preservation of the individual and this requires a strong belief in continuity of personhood.

Ascendancy of Yahweh

> *Yahweh is once again viewed as breathing smoke and fire, mounted on a cherub, flying on the wings of the wind. Yahweh is surrounded with the dense, dark clouds containing raindrops. He thunders from the heavens projecting his voice like Baal.* [230]
>
> – Alberto Ravinell Whitney Green

Yahweh, also YHWH to the Jews and Jehovah to the Christians, is the last storm god and achieved supremacy at the end of an unbroken chain of similar gods from Enlil of the Sumerians. In parallel the supreme storm god gradually replaced all local gods by absorbing their roles.

The Old Testament has 89 references to Baal, the Canaanite high god, all brief and polemic in style relating the eclipsing of him by Yahweh. Baal had mythically fought and tamed Mot (death) and had many devoted followers, so he was only reluctantly abandoned. He was also strongly associated with the fertility goddess Asherah, mentioned 40 times the Old Testament. Altars to Baal and their associated Asherah poles are described in Kings I and II, Chronicles II and Judges 6:28-30:

> *And when the men of the city arose early in the morning, behold, the altar of Baal was cast down, and the grove was cut down that was by it, and the second bullock was offered upon the altar that was built. [...] Then the men of the city said unto Joash, Bring out thy son, that he may die: because he hath cast down the altar of Baal, and because he hath cut down the grove that was by it.*

Different protagonists destroy these early shrines, while antagonists reinstate them, illustrating a theological struggle. In most biblical translations Asherah is symbolised as a pole, but also as a grove, or holy tree. As a fertility goddess she was represented in wooden motifs: poles (possibly asherim) or totemic carvings which are all associated with plant renewal and agricultural fertility.

What is omitted from the Bible has been found by archaeology. In a ruined fort at Kuntillet Ajrud, north-east Sinai, Egypt, two large pots with inscriptions mentioning "Yahweh and his Asherah" were found dating to about 800 BCE. At a second site, Khirbet al-Qom, tombs were found with similar inscriptions. The anthropologist and historian Raphael Patai, in *The Hebrew Goddess* describes these texts:

> *At Khirbet al-Qom, a site some nine miles west of Hebron, another inscription was found. It reads: 'Uriah the rich has caused it to be written: Blessed be Uriah by Yahweh and by his Asherah; from his enemies he has saved him?' These inscriptions show that in popular religion the Goddess Asherah was associated with Yahweh, probably as his wife, and that 'Yahweh and his Asherah' were the most popular divine couple.* [321]

This is physical evidence that, like Baal, Yahweh coexisted with the fertility goddess Asherah in the eighth century BCE. Asherah may have been the consort of Yahweh, but this is uncertain. In any case, the Jews worshipped them jointly until the reforms made by the kings Hezekiah in 700 BCE and Josiah in 621 BCE. Two silver amulets with inscriptions to YHWH as the supreme God have been found in a grave at Ketef Hinnom dating to about 600 BCE.

Shaun Aster, a biblical scholar, assesses the chronology of all the inscriptions:

> *First, we have the purely monotheistic inscriptions. These include the Ketef-Hinnom amulets, 'Ein Gedi, and Khirbet bet-Lei. Next, we have the henotheistic inscriptions, or those that are monotheistic with the trappings of polytheism. These include Kuntillet 'Ajrud and Khirbet el-Qom. Lastly, we have the single inscription that exhibits pure polytheism, Kuntillet 'Ajrud Plaster B. Chronologically, it is interesting to note that all monotheistic inscriptions date to after the Hezekian reform, while all inscriptions containing polytheistic elements clearly fall before the Hezekian reform.* [322]

There are many Biblical passages where Yahweh assures providence and fertility, usurping of the role of Asherah, too. So, Yahweh absorbed all the cultic gods and the journey on the road to monotheism was complete by 600 BCE. It appears that through royal intervention the Jewish religion had been largely successful in ensuring Yahweh was supreme, just before the Babylonian exile in 587 BCE.

The shock of the Babylonian exile was matched with dismay over how belief in Yahweh had not been enough to prevent it happening. This was expressed in the setting back of Yahwism and was still felt as late as 170 BCE as the bodies of some Israeli soldiers, fallen in battle, were found with tokens of the cultic god Jamnia in their clothes.

However, at the time of the emergence of Christianity the concept of a single supreme god had been firmly re-established.

Old Aramaic was the Near Eastern *lingua franca* in the final centuries BCE and much cross-fertilization occurred into the emerging Arabic language. Timothy Tennent, theologian, identifies the origin of the word "Allah" with the Aramaic "el", "eloah" and "elohim" citing continuing cultural exchange between the Canaanites and Arabs:

> *The word "Allah" was used to translate the broad concept of God; it was not used to translate the personal, covenantal name revealed to Moses, YHWH. The Jews, in turn, applied elohim to both their covenantal God, Yahweh, as well as to false gods, using*

> *elohim in much the same way as we use the generic English word "god." In contrast, "Muslims never use Allah to refer to a false god, but is used only of the one true God."*

At the point when Yahweh, the last storm god, assumed the roles of all lesser gods, true monotheism had arrived. Therefore, even before the advent of Islam itself, monotheistic religion was also established in some parts of Arabia with Allah as the *concept and name* of God.

Roles of the Supreme God

> *This great change in our notion of the way the world works is of fundamental importance for biblical criticism, because the Bible is largely a tissue of miracle stories. The creation, the expulsion from Eden, the flood, the conversations with the patriarchs, the cell of Moses, the plagues on Egypt, the division of the Red Sea, the epiphany on Sinai, the giving of the law – these are all miracle stories, magnalia Dei.* [323]

> – Morton Smith

As Morton Smith makes clear – the miracle stories in the Bible were all written to give glory to Yahweh. From the perspective of the GMR we can now add further background: that the miracles are a class of magic conceived within the spiritual worldview and the change in our notion of the way the world works is the paradigm shift to the science worldview. It is only from the science worldview that pressure for a technically sound explanation of miracles is required by some believers today.

Miracles are expressions of the power of God, but generally they are discretionary. There are, however, critical tasks that are expected of God by all believers.

A "god role" is where supernatural, god-like powers are needed to facilitate a paradigm of belief within religion. The GMR shows that the Abrahamic God of Judaism, Christianity and Islam, and Ahura Mazda of Zoroastrianism have several essential roles in religion.

Table 7.1 (next page) details the four discrete roles in Mantle Religion and one of Tectonic Religion which, are assumed by that of the monotheistic supreme God.

GMR:7.1   **GOD ROLES IN MONOTHEISM**

GOD ROLE	RELIGIOUS BELIEF	LAYER
World Creation	Spiritual Worldview. *Explanation* for the existence of the sky, earth, underworld and humanity	Mantle Religion
Spiritual Judgment	Supernatural agency to deliver temporary and purgative external judgment in spiritual afterlife	Lower Mantle Religion
Resurrection Afterlife	Supernatural agency to *perform the reversion process of resurrection* from spiritual to physical afterlife	Upper Mantle Religion
Physical Judgment	Supernatural agency to *deliver final external judgment* in physical afterlife	Upper Mantle Religion
Universe Creation & Intelligent Design	Pseudoscience in a Quasi-Worldview. *Explanation* for the existence of the universe and evolved humanity	Tectonic Religion

These roles are all assumed into that of the one God because of the constraint of monotheism, and are still conceptually valid to many millions of believers despite the paradigm shift to a science worldview. The reason is that science has not yet answered them all – in particular: resurrection afterlife. The creation of the world is, however, well explained and so is the origin of humans. Hence, the TR quasi-worldview is required by most modern believers in order to maintain a coherent context to the spiritual worldview.

Secular judicial judgment appears to be a sufficient substitute for afterlife judgment in the maintenance of large, stable, semi-physicalist societies where living standards are high. When there are low living standards and a secular judicial system crippled by corruption, afterlife judgment is essential to avoid anarchy and the splintering of society into groups below Dunbar's Number in size.

Resurrection Afterlife Paradigm

Based on various New Testament sources, fundamentalists believe that Jesus was physically resurrected. [...] Nonfundamentalists who believe in the physical resurrection of Jesus might acknowledge its implausibility but believe that it is

> *not so inherently unreasonable that it needs to be rejected outright. They might embrace the belief in a spirit of hope or longing, rather than certainty. If indeed Jesus' death was not final, then the death of others, especially the righteous, might not be final either.* [324]

– Solomon Schimmel

In the spiritual worldview resurrection is performed magically, by the power of God, and the details can remain shrouded in mystery. It is only under the pressure of the paradigm shift to the science worldview that resurrection needs to be defined technically in terms of reanimation, replication or reconstitution. Where such definitions are attempted, and do not conform to the accepted corpus of science, then this belief is pseudoscience and falls within the quasi-worldview of Tectonic Religion.

Christianity has the opaque concept of Trinity as a god-head: Father, Son and Holy Spirit, where three are one and one is three. This leaves open the possibility that a discrete god-role is handled by just one of the Triune. We see this especially with Christ who not only assumes the role of facilitating resurrection afterlife in the Book of John 11:24-25, but actually demonstrates it too:

> *Martha saith unto him, I know that he shall rise again in the resurrection at the last day. Jesus said unto her, I am the resurrection, and the life: he that believeth in me, though he were dead, yet shall he live.*

Martha was mourning her brother Lazarus who had died four days earlier. Christ followed up on his words by resurrecting Lazarus to physical life, after three days – which is believed to be even harder as Lazarus' spirit had to be recalled back to his body. This is a very interesting development because Christ's own resurrection is evidence to believers for the resurrection afterlife paradigm. There is a process going on which is a partial eclipsing of Yahweh by Christ, this time by a better god of resurrection.

There have long been different views on how important a deceased's corpse is to their afterlife. If it is believed that a spirit has its destiny tied to the physical remains until final judgment, then reasonable efforts must be made for preservation at death, such as embalming and burial rather than cremation. Catholicism has this emphasis, whereas

Protestantism readily accepts cremation with an emphasis of resurrection drawn from spirit alone.

The resurrection afterlife paradigm itself keeps evolving too.

There are different views on how "conscious" spirits are in the intermediate state between death and resurrection. John Cooper addresses this in *Biblical Anthropology and the Body-Soul Relation*:

> *It is interesting to note that the dead are sometimes said to be sleeping even when they are conscious during the intermediate state. "Sleep" in reference to death, then, is not necessarily a euphemism for nonexistence or unconscious existence. Rather, it can suggest the bodily inactivity and dreamlike quality of consciousness during the intermediate state.* [325]

Perhaps this best describes the majority view of Christians today. In the medieval period spiritual afterlife was considered to be very active with heavenly bliss or purgative judgment occurring. This is famously illustrated in Dante's Inferno. Active spirituality before resurrection is a view still current in Islam.

The matter is more complex in Judaism. The medieval Jewish theologian Maimonides determined that there was only a spiritual resurrection and that ascended spirits would unite with God. His teachings had a profound effect upon the direction of Rabbinic Judaism, such that both spiritual and physical resurrection afterlife is acceptable belief, perhaps because of this inconsistency many Jews focus on the current life rather than the nature of the next.

Conversely, a few Christian denominations, such as Jehovah's Witnesses, have dispensed with the concept of spirit entirely and consider that death is temporary oblivion, which also substitutes for Hell, and that God will resurrect those to be saved from his memory of them. The continuity of personhood is achieved in *God's mind* instead of spiritually and this still preserves personhood as a disembodied identity.

As mentioned in Chapter One, Mormonism allows for translation afterlife, where an individual can become immortal through divine intervention, without dying first, and it is believed this happened to Enoch and a few others.

A further revision, especially in recent centuries, is the meme of rejuvenation in afterlife, which increases in importance as life expectancy increases. The belief is that people will be resurrected at an optimal age, sometimes said to be equivalent to 33-years-old, with lost faculties restored. So, a person dying aged 80 with Alzheimer's disease, physically diseased and crippled, will be restored to youthful exuberance in the afterlife. It is rejuvenation which defines the end point for the evolution of resurrection belief, because *physical immortality*, in a *rejuvenated state*, in *paradise* cannot be improved upon as a solution to personal mortality.

Purgative and Final Judgments

> *In the Gathas we have the idea that at death the person's soul is presented at this bridge or "crossing"; the crossing can either lead to the House of Song (heaven) or the House of Lies (hell). The "separator" itself may have been the enormous chasm that may be supposed to exist between the House of Song and the House of Lies, for some versions of the myth state that the soul destined for damnation will find that the bridge contracts to such a degree that it is impossible to remain on it; and so the soul will fall off and plunge down to hell.* [326]

– Peter Clark

The Gathas, the earliest Zoroastrian scripture, describe a purgative process in spiritual afterlife. Here, the plunge from the Chinvat Bridge to hell is not forever, only for a prescribed period or until final judgment.

Like the Dharmic reincarnation religions the resurrection religions have also, to some degree, developed the doctrine of two-phase judgment. First, there is spiritual judgment immediately after death, the consequences of which are regarded as temporary, where it is often a purgative or corrective process. Secondly, in resurrection belief after physical immortality is achieved, there is a final judgment which occurs for everyone at once. This last phase is what differentiates resurrection religions from everything previously seen and is collectively known as apocalyptic eschatology. Clark also relates the final physical judgment in Zoroastrian belief:

> *..later Zoroastrian apocalyptic mythology, rooted in Zarathushtra's Gathic teachings, speaks of a universal trial by molten metal, whereby all men and women will be subjected to a general judgment; men and women who have lived good virtuous*

lives will be made to pass through the metal and to those people it will seem like "warm milk". Those who have lived evil lives, however, will not be so fortunate, for to them the metal will be agonizing and will destroy them. [326]

The role of gatekeeper to pleasant afterlife is one of judge, jury and executioner. Ahura Mazda was always seen as good and benevolent, although clearly punishment could be meted out by him. This also means the Abrahamic God can be at once infinitely merciful and yet vengeful and jealous (of false idols). Additionally, a supreme God of judgment is most effective, powerful and believable if he also has the role of Creator.

Most believers will put their chances of afterlife at close to 100 per cent. However, what chance of a pleasant afterlife? If they are brave they might hazard over a 50 per cent chance. They might also decline to be so presumptuous. Why? As their thoughts and words are laid bare to God they risk sanction for second-guessing his intentions.

Such is the powerful effect of the meme of judgment maintained by natural selection in individuals through 8000 long years of multilevel natural selection between competing societies.

Creation of the World

Creation is the least important of the god roles, and this belief is properly a component of the general spiritual worldview, not eschatology. It has however, contributed to the rise of monotheism and the buttressing of it ever since. Creator gods appear in almost every culture and similarly in the Near East except that it also established henoism there. In the evolution of religion, henoism is a high god existing above all others, conceptually partway between polytheism and monotheism. John Pleins, an archaeologist and biblical scholar summarizes:

A corollary to monotheism is the idea that God is the sole Creator of the world. It is true that the idea of a singular creator God is in the Near East, except perhaps for the Egyptian heresy of Pharaoh Akhenaten, who worshiped only the sun disk Aten. But it is also the case that many ancient Middle Eastern myths elevate the creative action of one god above all the others, even when the belief

> *system admitted many gods into the pantheon. In this is a valuable clue to the origins of biblical monotheism.* [327]

The Abrahamic God prevailed because he became much more than a creator; he became a god of judgment and of resurrection afterlife. Any god which cannot deliver one of these is doomed to be a lesser god, and will eventually fade away completely.

Creation in Judaism and Christianity is famously described in the *Book of Genesis*, common to the Old Testament and the Hebrew Bible. Analysis of it is a well-worn path, so all we need to do here is affirm that it is an essential of these religions that the God of creation, of the beginning, is the same as the God of eschaton, of the ending. Creation in Islam is not detailed nearly so fully in the Holy Quran, but enough is present to see it asserts that the world was created by Allah.

The concept of creation itself was transformed in the paradigm shift to the science worldview and has become firmly redefined in religion as a pseudoscientific process, and this is discussed in Chapter Eight on Concepts from Science.

Resurrection Religions

The three Abrahamic religions and Zoroastrianism promise resurrection afterlife, and all require a supreme God. It is the sheer number of adherents to this afterlife paradigm, over 3600 million people, which makes the Abrahamic God in particular *appear* central to religion itself.

The four monotheistic resurrection religions are listed in the chronological order that this last afterlife paradigm is attested to in their scripture. Again, thousands of books exist about these religions. Here, we are just reviewing the mainstream denominations and their doctrine on afterlife and judgment eschatology, and creation – their *raison d'être*.

Zoroastrianism

> *Zoroaster was thus the first to teach the doctrines of an individual judgment, Heaven and Hell, the future resurrection of the body,*

> *the general Last Judgment, and life everlasting for the reunited*
> *soul and body.* [257]

> – Mary Boyce

One of the two earliest resurrection religions is Zoroastrianism, the primary religion of Persia until Islamic times; some 2.6 million people adhere to it today, mostly in Iran and India, where they are known as Parsis.

The origins of Zoroastrianism are in Central Asian polytheistic pagan traditions influenced by the Vedas of Hinduism, and it dates from about 1500 BCE. However, it was only during the priesthood of Zoroaster, also known as Zarathustra, who probably lived between 1400 and 1100 BCE, that Zoroastrianism became a significant religion. Zoroaster wrote much of the Gathas, five hymns of Old Avestian scripture, and recognized Ahura Mazda, also called Ormazd in the Pahlavi language, as the supreme deity, creator of the spirits and immortals. He also described the world in terms of a battle between good and evil personified. The Gathas, however, make no mention of resurrection afterlife and this is probably because it was a later development, rather than the Gathas being incomplete today.

Mary Boyce, a professor of Iranian studies who spent years interviewing adherents in Yazd region, asserts that Zoroaster preached physical resurrection, but it is far from certain. It may well have been that he considered only spiritual afterlife with a final spiritual judgment applying. His major novel contribution to Persian belief is that *only one physical life was permitted*. This is described by Selwyn Champion and Dorothy Short:

> *Later Zoroastrianism taught also the resurrection of the body, and*
> *there were prophesies as to the coming of a kind of Saviour called*
> *Saoshyant, who would assist in the final judgment. [...] In*
> *Zoroastrianism it is the importance of each man's soul which*
> *counts most; the soul exists eternally, and an irrevocable choice*
> *has to be made in the one earth-life.* [328]

Zoroastrianism became the state religion of three successive Persian empires between about 600 BCE and 700 CE. It was during the first, the Achaemenid dynasty, that the Avestian text, Zamyad Yasht, was written. Religion was focused upon the king, so it is in the context of his afterlife that resurrection is described as a gift of Ahura Mazda:

> *...in order for (His creatures and creations) to make existence brilliant, not aging, imperishable, not rotting, not putrefying, enjoying eternal life, enjoying eternal benefit, enjoying power at will, so that the dead will rise again, imperishability will come over the living, (and) existence will be made brilliant in value.*

The Achaemenid dynasty ended in Alexander the Great's conquest of Persia by 330 BCE, which subsequently saw a change in the focus of Zoroastrianism from the king to God.

The next apparent reference to resurrection is in the Vendidad text (18, 51), dated to the second century BCE, which describes the spirit of Holy Devotion, personified, being invoked to ensure a deceased person is worthy of a successful afterlife. However, it may be read as ensuring that the deceased was recognized during spiritual judgment to have been diligent at performing the essential daily prayers during life.

Afterlife judgment in Zoroastrianism has been described earlier, but an extract from Fravardin Yasht, related by the theologian and Methodist minister John Waterhouse, shows how high the bar is raised:

> *Zoroaster knew that the God whose eye nothing escaped, hated falsehood outward and inward : "Whatsoever open or secret things may be visited with judgment, or what man for a little sin demands the heaviest penalty – of all this through the Right thou art ware, observing them with flashing eye".* [329]

A little sin demanding the heaviest penalty is the language echoed in Christian and Islamic scripture.

Zoroastrianism in its earliest form was henoistic and Ahura Mazda was the high god but there were other lesser gods, the personification of evil, and immortals. The equality in afterlife for women with men was an important early advancement made by Zoroastrianism. An echo of ancestor worship survived into later times in the form of fravashis which are personal guardian spirits, referred to in the female gender. The actual symbol of Zoroastrianism is the faravahar, a man on a winged mount. It may have originally represented the fravashi of the king. It also reused the imagery of Ashur, the city god of Assur, which is the capital of Assyria. As the Assyrian empire grew Ashur gradually assumed the role of Enlil, the Mesopotamian god of air and storms.

The Zoroastrian creation myths evolved from pagan times. Diané Collinson and Robert Wilkinson describe the earliest creation myth, prevailing when Zoroaster lived:

> *Zoroaster held to the ancient belief in a sevenfold creation in which there was first the enclosing shell of the sky, made of stone, then the world within it, then water in the shell, followed by the earth flat upon it; then a plant, an animal and a man in the centre of the earth. The gods were believed to have crushed and sacrificed these last, thereby causing their multiplication and beginning the cycle of life and death.* [330]

Subsequently, it was Ahura Mazda who was the architect of creation, the act of which had the side effect of awakening a near equal personification of evil, Angra Mainyu. This set up a long struggle for control of the Zoroastrian worlds in the SEU paradigm. A succession of prophets or saviours is predicted, of which Zoroaster was the first and Saoshyant will be another, culminating in an epic conquest of evil and then final judgment.

Judaism

> *And I will lay sinews upon you, and will bring up flesh upon you, and cover you with skin, and put breath in you, and ye shall live; and ye shall know that I am the Lord. So I prophesied as I was commanded; and as I prophesied, there was a noise, and behold a commotion, and the bones came together, bone to its bone. And I beheld, and, lo, there were sinews upon them, and flesh came up, and skin covered them above; but there was no breath in them. Then said He unto me: "Prophesy unto the breath, prophesy, son of man, and say to the breath. Thus saith the Lord God: Come from the four winds, O breath, and breathe upon these slain, that they may live." So I prophesied as He commanded me, and the breath came into them, and they lived, and stood up upon their feet, an exceeding great host.*
>
> – Ezekiel 37:6-10, Hebrew Bible

Judaism is certainly the world's most influential early religion and it traces its legendary origins to Abraham in texts written in the sixth century BCE. Today, it has about 14 million adherents across various denominations. Modern Rabbinic Judaism is the main form, arising from classical Pharisaic Judaism.

The Hebrew Bible is the collection of sacred texts in Judaism comprising books of the Law, Prophets and Writings, all brought into a final canon about 90 CE. There is much overlap with the Old Testament of Christianity, although some books are omitted and some added. Judaism holds to an ancient covenant between Yahweh and the nation of Israel where Israelis are the chosen people of God, leaving everyone else (gentiles) excluded. This means it is necessary to be born a Jew to worship within Judaism.

How important Yahweh was in the First Temple period is unknown as polytheism had not yet been extinguished when Israel was broken into two in 721 BCE. At the time, Solomon's rich temple would have been unsuited to the austere Yahweh cult alone. As we have seen, the royal reforms held Yahweh as supreme during the century to 600 BCE and monotheism was established.

Soon after this, in 587 BCE, during the reign of Nebuchadnezzar II, the Kingdom of Judea was conquered and the surviving nobility taken into Babylonia as captives. It is during this painful exile that some degree of influence from Persian Zoroastrianism is thought to have occurred. However, Babylonia still held to the Mesopotamian pantheon and perhaps it was Jewish awe and gratitude to the Persian king Cyrus the Great which encouraged them to learn from his religion instead. Cyrus liberated them and some returned home where, after 60 years, they found the Jewish religion much weakened amongst those who remained. Some had married gentiles, so were expelled from Jewish society altogether.

Key similarities exist between Judaism and Zoroastrianism. They both formed a view of physical resurrection at roughly the same time. The Zoroastrian Zamyad Yasht is contemporary with Ezekiel's powerful vision of the Valley of Dry Bones. Written during the exile Ezekiel's vision may have been first an allegory for the eventual restoration of Israel to the Jews, but it is undeniably a description of physical resurrection too. Yet, there is no sky realm either – it is resurrection to the earthly world with no mention of afterlife judgment.

The verses of Ezekiel, and indeed the whole Bible, show the conflation of breathing symbolism with spirit and the spark of life, a concept seen throughout Semitic cultures inherited from Neolithic times. Also, like the Zoroastrians, the Jews believed that after death the spirit remained with the deceased for three days before journeying on.

The re-establishment of the Judean state after the return from exile is known as the Second Temple period which began in 530 BCE, continuing until Judea was fully subjugated as a Roman province, and the temple destroyed again, in 70 CE.

Judaism also developed a view of spiritual purity which is reminiscent of the period in Zoroastrianism when Ahura Mazda asks the spirits to suffer, returning to the earthly world clothed in flesh to join the fight against evil. The *New Standard Jewish Encyclopedia* describes this paradigm:

> *The soul is regarded as an immaterial substance whose relationship to a particular body is more or less incidental. According to this view existence before birth and after death is a matter of course and it is the soul's descent into matter and the mortal body that requires explanation. The moral and religious task of life is to protect the soul from losing its purity while in the material world.* [331]

By the middle of this period, 300 years after Ezekiel, afterlife was still considered to be a spiritual existence in Sheol, similar to the Mesopotamian underworld and Greco-Roman Hades. Graves were gateways to it and possible physical resurrection an exceptional event. The early concept of levels in Sheol existed where spirits were separated and it was considered that those consigned to the lowest, fourth level were unlikely to return to life on earth. It was a place where they sat in darkness and ate dust.

Ben Sira, a rabbi and author, wrote the *Book of Sirach* between 200 and 175 BCE with this long established view in mind. His text was not included in the Hebrew Bible but it was later amended – as identified by Alan Avery-Peck, a professor in Judaic studies:

> *In Sirach 7:17, there is an addition of "fire" to the "worms" that await human beings in the afterlife. Worms cause no surprise; they formed part of the imaginative personification of death/sheol that begins in the grave. But fire is probably an addition that comes from a mentality that distinguished between reward and punishment in the next life.* [332]

Judaism then fully adopted the SEU paradigm with corresponding different realms for spirits depending upon the result of judgment. Avery-Peck also describes this change:

> *Nevertheless, once "Sheol" ceases to be seen as a neutral place, accommodating good and wicked alike, and becomes a place of punishment – called Abaddon, or Gehenna, or "the pit" – as was commonplace at the time of writing of the Qumran scrolls, then the heavens correspondingly invite the righteous, as the place of eternal bliss for the righteous.*

Chapter 12 of the Book of Daniel has a later addition at this time too. It is a reference to resurrection afterlife, and importantly the first to imply a *final judgment*. Robin Lane Fox, classical historian and writer, puts it into context:

> *In the 160s the belief hardened. During the Jews' great war of resistance, martyrs were dying valiantly, but surely they were not dying forever? Our Bible's first clear account of a bodily resurrection and eternal life for saints and sinners is in a text as late as the 160s B.C. It was impelled by a historical crisis and, in order to impose itself, was palmed off on someone who never wrote it.* [333]

The Jewish war of resistance, the Maccabean Revolt, was against the Seleucid Empire run by the Greek heirs and generals of Alexander, who had died relatively young. Ultimately, the revolt was successful and by 140 BCE led to the establishment of the Hasmonean dynasty of Jewish kings. Judea existed independently for the first time in nearly 600 years but it was short-lived as the Romans, under General Pompey, conquered it in 37 BCE.

During the Second Temple period, there was a conflict between two principal sects with their competing schools of thought. The Pharisees who believed in afterlife, spirituality, resurrection and judgment, and the Sadducees who believed in none of those things, and could be best described as secular aristocrats who followed the Law of Moses. It was the Pharisees which prevailed. This is consistent with multilevel natural selection. Pharisee theology was superior to that of the Sadducees because it provided a better basis of social cohesion: afterlife and judgment. When these two sects competed the outcome was a foregone conclusion. Two thousand years later mainstream Judaism is from the Pharisees. It is a microcosm of the power of a religious society overcoming a weakly religious one.

Christianity

All who read and understand this shall attain immortality, and never die.

– Gospel of Thomas

Christianity is the largest religion in world history with 2500 million adherents today. It developed from Judaism with a final schism in the second century CE, becoming the state religion of the Roman Empire in the fourth century. It now exists in cultures all over the globe, due to European colonization in the last 500 years. The principal denominations: Catholic, Orthodox and Protestant still have a strong alignment in doctrine.

Understandably, the loss of freedom in Judea after Roman conquest in 37 BCE ushered in a Messianistic period where the people were hoping and expecting the arrival of a new king, an heir of King David, who was able to marshal divine power to eject the Romans for good. Some expected an imminent divine kingdom, assuming that they were living close to the eschaton, or end of times.

Lane Fox concludes that Christ was born about 12 BCE and was about 50-years-old when he died. [333] If this is correct, attaining such an age is quite an achievement in the first century CE, when life expectancy was 30. He would have possessed much wisdom and experience standing before his followers, listening intently.

It was during this period of oppression that Christ conducted his rabbinical ministry. The Pharisees observed it from the beginning and, originally, had a lot in common with Christ who visited their houses, but differences soon became apparent, as described by the theologist Brennan Hill:

He challenged them as the accurate interpreters of the law, did not place the same emphasis on the scribal oral tradition, and was not as rigid when it came to observing purity regulations and Sabbath laws. Jesus preferred to teach his own version of the law on his own authority, and laid the foundations for the eventual setting aside of the Torah and the scribal tradition for his own oral tradition. As to following the law in everyday life, Jesus displayed even more liberal views than the Pharisees. He shocked and angered some of them by his willingness to cure on the Sabbath.

> *Moreover, he went beyond their open table ministry and included prostitutes (the story at Simon the Pharisees house) and tax collectors. Jesus also went beyond the Father God of the Pharisees and called God by an even more intimate name, Abba.* [334]

Christ lived at the time when Judaism had various competing sects practising their own doctrines; the Hebrew Bible was still in flux. However, the Pharisees, Sadducees, Essenes and Zealots were all sects tolerated within greater Judaism, but Christ founded one where he, the chief rabbi, called himself the Son of God, and this was beyond accommodation.

He was on a collision course with religious and political hierarchies which inexorably led to crucifixion.

Jesus Christ was the founder of Christianity but it was another who set this emerging religion on a course to global success instead of distant obscurity. Paul the former persecutor may have been a temple guard when Christ was arrested, but later had a vision on the road to Damascus and became Apostle to the Gentiles. He was instrumental in spreading the powerful concept of *resurrection afterlife into paradise* to the Greeks and Romans.

The archaeologist and New Testament scholar William Ramsay interprets the account of Paul's sermons in Antioch of Pisidia reported in the Acts of the Apostles:

> *[Luke] places the speech at the beginning of Paul's work among the Gentiles as a typical example of the way in which Judaism and the promises of God were made universal by him. The Jews as a body did not perceive the deep-lying suggestiveness of Paul's inclusion of the Gentiles; but the Gentiles saw it, and on the next Sabbath almost the whole city flocked to the Synagogue. It was now clearly apparent what interpretation was put on the words of Paul. Even the Gentiles who had not previously been attracted within the circle of the Synagogue came to hear the new message of a widened Judaism.* [335]

Judaism was only for the Jews, because of Yahweh's covenant with Israel, and would always be limited by this but, intolerably, there was now a sect which admitted anyone. It could only lead to total schism and a new religion.

Paul was not only a tireless preacher, but a writer of letters and sermons, called *epistles*, directed to various peoples, which must have been publicly read to crowds in many places by his followers. The consensus is that most of the Pauline Epistles were written by him between 50 and 60 CE and establish him as the first missionary, the first of millions.

When Paul reached Rome in 60 CE, news of emerging Christianity and adherents to it had already arrived. Despite vigorous persecution of martyrs, the seeds were sown such that it was inevitable that the Roman Empire would become Christian. This is because physical resurrection in paradise is always a superior afterlife to a spiritual experience in Hades. It is surprising that the process took as long as 300 years, although the Roman emperors usually believed they were themselves gods and this made it difficult for them to accept the monotheistic Abrahamic God. Constantine permitted Christian worship in 313 and it became the state religion of the empire in 380. The centre of gravity of Christianity had moved from the Levant to Rome and has remained there ever since.

About 65 CE Paul died. Between his death and 100 CE the four canonical gospels were written, focusing on Christ's birth, ministry and death. However, they also reflect the firm belief that Christ was divine during life and possessed god-like powers with respect to the afterlife. They provide justification that he was at once a king of the Jews, by patriarchal descent from King David, and also divine by benefit of a virgin birth. There are two different royal genealogies of his father Joseph and an explanation of virgin conception which sidelines Joseph entirely, all to prove divine kingship.

In the gospels, Christ was now considered to have proven that resurrection worked with an act of *coup de grace* by undergoing it *personally*, then returning to his followers afterwards – no mean feat when executed by the Romans who invented genocide and were thorough in making sure that those they meant to kill became well and truly dead.

From the start of Christianity, the SEU paradigm was integral to it but, because this was a young religion, certain ancient matters were unresolved. The *First Epistle of Peter* chapters 3 & 4 mention Christ preaching to the spirits of the dead and this was a key concept. It is an early belief that between Christ's death and resurrection his spirit descended to Hell. The *Catechism of the Catholic Church* summarizes:

> *In his human soul united to his divine person, the dead Christ*
> *went down to the realm of the dead. He opened heaven's gates for*
> *the just who had gone before him.* [3]

All the people who died before the Christian era are believed to have heard Christ's sermons as he had preached to spirits in Hell, and further, that the Old Testament patriarchs, who held true to Yahweh, were freed and admitted to Heaven.

The Bible gives no clear description of Satan and the 49 mentions of him are largely personifications of evil or sin. Nevertheless, Christian art depicts Satan as horned and cloven-hooved. The astute observation made by the Egyptologist Margaret Murray must apply here: "*The gods of the old religion become the demons of the new religion.*"

As Christianity spread in Europe, one way the resistance it encountered was dealt with was to reuse elements of some NST. Antlered and horned gods, such as the Greco-Roman Pan or Faunus and the Celtic Cernunnos, were demonized in order to turn people from their old pagan spiritual and nature religions.

The Book of Revelation, also written by 100 CE, paints images of the overarching apocalyptic eschatology which has defined the relationship between Christianity and its followers for nearly 2000 years. It has many prophesies of the end times, turbulence and upheaval, the second coming of Christ, of the battle with evil personified and of a divine kingdom where resurrection precedes final judgment. The Catechism continues:

> *The resurrection of all the dead, "of both the just and the unjust",*
> *will precede the Last Judgment. This will be "the hour when all*
> *who are in the tombs will hear (the Son of man's) voice and come*
> *forth, those who have done good, to the resurrection of life, and*
> *those who have done evil, to the resurrection of judgment." Then*
> *Christ will come [...] And they will go away into eternal*
> *punishment, but the righteous into eternal life.*

Yahweh, now mystically bound within the Trinity, with Christ and the Holy Spirit, is at once infinitely merciful yet capable of extreme vengeance against all sinners. Judgment in afterlife is writ large in the mind of every potential sinner in Christendom.

In the GMR, the observation is now possible that multilevel natural selection in competing societies reached a local maxima, or temporary endpoint by 100 CE. In the buttressing of society by the morality of constraint through afterlife judgment nothing could trump Christian eschatology.

Christianity sailed serenely on despite the apparent clouds of schisms. Egypt in the fifth century was about 80 per cent Christian, but it seems the Arab cultures were a bridge too far. The first break was with the Copts there, and the church in Syria, along with other related churches now grouped as Oriental Orthodox. The Great Schism between East and West in the eleventh century formally established Catholicism and Eastern Orthodox. In Northern Europe, Protestantism followed in the sixteenth century. Even the thousand-year arm wrestle in North Africa, Fertile Crescent, Iberia and the Balkans, with its new and formidable rival, Islam, did not prevent Christianity's long-term success.

The principal struggle came from elsewhere: science. First, it was unperturbed after Copernicus' description of the heliocentric Solar System, which was published by him in 1543, the year of his death. Interestingly, this significant discovery did not meet with doctrinal opposition from the established church until over 60 years later.

The GMR holds that the reason for this hiatus was that the Copernican Revolution was still tolerable within the spiritual worldview. It was only after the science worldview first emerged, arguably sparked in the year 1608, that the Christian church encountered the wavefront of this paradigm shift, then correctly reinterpreted the heliocentric Solar System as part of this change, and swiftly reacted – as soon as 1609. This is discussed in Chapter Eight on Concepts from Science.

Islam

Again, on the Day
Of Judgment, will ye be
Raised up.

– *The Holy Quran*, 23:16, Trans. by Yusuf Ali, 1934

Islam is the world's second largest, and presently the fastest growing, religion with 1500 million adherents.

It was founded by the Prophet Muhammad who was born circa 570 within the Quraysh tribe dominant in Mecca at the time. He is believed to have received divine revelations, from God, comprising the Islamic faith between 610 and his death in 632. His oral quotes from these revelations were posthumously compiled to form the *Holy Quran*, the essential sacred text of Islam. Many additional teachings are codified in the extensive *Hadith*.

In Arabia, in the fifth and sixth centuries, before Islam, there was still much polytheism but also a predisposition to monotheism, partly due to some inhabitants adhering to one of the major resurrection religions. Jonathan Berkey writes in *The Formation of Islam*:

> *Penetration of Arabia by the Roman and Sasanian empires, and by Christianity, Judaism, and Zoroastrianism, was always tentative, its implications and consequences always ambiguous.* 336

Berkey continues describing a process of development from longstanding Arab cultural themes:

> *Islam was not fully formed at the death of the Prophet Muhammad in 632, nor a few years later when it burst out of its Arabian homeland, nor even many decades later when it was clear that the rule of those who called themselves "Muslims" was permanent.*

Michael Haag, a writer of history, relates a contemporary insider perspective on the emergence of Islam. The Byzantines considered that Islam was a form of Christianity called Arianism where the divinity of Christ was rejected:

> *Even someone who saw things from up close, such as John of Damascus (c676-749), a Syrian Christian theologian who lived entirely under Muslim rule and served as counsellor in the court of the Umayyad caliphs, did not regard Islam as a new religion but considered it a deviation from orthodox Christianity similar to other early heresies.* 337

Despite this, the new religion was becoming very distinct to its followers.

Islam, from its beginning, maintained the purest form of monotheism. It rejected the Zoroastrian concept of a duality, where evil personified is a match for God. It also rejected the Christian concept of Trinity, instead establishing Christ as an important but mortal prophet, not divine. Christ is recognized without god-like power over afterlife, which is vested in Allah only. The legendary Canaanite patriarchs are still honoured: Adam, Noah and Abraham (known as Ibrahim) giving rise to continuity from the Abrahamic tradition.

Of the major religions, Islam has also most comprehensively rejected the old symbolism of the NST. Nowhere is the shell, egg or leaf symbolism still as recognizable as they are in Christianity. Where cathedrals have been converted to mosques, such as in Nicosia, all traces of un-Islamic symbolism is erased, even acanthus leaves atop columns are chiselled out.

There is no formal hierarchy of priesthood, and although all adherents to the faith, the ummah, are meant to be united within a single caliphate this has not been fully realized since the seventh century. This is primarily because there was an early schism centred on the dispute between Muhammad's companions and descendants. The orthodox, or Sunni, hold to the traditions of descendants from Abu Bakr of his companions. The Shia followers are those who hold to the succession of descendants from Ali, Muhammad's cousin.

Additionally, the new religion spread like a wildfire westward through North Africa, north to Anatolia and eastwards through Central Asia, the Indian subcontinent and eventually South East Asia. Having quickly dispersed over so many different cultures it made a unified orthodoxy impossible to achieve.

Judgment is very strongly expressed in Islam and, significantly Islamic countries still maintain Islamic Law (Shari'ah) at the state or regional level, thus maintaining close links between law and religion. This importance to social cohesion is widely recognized and described here by the sociologist Abdullah Al-Khalifah:

> *But, most importantly, the concept of punishment has a unique feature: a religious dimension that allows one's avoidance of punishment to increase one's conformity to the Islamic social order. In this case, punishment is considered to be of two types: divine and worldly. Divine punishment is what awaits each individual who failed to live in accordance with the Shari'ah but managed to escape punishment during his/her lifetime. This divine punishment is viewed as severe and eternal, for those who are guilty of violating the law of God and sought to escape the Day of Judgment.* [338]

Having both divine and worldly punishment firmly imposes the morality of constraint upon adults, and this is the most complete system as it sanctions believers twice.

A central feature of the GMR is that judgment in afterlife (or judgment from the afterlife) is the fundamental driver of social cohesion in large societies, and is a fundamental driver of the spiritual worldview. In Western society with Christianity, the secular judicial system is now divorced from religion. In the case of non-believers, physicalists, only the worldly punishment is observed – but this is a later phenomenon. A successful model of secular law can only develop after first passing through a dualistic phase, and this is still seen in Islamic countries.

There has long been debate between Islamic scholars about reconciling predestination by God and free will in people. Judgment requires people to be accountable for their actions and this can be interpreted as people choosing their actions but God determining the consequences. Alternatively, the binary view exists where everything is preordained by God and that free will is an illusion except in one respect – the ability to accept or reject God. The consequences for Muslims who later make the wrong choice hardly needs spelling out.

8 ◆ TECTONIC RELIGION: CONCEPTS FROM SCIENCE

The Second Great Paradigm Shift

We are living in that rarest of times: during a worldview paradigm shift. The science worldview is very much incomplete for the reason that it has not yet delivered a solution for mortality, equivalent to the afterlife that the spiritual worldview promises. Therefore, at the present time it is natural that many people have a conceptual imperative to reconcile the old and new paradigms. The result is described the GMR as Tectonic Religion (TR), a transitional quasi-worldview which is a thin pseudoscientific layer over the vast, spiritual, Mantle Religion. It is analogous to the earth's crust wrapping the mantle. Concepts such as Cartesian Dualism, with separation of matter and spirit, flower in the present quasi-worldview.

Emergence of Science

Science is viewed as a mixed blessing for religion. It clearly benefits humanity's living standards yet, at the same time, casts strong doubt upon the validity of most aspects of its religious belief. There is widespread opinion that science and religion are adversaries, more often than not. However, one of the important conclusions from the GMR is that it reveals science and religion are in a deep and ancient *partnership*. Religion is directly responsible for formulating conditions within which science has been able to flourish. Science is the butterfly emerging from the chrysalis of religiously buttressed large societies and civilizations.

Logic and mathematics need to be considered separately from the scientific worldview, especially as maths is the language of science, and they both transcend the science worldview itself. Logic and maths are just as valid in the life-force and spiritual worldviews as they would be in any theoretical post-science worldview (in the unlikely event this universe is just a simulation). For this reason, the early scientists are more accurately termed logicians and mathematicians. Trigonometry, geometry and other research work they did was more than tolerable within the spiritual worldview and did not challenge it.

An example is the ratio of a circle to its diameter, pi, which was used even in the time of ancient Egypt. Pi would have been thought of as a magical number between three and four of which the closest approximate fractional value was esoteric knowledge.

Miletus, a prosperous port city of the Greek colony on the western coast of the Anatolian mainland, seems to have been a special place. In the sixth century BCE its population is estimated at 30,000. It was larger than Athens in Greece.

Often described as the world's first scientist or the "Father of Science" Thales of Miletus, circa 624 to 546 BCE, attempted to describe nature though mathematics, logical analysis and experiment. In particular, he was the first to do this without recourse to religious mythology. Thales is only known of through anecdotes and writings by others as his works are lost to history. Hippodamus, of the same city, lived shortly afterwards circa 500 to 440 BCE, and has been called the "Father of Town Planning".

What these pioneers achieved was primarily in the disciplines of logic and maths.

In the Medieval period, Arab Islamic culture was a centre of excellence for mathematics and early science. The decimal numbering system, including the placeholder concept of zero, were defined, algebra and medicine were researched and taught. Circulation of the blood around the human body and the relationship between the lungs and heart were properly identified, 300 years before the same discovery was determined in Europe. All of this was still tolerable within the spiritual worldview.

The origin of the science worldview is arguably the year 1608 when the first telescope was described in a patent application in the Netherlands. It had four-fold magnification and news of this impressive device spread very quickly. The first microscope was also constructed at this time but it was half a century later before its full potential as a tool for scientific enquiry was properly recognized. During this period the practice of publishing scientific papers was invented.

This is the point where technology – applied science – made the further advancement of science possible by going beyond the limits of the human senses. Where science departs completely from magic is the use of instrumentation. The five senses can only distil a certain amount of information about nature, and early assumptions drawn from sensory data alone were usually erroneous; examples of which are the sun and moon travelling over the earth, and there being only four elements: earth, fire, air and water. It is only with the invention of ever better tools to augment the human senses, especially the many forms of telescopes and microscopes that science can continue in a step-by-step progression.

So, instrumentation used in scientific research sparked the science worldview and brought about a profound challenge to the spiritual worldview, and therefore to religion. The forefront of the challenge was astronomy, where the spiritual worldview included the Aristotelian view that the earth was at the centre and the heavenly bodies revolved around it.

Galileo Galilei, mathematician and philosopher, saw the potential of long-distance magnification immediately and used his superior skills of craftsmanship to make a series of improved telescopes, up to 30-fold magnification, and performed new astronomical research. He was, though, a good Christian and never intended to upset religious orthodoxy. The science journalist David Zax describes the situation leading to charges of heresy:

> *The Aristotelian worldview had been integrated with Catholic teachings, so any challenges to Aristotle were potential heresy. That Galileo had revealed flaws in celestial objects was bothersome enough. But some of his observations, especially the changing phases of Venus and the presence of moons around other planets, lent support to Copernicus' heliocentric theory, which ran afoul of the church's teachings. Biblical literalists pointed to the book of Joshua, in which the Sun is described as stopping, miraculously, "in the midst of heaven, and hasted not to go down about a whole day." How could the Sun stop if, as Copernicus and now Galileo claimed, it was already stationary?* [339]

Although the Copernican heliocentric Solar System was known about for decades, it was still a hypothesis. It was only the telescope which could prove it right beyond reasonable doubt. The Aristotelian view was only vigorously challenged in 1609, probably when the first telescopes were used to examine the night sky. Charges of heresy were levelled against Galilei in 1613 and never went away in his lifetime.

As the science worldview continued to develop, it enveloped other areas, and none more contentiously than the origin of humanity.

Evolution, first detailed in print by Charles Darwin in 1859, also attracted vigorous condemnation from church orthodoxy.

It is within the TR quasi-worldview, a temporary phase, where the religious resolution to these matters can be found. In 1992, Pope John Paul II issued a statement of regret over Galilei's treatment, and this was possible because the Catechism of the Catholic Church was then being revised to change the emphasis from God's *creation of the earth*, to God's creation of the universe *containing the earth*. It is a position which now tolerates heliocentricity. It is not yet orthodoxy but intelligent design also resolves the problem of human evolution in a manner compatible with the spiritual worldview.

In areas unrelated to afterlife, judgment and creation, the progress of science is non-contentious. Overall, the requirement upon religion to explain nature has weakened considerably. For example, religion is no longer expected to explain why it does not rain and, crop destroying droughts happen. Nor are ritual ceremonies invoked to break droughts which threaten food shortages.

From the perspective of multilevel natural selection between competing societies, science and technology were, and still are, very powerful fitness factors. Any culture which made limited use of these was doomed to become marginal and risked extinction. A further competitive advantage is by multilevel natural selection between sub-units of society, corporations in a capitalist framework – which has further accelerated science and technology.

Aspects of the TR Quasi-Worldview

The first part of Tectonic Religion (TR) is the religious response of existing religions inspired by pseudoscientific interpretations of the emerging corpus of science.

Universal Creation

The question about the origins of the world and of man has been the object of many scientific studies which have splendidly enriched our knowledge of the age and dimensions of the cosmos, the development of life-forms and the appearance of man. These discoveries invite us to even greater admiration for the greatness of the Creator, prompting us to give him thanks for all his works and for the understanding and wisdom he gives to scholars and researchers. [3]

– Catechism of the Catholic Church

The distinction between Universal creation and creation science is that Universal creation accepts the scientifically determined multi-billion year age of the universe and the earth, but asserts that this universe was created by God with later interventions. Creation science asserts instead that the universe, earth and everything on it is less than 10,000 years old.

The sky, earth and underworld (SEU) were everything to the ancients, therefore the many creation myths of religions in the spiritual worldview only attempt to explain the origin of the *world*: the earth and its spiritual realms. Until the invention of ever better telescopes the universe we recognize today was simply unknown. So, the universe has been discovered by science, largely in the last century, wholly within the scientific worldview.

Most authors on religion fail to distinguish between the ancient SEU world and the universe discovered by science. This is unhelpful confusion of terminology as seen in *The Encyclopedia of World Religions*:

Religions explain the origin of the universe in different ways. One familiar way is creation by a God. This may be creation from nothing, as Jews, Christians, and Muslims usually think today, or it may also involve creation by a god who works on pre-existing matter, which is one way to read the first verse of Genesis. [340]

When religion needs to explain the origin of the universe, it is responding to the corpus of recently acquired scientific knowledge. Hence these religious explanations are part of Tectonic Religion. Christianity is one of the few to have formally accepted this change as doctrine.

If believers consider that God has created the universe, which is now even Catholic orthodoxy, then this belief is consistent with God subsequently monitoring and intervening in the affairs of the world. This allows for continued belief in spiritual afterlife, judgment and resurrection.

It is a common belief amongst modern populations who are only notionally religious or even agnostic that God created the universe but has since let it run without intervention. This concept almost merges with the Strong Anthropic principle which is fringe science. The Strong Anthropic principle lends great weight to the laws of physics, which appear finely tuned to support the existence of humans, but falls short of specifying God, instead implying an anonymous directive quality inherent in the universe itself.

Creation Science

Biblical creationism is the belief that the world was created by God as described in Genesis in the Judeo-Christian bibles, within the last 10,000 years. This includes the creation of humans and the Great Flood. In the GMR, this belief is a component of the spiritual worldview in Mantle Religion, and sits amongst analogous beliefs found in other non-Abrahamic religions.

It was still during the formative period of the scientific worldview, the late nineteenth century, when the great age of the earth was determined. Yet, this was still reconcilable within the spiritual worldview as each biblical "day" of creation was considered an "age".

Creation science is a late twentieth century development where creationism has adopted concepts from the science worldview. This is described by Ronald Numbers in his historical treatment:

> *Besides the unexpected revival in recent years, which caught even enthusiasts by surprise, the most striking development in the history of twentieth-century creationism is the ascendancy since the early 1960s of a distinctive brand of creationism known as "scientific creationism" or "creation science."* [341]

Numbers describes the issuance of many creationist books in the United States such as flood geologies, reviving creationist thinking in the public and in churches. Perhaps it was the pressure from 100 years of incremental advances in Darwinist thinking concerning the evolution of humans from early primates that finally drove the events leading to creation science. Clearly a meme was sparked, which has persisted and spread internationally.

The ascendancy of creation science is typical of developments in religious thinking during a worldview paradigm shift where concepts from the old paradigm are reinterpreted within concepts from the new paradigm in order to maintain the viability, to believers, of the religion in question.

Intelligent Design

Now intelligent design does just this – it puts our native intellect to work and thereby confirms that a designer of remarkable talents is responsible for the physical world. How this designer connects with the God of Scripture is then for theology to determine.[364]

– William A. Dembski

Intelligent design (ID) is a Christian creationist response to the scientific process known as evolution which describes the emergence of highly complex life on earth from simple organic chemicals. It is an attempt to explain the key element of natural selection within evolution as a series of interventions by an abstract intelligence.

Dembski makes clear the strategic direction of ID against its categorization as religious pseudoscience. It is by defining ID as being determined scientifically, and only subsequently inviting theologians to associate it with the Abrahamic supreme God.

In the GMR, an inevitable consequence of ID containing the fundamental scientific concept of design is that it becomes, by definition, a component of Tectonic Religion. In the spiritual worldview of Mantle Religion the earth, people and anything in it can simply be created by gods, not requiring any design. Where religion requires design, it is also adopting the important technical principle of design itself. Design is a very human activity required to overcome incomplete information and self-doubt to perform problem-solving.

NDE as Afterlife Evidence

The great religions have always spoken to the belief in God and an afterlife. The evidence of near-death experiences points to an afterlife and a universe guided by a vastly loving intelligence.

> *Near-death experiences consistently reveal that death is not an end but rather a transition to an afterlife.* [342]

– Jeffrey Long and Paul Perry

A near-death experience (NDE) is a conscious experience when in an unconscious state close to clinical death. Usually this is reported by patients who have revived after a short failure of respiration in a hospital or other medical facility. Those revived with this experience relate one or more events, such as having seen their body externally, floating above it, seeing a tunnel of light or feeling gloom and fear, or even meeting the spirits of deceased relatives. NDEs are reported very frequently since the twentieth century because modern medicine is recovering many more patients from situations warranting intensive care.

In the spiritual worldview, progression to and from afterlife is a magical process. The description below of the NDE phenomenon by Ornella Corazza is securely within that worldview:

> *In Tibetan tradition, there is an interesting phenomenon called delok, which literally means 'returned from the dead'. The name deloks is given to people who seemingly 'die' as a result of an illness, and find themselves traveling in the Bardo, before returning to life again. His Holiness the Dalai Lama observed that this argument could offer some interesting parallels with the NDE.* [343]

The mainstream perspective from science is clear. An NDE is considered by neuroscientists to be an artefact of the mind when the brain is deprived of oxygen, the normal brainstem capability of differentiating REM sleep and the wakeful state is disturbed, and the temporoparietal area of the brain, which maintains self-awareness of the body, is abnormally stimulated.

However, this is disputed by those who look for explanations elsewhere. In *Evidence of the Afterlife: The Science of Near-Death Experiences* the medical practitioner Jeffrey Long and film producer Paul Perry assert that NDEs are evidence for afterlife, and use concepts from science to support it. In the GMR, this belief falls within Tectonic Religion.

A second phenomenon which is interpreted as evidence for afterlife is past-life memories. These experiences are usually related by children who claim prior memories of other places, providing evidence that the integrity of adult memories and personality are partially preserved through the Dharmic cycle of samsara, death and rebirth. There is a cultural bias as these are mostly researched in India rather than Western countries. Similarly, though, where concepts from science are employed in evidencing past-life memories, and this becomes part of religious belief in reincarnation, this is also Tectonic Religion.

Quantum Mechanics in Dharmic Religions

Finally, we ought to remember that Madhyamaka, like all of Buddhism, is intended as a means to liberation, whereas physics has more modest aims. Buddhism and Western physics have come out of different cultures, and they have different starting points, methods, and goals. This makes it all the more remarkable that they have produced some very similar ideas. [344]

– William L. Ames

The Dharmic religions: Hinduism, Jainism, Buddhism and Sikhism have found it easier to coexist within the science worldview than Christianity. Likely, this is because of the absence of early points of conflict – no young-earth doctrine or apocalyptic end-of time involving resurrection – and the remoteness from the centres where Western science developed – until recently.

Madhyamaka is a philosophy concerning the attainment of wisdom, part of the Mahayana Buddhist school originating in the second century CE. One of the features of it is that instead of a spirit which survives death, there is considered to be a disembodied identity that is at once a "mental-physical state" (which is considered not self-aware) and "empty" (which is considered not the same as nothing, and explanations struggle here). The duality of this thinking, as well as the duality between matter and emptiness in Buddhist concepts of reality, finds an attractive parallel in the properties of quantum mechanics.

Quantum mechanics underpins reality in the science worldview and is a twentieth century discovery which defies easy explanation. It is sufficient for usage here to note that it has properties of wave and particle duality, uncertainty in particle position, and particle or energy emergence from a vacuum. From the perspective of science, such parallels with concepts in Buddhism are usually considered to be coincidence.

Increasingly, however, linkage is made between the two, as implied by the journalist and philosopher Charles Johnson:

> *Even though we can say that each person has a "separate" history, the dharma teaches — as does quantum mechanics — that we are really a process, not a product: We are each an "individuality," ever arising and passing away, every one of us a "network of mutuality," as Martin Luther King, Jr., famously said.* [345]

The astrophysicist Piet Hut comments:

> *Whether a scientific worldview leaves room for a Buddhist way of looking at the world is a more difficult question. In fact, the very question is already wrongly posed, since there is as yet no scientific worldview, and I don't expect there to be one for at least a century. For an approach to reality to be comprehensive enough to be called a worldview, at the very least such a view should have room for human life, meaning, dignity, responsibility, and other aspects of what it means to be human.* [346]

In the GMR, the science worldview is, of course, wholly evident and has done nothing but improve living standards, dignity and other important aspects of humanity for 400 years. The Buddhist worldview is still part of the spiritual worldview paradigm, even if the concept of spirit is rejected and replaced with analogous ideas of mental-physical states.

The incorporation of quantum mechanics into Buddhist and other Dharmic theology is the borrowing of concepts from science and is therefore part of Tectonic Religion.

Universal Apocalyptic Eschatology

Due to some inexorable aspects of fundamental physics: entropy, gravitation and dark energy, science has determined that the universe has a finite lifespan. This is calculated to be, at minimum, some 60 billion years in the future, although still possibly thousands of times longer. This is mainstream science, but pseudoscience is drawn from it to reconcile Christianity with the post-spiritual worldview.

This religious response is subscribed to by John Polkinghorne, a theoretical physicist and Anglican priest who writes:

Yet science tells us most surely and clearly that the end of present physical process lies in futility, the bang of cosmic collapse or the whimper of cosmic decay. Carbon-based life will have its day and then it will disappear for ever. I mentioned these problems in the first chapter. A credible eschatology, which takes account of the eventual death of the universe and looks beyond it to God's new creation, is surely an indispensable component in realistic Christian thinking. [347]

Of course, the universe is only known to religion because it was discovered by science. In the GMR, where the death of the universe is included into, and subordinated within Christian end-of-times eschatology, such as the final judgment and God's kingdom, this is religious belief which exists within the quasi-worldview of Tectonic Religion.

Pseudoscientific Religions

The second part of Tectonic Religion is the emergence of entirely new religions which are significantly or wholly inspired by pseudoscientific interpretations of the expanding corpus of science. This includes religion inspired by science fiction. To modern minds a new religion is not credible unless it is appears compatible with science – current or future.

Falun Gong

I submit that viewing Falun Gong as anything other than a religious movement, concerned with moral purpose and the ultimate meaning of life and death (and not—at least at the movement's beginning—with the organization of power in this world), is ultimately limiting; there is no other way to understand its attraction without denying the humanity of its practitioners. [348]

– David Ownby

Falun Gong was founded in the early 1990s by Li Hongzhi, a student of Buddhist and Taoist schools. It is an international religion with an uncertain number of adherents, perhaps currently several hundred thousand active believers. In China, where it experienced a rapid growth in popularity in 1990s, it was briefly practised by tens of millions, but the numbers collapsed after it suffered significant repression.

The term qigong is a modern reinterpretation of the ancient concept of qi, also known as Ch'i, mentioned earlier as a belief in an invisible life-giving essence analogous with spirit. Qigong traditions date from the Maoist era of the 1950s and are a collective name for various ideas concerning cultivation of Chinese herbal medicine and alternative healing practices.

In Falun Gong, traditional Chinese medicine assists in the analysis and promotion of the various types of Ch'i which makes up each individual; where every organ has its own type of Ch'i. It is a central assertion of the religion that Ch'i has been found experimentally using scientific methods. Even a research foundation and laboratory has been set up to further this discovery.

Breathing exercises in open spaces is a popular daily practice of Falun Gong adherents, which seems innocuous, but its sudden decline was due the official response to its social organizational message, very much seen in China as a political threat.

Falun Gong is firmly rooted in existing qigong traditions, but it incorporates the Dharmic reincarnation afterlife paradigm and karmic self-judgment. Because it is also strongly aligned to concepts borrowed from science it is categorized in the GMR as a Tectonic Religion.

Scientology

> *The ultimate goal – Scientology's equivalent of salvation is to enable the individual's thetan, the equivalent to the soul in other religious systems, to move freely in time and space as it once did countless existences ago before it was bound to its current state of existence in the material universe.* [349]
>
> – James R. Lewis

The Church of Scientology was founded in 1954 by L. Ron Hubbard, writer and adventurer, and has about 500,000 adherents today. It emerged from the Dianetics movement Hubbard started some years earlier. While Dianetics is intended to provide therapeutic benefits for troubled minds and solve psychological disorders, Scientology is oriented towards spiritual matters.

James Lewis, writer and researcher of modern religion, identifies a movement within New Age, twentieth century religions which attempted to investigate mind and spirit in a scientific way. He observes that Scientology went beyond the others by describing their therapeutic practices as technology and actively attempting to improve the human mind.

The central afterlife belief of Scientology is that spirits, known as thetans, are immortal and undergo a Dharmic-like reincarnation cycle. Hubbard's science fiction works are codified into a religious history where many thetans, millions of years old, came to be dispersed across the world from an extraterrestrial source.

Thetans, when trapped in a human body, are limited, unless Dianetics is employed to completely free the person's mind from previous mental trauma, at which point they can achieve their full spiritual potential and escape the reincarnation cycle. Part of this process involves adherence to a moral code of behaviour defined by Hubbard.

From the perspective of the GMR, the strong afterlife theology and moral code within a framework of concepts from science, and the use of religious technology, defines Scientology as a Tectonic Religion.

Various UFO religions

> *UFOs in fact offer a substitute "deity" for those who (can) no longer believe in a "God who intervenes in history." Indeed, there is a remarkable overlap between some UFO scenarios and the equally popular "Premillennial dispensationalists."* [350]

> – Richard Allen Landes

In the twentieth century, many small religions and cults were founded with the idea that the earth has been subject to visits by extraterrestrials. Because there have been many thousands of unidentified flying object (UFO) sightings and not all are easily explained, these ideas fall on receptive minds influenced by modern popular culture. UFO-oriented religions exist within the spiritual to science worldview paradigm shift as they draw upon elements from both and find a much more benign environment to grow in than would otherwise be the case.

The premillennial dispensationalism that Landes refers to is the Christian belief late in the twentieth century that, as 2000 years since Christ's birth approached, the apocalyptic end-times were imminent. This theme is seen in most UFO religions where the expected arrival of extraterrestrial figures will result in a similar apocalyptic end-time. Landes continues:

> *On the one hand, the suicides at Heaven's Gate believed that a ship would take them off the earth before it was "plowed under" with all its inhabitants, while preachers like jack Van lmpe believe that God will "rapture" a chosen few (presumably including him and his wife Rexilla) before visiting a terrible Tribulation upon the world. A common apocalyptic archetype informs both these "prophecies".*

Landes considers UFO cults to be millennialist and also finds the same theme of divine intervention occurring throughout history, from Roman times until today. This is more an expression of how the priesthood of many religions finds leverage amongst believers, maintaining their adherence at a period when end-times are considered to be imminent.

UFO religions borrow heavily from pseudoscience and fiction with highly unorthodox afterlife doctrines. James Lewis describes the central belief of the Raelians:

> *Denying the existence of God or the soul, Rael presents as the only hope of immortality a regeneration through science, and to this end members participate in four annual festivals so that the Elohim can fly overhead and register the Raelians' DNA codes on their machines. This initiation ritual, called "the transmission of the cellular plan," promises a kind of immortality through cloning.* [351]

Adherents to the Aetherius Society, formed in the 1950s, do, however, believe in spirits and their existence in the realm of the dead, but, again, have an extraterrestrial origin for their major religious figures.

Belief in afterlife achieved within a framework of concepts borrowed from science fiction and pseudoscience firmly categorizes, within the GMR, the various UFO religions as Tectonic Religion.

Limit of the Geologic Model of Religion

It is here, at the edge of Tectonic Religion, that the presentation of the GMR itself comes to an end. I hope that you have found the journey along the long road of religion from the remote prehistoric past to the present day interesting, and dare I say enlightening?

Having constructed a model, one of the main benefits is using it to make predictions. Hitherto, all we have done is interpreted the past. We can use the GMR to make a prediction, and the principal prediction from it must be: How long will religion continue? If this question intrigues, then hopefully you will find a short excursion into the near future, interesting too. Regrettably, here I risk splitting my readership into numerous groups. Some may accept or reject the thrust of the GMR itself, but now a similar choice presents itself with the epilogue.

Because science is outside of religion, the question can be rephrased: When will the paradigm shift from spirituality become complete? This can be indirectly determined by examining how the science worldview is dealing with the age-old problem of personal mortality, which originally sparked religion so many long years ago.

EPILOGUE ◆ SCIENCE WORLDVIEW

Physicalism and Personal Mortality

The GMR encompasses the life-force and spiritual worldviews, and the two great paradigm shifts: one from life-force, and one from spirituality. The third worldview, science itself, is external to it. So, physicalism and patternist philosophy are also external to the GMR.

Life and Death in Flux

"Wayfarer, do not pass by my epitaph, but stand and listen, and then, when you have learned the truth, proceed. There is no boat in Hades, no ferryman Charon, no Aeacus keeper of the keys, nor any dog called Cerberus. All of us who have died and gone below are bones and ashes: there is nothing else. What I have told you is true. Now withdraw, wayfarer, so that you will not think that, although dead, I talk too much." [352]

– Second century Roman tombstone, Trans. R. Lattimore

When the Italian occultist, polymath, collector, researcher and writer Athanasius Kircher passed away in 1680 the time had gone when it was possible for a single individual to understand all of discovered knowledge. [353]

Currently, it would take hubristic bravery to claim to understand a millionth of all knowledge, and it is still growing very fast. Some observers report information doubling times are currently at two years or less. Information alone is an inadequate metric as it is often partially random or duplicated data. This is not valuable knowledge. Measured by the number of peer-reviewed and published scientific papers, which is a challenging task with highly variable results by discipline, the average doubling time of scientific knowledge proves to be 15 years. Therefore, as much scientific knowledge was acquired between 1997 and

2012 than all the period up to 1997. As the science worldview is truly vast in size, we are only going to consider a small but important portion of it.

For the purpose of the GMR we wish to determine a prediction for when the Second Great Paradigm Shift will complete. The spiritual worldview will not have run its course until science answers the most important question of all, the one perhaps first considered by the long extinct *Homo erectus*, and originally sparked the age-old fire of religion: What is the solution to personal mortality?

In the life-force worldview the solution was rebirth, in the spiritual worldview the solution was air as spirit (preservation as a disembodied identity). In the science worldview the solution requires technology which does not yet exist, however we can already determine its theoretical basis. This has become apparent since the 1990s.

Before science can solve personal mortality it requires an accurate definition of death and this first step has proved, until recently, very problematic. The scientific definition of it has been constantly changing over the years.

For centuries absence of vitality was considered absence of life. The failure of respiration, pupil dilation and lack of pulse or heartbeat were long known as hallmarks of a fatal state. When electricity was discovered in the early nineteenth century it was first thought that this was the vital essence of life and could reanimate corpses. Such experiments were unsuccessful. In the twentieth century improved medicine and life-support technology eventually meant the old hallmarks of life were insufficient. Radical surgery, such as heart transplants, transformed thinking on the matter.

The first heart transplant, performed by Dr Christian Barnard in Cape Town in December 1967, attracted questions over death and identity as much as those about the ground-breaking technical difficulties he overcame. Was the patient the same person? Did he die and come back to life?

Brain death steadily became the best measure for establishing legal death in humans; however, acceptance of cessation of brain function as final arbiter has been fought at every step, as seen in the view held by rabbi and lawyer Michael Broyde:

> *A determination of death is a legal determination that a collection*
> *of living cells is no longer entitled to the rights granted to human*
> *beings, rather than a scientific or medical determination that all*

> *biological life has ended. [...] The question is, at its core, not a*
> *medical question but a moral or religious one.* [354]

So, brain death was only officially recognized in the United States as late as 1981. Other countries have lagged further, for example India accepting this definition in 1996 and Japan in 1997. In the science worldview the determination that biological life has ended can only be a scientific one. To pretend otherwise is being politically correct to non-scientific cultural biases, or to persist in the conflation of the spiritual worldview with the scientific paradigm. A further difficulty is that as science tries to determine the point of no return back to physical function, the goalposts keep moving away as life-support technologies improve. Cryonics, the suspended animation of vitrified deceased humans at liquid nitrogen temperatures, puts a coach and horses through the current definition of brain death – if such people can be restored to function through advanced molecular technology.

From the direction opposite to defining death and performing life support, life-extension technologies attempt to keep people vigorously healthy and rejuvenated as long as possible.

A few hundred years ago most people were cut down in their prime, in their thirties; lifespan today is more than double that. Few areas of science have been pursued more vigorously than the development of pharmaceuticals to arrest disease and disorders. This means that most people encounter failing health from age-related terminal disorders in their seventies and eighties. Since the advent of modern medicine, particularly in the twentieth century, life expectancy has increased close to natural limits where the battle is now up against the aging process itself. Aubrey de Grey, theoretical gerontologist, coined the term "pro-aging trance" and vigorously writes against its effects. He finds that the trance is induced because aging is seen as so inevitable that people prefer to come to terms with it as natural, rather than see it as a horrible affliction.

There are many new technologies which promise to delay the onset of aging and reduce the rate of growth of its accumulated pathologies. Action at the cellular level has seen radical advances with stem cell therapies, which promise the ability to regrow new organs and connective tissues though a model of repair by "spare parts". However, the most ambitious anti-aging program is that offered by the SENS Foundation.

The Strategies for Engineered Negligible Senescence (SENS) are a set of research programs breaking down the human aging process into its discrete elements and developing pharmacological solutions to each one. The aging process is the effect of a varied collection of different pathologies. One example is accumulation of lipofuscin, mitochondrial and other organic waste residue mixed with trace inorganics from cellular functions. The body lacks appropriate enzymes to process these materials for recycling or excretion so they slowly accumulate over a lifetime leading to many degenerative diseases. SENS proposes a form of enzyme replacement therapy, from bacterial prototypes, to digest these substances. Although other pathologies offer greater resistance to therapy, in principle they can all be dealt with, potentially increasing human lifespan to a thousand years. [355]

All of the existing and theoretical interventions by science against mortality with the goal of preserving physical life are still tolerable within the spiritual worldview because advanced medicine still does not guarantee immortality. Even a person who can live a thousand years may still have his or her life extinguished in an air accident or by murderous actions against them. Do these life-threatening possibilities leave spirituality as the only enduring solution to mortality?

It appears not. A review of mortality within the science worldview indicates that immortality is achievable.

Consciousness and Mind

> *We would like to believe that consciousness is an emergent phenomenon of a neurobiological process. While fundamental philosophical difficulties in defining consciousness remain, to study the neural correlates of anesthetic-induced unconsciousness there is no alternative to adopting a mechanistic working hypothesis, similar to what was suggested for studying the neural correlates of consciousness itself (Crick and Koch 2003).* [356]

> – Anthony Hudetz and Robert Pearce

The following are relatively new areas of research which enable a new perspective on the understanding of consciousness, mind, identity, death and immortality within the scientific worldview. This understanding is incomplete, but in the last two decades the direction from which science is addressing the fundamentals of the human condition has become apparent.

Despite the processes underpinning the emergence of consciousness not yet fully decomposed though scientific research, we do already have evidence that consciousness has an electrochemical basis. It comes from anaesthetics. Rendering patients unconscious for operations is critical to modern medicine. Two of the best anaesthetics are nitrous oxide and xenon. This is very interesting as both are inert in the human body and do not chemically react. In fact xenon is one of the noble gases and is never found naturally in a compound. So, it can only act mechanically, like a wrench between two gears. The nitrous oxide molecule and xenon atom are a similar size, at four angstroms in diameter. They work by blocking a suitably sized protein receptor in the brain, likely NMDA. [357]

Molecules at room temperature move extremely fast, they do not just sit in a receptor but are oscillating in and out. Dozens of different molecules of the anaesthetic gas will be blocking the same receptor, every second. Because there are enough gas molecules to swamp the billions of protein receptors, they have a global effect, which means emergent properties are quashed. Consciousness vanishes by mechanical means!

The concentration of gas rises after first intake and then falls as diffusion occurs. The skill of the anaesthetist is crucial in monitoring the reduced levels of electrical activity in the brain, as too high a concentration results in likely brain death when electrical activity stops. Done properly, the inert anaesthetic gas is purged from the body via respiration, reducing its concentration and number of instances where the receptors are blocked. The patient then revives, regaining full consciousness.

The temporary suspension of conscious and subconscious properties of a brain shows continuity of consciousness is an illusion and can't be relevant to preservation of individual identity. Consciousness clearly emerges from electrochemical processes. Anaesthetics continue to prove it in surgeries of hospitals around the world, every hour of every day.

Hudetz and Pearce, anaesthesiologists and biophysicists, discuss consciousness in terms of information processing:

> *Tononi (2004) defined a conscious system by its capacity to integrate information. The latter definition implies that consciousness is a graded phenomenon, with more integrated*

information comes, in some sense, more consciousness. Conversely, consciousness is reduced either when the available information is reduced or when the capacity of the system to integrate is reduced. This model was recently applied to illustrate how anesthetic agents may suppress consciousness (Alkire, Hudetz, and Tononi 2008). [356]

An analogy is appropriate here. Consciousness is similar to a computer's operating system which processes environmental information but runs on biological hardware instead of silicon-based substrate. The operating system that is consciousness is exactly the same version for all humans and, indeed, for all animals which have a large enough brain to support its emergence. Each brain has a different instance of consciousness, and it can be switched off and on mechanically by several means such as anaesthetics, hypoxia, shock or cold. The smaller and less complex a brain is, the more degraded is the instance of consciousness it can support.

Unlike computers, however, where each example of a specific make and model are identical, every brain is physically unique. It is the physical differences in the brain cells, particularly the synaptic connections of axons and dendrites of neurons, which encode the many pattern layers of personality and memory. It is this that makes everyone different and represents their identity. The evolved benefit of consciousness is to better support the interaction of a stored identity pattern with the environment. A stored identity pattern has an initial genetically determined state but slowly develops and modifies from infancy onwards through feedback from the environment.

The environment is not perceived directly, as explained by the physicist and engineer Scott Tyson who gives the example of cascading sound waves from a falling tree reaching an observer:

The vibrations are then transferred to the ears' tympanic membranes, which begin to resonate. These motions are transferred through the bones and apparatus of the ear until they reach the cochlea. The cochlea then translates these vibrations into electrochemical impulses, which travel along nerves of the central nervous system until the signals reach the auditory processing center of the brain. This part of the brain then interprets the incoming electrochemical signals into a form of information that

> *is useful to us. This information is transferred to our*
> *consciousness where, finally, we perceive sound.* [358]

It is the emergent property of consciousness interacting with the underlying biologically-stored identity pattern that together functionally constitute a mind, which can then think and perceive perceptions of the environment. Pushing the computing analogy further, a mind is the suite of applications which run within an operating system, some of which are foreground tasks and some, are background (in a mind: subconscious) tasks.

Ben Goertzel, in his work *The Hidden Pattern* introduces and explains his patternist philosophy, which describes reality as layers of interacting patterns of many types and scales. His area of focus is, however, how mind and intelligence comes about:

> *Patternist philosophy states that mind is made of pattern, and*
> *that intelligent systems are involved in recognizing and creating*
> *patterns in their environments in the service of achieving more or*
> *less complex goals.* [359]

Goertzel is developing computer software utilizing patternist principles for its design. The aim is to create an artificial general intelligence and this project is well advanced.

Unlike computers, where the hardware remains stable, when a biological mind is working, modifications continually occur to the underlying patterns of personality and memory as a result. An identity pattern can also be described as a special type of information and therefore will conform to the principles of information theory.

Death Redefined

Thus far, across the millennia, people have always thought of life and death as two distinct situations, a duality. Someone is either alive or dead. They might be barely alive, and nearly dead, if fatally wounded or terminally diseased. When very sick, death feels close, ready to snuff out the flickering candle of life. Similarly, the transition from life to death is assumed to be much like a light bulb turning from lit to unlit, on to off.

Death is supposed to be a sudden event – no heartbeat, no breathing and no brainwaves. When the triangle of vitality is broken, the individual becomes no more. Socially, medically, religiously, legally and emotionally in the vice-like crush of greatest personal grief, railing against the darkness – this duality defines our existence.

Based upon information theory within the scientific worldview, this is incorrect. Almost everyone who has contemplated death has misunderstood its true nature. This is the case for atheists and religious believers alike.

Consider the light bulb again. It might seem to have two states: on and off, but more accurately, it has *three*: on, off and broken. There is a fundamental difference between off and broken. When a light bulb is off it can be switched on again and will function normally. When a light bulb is broken it can no longer be switched back on. Perhaps it could be repaired, you might think, but this is infinitely harder than just turning it back on. It requires advanced knowledge and specialist equipment. Even then the end result can be considered a different light bulb from the original. As we will see, the states of on and off are far closer to the same state – than off is to broken.

A light bulb has three recognizably distinct states. This is also the case with all humans, animals, plants, fungi, bacteria, computers, machinery, or any complex functional structure. They can be alive (on), dormant (off), or destroyed (broken). Just because humans, and some animals, are the only functional structures complex enough to be self-referential does not mean this principle applies differently.

What people have thought of as death, for tens of thousands of years, is a combination of dormant and destroyed. Those two concepts have been mixed together to the point where most people consider death to be a single, quick transition from the state of being alive.

Another way of thinking about this is the difference between form and function. A glass globe with a fixing base containing a filament in a vacuum is the form of a light bulb. The function is conducting electricity through resistance to emit light, which is something that can be switched on and off hundreds of times, until such time as the form of the light bulb radically changes. This happens if the filament erodes through due to oxidation and then the light bulb is broken, or "dead". Its function is lost.

The same principle applies to human brains. The form of personal identity, as we have just seen, are semi-fixed patterns across millions of neurons. Consciousness and mind are the functions of the brain – expressing the stored patterns as an individual identity, now able to be active in the environment. Consciousness and mind can be switched on and off hundreds of times, until such time as the *form* of the stored identity patterns changes too radically.

If a brain is physically damaged, perhaps by receiving too much anaesthetic gas during an operation, and it can no longer produce consciousness, let alone a thinking mind, then its function has been lost. This would be considered medically as death, but in terms of information theory very little data is lost at this point. Because the neurons are still intact, the patterns are persistent but, temporarily, as they begin a process of disintegration through entropy. The identity held by this brain is dormant but not immediately destroyed.

Destruction and information theoretic death depends upon the physical structure of the patterns, as to how quickly something dormant then becomes destroyed. Machinery made of steel remains stable when switched off and only slowly rusts away. Machinery of carbon – biology – is far more fragile as it must remain in homeostasis. This is a fine balance of chemical concentrations and reaction pathways. All advanced, multi-cellular living organisms depend upon homeostasis for smooth functioning. Evolution has generated a sophisticated and delicate level of homeostasis in advanced organisms because the process of natural selection works only step by step. The biological structure of the human body is so complex that absence of respiration quickly disrupts the balance of homeostasis.

In the event of loss of respiration chemical processes that normally work in a manner of circular feedback become open-ended, one-way, and destructive to the fabric of the biological organism. This speed of destructive processes also depends upon ambient temperature, according to the Arrhenius equation, and the presence of agents such as microbes.

Death is not a force of nature claiming a life any more than a "force of darkness" overcomes a light bulb when it is switched off. Real death means destruction. Destruction is the randomizing of an identity pattern. It is information loss. Like a jigsaw, there are millions more ways that pieces of a pattern can be scattered than they can be assembled into a coherent picture. Once information is lost randomly into the environment it is virtually impossible to recover. This is the physicalist, science worldview definition of death.

Completion of the Second Great Paradigm Shift

The paradigm shift underway at present means that the situation current in the early twenty-first century is life-extension by science and afterlife via spirituality combined in a quasi-worldview. This will persist until the science delivers true immortality. Only then, after several hundred thousand years, will religion itself fade away, but only because it has indirectly succeeded in the respect that humanity will have finally overcome mortality.

Personal Identity Patterns

> *Informational Continuity: Physical structure may be destroyed, but all the information necessary to potentially allow reconstruction of the brain (or other consciousness-support structure) and thus restoration of its function persists.* [360]

> – Max More

Water passing by a rock in a stream creates a constant pattern of ripples. This pattern may persist for years, although each water molecule flows past in seconds. The pattern may distort as the water level lowers, and return as the level climbs. The persistence of patterns is the key to the persistence of a complex organism. Cells and proteins within cells are constantly being replaced and rebuilt. Depending upon the tissue type, it is all turned over in time. So, the person you are today is, on a molecular level, almost completely different to that of last year. What has persisted is the pattern of your body. Because you are still a very similar person as last year – what has also persisted is the personal pattern of information stored in neurons in your brain.

A personal identity pattern is used in the singular here because one identity is being discussed; however, in a brain, thousands of information patterns overlay each other and the entirety constitute the individual. Therefore, the quality of being alive is a functioning identity pattern. Dormant is a non-functioning identity pattern. Death and destruction is the randomizing scattering of a previously functioning identity pattern.

Arguably, there is growing support for the concept of information theoretic death – that death will be redefined to mean only destruction of a personal identity pattern, the permanent loss of information about an individual's identity. If this becomes mainstream thinking then it must significantly direct the future of humanity in this century.

The practical work to uncover the physical basis of personal identity patterns is a new area of research concerning the "connectome". In *Connectome: How the Brain's Wiring Makes Us Who We Are* Sebastian Seung summarizes this concept:

> *...a connectome is the totality of connections between the neurons in a nervous system. The term, like genome, implies completeness. A connectome is not one connection, or even many. It is all of them. In principle, your brain could also be summarized by a diagram that is like the worm's, though much more complex.* [361]

The assertion is that our connectomes encode patterns of our unique memories and personalities. These patterns, are in turn, interpreted by our minds and make each of us unique to the outside world. Decoding, by slicing and scanning the detail of a human connectome, is such a challenging task that Seung considers it may not become routine, even in the twenty-first century. However, in the timeframe of the transcendence of the scientific worldview this is still not a long period.

Decoding a connectome means that it then becomes stored digitally as a computer file. The difference between pattern and substrate becomes clear when it is considered that it is likely a personal identity pattern will eventually be "read" from the information stored in such a file. Thus far, most life-extension technologies are concerned with preserving human identity in its existing biological substrate.

At this point the science worldview can only be explored further by projecting future trends. It becomes a much more challenging task than interpreting the past, so only a very short section will be devoted to this area. Finally we will speculate upon the implications if a break is made with the dependency of human minds relying upon biological bodies.

Immortality and Singularity

> *What does it really mean to want to live forever? Delving into the meaning of "live" and "forever" isn't that fascinating to me in*

> *this context, [...] What intrigues me more is digging into the "I"
> who wants to live forever. What exactly is it that's being
> perpetuated, in the hypothesis of eternal life? How can we tell
> whether, in a particular scenario, this "I" is really being
> perpetuated or not? [...] It seems very clear to me that
> pharmacology or nanomedicine will eventually enable human
> physiological immortality – and that uploading will eventually
> allow humans to copy their minds into computers of some sort.* [359]
>
> – Ben Goertzel

Afterlife is fundamental to religion, only because it is the best proxy for immortality within the pre-scientific worldviews. Immortality is theoretically possible in the science worldview if it is accepted that a person's identity can be reduced to data and stored digitally. Inevitably this includes storage on the internet.

Subsequent instantiation of a mind in an artificial substrate, making use of a stored pattern, is itself a major technical challenge, but may be easier than connectome scanning, as the problem is then primarily one of software. If successful, then an instantiated mind might also enjoy a renewed physical existence with a reconstructed biological or inorganic analogue body, perhaps fashioned through nanotechnology.

A common argument against the benefit of instantiation of minds in a separate substrate is that there must be a break in *continuity of consciousness*. In the previous section this is seen to be an illusion. There are many people alive today who have not only had complete loss of consciousness, but a loss of electrical function of the brain during anaesthetic or hypothermic conditions. Upon revival they consider themselves the same person as before. The only continuity required was preservation of their identity pattern. Additionally, it makes no functional difference whether identity patterns are stored in atoms of carbon or silicon.

Once human personal identity patterns are uploaded into computers and distributed across the internet, then it will be almost *impossible to die*. The problem of fatal accidents is overcome because there could be real-time backup facilities and therefore recoverable backups available. Even if someone was unlucky enough to be vaporized in a nuclear explosion, they could be recovered from a remote backup missing only the last few seconds of personality and memory changes. The unlikely destruction of the earth itself is not a problem for survival, as within a few hundred years from now the growing data-sphere of human exploration in space will mean that many repositories for billions of uploaded identity patterns will exist in the Solar System and beyond. Pattern updates would then be cascaded from repository to repository at the speed of light. Even if it takes days or weeks for the signal to reach its furthest point, the information is conserved.

There would be great difficulty in committing suicide. Anyone who was genuinely tired of existence would presumably have to take steps to reduce the probability of revival from uploaded copies. Accessing all uploaded copies of a single identity pattern would be almost impossible as off-line storage sites will exist to deliberately protect against systemic viral threats. There would need to be a requirement for a new human right – a *right to permanent termination*. Safeguards would also be needed, just as today, as there is a debate over the safeguards around voluntary euthanasia for the terminally ill.

The patternist, information theoretic view shows that individuals can be preserved for thousands or even millions of years – this being only a question of technology. It is a time period so much greater than the seventy years afforded to humans by evolution that for all practical purposes it can be considered indefinite. Information-based immortality provides just as much of an extension to existence as that postulated by spirituality.

Brain scanning and digitally instantiating minds are presently exuberant science fiction and seemingly well beyond the lifetime of people today. Ray Kurzweil, inventor and futurologist, argues that such thinking is projecting the growth of technology linearly, whereas technology has been advancing exponentially for centuries and the present time is within the knee of the technological curve:

> *What, then, is the Singularity? It's a future period during which the pace of technological change will be so rapid, its impact so deep, that human life will be irreversibly transformed. Although neither utopian nor dystopian, this epoch will transform the concepts that we rely on to give meaning to our lives, from our business models to the cycle of human life, including death itself.*
> 362

The approach of a technological singularity will make a reality of many of the theoretical solutions to advanced problems, perhaps including digitally instantiated minds. Kurzweil continues:

The Singularity will allow us to transcend these limitations of our biological bodies and brains. We will gain power over our fates. Our mortality will be in our own hands. We will be able to live as long as we want (a subtly different statement from saying we will live forever).

The Singularity is projected to occur about 2045, with many informed predictions between 2030 and 2080. [363]

If and when this transpires, the paradigm shift from the spiritual worldview will be complete. The transitional quasi-worldview of Tectonic Religion will also, by definition, come to an end. This will only be after such extreme life-extension is recognized by almost everyone as an unequivocal success. The process is inexorable, as not only is immortality central to religion, it is central to science as well. They are in harmonious alignment that this is the natural, destined, objective for humanity.

♦

GLOSSARY

Animal Renewal Traditions (ART) is a Palaeolithic belief system within ICR as it assists with attaining afterlife. ART has the major belief sub-system of harnessing the life-giving power of eggs in funerary ritual, usually with egg representations of shells and teeth, to functionally ensure that physical rebirth occurs. Antler renewal drives a second belief sub-system for the same purpose.

Breathing Holes Hypothesis (BHH) is the interpretation of cupules, hammered depressions in ancient rock art, as functional representations of breathing holes. There are two types: *landscape cupules* which bring rock surfaces alive in sympathy with the life-force worldview, and *funerary cupules* which ensure rebirth by breathing life into human remains in burials and excarnation sites. Associated grooved lines, spirals and ring marks are representations of air-flows. In the spiritual worldview, landscape cupules became obsolete while funerary cupules were conceptually transformed to assist with spiritual progression or partial reincarnation.

Core Religion (CR) groups afterlife belief systems within naturalistic animism, also known as the life-force worldview. This model of reality has the environment consisting of living things. CR includes the ICR and OCR divisions of belief systems. The naturalistic animism worldview prevailed from the emergence of *Homo sapiens* until the Neolithic revolution.

Enhanced Rebirth Afterlife (ERA) is a Palaeolithic belief system within OCR as it assists with improving afterlife. ERA has the beliefs that animal parts, as grave goods, imbue strength or speed, and similarly that artefacts or tools imbue skills or learning. All were to enhance capabilities for the deceased when growing up after physical rebirth.

The **Geologic Model of Religion (GMR)** decomposes religious belief systems within worldviews, and defines chronological divisions in the development of paradigms of how the processes of afterlife work. It uses a structure analogous to the interior of the planet earth.

Inner Core Religion (ICR) is the division of naturalistic animism belief systems for achieving rebirth afterlife. It comprises the NRT which are associated with accelerating or ensuring that rebirth afterlife occurs.

Lower Mantle Religion (LMR) is the division of spiritual religions which offer a spiritual afterlife. It includes ancestor worship and formal religions which offer a purely spiritual existence, also partial reincarnation where the spiritual identity fades away and personal identity is not preserved.

Mantle Religion (MR) groups afterlife belief systems within the spiritual worldview, which is that spirits – disembodied identities – exist in the environment. MR includes spiritual worlds seen in the SEU paradigm, and LMR and UMR afterlife paradigm divisions. Nearly all formal religions today are within MR.

Natural Rebirth Traditions (NRT) falls within ICR. They are the four prehistoric belief systems (ART, PRT, ROT and SBT) which harness the various renewal powers of nature, in funerary ritual, to ensure rebirth afterlife occurs.

Natural Spiritual Traditions (NST) emerge in the Neolithic and are the Natural Rebirth Traditions, including Enhanced Rebirth Afterlife, fully transformed into facilitating spiritual afterlife and partial reincarnation within the spiritual worldview.

Outer Core Religion (OCR) is the division of naturalistic animism belief systems for improving rebirth afterlife. It comprises ERA and RFB which are associated with the post-rebirth state: either enhancing the next life or interpreting its success.

Plant Renewal Traditions (PRT) is a Palaeolithic belief system within ICR as it assists with attaining afterlife. PRT harnesses the life-giving renewal power of plants, usually by green stones and flowers, to ensure rebirth afterlife occurs.

Rebirth Feedback Belief (RFB) is a hypothetical Palaeolithic belief system within OCR, driving self-selection within early modern humans. This is where specific young adults are interpreted as being from successful rebirths and treated favourably. Such self-selection exaggerates gracile, neotenous traits – finally producing today's fully modern humans.

Red Ochre Tradition (ROT) is a Palaeolithic belief system within ICR, as it assists with attaining afterlife. ROT harnesses the life-giving power of blood using ochre or other red pigments in funerary ritual to ensure rebirth afterlife occurs.

Rot-Art is Palaeolithic amulets combining elements of NRT: blood, animal renewal and breathing symbolism. Commonly, they are red ochre-stained shells, often perforated with breathing holes and probably considered as a life-giving object.

Stone Breathing Traditions (SBT) is a Palaeolithic belief system within ICR, as it assists with attaining afterlife. SBT harnesses the life-giving power of air, usually by charcoal, burnt bone, perforated objects, and funerary cupules or grooves in rock art as per the BHH. All were considered functional in ensuring that rebirth afterlife occurs for the deceased.

Sky, Earth and Underworld (SEU) is a paradigm of the MR spiritual worldview which includes spiritual realms alongside the normally perceived realm of the earth. SEU realms are ruled by gods and inhabited by the dead.

Tectonic Religion (TR) is the division of religious belief which exists within the quasi-worldview of conflated spiritual and science worldviews. These are either new religions or subsets of MR religions, which arise purely as a response to science, pseudoscience or science fiction.

Upper Mantle Religion (UMR) is the division of formal spiritual religions, which offer a physical afterlife by way of reincarnation or resurrection, while also properly preserving personal identity. UMR is the higher religions of today which have adherents comprising 75 per cent of the world's population.

BIBLIOGRAPHY

1.   Green REea. A Draft Sequence of the Neandertal Genome. Science. 2010;5979 pp. 710-722.

2.   Price MC. Many Worlds Quantum Theory. Feb 1995. http://kuoi.com/~kamikaze/doc/many-worlds-faq.html. Accessed November 17, 2011.

3.   Vatican. Catechism of the Catholic Church; 2002.

4.   Dawkins R. Unweaving the Rainbow; 1998.

5.   Boyer P. Religion Explained; 2002.

6.   Spengler O. The Decline of the West; 1926.

7.   Hovey JD. Religion And Suicidal Ideation In A Sample Of Latin American Immigrants. Psychological Reports. 1999:171-177.

8.   Dervic K, al. e. Religious Affiliation and Suicide Attempt. The American Journal of Psychiatry. 2004;12.

9.   Beit-Hallahmi B. Religion And Suicidal Behavior. Psychological Reports. 1975;3f.

10.   James EO. The Beginnings of Religion; 1973.

11.   Frazer SJG. The Golden Bough: A Study in Magic and Religion; 1905.

12.   Dennett D. Breaking the Spell: Religion as a Natural Phenomenon; 2007.

13.   Haycock D. Being and Perceiving; 2011.

14.   Churchward A. The Origin and Evolution of Religion; 1924.

15.   Marshall H. The Religious Instinct. Mind. 1897;21.

16.   Barraclough H. The Religious Instinct. New Zealand Medical Journal. 1905;16:211-212.

17.   Abel DC. Freud on instinct and morality. New York: State University of New York Press; 1989.

18.   Brodie R. Virus of the Mind; 1993.

19.   Roossinck MJ. The good viruses: viral mutualistic symbioses. Nature Reviews Microbiology. 2011:99-108.

20.   Dunlap Kea. Endogenous retroviruses regulate periimplantation placental growth and differentiation. Proceedings The National Academy of Sciences. 2006.

21.   Simpson C. Adam in Ochre; 1951.

22.   Pearson MP. The Archaeology of Death and Burial; 1999.

23.   Karsten R. The origins of religion; 1935.

24.   Clark R. The Multiple Natural Origins of Religion; 2006.

25.   Fowler C. The Archaeology of Personhood: An anthropological approach; 2004.

26.   Bednarik RG. South African Archaeological Bulletin. 1998;53(167): 4-8.

27.   L M. A Comparison of Encephalization between Odontocete Cetaceans and Anthropoid Primates. Brain, Behavior and Evolution. 1998;51:230-238.

28.   McHenry HM, Katherine C. Australopithecus to Homo: Transformations in body and mind. Annual Review of Anthropology. 2000:29:125–46.

29.   Asfaw WLLSS. Australopithecus garhi: A NewSpecies of Early Hominid from Ethiopia. Science. 1999;p 629.

30.   Oakley KP. Emergence of Higher Thought 3.0-0.2 Ma B.P. Philosophical Transactions B. 1981;1057.

31.   Walker A, Shipman P. Wisdom of the bones; 1996.

32.   Morell V. Ancestral passions: the Leakey family and the quest for humankind's beginnings; 1996.

33.   Cameron D, Groves C. 'Bones, stones, and molecules: "out of Africa; 2004.

34.   Lucassen J. Migration history in world history: multidisciplinary approaches; 2010.

35.   Bednarik R. Replicating the first known sea travel by humans: the Lower Pleistocene crossing of Lombok Strait. 2000.

36.   Tarlochan F, Ramesh S. Heat Transfer Model for Predicting Survival Time in Cold Water Immersion. Biomedical Engineering - Applied, Basis & Communications. 2005:159-166.

37.   Templeton A. Out of Africa again and again. Nature. 2002:45-51.

38.   Jurmain R, al. e. Introduction to Physical Anthropology 2011-2012; 2011.

39.   Harvati K, Harrison T. Neanderthals revisited: new approaches and perspectives; 2006.

40.   S. S, J. G, J. S, J. A. Human Awareness of Mortality and the Evolution of Culture. The psychological foundations of culture; 2004.

41.   Bahn PG, Vertut J. Journey through the Ice Age; 1997.

42.   Bednarik RG. The 'Australopithecine' cobble from Makapansgat, South Africa. South African Archaeological Bulletin. 1998:4-8.

43.   Bednarik RG. The calibrated dating of petroglyphs. The Artefact. 1993;61.

44. The Humans of Sima de los Huesos. Available at: http://www.amnh.org/exhibitions/atapuerca/simahumans/index.php. Accessed November 15, 2011.

45. Lumley d. A Palaeolithic camp at Nice. Scientific American. 1969;5.

46. Clark JOKWL&MJ. New studies on Rhodesian Man. Journal of the Royal Anthropological Institute. 1947;77.

47. Deino AL, McBrearty S. 40Ar/39Ar dating of the Kapthurin Formation, Baringo, Kenya. Journal of Human Evolution. 2002;pp 185 - 210.

48. L. B. Systematic Pigment Use in the Middle Pleistocence of South-Central Africa. Current Anthropology. 2002.

49. A. M. On Paleolithic Ochre and the Early Uses of Color and Symbol. Current Anthropology. 1981;2:188-191.

50. Paddaya. The Acheulian culture of the Hunsgi Valley. 1982.

51. Roebroeks W, al. e. Use of red ochre by early Neandertals. 2011.

52. Van Peera Pea. The Early to Middle Stone Age Transition and the Emergence of Modern Human Behaviour at site 8-B-11 ,Sai Island, Sudan. Journal of Human Evolution. 2003;45, 187–193.

53. Marean CWea. Early human use of marine resources and pigment in South Africa during the Middle Pleistocene. Nature. 2007;905 - 908.

54. Dart R.A. BP. On a further radiocarbon date for ancient mining in southern Africa. South African Journal of Science. 1971;67.

55. C H. A 100,000-Year-Old Ochre-Processing Workshop at Blombos Cave, South Africa. Science :219-222.

56. Morris M, Linnegar J, Education SAMo. Every step of the way: the journey to freedom in South Africa; 2004.

57. Wymer J. The Palaeolithic Age; 1982.

58. Vianello A. Stone Age symbolic behaviours: questions and prospects. The Criteria of Symbolicity. April 13, 2004. Available at: http://www.semioticon.com/virtuals/symbolicity/behaviours.html. Accessed December 02, 2011.

59. Kagan S. The birth of Art: Journey in an archeological controversy. 2002. http://sachakagan.chez-alice.fr/docs/birthart.pdf. Accessed December 08, 2011.

60. Lanyon SJ. A Saltationist Approach for the Evolution of Human Cognition and Language. Proceedings EVOLANG 6. Rome; 2006.

61. Darvill T. The concise Oxford dictionary of archaeology; 2008.

62. Ritchie J. Cup-Marks on the Stone Circles and Standing Stones of Aberdeenshire and Part of Banffshire. Proceedings of the Society of Antiquity, Scotland. 1918.

63.   Bednarik RG. Auranet Library. 2007. http://mc2.vicnet.net.au/home/aura/web/info.html. Accessed January 28, 2012.

64.   Singh U. A History of Ancient and Early Medieval India:From the Stone Age to the 12th Century; 2008.

65.   Lenik EJ. The Bald Friar Petroglyphs of Maryland. The Rock art of Eastern North America: Capturing Images and Insight; 2004.

66.   Defleur A, al. e. Neanderthal Cannibalism at Moula-Guercy, Ardèche, France. Science. 1999;5437 pp. 128-131.

67.   Russell MD. Mortuary practices at the Krapina Neandertal site. American Journal of Physical Anthropology. 1987;3 pp 381-397.

68.   Zilhão J. Burial evidence for the social differentiation of age classes in the early Upper Paleolithic. Etud Res Archéol Univ Liège. 2005;111:231–241.

69.   Louwe Kooijmans YSRSSPVTWRHG. On the Evidence for Neandertal Burial. Current Anthropology. 1989;3.

70.   Trinkaus E. The Emergence of modern humans: biocultural adaptations in the later Pleistocene; 1989.

71.   Mellars P. The Neanderthal legacy: an archaeological perspective from western Europe; 1996.

72.   Levy TE. The archaeology of society in the Holy Land; 1998.

73.   RH. G. Middle Palaeolithic burial is not a dead issue: the view from Qafzeh, Saint-Césaire, Kebara, Amud, and Dederiyeh. Jornal of Human Evolution. 1999;(1):27-90.

74.   Erella Hovers SIOBYaBV. An Early Case of Color Symbolism: Ochre Use by Modern Humans in Qafzeh Cave1. Current Anthropology. 2003;4.

75.   Dederiyeh Cave and Excavations. 2003. Available at: http://www.kochi-tech.ac.jp/akazawa/english/1.html. Accessed April 27, 2012.

76.   Bar-Yosef, et.al. The role of western Asia in modern human origins. Philosophical Transactions of the Royal Society B: Biological Sciences. 1992.

77.   Cartmill M, Smith F. The human lineage; 2009.

78.   Milisauskas S. European Prehistory:; 2011.

79.   Ritter E. New Perspectives on People and Forests; 2011.

80.   Green MA. An Archaeology of Images: Iconology and Cosmology in Iron Age and Roman Europe; 2004.

81.   Botha RP, Knight C. The Cradle of Language; 2009.

82.   Bahn PG. Prehistoric Rock Art: Polemics and Progress; 2010.

83.   Mithen S. Symbolism and the Supernatural. The evolution of culture: an interdisciplinary view; 1999.

84.   Barton N. Book of stone age Britain; 1997.

85.   d'Errico F, Henshilwood C, Lawson G, et al. Archaeological Evidence for the Emergence of Language, Symbolism, and Music — An Alternative Multidisciplinary Perspective. Journal of World Prehistory. 2003;1.

86.   Bellah RN. Religion in Human Evolution: From the Paleolithic to the Axial Age; 2011.

87.   Bradley R. The significance of monuments:on the shaping of human experience in Neolithic and Bronze Age Europe; 1998.

88.   Bonsall C. The Mesolithic of the Iron Gates. Mesolithic Europe; 2008.

89.   Peabody C. Red Paint. Journal de la Société des Américanistes. 1927.

90.   Zagorska I. The Use of Ochre in Stone Age Burials of the East Baltic. The Materiality of Death: Bodies, Burials, Beliefs; 2008.

91.   Hovers E, Vandermeersch B, Bar-Yosef O. A Middle Palaeolithic engraved artefact from Qafzeh Cave, Israel. Rock Art Research. 1997;2:79-87.

92.   Grün R, P. B. Border Cave revisited: a revised ESR chronology. Journal of Human Evolution. 2001.

93.   Aldenderfer M, et.al. World History Encyclopedia, Volume 10; 2011.

94.   Bowler JMea. New ages for human occupation and climatic change at Lake Mungo, Australia. Nature. 2003:837-840.

95.   Jacobi RM&HTFG. The "Red Lady" ages gracefully: New ultrafiltration AMS determinations from Paviland. Journal of Human Evolution. 2008:898-907.

96.   Einwögerer Tea. Upper Palaeolithic infant burials. Nature. 2006;285.

97.   Vincenzo F, et. al. The Upper Paleolithic triple burial of Dolní Věstonice: Pathology and funerary behavior. American Journal of Physical Anthropology. 2001.

98.   Cidália Duarte JMPBPPSETHvdPaJZ. The early Upper Paleolithic human skeleton from the Abrigo do Lagar Velho (Portugal) and modern human emergence in Iberia. Procedures of the National Academy Sciences, U S A.. 1999 June 22:7604–7609..

99.   Lee YK, Zhu N. Social Integration of Religion and Ritual in Prehistoric China. 2002.

100.   Orschiedt J, von Berg A, Flohr S. Human remains from the late Upper Paleolithic of Irlich, Germany – A preliminary repor, 2011; Herne.

101.   Belcastro MG, Condemi S, Mariotti V. Funerary practices of the Iberomaurusian population of Taforalt (Tafoughalt, Morocco, 11-

12,000 BP): the case of Grave XII. Journal of Human Evolution. 2010;6.

102. Buchvarov K. Intramural burials in Bulgaria in their southeast European and Anatolian context; 2003.

103. Stoliar AD. Milestones of Spiritual Evolution in Prehistoric Karelia. Folklore. 2001.

104. Morris R. A Shroud of Ochre: A Study of Pre-Contact Mortuary Ochre Use in North America; 2010.

105. Albrethsen SE&EBP. Excavation of a Mesolithic cemetery at Vedbæk, Denmark. Acta Archaeologia. 1976;47:1-8.

106. Wreschner E. Red ochre and human evolution: a case for discussion". Current Anthropology. 1980;5.

107. Andrew Jones GM. Colouring the past: the significance of colour in archaeological research; 2002.

108. Dickson BD. The Dawn of Belief: Religion in the Upper Paleolithic of Southwestern Europe; 1992.

109. James EO. Prehistoric Religion; 1957.

110. Pettit RB, Richards M, Maggi R, V. F. The Gravettian burial known as the Prince (" Il Principe"): new evidence for his age and diiet. 2003.

111. Lubell D. Late Pleistocene - Early Holocene Maghreb. Encyclopaediaof Pre-History. Vol 1. New York; 2001.

112. Balout L. The Prehistory of North Africa. General History of Africa: Methodology and African prehistory; 1981.

113. Knight C, Power C, Watts I. The Human Symbolic Revolution: A Darwinian Account. Cambridge Archaeological Journal. 1995;1:75-114.

114. Peasnell B. Iranian Chalcolithic. Encyclopedia of Prehistory: South and Southwest Asia. Vol 8; 2002.

115. Straus LG. Humans at the end of the Ice Age: the archaeology of the Pleistocene-Holocene transition: Springer; 1996.

116. Naumann N. Japanese prehistory: the material and spiritual culture of the Jōmon period; 2000.

117. Viet N. Archaeology of Death in Vietnam. Paper presented at: SEAEAA conference, 2002; Sigtuna, Sweden.

118. Higham C. The archaeology of Mainland Southeast Asia:; 1991.

119. Hiscock P. The archaeology of ancient Australia; 2008.

120. Weber G. Pericu People (Baja California Sur, Mexico). George Weber's Lonely Islands. Available at: http://www.andaman.org/BOOK/chapter54/text-Pericu/text-Pericu.htm#pericu. Accessed January 12, 2012.

121.   Morris DP, Erlandson JM. A 9,500 Year-Old Human Burial from CA-SRI-116, Santa Rosa Island. Journal of California and Great Basin Anthropology,. 1993;1.

122.   Snow DR. Differentiation of Hunter-Gatherer Cultures. The Cambridge History of the Native Peoples of the Americas: North America; 1996.

123.   Paine RR, Lewis PJ. An archaic human burial from Yoakum County, Texas: the crossroads of bioarchaeology and forensic anthropology. The Texas Journal of Science. 2000.

124.   Darchuk L, al. e. Composition Of Pigments On Human Bones Found In Excavations In Argentina Studied With Micro-Raman Spectrometry And Scanning Electron Microscopy. Paper presented at: Infrared and Raman Users' Group (IRUG), 2008; Vienna.

125.   Clottes J. Spirituality and Religion in Palaeolithic Times. The evolution of rationality; 2007.

126.   Nadel D, al. e. The Late Natufian at Raqefet Cave: The 2006 Excavation Season. Journal of The Israel Prehistoric Society. 2008.

127.   Belfer-Cohen A. The Natufian Graveyard in Hayonim Cave. Paléorient. 1988;2.

128.   Bradley R. Rock art and the prehistory of Atlantic Europe: signing the land; 1997.

129.   Svoboda JA, van der Plicht J, Kuzelka V. Upper Palaeolithic and Mesolithic human fossils from Moravia and Bohemia (Czech Republic): some new [sup.14]C dates. Antiquity. 2002.

130.   Cartier R. The Sunnyvale Red Burial, CA-SCL-832. Proceedings of the Society for California Archaeology. 2002;15:49-52.

131.   Schulting R, Wysocki M. The Mesolithic Human Skeletal Collection From Aveline's Hole: A Preliminary Note. Proceedings of the University of Bristol Spelaeology Society. 2002;3.

132.   Poikalainen V. Palaeolithic Art from the Danube to Lake Baikal. Folklore. 2001.

133.   Werness HB. The Continuum Encyclopedia of Animal Symbolism in Art; 2006.

134.   Eliade M. Images and symbols: studies in religious symbolism; 1991.

135.   Ashton N, Lewis SG, Stringer C. The Ancient Human Occupation of Britain. 2010.

136.   Cauvin J, Watkins T. 'The Birth of the Gods and Origins of Agriculture; 2000.

137.   Kabu J. Ancient Jomon of Japan; 2004.

138.   Claasen C. Shells; 1998.

139.   McCown TD. Mugharet Es-Skhul. Description and Excavations. The Stone Age of Mount Carmel. Vol 1; 1937.

140.   Witter D, Fullagar R, Pardoe C. The Terramungamine Incident: a Double Burialwith Grave Goods near Dubbo, New South Wales: Records of the Australian Museum; 1993. 0 7310 0280 6.

141.   Tilley C. An Ethnography of the Neolithic: Early Prehistoric Societies in Southern Scandinavia; 2003.

142.   Thorpe IJ. The Origins of Agriculture in Europe; 1999.

143.   Gurina NN. Oleneostrovski mogilnik. Materialy i issledovania po arkheologii SSSR. 1956.

144.   A Paleoindian Grave. Texas Beyond History. December 2010. Available at: http://www.texasbeyondhistory.net/horn/burials.html. Accessed October 19, 2011.

145.   Lubell D. Prehistoric edible land snails in the circum-Mediterranean : the archaeological evidence. 2004.

146.   Spiers M. LD,GMAN,DA,BCA. Nahal Ein Gev I : A Late Upper Palaeolithic Site by the Sea of Galilee, Israel. Paléorient. 2004;1.

147.   Vercellotti G, al. e. The Late Upper Paleolithic skeleton Villabruna 1 (Italy): a source of data on biology and behavior of a 14.000 year-old hunter. Journal of Anthropological Sciences. 2008;86:143-163.

148.   Glorstad H, Nakrem HA, Torhaug V. Nature in Society: Reflections over a Mesolithic Sculpture of a Fossilised Shell. Norwegian Archaeological Review. 2004;2.

149.   Shearin N, Loveland C, Parr R, Sack D. A Late Archaic Burial from the Thursday Site, Utah. Journal of California and Great Basin Anthropology. 1996;1.

150.   Bogucki P. The origins of human society; 1999.

151.   Barich BE. People, water, and grain: the beginnings of domestication in the Sahara and the Nile valley; 1998.

152.   Solecki. Shanidar, the First Flower People.

153.   Sommers J. The Shanidar IV "Flower Burial": A Re-evaluation of Neanderthal Burial Ritual. Cambridge Archaeological Journal. 1999; pp 127-129.

154.   Schwarcz HP, Skoflek I. New dates for the Tata, Hungary archaeological site. Nature. 1982:590 - 591.

155.   Farrington O, Field H. Neanderthal (Mousterian) Man. 1929.

156.   Walker M, al. e. The excavation of buried articulated Neanderthal skeletons at Sima de las Palomas. Quaternary International. 2011.

157.   Wynn T, Coolidge F. How to Think Like a Neandertal; 2011.

158.   Schulting RJ, al. e. Stable carbon and nitrogen isotope analysis on human remains from theEarly Mesolithic site of La Vergne

(Charente-Maritime, France). Journal of Archaeological Science. 2008:763-772.

159. Valdeyron. The Mesolithic in France. Mesolithic Europe; 2008.

160. Peregrine PN, Ember M(). Encyclopaedia of Prehistory. Vol 6 North America; 2001.

161. ARIAS P, al. e. Burials in the cave: New evidence on mortuary practices during the Mesolithic of Cantabrian Spain. Mesolithic Horizons: Papers presented.at the Seventh International Conference on the Mesolithic in Europe; 2005.

162. Swiny S. That Cat from Shillourokambos. Caari News. 2004;28.

163. Maher LA SJFSHJMPea. A Unique Human-Fox Burial from a Pre-Natufian Cemetery in the Levant (Jordan). PLoS ONE 6(1): e15815. doi:10.1371/journal.pone.0015815. 2011.

164. Underhill AP. An analysis of mortuary ritual at the Dawenkou site. Journal of East Asian Archaeology. 2000;2.

165. Rice M. Egypt's legacy: the archetypes of western civilization 3000-30 BC; 1997.

166. Radovanic I. The Iron Gates Mesolithic. InternationalMonographs in Prehistory, Archaeological Series ll. 1996.

167. Grosman L, Munroe ND, Belfer-Cohen A. A 12,000-year-old shaman burial from the southern Levant (Israel). Proc. Natl. Acad. Sci. USA. 2010;35:15362-15366.

168. Enoch JM. A Mesolithic (Middle Stone Age!) Spanish artificial eye: please realize this technology is circa 7000-years-old!. Hindisght. 2009;2.

169. Bednarik RG. The Human Condition; 2011.

170. Disposing of the dead - Burial. January 07, 2010. Available at: http://australianmuseum.net.au/Disposing-of-the-dead-Burial. Accessed January 23, 2012.

171. Fiorenza L BSTJKOBTea. Molar Macrowear Reveals Neanderthal Eco-Geographic Dietary Variation. PLoS ONE 6(3): e14769. doi:10.1371/journal.pone.0014769. 2011.

172. Van Peer P, Vermeersch PM, Paulissen E. Chert Quarrying, Lithic Technology and a Modern Human Burial at the Palaeolithic Site of Taramsa 1, Upper Egypt; 2010.

173. Schmidt K. Göbekli Tepe – the Stone Age Sanctuaries.New results of ongoing excavations with a special focuson sculptures and high reliefs. Documenta Praehistorica. 2010.

174. Schmidt K. Gobekli Tepe and the Early Neolithic Sites of the Urfa Region: a Synopsis of New Results and Current Views. Neo-Lithics: A Newsletter of South-West Asian Research. 2001.

175.   Özdogan A. ÖM. Çayönü. A Conspectus of Recent Work. Paléorient. 1989;1:65-74.

176.   Freedman M, Skinner GW. The Study of Chinese Society: Essays; 1979.

177.   McClelland NC. Encyclopedia of Reincarnation and Karma; 2010.

178.   Voltaire. A philosophical dictionary, Volume 6; 1824.

179.   Wasserman J. The Egyptian Book of the Dead: The Book of Going Forth by Day; 2009.

180.   Voorst REV. Anthology of World Scriptures; 2007.

181.   Loewe M, Shaughnessy EL. The Cambridge history of ancient China: from the origins of civilization to.

182.   Ferguson TJ, Dongoske KE, Kuwanwisiwma LJ. Hopi Perspectives on Southwestern Mortuary Studies: Archaeology, Physical Anthropology, and Native American Perspectives. Ancient Burial Practices in the American Southwest; 2004.

183.   Staller JE, Tykot Robert H. BBF. Histories of maize: multidisciplinary approaches to the prehistory; 2006.

184.   Middleton J. Lugbara Religion: Ritual and Authority Among an East African People; 1999.

185.   Lenneis E. Mesolithic heritage in early Neolithic burial rituals and personal adornments. Documenta Praehistorica. 2007.

186.   Richter T, Stock JT, Maher L, Hebron C. An Early Epipalaeolithic sitting burial from the Azraq Oasis, Jordan. Antiquity. 2010.

187.   Shahmirzadi M. Tepe Zagheh: A sixth millennium BC village in the Qazvin plain of the central Iranian plateau 1977.

188.   Smith RD. Neolithic Art and Ideology. www.dibonsmith.com. 1990-2012. www.dibonsmith.com/neo_art.pdf. Accessed June 06, 2012.

189.   Bailey DW. Balkan prehistory: exclusión, incorporation and identity; 2000.

190.   Richards MP, Price TD, E. K. The Mesolithic and Neolithic Subsistence In Denmark: New Stable Isotope Data. Current Anthropology. 2003;2:288-294.

191.   Hall JW. The Cambridge History of Japan: Ancient Japan; 1993.

192.   Oxenham MF, Matsumura H, Dung NK. Man Bac : the excavation of a neolithic site in northern Vietnam. Terra Australis. 2011.

193.   Price TD. The Chemistry of prehistoric human bone; 1989.

194.   Dunbar R. Coevolution of neocortex size, group size and language in humans. Behavioral and Brain Sciences. 1994;4: 681-735.

195.   Gonçalves B PNVA. Modeling Users' Activity on Twitter Networks: Validation of Dunbar's Number. PLoS ONE 6(8): e22656. doi:10.1371/journal.pone.0022656. 2011.

196.   Keightley DN. Sources of Shang history: the oracle-bone inscriptions of bronze age China: University of California Press; 1985.

197.   Moore C. A timely recounting of the Weimar disaster that aided Hitler's rise to power. The Telegraph. August 02, 2010. Available at: http://www.telegraph.co.uk/comment/columnists/charlesmoore/792 1664/A-timely-recounting-of-the-Weimar-disaster-that-aided-Hitlers-rise-to-power.html. Accessed August 02, 2010.

198.   Krebs D, Janicki M. Biological Foundations of Moral Norms. The psychological foundations of culture.

199.   Richerson PJ, Boyd RPD. Not by genes alone: how culture transformed human evolution; 2004.

200.   Wilson DS. Darwin's Cathedral; 2003.

201.   Donohue K. Density Dependent Multilevel Selection in the Great Lakes Sea Rocket. Ecology. 2004;1:180–191.

202.   Pletcher K. The History of India; 2010.

203.   Drew D. The Lost Chronicles of the Maya Kings; 1999.

204.   Pearson MP. Death, being, and time: the historical context of the world religions. Archaeology and World Religion; 2001.

205.   Akkermans PMMG, Schwartz GM. The Archaeology of Syria: From Complex Hunter-gatherers to Early Urban Socieites.

206.   Bottéro J, Herrenschmidt C, Vernant JP. Ancestor of the West: writing, reasoning, and religion in Mesopotamia, Elam, and Greece; 2000.

207.   Hancock P. The Code of Hammurabi; 1903.

208.   Gunn B. The Instruction of Ptah-Hotep and the Instruction of Ke'gemni; 1907.

209.   Turner SP. Emile Durkheim: sociologist and moralist; 1993.

210.   Gaume JJ(). Ep. Ad Ephes. Hom. XI. Vol XI. Paris; 1838.

211.   Shushan G. Conceptions of the afterlife in early civilizations: universalism, constructivism, and near-death experience; 2009.

212.   Hall S. Burial and Sequence in the Eastern Cape Porvince. The South African Archaeological Bulletin. 2000:137-146.

213.   Kendall MB. "Rivière De Précourt, Émile-Valère." Complete Dictionary of Scientific Biography. 2008. Available at: http://www.encyclopedia.com/doc/1G2-2830903693.html. Accessed October 11, 2011.

214.   Perles C. The early Neolithic in Greece: the first farming communities in Europe; 2001.

215.   Doninger W(). Merriam-Webster's Encyclopedia of World Religions; 1999.

216.   Eller JD. Cultural Anthropology: Global Forces, Local Lives; 2009.

217.	Anderson L. Karma; 2002.

218.	Soustelle J. Daily Life of the Aztecs, on the Eve of the Spanish Conquest; 1970.

219.	Portilla ML. Aztec Thought and Culture: A Study of the Ancient Nahuatl Mind; 1963.

220.	Phillips C. The Lost History of Aztec and Maya; 2004.

221.	Josephus F. The Works of Flavius Josephus, the Learned and Authentic Jewish Historian; 1841.

222.	Bongmba E. "Religion: Africa." Encyclopedia.com:. 2005. Available at: http://www.encyclopedia.com/doc/1G2-3424300674.html. Accessed November 18, 2011.

223.	Encyclopaedia perthensis, or, Universal dictionary of the arts, sciences, literature, etc. : intended to supersede the use of other books of reference; 1816.

224.	Brandon SGF. The Judgment of the Dead; 1967.

225.	Soni M. Mystic Chords; 2002.

226.	Nichols T. Death and Afterlife: A Theological Introduction; 2010.

227.	Middleton P. Martyrdom: A Guide for the Perplexed; 2011.

228.	Leeming DA, Leeming MA. A Dictionary of Creation Myths; 1994.

229.	Juergensmeyer M. Religion In Global Civil Society; 2005.

230.	Green ARW. The storm-god in the ancient Near East; 2003.

231.	Taracha P. Religions of second millennium Anatolia; 2009.

232.	Lipinkski E. The Aramaeans: Their Ancient History, Culture, Religion; 2000.

233.	Smith MS. The Early History of God: Yahweh and the Other Deities in Ancient Israel; 2002.

234.	Cumont F. After Life in Roman Paganism; 1922.

235.	De Grummond NT. On Mutilated Mirrors. Votives, places and rituals in Etruscan religion: studies in honor of Jean MacIntosh Turfa; 2009.

236.	Ghosh A. An Encyclopaedia of Indian Archaeology; 1990.

237.	Daniell C. Death and Burial in Medieval England, 1066-1550; 1997.

238.	Simoons FJ. Eat not this flesh - Food Avoidances from Prehistory to the Present; 1994.

239.	Zettler RL, Horne L, Hansen DP, Pittman H. Treasures from the Royal Tombs of Ur; 1998.

240.	J. MK. The Star-Crossed Stone: The Secret Life, Myths, and History of a Fascinating Fossil; 2010.

241.	Baccolini G. The Symbolic Meaning of the Oval Stone and of the Egg in the Etruscan Religion. Monovolo Retreats. March 2004. Available at: http://ms.fci.unibo.it/~baccolin/tomba%20leopardi/montovolo-retreat-10-en.htm. Accessed May 12, 2010.

242. Fitzsimmons JL. Death and the Classic Maya Kings; 2009.

243. Meyer MW. China: A Concise History; 1994.

244. Aguilar-Moreno M. Handbook to Life in the Aztec World ; 2007.

245. Guderjan TH. The Nature of an Ancient Maya City: Resources, Interaction, and Power at Blue Creek, Belize; 2007.

246. Foster LV, Mathews P. Handbook To Life In The Ancient Maya World; 2005.

247. Neill MG. The communion of scholars: Chinese art at Yale; 1989.

248. Ward W. Scarabs. Near Eastern Archaeology: A Reader; 2003.

249. Egan RB, Joyal M, Berry EG. Daimonopylai: essays in classics and the classical tradition presented to Edmund G. Berry; 2004.

250. Strong E. Apotheosis and After Life; 1915.

251. Strong A. The Exhibition, illustrative of the Provinces of the Roman Empire, in the Baths of Diocetian, at Rome. The Journal of Roman studies. 1911.

252. Anderson W. Green Man: The Archetype of our Oneness with the earth; 1990.

253. Basford K. The Green Man; 1978.

254. MacLeod SP. Celtic Myth and Religion; 2011.

255. Davidson H. The Lost Beliefs of Northern Europe; 1993.

256. Horwitz LK, Goring-Morris N. Animals and ritual during the Levantine PPNB : a case study from the site of Kfar Hahoresh, Israel. Anthropozoologica. 2004;1:165-178.

257. Boyce M. Zoroastrians: Their Religious Beliefs and Practices; 2001.

258. Braim TH. A history of New South, Wales: from its settlement to the close of the year 1844; 1846.

259. Jacob TK. In the Beginning: A Perspective on Traditional Aboriginal Societies; 1991.

260. Castleden R. The Stonehenge People: An Exploration of Life in Neolithic Britain 4700-2000 BC; 2002.

261. Akkermans PMMG, Schwartz GM. The Archaeology of Syria: From Complex Hunter-Gatherers to Early Urban Societies (C. 16,000-300 BC); 2003.

262. Bar-Yosef O. The Natufian Culture in the Levant, Threshold to the Origins of Agriculture. Evolutionary Anthropology. 1998.

263. Mellaart J. Excavations at Catal Huyuk, 1963: ThirdPreliminary Report. Anatolian Studies. 1964;14.

264. Hodder I. Çatalhöyük 2005 Archive Report. Çatalhöyük: Excavations of a Neolithic Anatolian Höyük. 2005. Available at: http://www.catalhoyuk.com/archive_reports/2005/ar05_01.html. Accessed March 11, 2012.

265. McNamara P. Spirit possession and exorcism: history, psychology, and neurobiology; 2011.

266. Warburton DA. The Discovery of the Dawn of Consciousness. Textual, comparative, sociological, and cognitive approaches.

267. Cohen AC. Death rituals, ideology, and the development of early Mesopotamian kingship: toward a new understanding of Iraq's royal cemetery of Ur; 2005.

268. Lambert WG. Babylonian Wisdom Literature; 1960.

269. Black JA,CG,FHERE,aZG. The Electronic Text Corpus of Sumerian Literature. 1998. Available at: http://etcsl.orinst.ox.ac.uk/index1.htm. Accessed November 1, 2011.

270. Birmingham RA. Spirits of earth: the effigy mound landscape of Madison and the Four Lakes; 2009.

271. Wentink K. Ceci N'est Pas Une Hache: Neolithic Depositions in the Northern Netherlands; 2006.

272. Sorlini GB. The megalithic temples of Malta, an anthropological perspective. Archaeology and fertility cult in the ancient Mediterranean: papers presented at the first International Conference on Archaeology of the Ancient Mediterranean, University of Malta, 2-5 September 1985.

273. Cremin A. Archaeologica; 2007.

274. Faulkner R, Goelet O, Andrews C, Wasserman J. The Egyptian Book of the Dead: The Book of Going Forth by Day - The Complete Papyrus of Ani; 2008.

275. Griffiths JG. The origins of Osiris and his cult; 1980.

276. Stilwell GA. Afterlife; 2005.

277. Taylor JH. Death and the afterlife in ancient Egypt; 2001.

278. Oldstone-Moore J. Chinese Traditions. The Illustrated Guide to World Religions; 2003.

279. Brashier KE. Han Thanatology and the Division of "Souls". Early China. 1996.

280. Chamberlain J. Chinese Gods: An Introduction to Chinese Folk Religion; 2010.

281. Barnard A, Spencer J. Encyclopedia of Social and Cultural Anthropology; 2002.

282. Parpola A. Airāvati; 2008.

283.   Mahadevan I. Towards a scientific study of the Indus Script. The Hindu (Newspaper). 2007, Feb 4th.

284.   Richardson NJ. Early Greek Views About Life After Death. Greek Religion and Society; 1985.

285.   Castleden R. Minoans: Life in Bronze Age Crete; 1990.

286.   Kohler K. Heaven and Hell in Comparative Religion with Special Reference to Dante's Divine Comedy; 1923.

287.   Toynbee JMC. Death and Burial in the Roman World; 1996.

288.   DuBois TA. Nordic religions in the Viking Age; 1999.

289.   Peel JDY. Religious Encounter and the Making of the Yoruba; 2003.

290.   Asante MK, Nwadiora E. Spear Masters; 2007.

291.   Ilogu E. Christianity and Ibo Culture; 1974.

292.   Parrinder EGS. West African Psychology; 2002.

293.   Deacon HJ, Deacon J. Human Beginnings in South Africa: Uncovering the Secrets of the Stone Age; 1999.

294.   Lang A. Myth, Ritual & Religion. Vol 2; 1887.

295.   Whittlesey SM, Reid JJ. Mortuary Ritual and Organizational Inferences at Grasshopper Pueblo, Arizona. Ancient Burial Practices in the American Southwest:; 2004.

296.   Lowenstein T, Vitebsky P. Native American Myths and Beliefs; 2011.

297.   Markman PT, Markman RH. Masks of the Spirit: Image and Metaphor in Mesoamerica; 1989.

298.   Pool CAl. Olmec Archaeology And Early Mesoamerica; 2007.

299.   Demarest AA. Ancient Maya: The Rise And Fall Of A Rainforest Civilization; 2004.

300.   Craig RD. Dictionary of Polynesian Mythology; 1989.

301.   Oliver DL. Polynesia in early historic times; 2002.

302.   Drummond H. James Chalmers of New Guinea, missionary, pioneer, martyr; 1902.

303.   William C, Roussel H. Easter Island: the Rapanui speech and the peopling of southeast Polynesia; 1912.

304.   Earle A. Nine Months Residence in New Zealand in 1827; 1832.

305.   Best E. The Maori; 1941.

306.   Miller WM. The Baha'i Faith: Its History and Teachings; 1974.

307.   Major Religions of the World Ranked by Number of Adherents. Adherents. 2012. Available at: http://www.adherents.com/Religions_By_Adherents.html. Accessed May 07, 2012.

308.   Leeming DA. The Oxford Companion to World Mythology; 2005.

309. Van den Broek R. The myth of the Phoenix, according to classical and early Christian traditions; 1971.

310. Wilhelm R. Lectures on the I Ching; 2000.

311. Klenke K. Authentic Leadership: A Self, Leader, and Spiritual Identity Perspective. International Journal of Leadership Studies. 2007;1.

312. Renard J. Responses to One Hundred One Questions on Hinduism; 1999.

313. Sanghvi SJS. A Treatise On Jainism; 2008.

314. Uttal WR. Dualism: The Original Sin of Cognitivism; 2004.

315. Grover S. Reflections on Solitude and Other Essays; 2011.

316. Pratt JB. The Pilgrimage of Buddhism and a Buddhist Pilgrimage; 1928.

317. Heuser M, Klimkeit HJ. Studies in Manichaean Literature and Art; 1998.

318. Novák P. The Lost Secret of Death: Our Divided Souls and the Afterlife; 2003.

319. Singh K, Singh T, Fraser GS. Selections from the Sacred Writings of the Sikhs; 1960.

320. Giordano G. Everything You Need to Know About Wicca; 2001.

321. Patai R. The Hebrew goddess; 1990.

322. Aster SZ. Monotheism and Polytheism in Ancient Israel as Reflected in Epigraphic Material from the 9th to 6th centuries BCE. 2011.

323. Smith M. Studies in the Cult of Yahweh: Studies in the New Testament, Early Christianity, Magica; 1996.

324. Schimmel S. The Tenacity of Unreasonable Beliefs: Fundamentalism and the Fear of Truth; 2008.

325. Cooper J. Biblical Anthropolgy and the Body-Soul Relation. Soul, Body, and Survival: Essays on the Metaphysics of Human Persons; 2001.

326. Clark P. Zoroastrianism: An Introduction to an Ancient Faith; 1999.

327. Pleins JD. When the Great Abyss Opened: Classic and Contemporary Readings of Noah's Flood; 2003.

328. Champion SG, Short D(). The World's Great Religions: An Anthology of Sacred Texts; 2003.

329. Waterhouse J. Zoroastrianism; 2006.

330. Collinson D, Wilkinson R. Thirty-Five Oriental Philosophers; 2002.

331. Wigoder G, (eds.) ea. The New Standard Jewish Encyclopedia; 1992.

332. Avery-Peck AJ. Judaism in Late Antiquity, Part 1, Volume 49; 2000.

333. Lane Fox R. The Unauthorized Version; 1991.

334.   Hill B. Jesus, the Christ: Contemporary Perspectives; 2004.

335.   Ramsay W. The Cities Of St. Paul:Their Influence On His Life And Thought, The Cities Of Eastern Asia Minor; 1907.

336.   Berkey JP. The Formation of Islam: Religion and Society in the Near East, 600-1800; 2003.

337.   Haag M. The Templars: The History and the Myth - From Solomon's Temple to the Freemasons; 2008.

338.   Al-Khalifah AHM. Religiosity in Islam as a Protective Mechanism against Criminal Temptation. The American Journal of Islamic Social Sciences ;1.

339.   Zax D. Seeing What Galileo Saw; 2011.

340.   Ellwood RS, D. AG. The Encyclopedia of World Religions; 2007.

341.   Numbers RL. The Creationists; 1993.

342.   Long J, Perry P. Evidence of the Afterlife: The Science of Near-Death Experiences; 2010.

343.   Corazza O. Near-Death Experiences: Exploring the Mind-Body Connection; 2008.

344.   Ames WL. Emptiness and Quantum Theory. Buddhism & Science: Breaking New Ground; 2003.

345.   Johnson C. The Dharma of Social Transformation. The Best Buddhist Writing 2007; 2007.

346.   Hut P. Conclusion: Life As a Laboratory. Buddhism & Science: Breaking New Ground; 2003.

347.   Polkinghorne JC. Belief in God in an Age of Science; 2003.

348.   Ownby D. Falun Gong and the Future of China; 2008.

349.   Lewis JR. Scientology; 2009.

350.   Landes RA. Heaven on earth: The Varieties of the Millennial Experience; 2011.

351.   Lewis JR. The Gods Have Landed: New Religions from Other Worlds; 1995.

352.   Lattimore R. Themes in Greek and Latin epitaphs; 1962.

353.   Findlen P. Athanasius Kircher: the last man who knew everything: Routledge; 2004.

354.   M.J. B. The diagnosis of brain death [letter]. New England Journal of Medicine. 2001;345.

355.   de Grey A, Rae M. Ending Aging: The rejuvenation breakthroughs that could reverse human aging in our lifetime; 2007.

356.   Hudetz A, Pearce R. Suppressing the Mind: Anesthetic Modulation of Memory and Consciousness; 2009.

357.   Nagele P MLCC. Xenon acts by inhibition of non-N-methyl-D-aspartate receptor-mediated glutamate. Anesthesiology. 2005:103: 508-13.

358.   Tyson SM. The Unobservable universe:A Paradox-Free Framework for Understanding the universe; 2011.

359.   Goertzel B. The Hidden Pattern: A Patternist Philosophy of Mind; 2006.

360.   More M. The Diachronic Self: Identity, Continuity, Transformation. 1995. http://www.maxmore.com/disscont.htm. Accessed January 2011, 04.

361.   Seung S. Connectome: How the Brain's Wiring Makes Us Who We Are; 2012.

362.   Kurzweil R. The Singularity is Near; 2005.

363.   Smart J. Singularity Timing Projections. Acceleration Watch. 2012. Available at: http://www.accelerationwatch.com/singtimingpredictions.html. Accessed June 15, 2012.

364.   Dembski WA. Intelligent Design: The Bridge Between Science & Theology; 2002.

INDEX